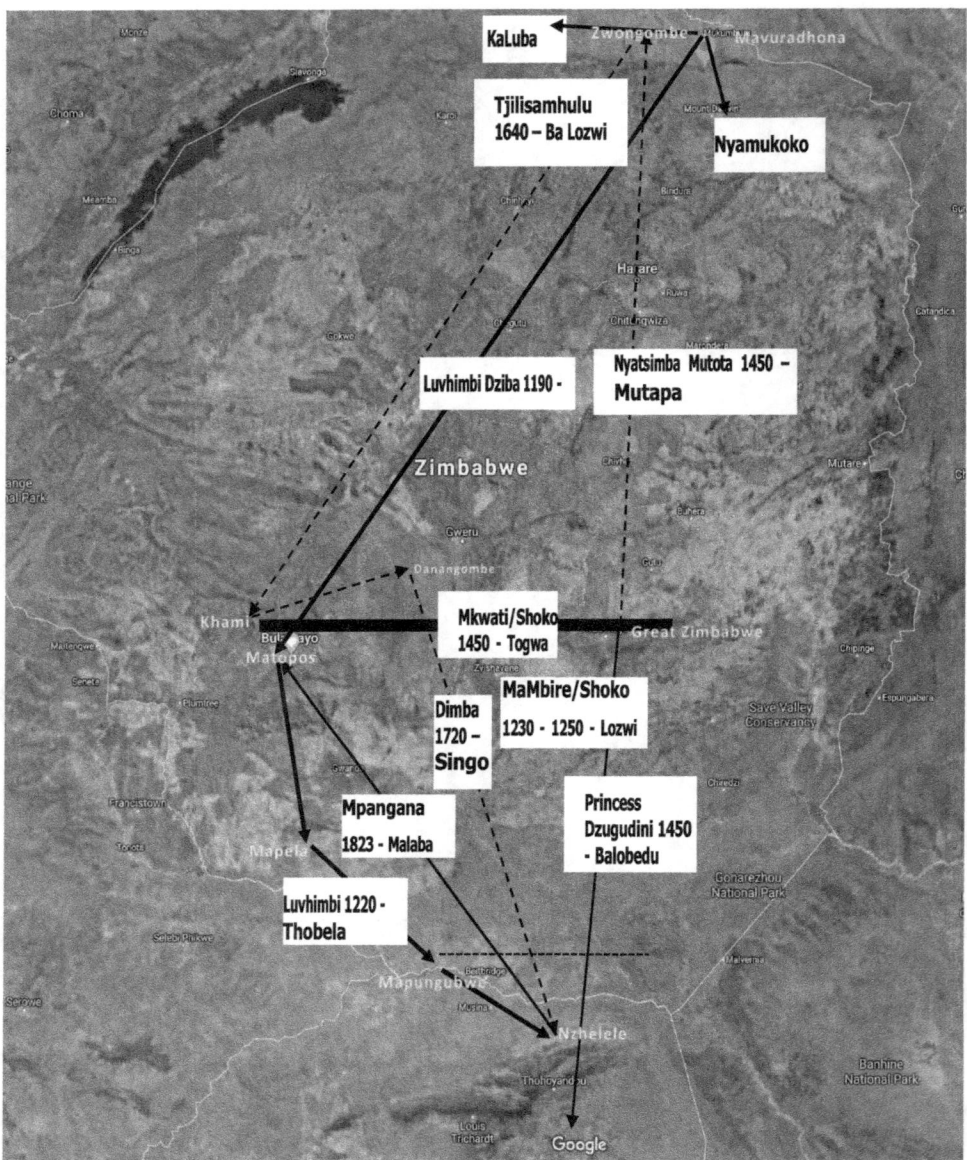

Figure 1. Map Showing Movements of Different Ancient Zimbabwean Clans

Published in @2021 by *Malaba Legacy Publishers*

Copyright © 2010 by Titshabona Ncube, Dr Matiwaza Ncube, Admire Ncube, John Ncube

All rights reserved. No part of this publication may be reproduced, distributed, or transmitted in any form or by any means, including photocopying, recording, or other electronic or mechanical methods, without the prior written permission of the publisher, except in the case of brief quotations embodied in critical reviews and certain other non-commercial uses permitted by copyright law. For permission requests, write to the publisher, addressed "Attention: Permissions Coordinator," at the address below.

info@malabalegacy.com

ISBN: 978-1-913713-62-1

For comments and notification of typos

info@malabalegacy.com

Dedication

We dedicate this book to The Malaba Clan in general and The Royal Malaba Family inparticular.

To our children:

Bridget Malaba

Wendy Malaba

Tsepiso Michele Malaba

Nkosikhona Malaba

Jason Mthandazo Malaba

Kimberley Tamusa Malaba

Nicole Malaba

Glenn Mninimuzi Malaba

Darren Tumelo Malaba

Lisani Malaba

Beverley Mihayedu Malaba

Indira Indie Malaba

Tiffany Tatjipiwa Malaba

Ludiyo Malaba

We are super proud of you. Keep questioning, learning, and discovering. It is a great big world out there and it is ready to be explored!

Acknowledgments

Most of all we would like to express our special thanks of gratitude to Kevin Njabulo Mathe, Thabani Hillary Moyo, Dickson Malaba Ncube, Henry Thobela Malaba, Brito Malaba Ncube, Hlanganani Malaba, Menzi Ndolo Malaba, Dingani Malaba Ncube, Linda Malaba Ncube and Christine Malaba-Nesongano for reviewing the draft work of the book, **The Malaba Clan: Heritage and Legacy: The Historical Perspective**. *We also wish to thank The Malaba Clan who gave us the golden opportunity to do this wonderful project which also helped us in doing a lot of research and came to know about so many new things. Thirdly, we would also like to thank our parents and families who helped us a lot in finalizing this project despite the pressure of family responsibilities.*

Table of contents

DEDICATION III
ACKNOWLEDGMENTS IV
TABLE OF CONTENTS V
TABLE OF FIGURES VII
LIST OF TABLES XI
FOREWORD XII
PREFACE XIV
CULTURE AND LANGUAGE XIX
INTRODUCTION XXII
IMPORTANCE OF WRITING THE MALABA HISTORY: DATA COLLECTION AND
ANALYSIS XXII
CHAPTER 1 1
MIGRATION 1
CHAPTER 2 10
BANTU MIGRATION 10
CHAPTER 3 13
THE ORIGINS OF THE MALABA PEOPLE 13
3,1. THE EMERGENCE OF THE RAINMAKERS 13
3,2. THE PEOPLE OF DZIBAGULU LEVULA 25
3,3. THE DZIBALEVULA-HUNGWE ALLIANCE 34
3,4. THE LUVHIMBI DYNASTY; MAPUNGUBWE SETTLEMENT 36
3,5. LUVHIMBI-MBEDZI ALLIANCE 46
3,6; THE CHILDREN OF MBEDZI-NKULU 60
3,7. MIGRATION FROM VENDA; THE JOURNEY 77
3,8. NCUBE YAKAMALABA 92
3,9. THE NCUBE YAKALUBIMBI/SABASWI/KOLE 93
3,10. THE NCUBE YAKATSHIMBA-BHANGWA 94
3,11. THE JOURNEY CONTINUES 97
CHAPTER 4 105
THE MALABA FINAL SETTLEMENT. 105
4,1. CHIEFTAINCY AND CHIEFDOM 105
4,2. HHOBHODO/HHOBA MALABA AND THE CLAN CHIEFTAINCY 141
4;3. LOBENGULA KHUMALO AND SARA LIEBENBERG AT THE MALABA KRAAL 143

4,4. The Potgieter Raid and Lobengula's Return to Esigodlweni 156
4,5. The Malaba Traditional Leadership 170
4,6. The Last Days of King Mzilikazi 175
4,7. Finding Tshidada Malaba 180
4,8. Lobengula is King 189
4,9. The Malaba and the Nketha Census 194
4,10. The Death of Mbikwa Tshimba 200
CHAPTER 5 208
THE MALABA LEGACY AND THE TEST OF TIME & THE EFFECTS OF THE NDEBELE WARS 208
5,1. Cecil John Rhodes 208
5,2; The Rudd Concession 212
5,3. The First Ndebele War 224
5,4. Umvukela WamaNdebele -The Ndebele Uprising 238
CHAPTER 6 258
THE MALABA PEOPLE AND LAND DISPOSSESSIONS 258
6,1. The Empandeni Settlement 258
6,2. Chief Ntelela Malaba 280
CHAPTER 7 293
THE NJELELE AND THE MALABA PEOPLE 293
7,1. Mwalism 293
7,2. The Malaba Clan and the Njelele Rainmaking Shrine 299
7,2. The Njelele Real Experiences 309
7,3. The Hosanna Real Experiences 311
7,4. Does the Njelele Shrine Hold the Future Key? 314
Appendix A 316
The Malaba people now 316
Genealogy and Malaba Prominent Individuals 316
1,1. Genealogy 316
1,2 The Malaba Prominent Figures 319
References 329
Written by: 340

Table of Figures

FIGURE 1. MAP SHOWING MOVEMENTS OF DIFFERENT ANCIENT ZIMBABWEAN CLANS i
FIGURE 2. MOTA WAS FOUND IN A CAVE, SITTING 6,440FT (1,963M) ABOVE SEA LEVEL IN SOUTHWESTERN ETHIOPIA'S GAMO HIGHLANDS. (PICTURE COURTESY OF THE DAILY MAIL.CO.UK) 3
FIGURE 3. THE IMAGE SHOWS AN EXCAVATION OF THE ROCK CAIRN UNDER WHICH THE BURIAL WAS FOUND (PICTURE COURTESY OF KATHRYN AND JOHN ARTHUR) 3
FIGURE 4. THE SKELETON FOUND IN MOTA CAVE IS RELATED TO THE ARI, WHO ARE MODERN-DAY ETHIOPIAN HIGHLANDERS (PHOTO COURTESY OF BEN PIPE/ROBERT HARDING) 4
FIGURE 5. THIS MAP SHOWS THE PROPORTION OF WEST EURASIAN COMPONENT, MOTA, LBK, ACROSS THE AFRICAN CONTINENT (PICTURE COURTESY OF THE DAILY MAIL.CO.UK, 2015). 6
FIGURE 6 MAP SHOWING EARLY HUMAN MIGRATION AROUND THE WORLD. IMAGE FROM WIKIPEDIA. 7
FIGURE 7. THIS MIGRATION FROM THE ANCIENT NEAR EAST AND FERTILE CRESCENT, ROUGHLY CORRESPONDING TO MODERN IRAQ, TURKEY, IRAN, AND SYRIA, RESHAPED THE AFRICAN CONTINENT'S GENETIC MAKEUP (PHOTO COURTESY OF THE DAILY MAIL.CO.UK) 8
FIGURE 8. MAP SHOWING MIGRATION OF THE EARLY MALABA PEOPLE FROM YEMEN TO THE GREAT LAKES REGION IN CENTRAL AFRICA. IMAGE COURTESY OF GOOGLE MAPS 12
FIGURE 9. MAP SHOWING THE CITY OF MALABA AND THE RIVER MALABA WHICH SEPARATES KENYA FROM UGANDA. IMAGE COURTESY OF GOOGLE MAPS 22
FIGURE 10. SHOWING THE MIGRATION OF THE MALABA PEOPLE FROM KENYA TO MALABA ZIMBABWE. IMAGE ADAPTED FROM GOOGLE MAPS, 2018. 23
FIGURE 11. SHOWING THE BUKUSU FAMILY TREE FROM MUNDU TO LUVHIMBI THE GREAT. ADAPTED FROM SIMIYO (1991). 24
FIGURE 12. SHOWING THE MAVULADONA (LITERALLY MEANS PLACE OF THE RAINDROPS) MOUNTAIN WHERE DZIBALEVULA IS BURIED. IMAGE ADAPTED FROM GOOGLE MAPS/IMAGES, 2018 29
FIGURE 13. THE MOVEMENTS OF DIFFERENT CLANS AND TRIBES IN BUKALANGA AND VHUVENDA, DRAWN FROM GOOGLE MAPS 31
FIGURE 14. MAPUNGUBWE-TYPE GLASS BEADS (B) WERE FOUND IN MAPELA HILL (A) - SHOWING THE SUMMIT, TERRACES, AND SURROUNDING FLATS (ADAPTED FROM CHIRIKURE ET AL, (2014)). 32
FIGURE 15. SHOWING THE MAPUNGUBWE HILL WHERE LUVHIMBI BECAME NYUNYIYEDENGA AND HIGH PRIEST. IMAGE ADAPTED FROM THE ENCYCLOPAEDIA OF ANCIENT HISTORY, 2020. 37
FIGURE 16. MAP OF MAPUNGUBWE (CE1220–1290). MAP COURTESY OF HUFFMAN, (2007). 39
FIGURE 17. STATUS AND HIERARCHICAL CHANGE IN THE VENDA SOCIETY. COURTESY OF LOUBSTER, 2008 40

FIGURE 18. ARTIST IMPRESSION OF MAPUNGUBWE SETTLEMENT - PICTURE COURTESY OF PININTEREST.COM 41
FIGURE 19. THE MAIN 11 TO 12TH CENTURY TRADE ROUTE CONNECTING MAPUNGUBWE AND THE ARAB NORTH (IMAGE DRAWN USING GOOGLE MAPS) 42
FIGURE 20. ABRAHAM ORTELIUS' 1570 MAP KNOWN AS AFRICAE TABULA NOVA SHOWING GREAT ZIMBABWE AS SIMBAOE. 45
FIGURE 21. MAP SHOWING THE SPHERES OF INFLUENCE OF THE MWALI RELIGION – ADAPTED FROM (DANEEL, 1970) 47
FIGURE 22. SHOWING A SKETCH OF THE LAYOUT OF THE ZIMBABWE STYLE TSHITAKA TSHA MAKOLENI LOCATED AT THE SUMMIT OF TSWINGONI MOUNTAIN. COPIED FROM THOMAS HUFFMAN SETTLEMENT HIERARCHIES IN THE NORTHERN TRANSVAAL: ZIMBABWE RUINS AND VENDA HISTORY. 53
FIGURE 23. SHOW THE AREAS SETTLED BY THE MBEDZI LUVHIMBI PEOPLE AS THEY ARRIVED FROM MALUNGUDZI, NORTH OF LIMPOPO. 59
FIGURE 24. THE MANELEDZI POOL ON RIVER MUTALE: WHERE THE "POOL CONTEST" TOOK PLACE. THIS SITE TOGETHER WITH TSWINGONI AND TSHILAVULU FORM A HOLY TRINITY OF THE SACRED CIRCUIT OF THE LUVHIMBI THEBULA RITUAL (COURTESY OF MANOMBE LUVHIMBI – VENDA) 63
FIGURE 25. AN ARTISTIC IMPRESSION OF MPANGANA MALABA: COURTESY OF AUTHOR LYNN BEDFORD HALL 92
FIGURE 26. A DEPICTION OF THE HOSANNA AT NJELELE: COURTESY OF WEEKENDPOST.BW 95
FIGURE 27. BAKALANGA OF BOTSWANA AND ZIMBABWE DOING HOSANNA DANCE; PICTURE COURTESY OF PAPERS.SSRN.COM 97
FIGURE 28. THE MAIN RETAINING WALL AT DANANGOMBE SHOWING THE PATTERNED WALLING. PICTURE COURTESY OF ZIMFIELDGUIDE HTTPS://ZIMFIELDGUIDE.COM/MATABELELAND-SOUTH/DANANGOMBE-MONUMENT-FORMERLY-DHLO-DHLO-RUINS 111
FIGURE 29. AN UNKNOWN ARTIST'S IMPRESSION OF KING MZILIKAZI KHUMALO THE KING OF MATEBELE, DIED 1868 – PICTURE COURTESY OF SOUTH AFRICAN HISTORY ONLINE, (2020). 128
FIGURE 30. THE MARSHALL HOLE CURRENCY OF 1900 IN BULAWAYO, COURTESY OF HTTP://WWW.RHODESIANSTUDYCIRCLE.ORG.UK/ 131
FIGURE 31. AN ARTISTIC IMPRESSION OF SARA THE DUTCH GIRL WITH PRINCE LOBENGULA UPON SPOTTING POTGIETER'S MEN. COURTESY OF AUTHOR LYNN BEDFORD HALL..... 156
FIGURE 32. THE WOOD OBJECT IS THOUGHT TO BE OLDEST EVER FOUND IN SUB-SAHARAN AFRICA (PHOTO COURTESY OF THE BBC) 159
FIGURE 33. PICTURE OF HENDRIK POTGIETER AND HIS WIFE SUSANNA MARIA DUVENAGE, COURTESY OF THE ZOUSTERNBURGER 164
FIGURE 34. PRE-COLONIAL MAP SHOWING INDICATING KALANGA AND NDEBELE AREAS. SOURCE; UNIVERSITY OF ROCHESTER PRESS 169
FIGURE 35. CHIEF NGUGAMA BANGO; PHOTO COURTESY OF WERBNER, 1991 174

FIGURE 36. MAP SHOWING THE JURISDICTION OF CHIEF MALABA & CHIEF HHOBHODO (WARDS, 5, 6, 7' RESPECTIVELY). ADAPTED FROM MATABELELAND SOUTH PROVINCE HTTPS://WWW.HUMANITARIANRESPONSE.INFO/SITES/WWW.HUMANITARIANRESPONSE .INFO/FILES/ZWE_MATSOUTH_PROVINCE_A0_V1.PDF 186

FIGURE 37. A PICTURE OF KING LOBENGULA AND ONE OF HIS WIVES – COURTESY OF ZIMBABWE ENVIRONMENTAL CONSULTANCY & HERITAGE TOURS 193

FIGURE 38. A DRAWING DEPICTING THE INAUGURATION OF KING LOBENGULA - FROM A DRAWING BY THOMAS BAINES. 194

FIGURE 39. A PAINTING SHOWING THE MANGWE FORT/PASS, PAINTING COURTESY OF MARULA WOMEN'S INSTITUTE, 1923 196

FIGURE 40. PRINCE TSHAKALISA SINTINGA; PHOTO COURTESY OF R.S. ROBERTS 206

FIGURE 41. CECIL JOHN RHODES (1853-1902) IS A PAINTING BY GRANGER. 208

FIGURE 42. RHODES' VISION WAS BRITISH DOMINION "FROM THE CAPE TO CAIRO". PICTURE COURTESY OF THE RHODES FOUNDATION... 211

FIGURE 43. A WHEEL FROM ONE OF THE CONCESSIONISTS CARTS IS KEPT BY THE MALABA PEOPLE AS A MONUMENT IN A HILLTOP IN MARULA (PHOTO COURTESY OF R. DOKO) 217

FIGURE 44. AN OLD MAP OF MATABELELAND – SOURCE UNKNOWN 218

FIGURE 45. A PICTURE OF THE MANGWE PASS – COURTESY MAPIO.NET 218

FIGURE 46. PICTURE OF THE LETTER SIGNED BY KING LOBENGULA. COURTESY OF SOUTH AFRICAN HISTORY ONLINE 220

FIGURE 47. MAP OF THE OCTOBER/NOVEMBER 1893 MATABELE WAR CAMPAIGN, PICTURE COURTESY OF DENNIS BISHOP 228

FIGURE 48. HADDON AND SLY LIMITED, PICTURE COURTESY OF RHODESIANSTUDYCIRCLE.ORG.UK 231

FIGURE 49. THIS PHOTO SHOWS THE TOWN OF BULAWAYO IN RHODESIA WITH A NUMBER OF HOMES, SHOPS, AND MILITARY BUILDINGS ON DISPLAY. PHOTO COURTESY OF THE DAILY MAIL.CO.UK 233

FIGURE 50. LOBENGULA'S SONS; PRINCE NGUBOYENJA (LEFT), PRINCE NJUBE (CENTRE) AND PRINCE MPEZENI (RIGHT) IN 1900. PICTURE COURTESY OF R.S. ROBERTS 236

FIGURE 51. A MAP SHOWS A PLACE THAT WAS PEGGED AS MALABA MOUNTAIN AS A WAY TO KEEP AN EYE ON THE MALABA PEOPLE DURING UMVUKELA WAMANDEBELE. MAP COURTESY OF FLETCHER AND ESPIN'S MAP OF MATABELELAND BY ROBERT ALEXANDER FLETCHER 245

FIGURE 52. DEPICTION OF BURNHAM AND ARMSTRONG AFTER THE ASSASSINATION OF MWALI HIGH PRIEST JENJE LUBIMBI. MATABELE WARRIORS IN HOT PURSUIT, DRAWN BY FRANK DADD. PIC, COURTESY OF WIKIVISUALLY.COM 250

FIGURE 53. FIG. THE EXECUTION OF SOME NDEBELE MEN AT THE 'HANGING TREE' IN BULAWAYO. PHOTO EXTRACTED FROM OLIVE SCHREINER'S BOOK ENTITLED TROOPER PETER HALKET OF MASHONALAND AND BELOW IT, STATUE OF ROBERT BADEN-POWELL HOLDING ON TO JENJE'S WALKING STICK IN POOLE ENGLAND 253

Figure 54. Picture: Ndebele chiefs and representatives gather for a meeting during umvukela wamandebele. (Photos by W. Rausch; Courtesy of the Daily Mail, UK). 254

Figure 55. A sketch of the 1896 peace Indaba. (Sketched by Lord Robert Baden-Powell). 255

Figure 56. Picture; The burial of Cecil John Rhodes. Photo Courtesy of Rhodesia.me.uk 256

Figure 57. Picture taken in March 1896; the Matabele revolted against the authority of the British South AfricaCompany (pictured. (Photos by W. Rausch; Courtesy of the Daily Mail, UK). 257

Figure 58. Picture - Chief Ntelela Malaba Portrait by D.J. Avery. Photo Courtesy of the Tshidada Family. 285

Figure 59. The traditional Zimbabwean system of governance 286

Figure 60. Picture - Chief Joseph Malaba. Photo Courtesy of the Tshidada Family 289

Figure 61. Picture: Joshua Mqabuko Nyongolo Nkomo Statue on Main Street Bulawayo renamed to Joshua Mqabuko Nkomo Street. Courtesy of RMF 292

Figure 62. Njelele Shrine; Image Courtesy of www.chronicle.co.zw 311

Figure 63. Suspected Mount Sinai picture courtesy of Google images 311

Figure 64. The Njelele Shrine located at the Matopo Hills. 314

Figure 65. Chief David Christopher Malaba at his birthday celebration. Picture courtesy of RMF 319

Figure 66. Chief Justice Luke Doko Malaba, Courtesy of www.zimbabwesituation,com 320

Figure 67. Hobodo Primary school named after chief Hhobhodo. 321

Figure 68. A sketchy art on the wall of Hhobhodo school showing chief Hhobhodo brewing tjathiyani/isathiyane. 322

Figure 69. The Chronicle cutting 5 May 2019, on the declaration of Misheck Ntundu Velaphi Ncube, as Zimbabwe's National Hero. He was the son of Mfihlo, grandson of Velaphi, great, grandson of Lungombe and great, great, great grandson of Mpangana Malaba. 325

Figure 70. Picture; St Joseph's Mission in Kezi; Picture. Courtesy of RMF 327

List of Tables

TABLE 1. SINGO LEADERSHIP LINEAGE, COMPILED BY DR MATIWAZA NCUBE FROM VARIOUS SOURCES 71

TABLE 2. SUMMARY OF CASUALTIES IN MATABELELAND AND MASHONALAND 1896-1897, DATA ADAPTEDFROM BEACH, 1975 257

Foreword

This is a summary of the history of the Malaba people or clan. It is a narrative that covers the Malaba people's existence and contributions to societies they have lived with or in and influenced from as far as admissible data could be gathered. The gathered data highlights a long migration pattern that stretches from the Middle East penetrating through East Africa and finally settling in the VhuVenda area before re-locating up north to the present-day Matabeleland. The book aims to recount the trials and tribulations of the clan, the spiritual battles, and physical challenges they encountered with conquests or none of that. The account presents a picture of how the clan managed to influence and shape other peoples and communities, specifically through their extraordinary gift of rainmaking and knowledge of African medicines.

It is herein this book a detail on the clan's existence in vhuVenda and around the Matobo areas of Zimbabwe where they co-existed with the BaKalanga, the Matabele of King Mzilikazi and Lobengula and under the British South Africa Company (BSAC) colonial rule. More importantly the book underscores the clan's ascendancy, prominence, and predominance in the political, religious, and social space, broadly in the Ndebele kingdom through the distinguished clan fathers like Mantsha, popularly known as Mpangana, through to Hhobhodo/Hhoba and to the contemporary Tshidada Malaba chiefdom.

Particular attention is paid on the Malaba clan and the establishment and sustained custodianship of the Njelele, a shrine located in the Mabweadziba site of the Matopos. The great influence of Mwalism and the Mwali religion in the region is deeply outlined in the book. This, nevertheless, should be noted that a separate book or document on the influence of Mwalism in general and the Njelele shrine, will be a necessity for a fuller comprehension of what the shrine stood for and should stand for.

The Malaba Clan: Heritage and Legacy: The Historical Perspective, is a rigorous and properly done original piece of work. The book represents one of the indigenous autobiographical pieces that are increasingly becoming important as new modes through which previously silenced voices are telling their own histories and stories that are counterhegemonic to hegemonic histories from colonizers and dominant ethnicities. That is to be the theoretical significance of the work as it answers a critical question of the "so what?" Why should I be interested in reading about the Malaba clan and their history? Relax for a journey into reading and enjoy the MALABA people from their own history by themselves.

By **John Malaba Ncube** (Chairman; The Malaba Royal Family Forum)

....

Preface

Elsewhere, someone once said that whenever a person undertakes to work on a program, they should at the outset, approach it with the underlying assumption that it was a puzzle with a solution. If one started a jigsaw puzzle not knowing whether all the pieces were in the box, it may turn out to be an unexciting exercise. Co-equally, for many history writers, fore gathering the history of the Malaba people has proven an equivalent to doing a jigsaw puzzle that has a million pieces and more so, not knowing whether all the pieces were actual in the box. To gain a comprehensive understanding of the history, heritage, and legacy of the Malaba people, it becomes critical to begin by answering a number of crucial and relevant questions before submitting a more concise summary of what basically defines the Malaba a people and a clan. The following sub-questions are narrower questions that provided the 'skeleton' around which information to answer the main research question on the *'History of the Malaba Clan'* were founded as this book is a piece of work which attempts to provide answers to the question that have always sought to find out *'Who are the Malaba People, and What is Their History, Heritage and Legacy?'*. This undertaking would be assisted by an attempt to answer the following further sub questions:

1. *What are the origins of the Malaba clan?*
2. *Who is Malaba?*
3. *What is their original totem?*
4. *Who are the known Malaba ancestors?*
5. *What were the reasons of their migration?*
6. *How did the Malaba legacy originate?*
7. *How and where does the rain making legacy begin?*
8. *What language and culture defines the Malaba clan?*
9. *What was the relationship between the Malaba and other nations?*
10. *What is the Malaba order of seniority?*

Although it could not be fully contended that the Malaba history commences at the point of answering the above questions, as a matter of fact, an attempt at answering the specific questions would, to a larger extent, assist with a better understanding of both the background and foreground of the Malaba clan history. The main question on *'Who the Malaba People are'*, and *'What Their History, Heritage and Legacy is'*, can be answered in various ways simply and/or comprehensively. A less complex answer to the question is presented in chief Ntelela Malaba interview with Author Cockcroft (Ntelela, 1976). Cockcroft quotes chief Ntelela to the effect that the Malaba clan *"had fought with their tribe"* in VhuVenda, which explains their resultant migration from VhuVenda to the present-day Zimbabwe. The same interview reveals that the Malaba *"were afraid that they would be followed hence the reason they changed their surname from Mbedzi/Ndlovu to Ncube"* (Cobbing, 1976).

The second section of Ntelela's answer indicates that the Malaba clan were at some point compelled to change the surname, a matter that ultimately leads to more supplementary questions; *what motivated them to change the surname? Is there any reason for the choice of the newly acquired name? Who and where were their so-called tribe? Why were they running away from the tribe and where to? Where do the Malaba people originate? And finally, who or what is Malaba?* Although they pertain to providing answers to only half of the Malaba people history, the above questions are principal as they become the first active step towards an answerable inquiry into the full and integrated history, heritage, and legacy of the Malaba people. Answering them becomes an essential springboard upon which further background information could be achieved.

The significant part of the contemporary Malaba clan's otherwise long history starts just before 1823, after Bepe Luvhimbi who was the last male in the Luvhimbi rainmaking dynasty realized an upcoming leadership vacuum that would be created through his death (Le-Roux, 1996, N. M. N. Ralushai, 1978). His death led to a succession contest that takes place in the sacred Maneledzi Pool, in the central Mutale River valley. It is an exceptional contest which is exclusive only to the male descendants of Luvhimbi, selected solely from the lineage of Mbedzinkulu's marriage to Luvhimbi's daughter Tshiembe.

Thobela Mbedzi's mother was also a MaLuvhimbi, born out of a marital alliance entered between the Luvhimbi and the Mbedzi clans. It is after his marriage to Tshiembe Luvhimbi, that Thobela Mbedzi become known as 'Mbedzinkulu' (an elevated and supreme Mbedzi), not only as a way of distinguishing him from the other Mbedzis, but also as an indication of change of status due to a paramount royal marriage. Marital alliances were routine informal, but strong, agreements or treaties between clans to marry within each other. This was done in accordance with keeping the cultural values intact, preserve family wealth, maintain geographic closeness, keep tradition, strengthen family ties, and maintain family structure. Marrying *'outside'* of the Alliance was perceived as potentially exposing the clan to the enemies. As shall be brought to light later, this cultural phenomenon over and above, draws attention to the Malaba clan's very origins.

The research findings reveal that the ancient story of the Malaba-*zinda* or *linga* legacy originated from *Wele* (God) Malaba, who was son of Sioka. *Wele* Malaba was an integral part of a Trinity system of the ancient Bukusu clan found in East-Central Africa (V. G. Simiyu, 1991). Like in the Christian doctrine, the Trinity system entailed that there is one Supreme Being but three Persons. In the Trinity, *Wele* (God) Malaba was given a role of looking after the welfare of people and their livestock as well as the vegetation. It is this role that led to the clan essentially being synonymous with the rainmaking tradition, a legacy they carried up to this day. It was this royal highness of *Wele* (God) Malaba that was to be recurrent through a deliberate system of revival or recreation whenever there was a requirement. Malaba means 'future' in the TshiLuba language of west and central Africa.

In the pool contest, the young Tshibi, from the Mpangana Malaba first house, wins the encounter in what was perceived to be a sacred decision taken by Mwali the Creator, God the Almighty. Tshibi ultimately assumes from the Great Luvhimbi, the ancient Malaba legacy, otherwise known as *linga* in TjiKalanga or *izinda* in siNdebele languages, respectively. According to tradition, the *linga/izinda* legacy had its emphasis on the spiritual power of a supreme and paramount ancestor, that was entrusted upon a qualifying descendant. The empowered descendant then assumes the role of that ancestor and in a special way of reversal of roles, becomes a *father even to his father*. The role involves assuming the all-important role as a custodian of values, customs and traditions of a clan, and the individual embraces the responsibility of providing guidance to the clan and other multitudes in general. After the pool contest victory, Tshibi's enacted legacy make him father to all the houses that arbitrarily fell under the Mpangana banner. Since the Malaba *zinda/linga* was supernaturally bestowed onto Tshibi, that meant thereupon, all the eight houses of Mpangana, and only those particular houses, were to assume the Malaba title, bequeathed and becoming heirs to the old Malaba royal and spiritual legacy with all its duties, functions, roles, and responsibilities. It was *Wele* Malaba's majesty and nobleness combined with being Mwali's chosen people that provided the clan with some special royalty that led to the clan referred to as the *Buhe gwakaMalaba*.

By the same token, Tshibi, assumes the form of a *bhaluli-umdabuli* or clan creator of the present day Malaba clan, a clan born exclusively out of the houses that arbitrarily fell under Mpangana as opposed to those houses arbitrarily falling under Mpangana's brothers or sisters. This, consequently, excluded the other houses regardless of whether they had competed in the pool contest or not. Accordingly, by default, Mpangana's siblings, Sabaswi-Kole Lubimbi, Tshimba- Bhangwa, Mufanadzo, Tshawwila and with their descendants and anyone else's families, were not entitled to this Malaba signature.

Therefore, to put it sacredly, in respect to the above revelations, the modern times Malaba clan presently found in parts of Matabeleland, Zimbabwe, were originated in VhuVhenda, in what is now known as the Limpopo Province of South Africa. However, the Malaba *zinda/linga* legacy is a phenomenon that in essence stretches back to the times of the ancient Bukusu tribes who existed in the ancient times in the proximity of Nam Lolwe, Nnalubaale, Nyanza or the present- day Lake Victoria in the peninsula of the African Great Lakes. The existence of the Malaba people themselves go beyond the Malaba legacy, and with the help of their cultural and religious traits, evidently traceable as far back as to a small ancient town of Sena in the present-day Republic of Yemen, a country at the southern end of the Arabian Peninsula in Western Asia.

Culture and language

Although the Malaba clan spoke and still speak the Kalanga language, they are technically of Venda origin, nonetheless. However, because they historically belonged to the ancient BaKalanga before being Venda, they ultimately make up a group of Southern African people naturally referred to as the Venda-Kalangas. The difference between the Lozwi-Kalangas and their Venda-Kalanga counterparts was significantly noticeable through the titles of their kings. The Venda-Kalanga kings were normally addressed as Thovhele/Thobela while the Lozwi Bakalanga's title for king was Mambo, although these titles were sometimes used interchangeably. As Beach points out, the Thovhela was not the same as the first Singo, for the connections between the Singo and the Changamire Rozvi are clear, whereas it is obvious from the Dutch reports of the 1720s that there was no political connection between the Thovhela and the Changamire and that there was probably no dynastic connection (D. Beach, N, 1980). The Venda language is not only one of seven known regional varieties of the main tjiKalanga language, but also a transformation of tjiKalanga and Sotho-Tswana, and the Venda society itself is a present-day variation of the Zimbabwe culture (Huffman and du Piesanie, 2011).

Dzibagulu levula is one of the founders of the BaKalanga people and his first son, Luvhimbi, undeniably spoke tjiKalanga as evidenced by their totems and the naming of people, features, and places. His descendants through the Luvhimbi dynasty of rainmakers, later spoke tshiVhenda, before riveting back to the original tjiKalanga language for religious reasons. Although living amongst the Venda and identifying as Venda, the restoration of tjiKalanga as the main language of communication was mandatory due to their role as rainmaking custodians. There's sufficient evidence of the clan speaking tjiKalanga from the days they lived in Bukalanga, to VhuVenda or Lukungurubwe and to as far as the modern times.

The evidence includes that many of the Malaba ancestor's names are in Kalanga and there is no evidence of the clan speaking any other language other than Kalanga or some of its dialects such as Venda, Lembethu or Tshimbedzi varieties. When Dzibalevula and his people arrived in the present-day Zimbabwe, they gave Kalanga names to places like Mavuladona, Matombo, Mabweadziba and others. The names of Luvhimbi's descendants are mostly in the tjiKalanga language. The Malaba *zwitemo* (totems), that chronicle their history, heritage and legacy are recited in Kalanga and no other language, and this is coupled with a notion that *zwitemo zwakaMalaba azwito tolikiwa* (the Malaba totems diction is not translative from Kalanga).

Nevertheless, some of the people who lived in Venda land were called vhaKalanga and like the Malaba clan, there are people in the Limpopo province of South Africa who still speak what is called *iKalanga* today and, like the Malaba clan, also practice similar traditions like the custom referred to as *tebula* (*thevhula*) or spilling, especially of sorghum. During the Tebula process young women are required to grind some mealies which have not been soaked and not fermented. People sit in a circle to take some black bovine or a black goat. The leader of the family or a village head would rise up and deliver a prayer specifically in the tjiKalanga language.

According to a BBC documentary, one of the main rituals performed at the Phiphidi waterfall in Thohoyandou is *Thevhula* (*tebula*), a rain ritual considered essential to ensuring a good harvest and rains (BBC, 2010). During *thevhula*, the women prepare unfermented beer to be poured into the ritual wooden plate which is kept for the purpose of contacting the ancestors for the purposes of thanksgiving and keeping out bad luck like diseases, bad harvests, natural catastrophes, accidents, or quarrels, disturb the harmony in the village. The same practice is still visible amongst the modern day Malaba people.

Some Venda informants revealed to the author that even those possessed with ancestral spirits in the contemporary Venda customary practices are considered as gods and are called *midzimu* or *vhakalanga*. They speak *tshikalanga* and deliver all their sermons in the tjiKalanga language. Coming from that background, it is not surprising that, despite being Venda by identity, the Malaba clan maintained the Kalanga language for so long against all odds. A quote from a 1905 report prepared for the General Staff of the British War Office, notes that the Lemba people living in VhuVhenda spoke "Lukalanga" therefore confirming that tjiKalanga was one of the languages spoken in VhuVhenda during that time and noticeably before. A conversation between Luvhimbi of the Mbedzis and the Vhatavhatsindi's Thengwe recorded in the Venda Milayo found at the Oxford Department of Anthropology, reveal a communication in the tjiKalanga language. Mwali the voice of Njelele spoke only in tjiKalanga and the collection of oral traditions by Mothibi (2006), notes that while Mwali of Njelele revealed himself in the Venda area before coming to BuKalanga, he arrived at Njelele Hill (the major shrine in the Matopos Hills) with the Malaba people from the Venda area already speaking iKalanga. Therefore, in essence, if the Malaba people had at some point lost their grasp of the Kalanga language, they either could also have lost grip of their rainmaking custodianship or at worse, the rainmaking culture and legacy could have gravely been compromised.

Historian Saul Gwakuba Ndlovu concludes that tjiKalanga was the proto or one of the proto- Bantu languages in pre-historic times especially in several regions south of the Great Lake's region (Sunday News, 2016). This explains the recurring signs and evidence of the tjiKalanga amongst the Malaba people despite the test of time as well as the constantly geographical relocations. The two basic Venḓa-speaking peoples were the Mbedzi and the Ngoṇa. Therefore, after being part of the original BaKalanga people, the Malaba people found themselves also as one of the original VhaVendas, hence, becoming a Kalanga-Venda clan.

INTRODUCTION

Importance of Writing the Malaba History: Data Collection and Analysis

Since we are not makers of history therefore, we are made by history (King, 1963), and because we are made by history this then means, those who do not remember the past are condemned to likely repeat the accidents of history (Santayana & Gouinlock, 2011). So, the venture towards a people to know its history is important than ever because while history represents human self- knowledge, it is essential for the people to know the past to understand the present and plan. Accordingly, with lack of knowledge of history, it becomes not only difficult to define humanity, but also becomes hard for humanity to claim ownership of what belongs to humanity.

A quote attributed to one Lt. Col Allen West pointed out that "*History is not there for you to like or dislike. It is there for you to learn from it. And if it offends you, then even better because then you are less likely to repeat it. It is not yours to erase. It belongs to all of us.*" This is a statement that teaches us to approach history with an awareness that it is both the ugly and the beautiful that encompasses it.

History is an essential clue to what man can do because history is what man has done. However, as Claudio Magris also notes, history does not only represent a collection of senseless and cruel events of the past, but also presents an opportunity to broadcast the broadest aspect of man's migrations from one environment to another, in such a way that it is difficult to state who is a foreigner. In other words, the awareness of history unites humanity (Magris, 1999).

The Malaba people have a history to be recorded. Through a linear tracking of the existence of a single most complete family, it is a history that presents a rare opportunity to understand, from an unexplored perspective, the lives of the BaKalanga, the Venda, the Shona as well as other tribes in Zimbabwe (Fig. 1). The

Malaba history has been kept as a *'secret'* for an exceptionally long time and therefore, its documentation presents an opportunity to make out other histories from its lineage as well as bridge any missing links in the history of Zimbabwe in general and histories of the VhaVhenda and BaKalanga in particular.

Like J.F. Kennedy once noted that history is a relentless master (Penrose, 1960), and the *'silence'* in the oral narrations of the Malaba history has always called for it to be researched and be documented, especially by members of the Malaba clan with the objective of unearthing what has always been buried beneath the mysteries of the so-called *'Malaba secrets.'* Hence, the undertaking of the *'The Malaba Clan: Heritage and Legacy: The Historical Perspective,'* piece of work. An African proverb goes that, until the story of the hunt is told by the lion, the tale of the hunt will always glorify the hunter.

In this book, the reader will be accompanied on a journey to the biography of selfless and great men who, from the wisdom of their yester lives, possessed the ability to see tomorrow, yet their story has been shrouded in secrecy for so long. This understanding of both the history of the Malaba clan and their cultural, political, and social era was based on gathering evidence regarding the clan's past and evaluating the evidence within the temporal scope of their history, heritage, and legacy. The evidence was then accessed on its contribution to the understanding of that history.

The research on the Heritage and Legacy of the Malaba clan relied on a wide variety of sources that included primary and secondary and oral traditions. Primary Sources comprised eyewitness accounts of events, interviews, oral or written testimony found in public records or legal documents, minutes of meetings, newspapers, diaries, letters, artifacts such as posters, billboards, photographs, drawings, papers located in various institutions.

Secondary sources included scholarly interpretations and critiques of the Malaba clan history. Oral testimonies and personal narratives were gathered from textbooks, encyclopaedias, journal articles, newspapers, biographies as well as in individuals and group interviews.

Considered relevant was the data appropriate to the theoretical questions that were posed prior to the Malaba clan history research. The data relevance was determined by how it was originally collected, or what meanings were embedded in the data at the time of collection. The interpretation and analysis of the collected data was based on a simple formula comprising three core principles for determining reliability.

The three core principles applied were mostly relating FORM, SPACE and TIME. For example, if the consulted sources all agreed about the FORM (that the person or thing existed), SPACE (existence location specified) and TIME (the period of existence specified), then the event was considered proven or on the brink of being proven. However, because the majority does not rule (Langlois & Seignobos, 1898), even if most sources related events in one way, that version could not prevail unless it passed the test of critical textual analysis by both the authors and the reviewers. When two sources disagreed on a particular point, the authors preferred the one source with the most authority.

Mainly that would be the source created by an expert or by an eyewitness (Howell, 2001). When two sources disagreed and there was no other means of evaluation, then the authors considered the source which accorded best with both LOGIC and common sense. Nevertheless, because the book's focus was on the Malaba clan history in relation to the other histories and nations, the authors considered HINDSIGHT as another important factor.

CHAPTER 1

MIGRATION

To understand the movement of the Malaba people and other tribes, a general seasonal movement of people from one region to another throughout history needs to be explained. Like various peoples in various histories, the Malaba clan's migration from one region to another was with the intention of settling permanently or temporarily at new locations for several reasons. For example, the first Agricultural Revolution of 10 000 BC, popularly known as the Neolithic Revolution, was a transition of many human cultures from a lifestyle of hunting and gathering to one of agriculture and settlement (McClellan & Dorn, 2006).

The population explosion that went with this period left a dramatic impact on the human gene pool. Proven by scientific studies, earlier on, the *Homo erectus* had also migrated out of Africa via the Levantine corridor and Ethiopia to Eurasia, the largest continental area on Earth, comprising all of Europe and Asia (Carotenuto et al., 2016).

The extinct ancient human *Homo erectus* was the first known group of modern humans to migrate out of Africa, and possibly the first to cook food. The *erectus species* consisted of several distinct species like the *Homo georgicus* and the *Homo ergaster*. Early archaeological excavations evidenced that the anatomical pattern of *H. erectus* had expanded out of Africa into Asia where they had evolved about two million years ago. The migration might have taken place because the environmental changes that provided suitable habitats and food sources stretched that far. For example, according to the Natural History Museum website, there are samples of some sabre-toothed cat remains that were found alongside *H. erectus* fossils in Georgia, and these were adjudged to have migrated from Africa.

Scientists determined that these types of cats were a specialised carnivore species that lacked the teeth to strip a carcass clean of its meat, thereby providing scavenging opportunities for early humans who deemed it necessary to follow them out of Africa (NHM, 2021).

Studies conducted by the American Association for the Advancement of Science have shown that after the great migration out of Africa as shown in (Fig. 6), came a period when populations started to move back into Africa (Llorente et al., 2015). A study of the Ethiopian genome by the American Association for the Advancement of Science (AAAS) revealed extensive Eurasian admixture in East African populations that helps explain a reverse migration into Africa that happened at about 3000 years ago. The research by nineteen researchers from the AAAS concluded that "ancient Ethiopian genome reveals a large Eurasian mixture throughout the African continent". The research is collaborated by studies conducted by Schlebusch and others (Schlebusch et al., 2017).

The genome study was based on a genetic sample from the remains of a hunter-gatherer man, known as the Mota man, who was found in a cave known as Mota in highland Ethiopia (Fig. 2 & 3). See also figure 5 on the proportion of West Eurasian component, Mota, LBK, across the African continent. According to the Llorente et al, the study was the first time an ancient human genome has been recovered and sequenced from Africa, the source of all human genetic diversity and the findings are published in the journal *Science* (Llorente et al., 2015).

Figure 2. Mota was found in a cave, sitting 6,440ft (1,963m) above sea level in southwestern Ethiopia's Gamo highlands. (Picture Courtesy of The Daily Mail.co.uk)

Figure 3. The image shows an excavation of the rock cairn under which the burial was found (Picture Courtesy of Kathryn and John Arthur)

The scientists analysed the genetic samples using radiocarbon analysis and the conclusion was that the Mota man had died around 2,500 BC and buried face-down 4,500 years ago in a cave cool and dry enough to preserve his DNA for thousands of years. The genetic analysis further demonstrated that the "man" was closely related to the modern Ari population living in the same area.

The modern Ari population represents an aboriginal African group with an undiluted bloodline (Fig.4.).

Figure 4. The skeleton found in Mota cave is related to the Ari, who are modern-day Ethiopian highlanders (PhotoCourtesy of Ben Pipe/Robert Harding)

Scientific evidence points to the fact that studies of African populations could provide a vital genetic baseline from which the story of human evolution could be developed (Llorente et al., 2015) as the DNA extracted from the Mota man's skull supports the theory that a wave of Eurasian farmers migrated back into Africa some 3,000 years ago during a process known as Eurasian backflow. The researchers also found that East African populations currently have as much as a quarter Euro and Asian ancestry while those in West and Southern Africa still have at least five per cent of their genome from Euro and Asian migrants (Gray, 2015). For example, the team also found vestiges of the 'backflow' migration in West Africans and in a Mbuti pygmy group in Central Africa.

However, despite its informative nature, this study was criticized by Pontus Skoglund, a population geneticist at Harvard Medical School in Boston who argued that he was surprised by the claim that as much as 6–7% of the ancestry of West and Central African groups came from the Euro and Asian migrants. He further argued that although "almost all of us agree there was some back-to-Africa gene flow, and it was a pretty big migration into East Africa, however, it did not reach West and Central Africa, at least not in a detectable way" (Callaway, 2016).

Despite the criticism, Skoglund praised the paper arguing that "the genome itself is just fantastic" in as far as proving that the "Eurasian backflow," occurred, especially when people from regions of western Eurasia such as the Middle East and Anatolia suddenly flooded back into Africa (Fig 7.). It was a reverse migration to that which led the first humans out of Africa about 100,000 years ago. The ancient genome study was also described as providing a direct window into the distant past because one genome from one individual could provide a picture of an entire population.

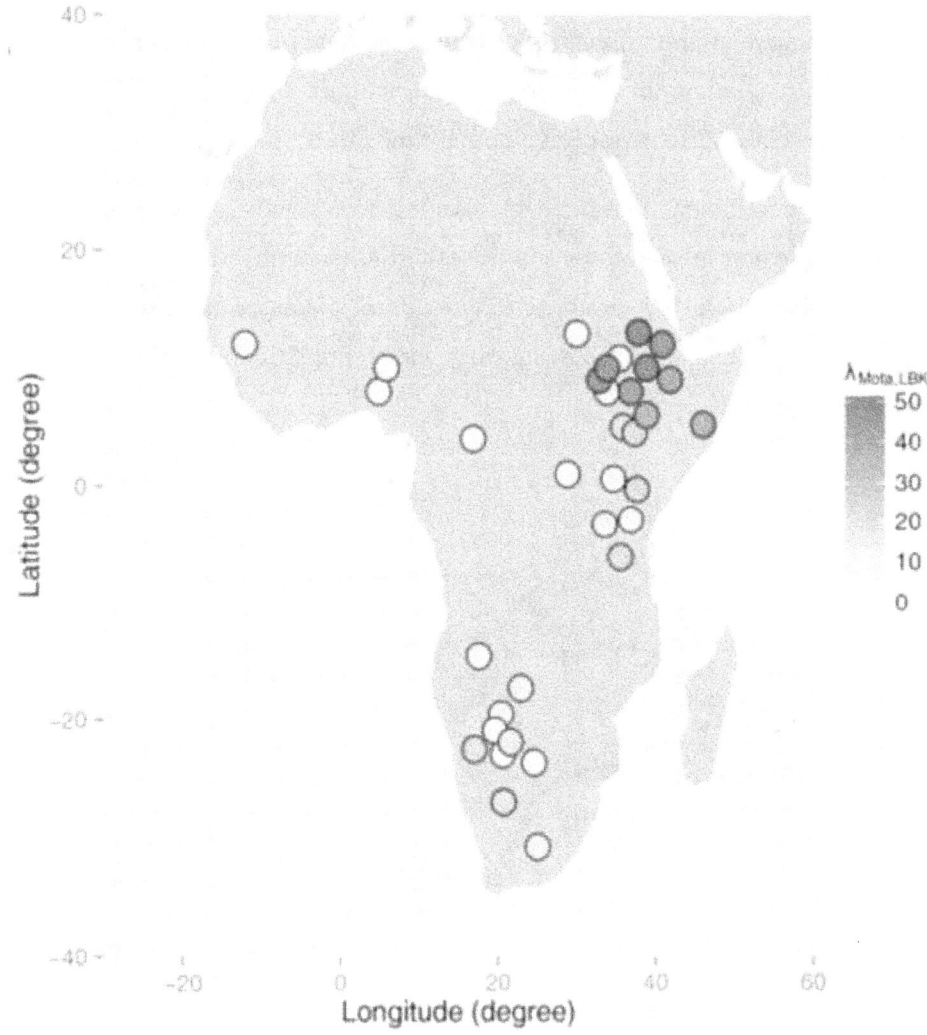

Figure 5. This map shows the proportion of West Eurasian component, Mota, LBK, across the African continent(Picture Courtesy of The Daily Mail.co.uk, 2015).

Accordingly, the wide diversity of human beings as seen in countries worldwide is evidence of human migration that took place throughout history. Among the main motivators of such migrations, was the First Agriculture Revolution of 10 000 BC as well as the Arab Agricultural Revolution of the 8th–13th century.

The growing populations permitted by farming would have, over time, caused territorial expansion in search for additional fertile land, absorbing or displacing particularly those with less productive agricultural practices in Europe, interior Asia, and Africa. See the map showing early human migration around the world in figure 6.

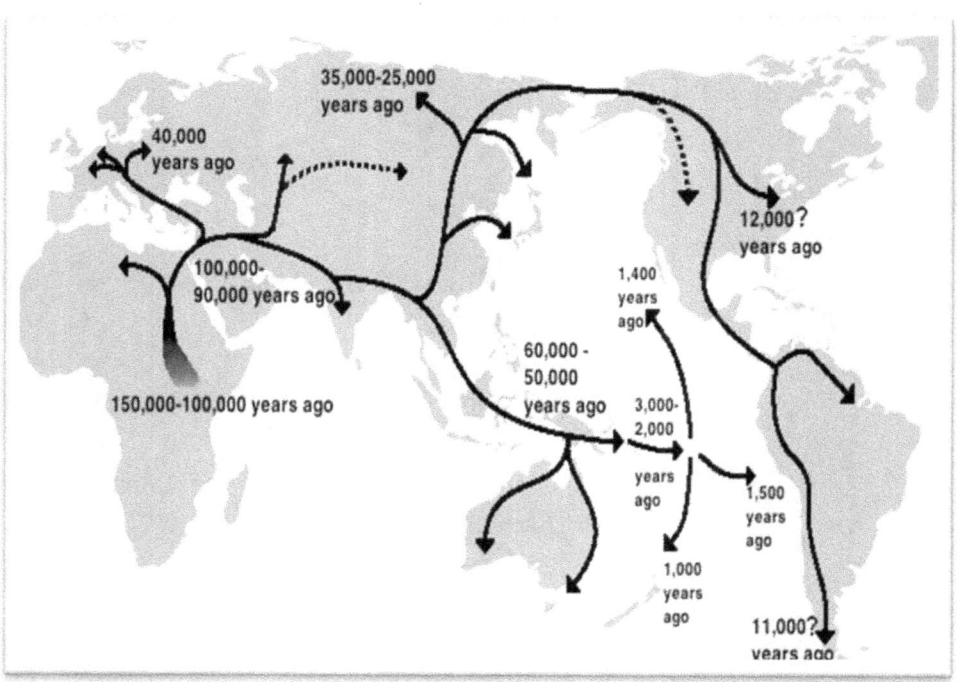

Figure 6 Map showing early human migration around the world. Image from Wikipedia.

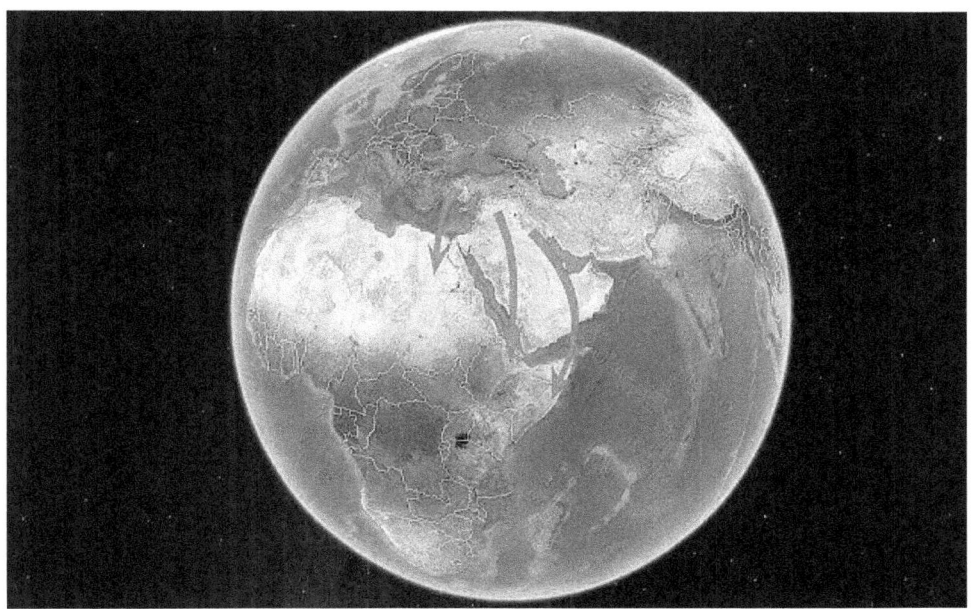

Figure 7. This migration from the ancient Near East and Fertile Crescent, roughly corresponding to modern Iraq, Turkey, Iran, and Syria, reshaped the African continent's genetic makeup (Photo courtesy of the Daily Mail.co.uk)

It has long been known that the final division of the Stone Age farmers from the Near East, including Yemen, where agriculture had developed following the end of the last glacial period, had moved into inner Europe and it is the same population that had brought agriculture to Europe about 7,000 years ago. One theory that has been suggested is that farmers looking for fertile land travelled up the Nile when wheat and barley, which first emerged in the Near East, appeared as crops along the Nile around 3,000 years ago.

However, it is also known that meanwhile a similar migration had taken place into Africa (Callaway, 2016), evidence of this being based on the presence of Eurasian genes in modern African populations.

The Mota study is a reminder that this movement did not take place only in one direction or at a single time. Its findings that the genes of the Stone Age farmers carried to Africa were closely related to the same population that had brought agriculture to Europe about 7,000 years ago. This means that modern-day migrants from East Africa crossing the Mediterranean to Europe were in fact distant cousins whose ancestors went the opposite way thousands of years ago (Llorente et al., 2015).

The genetic studies research conducted on contemporary African populations also demonstrates that, although the Eurasian mixture was greatest in East Africa, which is closest to the Near East, and it also reached the western and Southern Africa. Paul Heggarty, a linguist at the Max Planck Institute for Evolutionary Anthropology in Leipzig, Germany, also argued that the Euro-Asian backflow theory ties in with research about the spread of Semitic languages from the Near East to Ethiopia and to some Southern African countries (Associated-Press, 2015). This helps explain why in the book the reader shall be encountering the 2nd millennium Before the Common (or Current) Era (BCE) Bantu Migration starting north of Africa and slowly spreading southwards to finally reaching Southern Africa including, later, the Malaba migrants. Correspondingly, the study is relevant in this book as it assists in explaining the significant Semitic traits found amongst the Malaba clan cultural and religious practices.

A combination of these studies with many others, suggests that all modern humans trace their ancestry to a single spot, that is, Africa 200,000 years ago. The origin of the name "Africa" itself is greatly disputed by scholars. Although most believe it stems from words used by the Phoenicians, Greeks, and Romans. For example, the Egyptian word Afru-ika, meaning "Motherland"; or the Greek word meaning without cold. There is also a Latin word aprica, simply meaning sunny (National-Geographic, 2020).

CHAPTER 2

BANTU MIGRATION

Like many Bantu people, the Malaba people became part of the Bantu migration wave occurring in the mid-2nd millennium Before the Common (or Current) Era (BCE) and finally ending before 1500 Common (or Current) Era (CE). This migration pattern had occurred when the Bantu people, who originally lived in West Africa and/or beyond, had begun migrating towards the south and east.

This is highlighted in several studies that have previously shown that between 1000-1800 Anno Domini (AD), East Africa experienced a wave of migrations from different parts of Africa (Bentley, 1996). The migration is mainly attributed to the fear of famine which was breaking out because of overcrowding and drought, causing internal conflicts amongst people. People responded by literally migrating in search of greener pastures, either for themselves, their livestock or both.

Harzig *et el* note that the other reason could have been that the Arabs had migrated into West Africa at around 600 and 900 AD causing external pressure on local African populations which in turn acted as a push factor for further migration south or eastwards (Christiane Harzig, Dirk Hoerder, & Donna R. Gabaccia, 2009). However, as explained before, population pressure was not the sole cause of migration.

There is evidence that some of it was as a consequence of pandemics and diseases, natural disasters such as earthquakes, over flooding of rivers such as the river Nile in ancient times, unexplained illnesses, diseases such as malaria, sleeping sickness and other similar factors.

The love for adventure and group influence could not be ruled out as another factor for migration. Some migration experts believe that there was also a form of heroism associated with breaking into new areas and creating legacies for leaders.

However, more importantly, some migration by Bantu people was for commercial reasons as they travelled further to export their iron-working skills. It was during an era when people had discovered the knowledge of iron working and had invented iron tools. According to Ross (Ross, 2002), from the period starting 1400 and ending 1600, iron technology appears to have been one of a series of important social assets that facilitated the growth of significant centralized kingdoms, for example, in the western Sudan and along the Guinea coast of West Africa. These iron tools had transformed the agricultural sector by making the clearing of land from cultivation faster and more efficient.

This is a relevant point as the history of the Malaba people highlights a clan that was heavily involved in invention of iron tools and trade. An even great southward Bantu migration took place in the sub-Saharan Africa, over 2,000 years ago. With the development of the iron blade, farm reaping became easier for the Bantu people and agriculture took on a whole new meaning. Populations grew faster than before, and people began encroaching onto each other's land.

This necessitated an enlargement of territory, which led to the migration of black African tribes from the Great Lakes in central Africa, to the south of Africa. The Malaba ancestors were part of this migration which is described by the National Geographic Society (National-Geographic, 2020) as one of the largest human migrations in history.

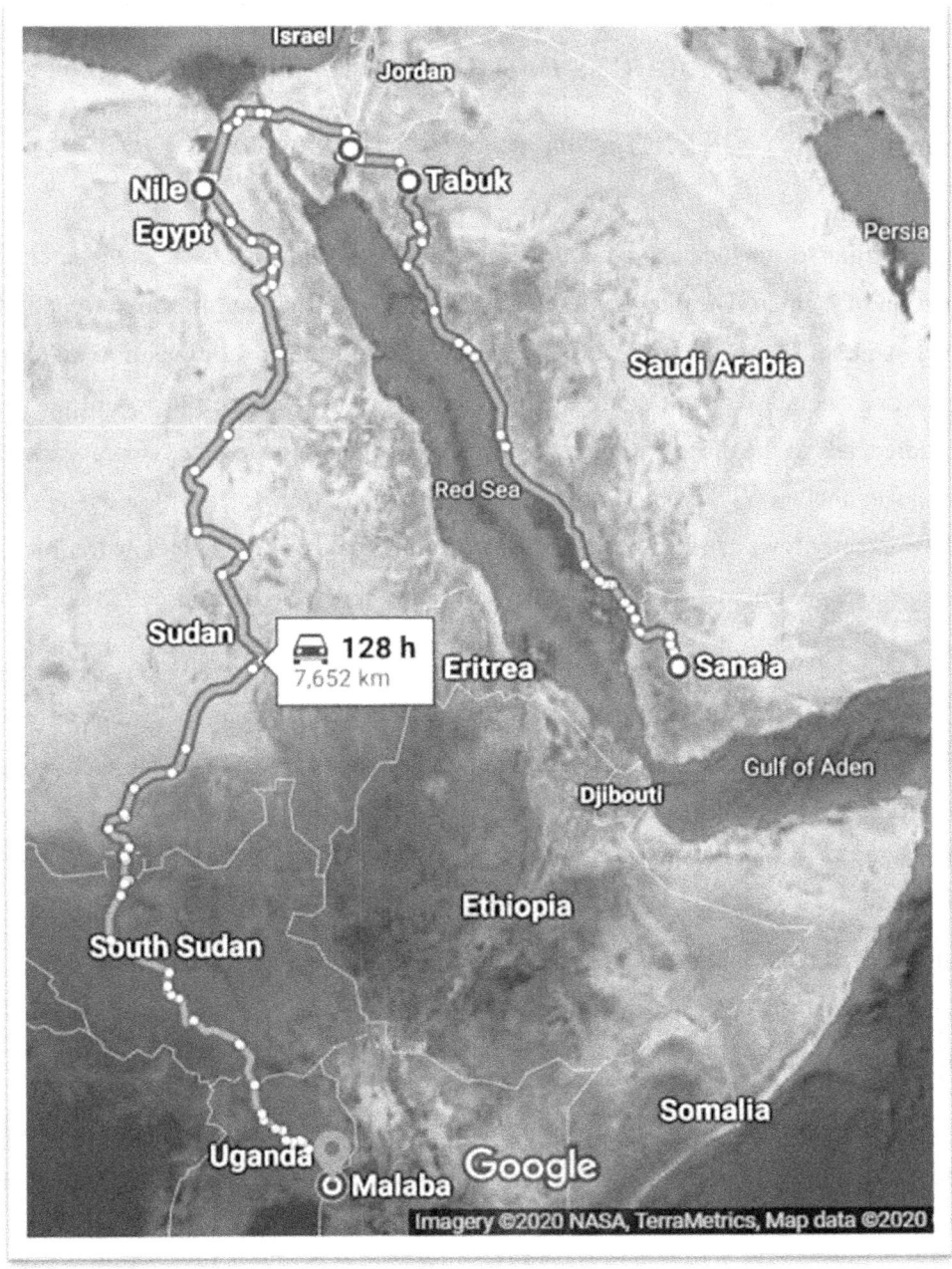

Figure 8. Map showing Migration of the early Malaba people from Yemen to The Great Lakes region in Central Africa. Image courtesy of Google maps

CHAPTER 3

THE ORIGINS OF THE MALABA PEOPLE

3,1. *The emergence of the Rainmakers*

The origins of the Malaba clan are trackable clearly to as far back as the ancient nation of Yemen. Despite that Yemen is a country located at the southern end of the Arabian Peninsula as shown in Figure 6, the Malaba religious and cultural practices notably reflect some distinct Semitic traits. An attempt to unfold the riddle leads to the discovery of several scholars who allude to a heavy presence of Jews in ancient Yemen but at the same note admitting the lack of knowledge on how exactly Jews came to settle in the Western Asian country. Yemenite traditions point to a period when a group of well-off Jews left Jerusalem in 629 BCE after hearing Jeremiah's prophecy of doom regarding the destruction of the Temple.

Some Historians argue that Jews were brought to Yemen from Judea around 900 BCE through King Solomon's trading networks. These Jews are said to have gone on to convert the Himyarite ruling family into Judaism. As a result, Judaism then became the ruling religion in Yemen until 525 CE after when the Christians from Ethiopia took over. The modern-day Jewish community in Yemen is exceedingly small and still shrinking as either most Yemenite Jews have left the country or have been airlifted to Israel since David Ben-Gurion, the head of the Jewish Agency, proclaimed the establishment of the State of Israel on the 14th of May 1948.

Like their Lemba kinsmen, according to oral tradition, the Malaba ancestors are said to have originated from a place called Sena in Yemen. Sena, Senna, Sanaw or Sanāw is a city that is located in Yemen's remote eastern Hadramaut valley, but it long has been abandoned. The Malaba link to Yemen can be qualitatively deduced using the sameness and/or correlation in religious practices, cultural traits, and ethnic descent. Applying the same principle, coupled with oral accounts, the Malaba storyline draw special attention to a footing whereby, from Yemen, the forerunners travelled southbound, making several stopovers, the symbolic one being the stopover at the Sinai Peninsula of Egypt where they possibly strengthened and maintained their faith in the God of the Mountain. The doctrine is later referred to as the Mwali religion, with most of its shrines based in the Matopo hills in the present-day Zimbabwe or the surroundings. The striking similarities between the religious activities at the Njelele shrine and Mount Sinai are also noticeable, indicating that the Njelele shrine, which ultimately was the Malaba clan's destination, is a sister hill to Mount Sinai and other similar ancient mountains of God.

The Malaba people's migratory patterns further highlight stopovers in Uganda and Kenya before reaching the present-day Zimbabwe and eventually South Africa, and again, back to Zimbabwe. To have a better understanding of the Malaba clan, one needs to time-travel back as far as 900 A.D. It is during that time that the Malaba can be traced to Kenya, where after arriving from Yemen via Egypt and Uganda, they had become part of a clan known as the Bukusu. The Bukusu people are said to be currently one of the seventeen Kenyan tribes of the Luhya Bantu people of East Africa, and calling themselves BaBukusu, they are currently the largest tribe of the Luhya nation, making up about thirty-four percent of the Luhya population (Mwakikagile, 2007).

A substantial number of southern African clans are descendants of the BaBukusu tribe. The culture and religious practices of the Bukusu clans possess characteristics that closely resemble that of the religious practices of the Malaba clan including the names of deities, places, and people. Just like the present-day Malaba clan, some sections of the Bukusu people still call themselves *baMwali* 'those of Mwali'.

There is a Bukusu clan oral tradition that traces the tribe's origin from Muntu we Entebe, who lived in Misri (Bulimo, 2013). They indicate that Misri simply means a 'place in the north'. Muntu was declaredly a great warrior who was later regarded as a god by the people of Misri. Some say the same Muntu is the father of all the Bantu people. His acclaim mainly emanated from his son Mwambu who married Sera, the granddaughter to Samba Ambarani. In addition, the oral traditions of the Bukusu tribe believe that Samba Ambarani was in fact the Biblical Abraham, the Hebrew. Cities of Kush, Nubia, Alwa and others including Soba and Balana were said to have been founded by Mwambu, a brother to Seela, the only girl in the family. He also had a brother, Mubukusu. Mwambu's brother Mubukusu had three sons, Malaba, Sioka and Silikwa. In his book *Luhyia of Kenya, The Cultural Profile*, Bulimo, to highlight the Bantu people progression, Bulimo, quotes oral traditionalist Osogo, as stating that other Luhyia subnations, except the Maragoli Idaho, Isukha and Tiriki, believe they are descendants of Akuru (Adam) and Muka (Eve) 'whose offspring Mungoma and Malaba populated the world' (Bulimo, 2013).

With benefit of hindsight, Malaba son of Mubukusu is the first recorded individual to be called by the title of *Malaba*, which later became some royalty title. A religious offering ceremony done for him is mentioned by Wandibbu in the book *Sacred Sites, Sacred Places* when he says "…the sacrifices offered in this shrine consisted of a small gourd (*nkombe/inkezo*) of milk or a spleen and a portion of the sacrificial animal's neck called enjasi (trachea), or *nhiya* in tjiKalanga (Carmichael, 1994). Such offerings were in the first place addressed to Malaba, a younger son of Mubukusu the founder of the Babukusu tribe. Although the practice of sacrificing was later banned and made a taboo in the Mwali religion, the small gourd (*nkombe/inkezo*) remains an essential component of the Malaba religious rites to this day.

According to history writer Makila, Sioka son of Mubukusu was an Omulako clan leader who led the Babukusu tribe during migration after the death of Walumoli, who was his half-brother, in a place called Ekukumayi (Makila, 1978). Sioka progressed on to later bear five sons, Walumoli, Wabutubile, Malaba, Sanjamolu and Misiulaliloba. Sioka's sons had necronyms or names of relatives who had died. As a way of honouring the deceased, it was a custom in some Semitic cultures to name a child after a beloved relative who had died. Malaba the third son of Sioka becomes the second recorded individual to assume the Malaba title, after Malaba the brother of Sioka. Sioka naming his son after his brother or any other relative is a situation that was to have a systematic fact of occurring again and again, standing the test of time to the modern- day generations of the Malaba clan. The recreation of the Malaba name became a tradition amongst most of the Malaba people scattered around the world. The significance of the phenomenon was that it was to be the beginning of a Malaba legacy recreation of which was to be recurrent in times of calm as well as in crises throughout the Malaba generations for years to come. Ritually, the legacy was referred to as '*linga*' in tjiKalanga or '*izinda*' in isiNdebele.

The *linga/izinda* was, and is still not only a legacy, but a spiritual power of a supreme ancestor that is bestowed upon a chosen descendant so that the descendant assumes the roles and responsibilities of that ancestor in the clan. To fully achieve this, ritual performances needed to happen after which the life of the 'receiving' descendant changes significantly as he assumes the all-important role of representing the clan in every aspect of life. From that time on, the entrusted individual is regarded and accepted as the custodian of customs and traditions of the clan, and/or the people in general. The individual ultimately assumes a responsibility of providing traditional guidance to the clan predominantly. The role is not a limited one as it is characterized by a diversity of functions ranging from simple administrative duties to much more extensive judicial and developmental duties. The Malaba *linga/zinda* involved a quite huge responsibility of both traditional leadership and most significantly, the authority to preside over the bigger responsibility of the rainmaking process. During history, the rainmaking phenomenon was not only limited to the Malaba clan in terms of effect and influence, but all the subjects, including all the peoples whose lives depended on tillage and cultivation for survival.

From Malaba the son of Sioka, more clans emerged. These included BaMalaba, BaNaela and BaNabayi, all whose main plank was disavowal of circumcision because they invoked the (*esichubo*) oath of Munyole. The disavowal of circumcision had started when the Bukusu sub nation had continued to maintain their Semitic culture, mainly the covenant of circumcision known as *brit millah*. However, at some point, the once united tribes broke up and the Malaba cluster followed a cultural conscientious objector and leader who was called Munyole. Munyole had become a rebel and choosing to disavow the traditional orthodox Jewish oath of circumcision. Some tribes like the Silikwa clans who were devoted to their heritage and took pride in Jewish oath of circumcision immediately cut ties with the Malaba cluster and began identifying themselves as *BaMwalie* (those of God) and emphasized it. By so doing they were implying that the Malaba cluster were no longer those of Mwalie because they had refused to obey the covenant of Yahweh, God the Almighty. Despite that set back, those of Malaba became even more powerful as Malaba son of Sioka later became associated with the paramount Bukusu Trinity.

Those who called themselves the Mwalie cluster went on to live at the base of the mountains they also named the Mwalie hills in the present-day Uganda. But their assumed power significantly reduced, and today, the BaMwalie people are known as Bayumbu people. However, to this day, some Bayumbu clans deny allegiance to the Bukusu sub-nation. Although the Malaba went on to maintain the disavowing of circumcision, some Munyole followers later joined Mango in reverting to circumcision after the fall of the snake dragon which was known as *Yadebe*. Oral traditions of the Bukusu people states that in the 1700s a man called Mango was born in the household of Bwayo Omukhurarwa, a clan that uttered sisiilao (oath) to Munyole cluster and a descendant of the first Malaba son of Sioka. This is the group that remained in Tanzania as Dzibagulu travelled down south. They lived in Mwiala, northward of Bwayi Hills (present day Amukura) in Mara Region of Tanzania. Mango's name meant a grinding stone or the process of grinding, loosely translated as Kuyani (The present-day Malaba also have a house of Kuyani). Mango is known to have been a brave young man who was popular among the peers. At the time, Wakhulunya was the tribal leader while Mango's father was an *omukasa* (elder).

Reports came in that Mango' son, whose name was Malaba had been killed by a snake called *endemu yadebe*. It is alleged that after learning of the death of his son Malaba, Mango had become so enraged that he swore to bring the snake down single-handedly. The local Barwa people joked with him that if he killed the serpent, they would get him circumcised and offered him a beautiful bride. Customarily, like the Luvhimbi clan, Mango belonged to the clan that swore by the oath of Munyole and never circumcised. So, Mango did wait for the snake at dawn and killed it single-handedly as it headed for its sleeping place. That act alone dawned the beginning of circumcision for Mango and his people, something the clan never did before.

The striking similarities between the oral traditions of Tshibi Malaba and Malaba son of Mango show a customary pattern that still existed amongst the two related groups but living in different parts of the world. This can only be explained in terms of similarities in religious beliefs which also confirms the two clans as just splinters from one family and still practiced similar religious and cultural institutions yet living from far apart. At that time, the Malaba who went down south still swore by the oath of Munyole and did not circumcise.

In the *Trans African Journal of History* journal, Simuyi, states that the BaMalaba's origins are indeed intrinsically traced to Malaba son of Sioka (V. Simiyu, Kireti, & Atinga, 1991). The venerated name of BaMalaba endured the test of time in that it is still used to this day as swearing allegiance to telling the truth by proclaiming *"BaMalaba tjose"* (I swear by my ancestors). Downstream, the title BaMalaba referred to the female members of the clan. Therefore, the Malaba clan that finally settled in the Southern Africa can be traced back directly to Malaba the son of Sioka not only through the name, but the umbilical cord link as demonstrated in religious and cultural practices of the current clan.

According to the Bukusu oral traditions, Malaba son of Sioka, became so great he was venerated as a saint or God. Nevertheless, his ultimate historical significance only arose when he was mentioned in the paramount Bukusu Divine Trinity. This trinity was a state whose genesis brought with it several doctrines. For instance, the number three became significant and symbolic in the Malaba generations to come. The Malaba oral narrations, however, allege the Trinity that predates their time in the Kenya or Uganda later became known as the paramount Malaba Divine Trinity. In the book, Luhyia Nation: Origins, Clans and Taboos, the Malaba God was viewed as the Almighty and a creator of all things. He was presented in a trilogy manner as a giver, omnipotent and good to Man (Bulimo, 2013).

According to the historian Simiyu, in his manuscript *'The Emergence of a Sub-Nation: A History of Babukusu to 1990*, the name given to the god was *Wele. Wele* was perceived as the Supreme Being and creator of the world and all things in it in a Trinity system (V. G. Simiyu, 1991). The Trinity was a typical creed that stated that there is one Supreme Being but three Persons. The Christian doctrine of the Trinity also holds that there is one God but three hypostases, the Father, the Son, and the Holy Spirit implying "one God in three Divine persons". At the top of the Trinity there was *Wele* Khakaba. *Wele* Khakaba was a Supreme Being, provider, the creator, and the maintainer of all forces that were good to man. After creating human beings, *Wele* retained control over their welfare including the power to make them prosper and had powers to give out life and to send death. He also ensured that whatever the gods imagined or implemented was in the best interest of their subjects and whatever they uttered was most pleasing. Below *Wele*, the Supreme Being, were two *Barumwa* or *batumwa* (messengers of God). *Wele* Mukhobe and *Wele* Malaba. Wele Mukhobe was God the Light and a guardian of rulers. He guided their wisdom and speech. Finally in the Trinity was *Wele* Malaba, from which the Malaba clan is derived. *Wele* Malaba was a guardian of human beings, animals, and vegetation. Writer Makila describes him as *Omurumwa Omwayi we Babandu*, meaning a messenger guardian who was bestowed a responsibility of looking after the welfare of the people, their livestock as well as of the vegetation. It was his advanced knowledge in medicine that also led him to be known as Mung'oma. The name Malaba means the future in the TshiLuba language of DRC.

This is fundamentally one of the first and earliest references to the name Malaba as cardinally associated to sacredness. Despite being part of the Trinity, Malaba was practically a demi-god, giving out life and death. He would apportion to each person wealth or poverty. The important role and responsibility of looking after the people and their livestock and the vegetation essentially required the abundance of water. Without water holding that responsibility was not going to be sustainable, because it is rain that is particularly important for sustaining life. All living organisms need water to live, therefore, Malaba had to acquire skills that would enable him to cause the rains to fall.

The rainmaking legacy that became synonymous with the Malaba clan and was inherited all the way to the establishment of the Mabweadziba shrine in the Matombo, to be known as Matopo hills centuries later, was acquired through the zeal to succeed in this role. It is the Mabweadziba shrine that later became known as the Njelele shrine.

The nature, essence, sum, and substance of the Malaba legacy through generations that came thereafter, was based on the character and spiritual characteristics of *Wele* Malaba. Throughout the course of history, his was a legacy that was to be revived and/or recreated whenever there was a requirement.

The journey of the Bukusu people is recorded both in literature and featured in oral narrations. Together with other Luhya sub-nations, the Bukusu are thought to have first settled north of Lake Turkana at a place called Enabutuku (Ndeda, 2019). They then relocated and settled in the Chereangani Hills at a place called Embayi, later to be known as Silikwa. It is believed that after evil and bad omens befell them, they dispersed taking six routes: five going around the western side of Mount Elgon (known to them as Masaba) and one via the eastern side of Mount Elgon. Those who went via the western side of Mount Elgon included the BaSilikwa, the BaNabayi, the BaNeala, the Bakikayi and those of Malaba, otherwise known as the BaMalaba (Kakai, 2016).

According to Simiyu, clans which claimed Mwali, were the Malaba and Nabayi who then moved towards Lake Victoria (V. Simiyu et al., 1991). They settled in the borders of Tanzania, Uganda, and Kenya, where they lived in the neighbourhood of non-circumcising Bantu peoples like the Banyole, Samia and other non-Bantu people such as the Luo. Their residence in these parts of the world is corroborated by existing names of places and natural features like mountains and rivers. A river found at the border between Uganda and Kenya is named Malaba. There is also a small Malaba town located in the vicinity as shown in the picture below (Fig 9.). Another place named Malaba is found near Kasongo in the Democratic Republic of Congo, indicating a southerly migration pattern.

They also show some indications of having further settled in place called Mbuji-Mayi in Luba country on the banks of the Sankuru River. In the local Tshiluba language Mbuji-Mayi is said to mean "Goat-Water", however, in the ancient Teso and/or modern-day TjiKalanga language 'Mbuji-Mayi' refers to a female goat.

One of the DRC informants cited that there is currently a gender-based project named after Malaba in the city of Mbuji-Mayi. Based on its inference, the name Kaluba, given to one of Dzibagulu-levula's sons could have been derived from 'Luba or TshiLuba'. Luba defines the collective term for the ethnic group, with name variations like Ba-Luba, Balouba, Baluba, Baluba-Bambo, Balubas, Kaluba, Kayumba *et cetera*. There are also several confirmed striking similarities in both language and culture of the modern and ancient Malaba tribes.

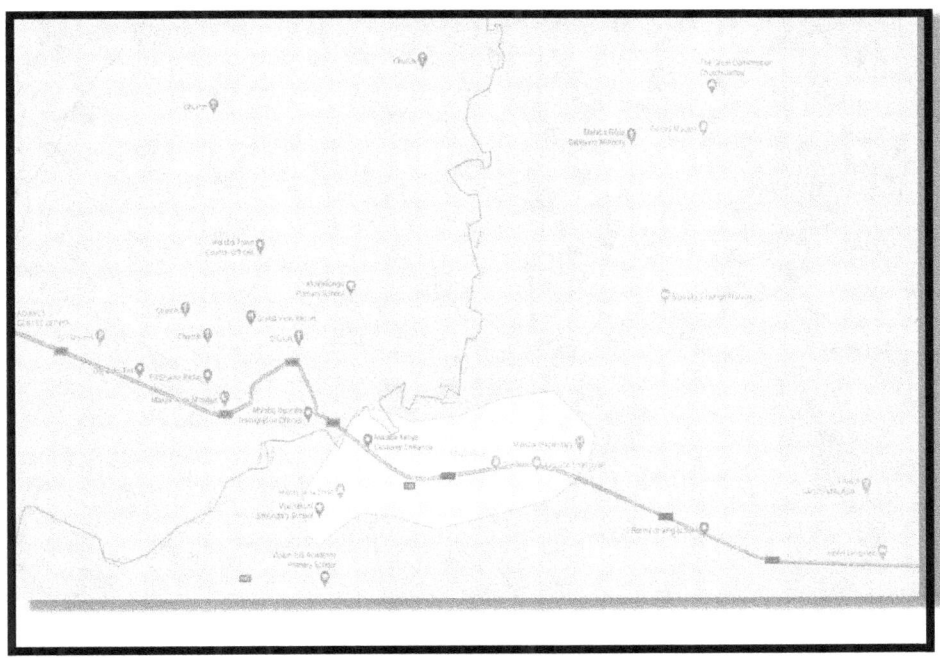

Figure 9. Map showing the city of Malaba and the river Malaba which separates Kenya from Uganda. Image courtesy of Google maps

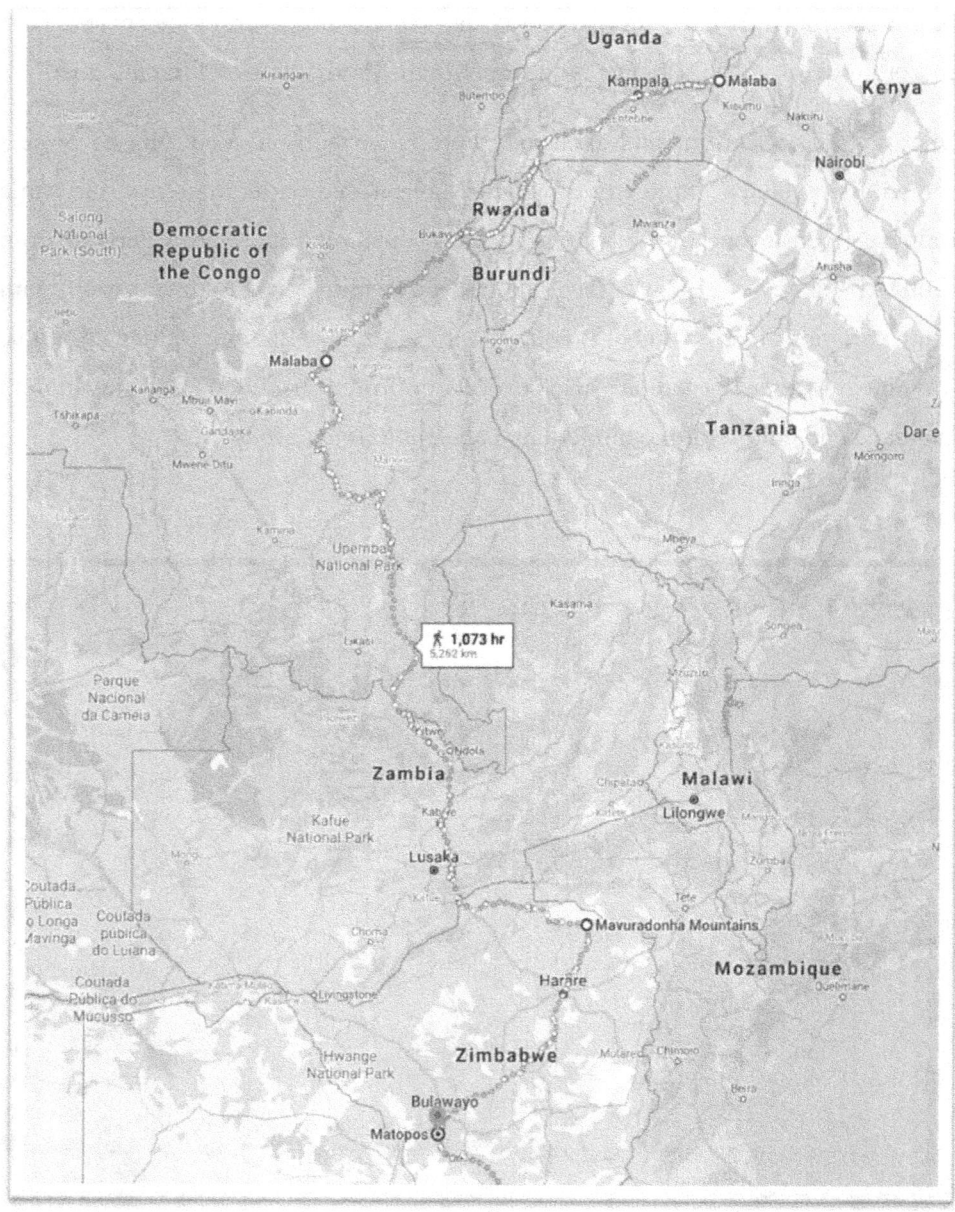

Figure 10. showing the migration of the Malaba people from Kenya to Malaba Zimbabwe. Image adapted from Google Maps, 2018.

Several centuries later, the BaMalaba continued to move on through Bugishu then Samoya then to Bukaya heading southwards until they ended up in the present-day Zimbabwe as shown in Figure 10. It was through their interactions with the Banyole, that they adopted the Banyole custom of non-circumcision. However, even though they invoked oath of Munyole in as far as circumcision practices were concerned, they later joined another Malaba descendant, Mango alongside Muyobo in new birth of circumcision after the fall of the snake dragon popularly known as Yadebe the snake dragon. These constituted the groups that were referred to as the Mwali believing clusters. The Malaba then took the eastern side route and settled at the hills later known as Mwali hills in Western Kenya where a significant figure Dzibagulu-levula emerged from the clan. He was known as the son of Mwali or at least he called himself that. Mwali's is a direct descendant of Muntu the great as shown in Figure 11.

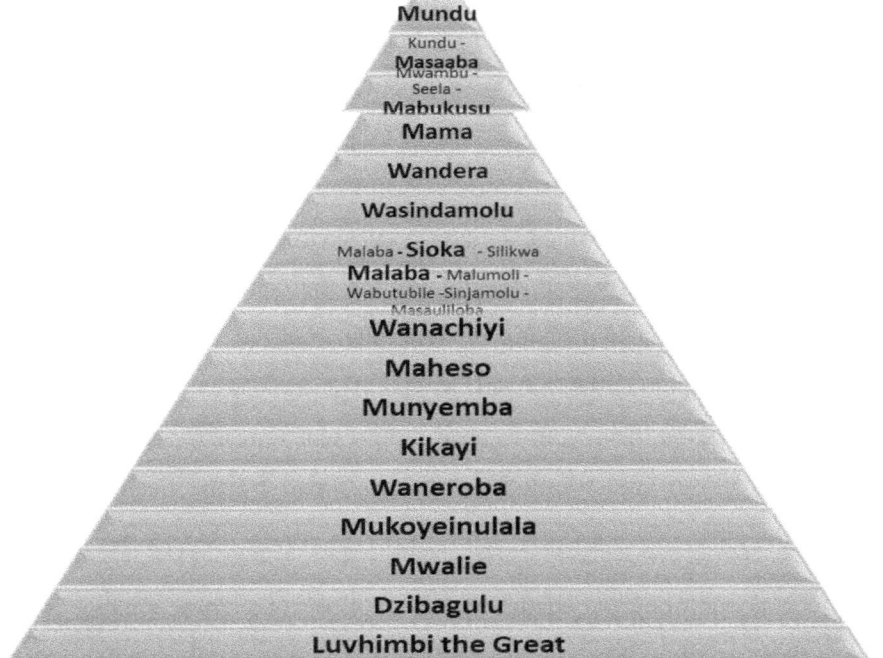

Figure 11. Showing the Bukusu Family tree from Mundu to Luvhimbi the Great. Adapted from Simiyo (1991).

3,2. The People of Dzibagulu Levula

Dzibagulu or Madziba or Dzibagulu levula called himself Mwali or rather as some would put it, son of Mwali. There are some historians who give his actual name as Mwalie, however since his history is traceable back to the BaMalaba of the Bukusu tribe and their relation to Mwali and the pool, both Dzibagulu levula and Mwalie could have been names that were assumed later in his life. This brings about the contention that Dzibagulu levula could have acquired and assumed the Malaba cultural and religious legacy through a pool contest. A pool contest was an ancient practice that was customarily triggered by a situation through which a successor to the throne could not be determined by natural processes. Such a situation would result in a situation whereby throne contestants would be armed with some firebrands and get into a pool of water (*dzibagulu levula*).

Whoever emerged at the other side of the pool end with some smoldering remains of the fire stick still in hand was deemed to have been selected by Mwali the Creator (God Almighty) and was considered to have won the challenge. The individual would then, as a rule, be coronated and be granted the Malaba Royal Highness and earning titles of Malaba or Mwali (*uNgwali*) and forthwith take over the cultural and religious responsibilities of leading the clan. The name *uNgwali* was to become synonymous with whoever was inheriting the Malaba rainmaking legacy, hence, Dzibalevula called himself Mwali. The trend was to be a common recurrence in the Malaba history up to until the present times. *Ngwali* was not a personal, but an official and traditional name assumed by the head priest on succeeding to the post.

According to oral traditions and written records, following a bateleur eagle of the air, which was an on flight symbolic bird of Mwali, the Dzibagulu Levula people had migrated from Yemen through the Arabian Peninsula across the Red Sea into

Egypt on way to Sudan before settling in the Lake Victoria peninsula. It is the stopover at Mount Sinai that the Dzibagulu levula people embraced and maintained the concept of the God of the mountain. The concept of God living on a holy mountain is a significant theme in the Yahwehist religion. From Sudan they followed a common migration route to Bale region of Ethiopia and lived in the present day Goba. From Goba, they moved into present day Lake Victoria and made a stopover at a place called Kaluba in Uganda.

Dzibagulu levula thereupon named his second son Kaluba or was the other way round. They crossed over into the Kenyan region through a port that later became known as the Malaba border post. According to Ugandan newspaper the *Daily Nation* (2014), Malaba is an ancient town that only boomed during the construction of the Kenya-Uganda railway in the 1900s. The newspaper further attests that the meaning of the name Malaba, remains a mystery amongst the local Iteso people. Nonetheless, the local oral history narrators allude that a popular witchdoctor and rainmaker by the name Malaba once lived in the area, entailing a Malaba diagnostic. The eastern Nilotic Teso language spoken by the local Iteso people also possess striking similarities with the present-day tjiKalanga language. These include words like *ngina*-enter, *(a)munyu*-salt, *inyama(t)*- food (meat), *batumwa* (messengers) and many others. Like the Malaba clan, the local people still practice an indigenous observation of meteorological event known as *khulula ifula*, meaning releasing the rains.

The Mwali cluster took the eastern side route and settled at the Mwali hills. As its also recorded in the Bukusu oral traditions, the group ultimately migrated and made a stopover in the deeper Ugandan region before proceeding down into the present-day Kenya where Dzibagulu Levula led his people further down south. It is cited that, carrying the sanctified Malaba traditional and religious legacy, Dzibagulu Levula used the feathers of the bateleur eagle (*njelele*) as his symbol of power and he wore it as a crown. The Dzibagulu Levula migration took many years but eventually reaching the Zambezi River at the time which is deductively carbon dated to approximately between 1210 and 1240AD. Eventually, after Dzibagulu levula's directive, the Dziba people crossed the great Zambezi River. In one of his writings, Pfebve, highlights that when Dzibagulu Levula reached the Zambezi region he did what he had to do and according to tradition, he pointed to the south of the Zambezi and said "there is our home (Pfebve, 2015). There we shall live and prosper." As they settled in the location, tradition mentions that it rained, and hence they named the place Vulayadona or Mavuladona (it has rained), later to be known as Mavhuradonha (Fig. 12). Lived and proper they did, and the clan became part of a nation known as the BaKalanga, making Dzibagulu-levula amongst the earliest founding fathers of the nation of BuKalanga.

Dzibagulu was one of the names used for Mwali the giver, and as indicated before, Dzibagulu himself called himself Mwali not because he was a god but either because of his father or ancestor by the name Mwali son of Mukoinelala or it was because he carried the burden of introducing Mwali the Creator, God the Almighty in this part of the world or most likely because of his triumph in a pool contest on way to win the rainmaking custodianship.

After inaugurating and stabilizing the Mwali religion in the Bukalanga area, Dzibagulu-levula became famous as a rainmaker while situated at the shrine at the base of the *Mavuladona* or *Vula ya dona* now known as Mavhuradonha Mountains range (Fig 12). Dzibagulu then moved further down into the Matombo, now known as Matopo hills, where according to oral traditions his people experienced the first landing of the Bateleur eagle (*njelele*), symbolizing not only the shrine's new location but the final permanent settlement for the Dzibagulu levula clan too. It is here that Dzibagulu levula established the Mabweadziba rainmaking tabernacle. Mabweadziba which means 'the sacred stones of Dzibagulu' is the same place that was renamed Njelele later in 1836.

The newly established Mwali religion had striking similarities with Yahwehism, further strengthening the narration that the Dzibagulu levula people indeed imported the religion into the vicinity. Beside the directive of the bateleur eagle, the pre-existing religious centrality of the Matopos could explain the Dzibagulu levula people's choice of the hills as the canonical location to establish the rainmaking shrine. It was from here that the religion spread to an extent that the sanctity of Mabweadziba became equivalent to what Mecca is to the Moslems and what the Vatican means to the Roman Catholics.

Like their ancestors and the importance of the number three, the Dzibagulu family maintained the Trinity and the significancy of the number three. Dzibagulu had three distinct sons, Lubimbi (Luvhimbi), Kaluba (Karuva) and Nyamukoko. Lubimbi was the elder son who distinctly trained to inherit the rainmaking skills and custodianship.

Kaluba was a diviner too, possessing a gift of creating mist as a method of confusing the enemy during conflicts. A place by the name Kaluba situated in Lake Victoria in the present-day Uganda still exists today rationally indicating where Dzibalevula's second son was born. The third son was Nyamukoko, and it is not clear how the name came about.

The name Lubimbi is argued to have been derived from the Banyoro people of Uganda where Dzibagulu-levula people had settled before. Lubimbi means a piece of arable land apportioned for the day, *ndima* or *indima* in Kalanga and Ndebele, respectively. As such in the Banyoro people, when the villagers are in the garden digging, each one uses a hoe or plough to till their portion or their olubimbi. Dzibagulu levula died and is buried in the *Mavuladona* or *Vulayadona* or *Mavhuradonha* in present day Zimbabwe.

Figure 12. Showing the Mavuladona (Literally means place of the raindrops) Mountain where Dzibalevula is buried. Image adapted from Google Maps/Images, 2018

It was when Dzibagulu died that his sons went separate ways. Lubimbi, the elder son assumed the title of *Hee* (chief) and led his people deeper into the land together with the family rainmaking legacy. Nyamukoko and Kaluba remained in the north, however, spreading inland in the Kingdom of Bukalanga. Kaluba later became the ancestor of the Tonga in Binga and the Tavara people living along the Dande river in Guruve. Some of Kaluba's Tonga descendants residing in Binga continued to identify with the name Lubimbi which is evidenced by Ward 4 in Binga which is known by the name Lubimbi. Some of the Tavara people are also found in Matabeleland, calling themselves the Mbano (*oMsendo*). The Mbano use *inyeluka* (eel fish) as their totem associating themselves with rainmaking as an eel stays inside a *dzibagulu levula*.

The descendants of Nyamukoko assumed the Gunguwo totem. The Kaluba people use that Gunguwo totem too to differentiate themselves from their Hungwe cousins so that they could intermarry. Intermarrying with the Hungwe people was evidently unavoidable considering that the only other tribes they could have married into were the Khoikhoi and the San. The San constituted micro-communities of hunters who had lived in the region from years back. After the San, another community of herder people called the Khoikhoi had emerged from the Nile Basin and migrated down south where they ultimately emerged with the San to form the Khoi-San community. After the creation of the Mwenemutapa kingdom, Kaluba's descendants became key political and religious advisers to the Mutapa kings and the Dzibagulu and Kaluba spirit mediums continued to be revered amongst the Tonga of Binga and the Tavara people to this day.

After Dzibagulu-levula's eldest son Lubimbi had assumed the leadership and the rainmaking custodianship, legend has it that the bateleur eagle resumed its flight, heading further down south. On account of that fact, Lubimbi found himself with an assignment of trekking down south as well, lingering behind the symbolic bird until he saw the setting up of the earliest southern African kingdom at a site where the njelele (bateleur eagle) bird landed for the second time. Its capital city was at Mapungubwe, just south of the Vhembe. The name Vhembe meant a river that crisscrossed many areas until it reaches the sea, (*Wone we wa vhimbila u tshi ya na lo u swika u tshiguma nga lwanzhe*) (Submission of the VaNgona nation to the south Africa parliament, 2018). The river Vhembe was later known as Limpopo, named after a Tsonga leader, known as Hosi Rivombo or Livombo. On way to the Mapungubwe settlement, the Lubimbi people made a stopover in the southern part of the present-day Zimbabwe where they built a stone-walled typical Leopard's Kopje Culture settlement known as Mapela hill (Fig. 13).

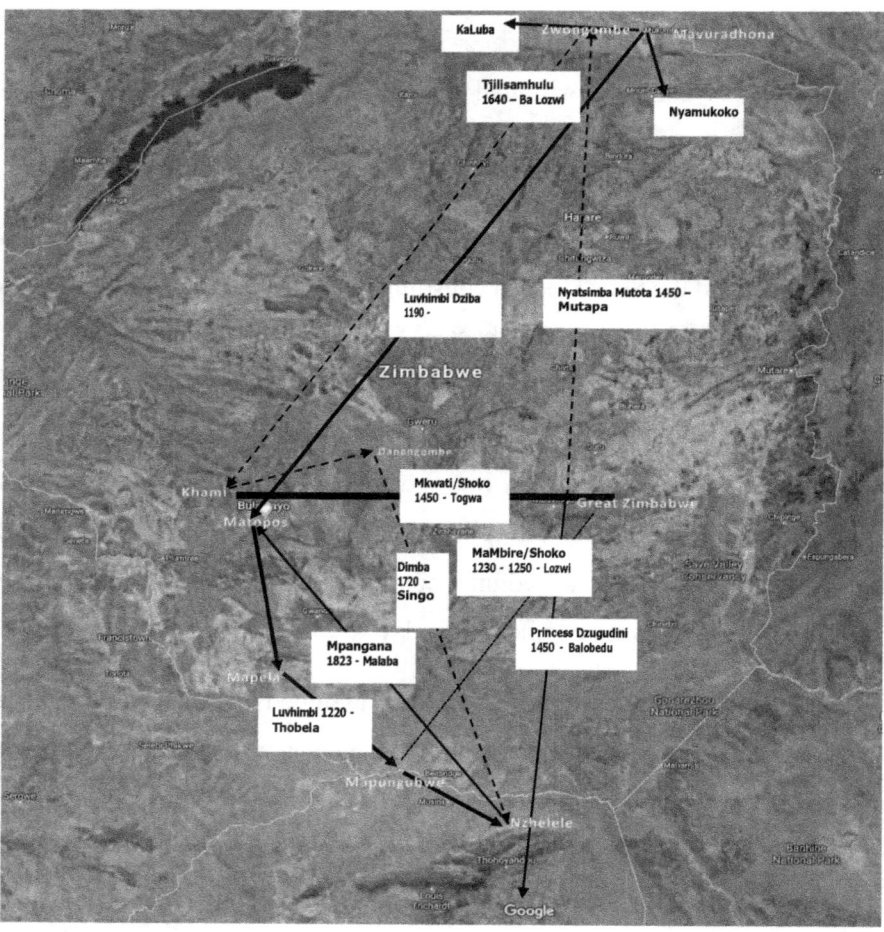

Figure 13. The movements of different clans and tribes in Bukalanga and VhuVenda, drawn from Google maps.

New research work at the Mapela hill has revealed that the stone-walled terraces of Mapela highlights a construction date of years earlier than Mapungubwe. The settlement also exhibits evidence of class distinction and sacred leadership built earlier than Mapungubwe (Chirikure et al, (2014). Class distinction and sacred positions associated with rainmaking found in the settlement were characteristics intricately linked to the Lubimbi family. Glass beads excavated on the edge of a lower terrace, northern side of Mapela (Fig.14) were also found in a rainmaking corner or tabernacle in Mapungubwe. Figure 14 also shows the organization of the settlement.

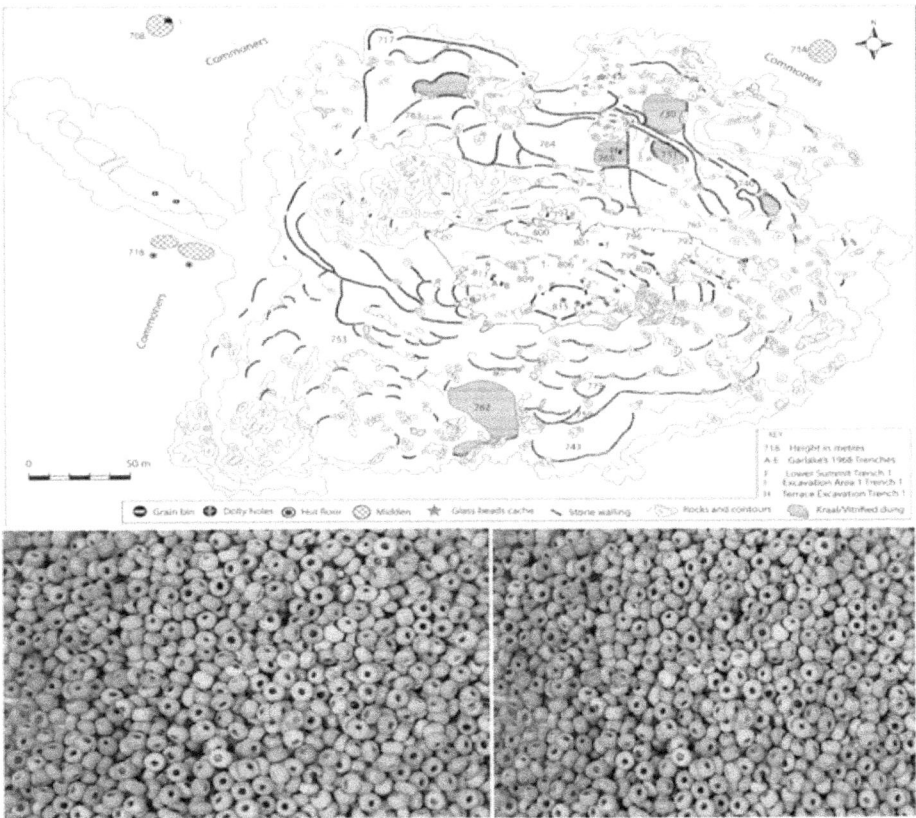

Figure 14. Mapungubwe-type glass beads (b) were found in Mapela hill (a) - showing the summit, terraces, and surrounding flats (adapted from Chirikure et al, (2014)).

Out of possession of Mabweadziba, Lubimbi exited Mapela at around 1230, with both the control-centrality of the rainmaking ceremonies in conjunction with its guardianship, finally seeing its re-establishment in the new Mapungubwe settlement in VhuVenda which was also known by the local VhaNgona as Lukungurubwe. Huffman confirms that archaeological evidence suggests that the people at Mapungubwe spoke an early form of Kalanga at this time (Huffman, 2011). Nevertheless, by and by the rainmaking shrine was to be re-instituted back in the Mabweadziba by 1836 where it endorsed Njelele as its new label. The title Njelele was adapted from the Dzibagulu levula symbolic rain bird, the bateleur eagle, known as *njelele* in the tjiKalanga language. Mapungubwe is also referred to as "Tshavhadzimu" which means "place of the gods" or a "revered place".

3,3. The Dzibalevula-Hungwe Alliance

To understand the relationship between the Malaba clan and other BaKalanga people, it is important to recognize the existing Hungwe mythologies. According to some legend, in olden times, a people known as the Dziba were dwelling on a mountain. They ate food raw because their chief, Dzibagulu levula, had lost the fire that his daughters had originally kept safely in a sealed horn containing oil. In the land, came some hunters from the north. These were Hungwe's ancestors. They had fire in their possession and ritually smoked a pipe to sustain their magical force. Their chief gave fire to Dzibagulu, who consequently married his daughter. The tribes united around Hungwe and Dziba and formed a union to be known as the Dziba-Hungwe alliance.

The Hungwe people are currently a tribe found across Southern Africa and believed to be amongst the earliest Bantu speaking inhabitants of modern-day areas south of the Zambezi River stretching to the Limpopo basin. They are amongst the original Bakalanga who according to Mazarire, later, among them Zwikono, Vunamakuni, Nkami and others become especially important Kalanga Mambo Tjibundule councillors. Some argue that their arrival was only preceded by the San, Khoi and the Dziba. The tribes united around Hungwe and Dziba and formed a union to be known as the Dziba-Hungwe alliance (-connect with-) that was established at a place that was given the name Moto usipo/Matosi-po (Matopos). It was after their alliance with the Dzibalevula clan that the Hungwe people remain connected by the common bond of the bateleur Eagle totem which transcends tribal, linguistic, cultural, and geographical boundaries (Makondo, 2009).

The Hungwe ancestors are believed to have inhabited a mythical place known as Guruuswa, the place of long grass, believed by Moyo, to be the land south of the Mupfure, 'stretching right down southwards to the area of the present Bulawayo and Fort Victoria" (Moyo, 2012). The Kaluba- Nyandoros are referred to as Maokomavi in their praise poetry, the praise name that is also used by the Hungwe. The Hungwe are also referred to as Chivara which is also synonymous with Ndoro, in their case referring to the white plumage of the Hungwe bird (Raftopoulos & Mlambo, 2009).

However, some scholars believe that Guruuswa stretched from the above-mentioned location up to the north of the Zambezi River towards Tanzania, yet the likes of Cox argue that Guruuswa was actually located in Tanzania. The 1512 Portuguese records refer to Guruuswa as Butua, a corruption of the Kalanga name 'buhwa' meaning, a place of grass. Abraham confirms that 'Butua' may have originated from 'Gunuvutwa' or Gunibuhwa, a name from the old Kalanga language which was what the Lower Zambezi Tonga and the Tavara people of Dzibagulu's son Kaluba would have spoken (Abraham, 1959).

We do not know what it was called by its own citizens at the time but with benefit of hindsight Guruuswa or Gunibuhwa could have been a reference to the long elephant-grass parts of the African Savanna region that stretches from Zimbabwe to Tanzania and into pats of Kenya. However, there are some scholars who referred to the place's name as Vhuhwa or Vhuxwa the place of dying -- because their king, the Ameer or Tjanga, and many of their people had died there (Mabogo, 2012).

3,4. The Luvhimbi Dynasty; Mapungubwe Settlement

Dzibagulu-levula's elder son Lubimbi settled in the Venda area south of the Limpopo River, at the Mapungubwe (Luswingo) Kingdom at around mid 1230AD and became known as Luvhimbi. This occurrence, however, was not a change of name but just a geo-linguistic change due to a speech sound variation. Mapungubwe, stretching from the Soutpansberg in the south, across the Limpopo River to the Matopos in the north (Huffman, 2005) marked the end of a multi-ethnic era and heralded "a new millennium to be characterised by stratification in the form of class divisions, differentiation and segmentation in the form of powerful ethnic identities. Basically, it heralded the era of chieftainships, state of kingdoms, and the formation of consolidated confederated empires (Mellet, 2018). At that time Mapungubwe was the centre of a kingdom with about 5,000 people living at its centre. The site was a prosperous trade centre with the people mining and smelting copper, iron, and gold, spun cotton, made glass and ceramics, grew millet and sorghum, and tended cattle, goats, and sheep.

The people of Mapungubwe are recorded to have been scientists with a sophisticated knowledge of the stars and this reading of the stars played a major role not only in their tradition and culture, but also in their day-to-day lives. Their trade was mainly with ancient Ethiopia through the ports of Adulis on the Red Sea and the ports of Raphta (now Quelimani) and Zafara (now Sofala) in Mozambique (Campbell, 2016). Continue Loving Mhlanga states that the Nguni Bantu called the kingdom "*Ebukhosini Bamaphungazwe* when the Nguni finally arrived in what we call South Africa today". They called the Mapungubwe residents *amaphungazwe*, 'Masters of Crossing the World' carrying goods and minerals with the trading Arabs who drove their camels and luggage. "From today's Insuza all the way to Palapye, to present day Gauteng province, to Mashaba was the Kingdom of Maphungazwe with its trade Centre at a hill we now know as Mapungubwe", Mhlanga explained (Conti Mhlanga, 2018).

Contrary to several scholarly impressions that Mapungubwe means 'hill of the jackal', given the bateleur eagle, which was the symbol of the early occupiers, Mapungubwe means 'hill of the eagle'. Although the Dzibagulu levula family had first settled at Mavuladona area, it is presented through oral traditions that the first landing of the Bateleur eagle (*njelele*), was in the Matopos area of the Kingdom of Bukalanga and symbolized the final permanent settlement for the Dziba clan. The second landing of the eagle was in Mapungubwe, therefore, explaining the argument that Mapungubwe refers to the hill of the eagle rather than that of the jackal. The name is a combination of two words, *ma-pungu* meaning bateleur eagle(s), and *bwe* which means stone (hill). In Tshivenḓa, the word means 'Place of Stone'.

Figure 15. Showing the Mapungubwe Hill where Luvhimbi became Nyunyiyedenga and High priest. Image adapted from the Encyclopaedia of ancient History, 2020.

The reasoning that Mapungubwe was extensively developed at the time of Luvhimbi and other early Bakalanga tribes' arrival in the area is backed by archaeological evidence showing that the aboriginal occupants of the Venda area were, stationed not in the Mapungubwe hill but at the adjacent site of Bambadyanalo. Like the Matopos and the Mapela settlements, historian (N. M. N. Ralushai, 2003) also attests that Mapungubwe had its capital at Mapungubwe hill, with its first king as Thobela or Thovhele, which are names identified with the Great Luvhimbi. Luvhimbi was also known as Nemapungubwe. In the Ngona language, the prefix *Ne* - means owner, that backs the argument that Luvhimbi is one of the originators of the Mapungubwe city. Historian Ralushai refers to the first people in Mapungubwe as early Iron Age settlers who inhabited the area from about 1000 AD to 1300 AD, before Iron Age subsistence farmers also settled in the area around 1500. Furthermore, the existence of the people of Mapungubwe is confirmed by the discovery by archaeologists of a few potsherds identified as Early Iron Age pottery on a hill shown in Figure 15.

This means that they manufactured their own pottery and metal tools. Ivory was traded with Arab merchants and contributed greatly to the wealth of the kingdom. It appears that it was after the arrival of the Luvhimbi group that the centre of the state shifted from Bambandyanalo to Mapungubwe hill in about 1230 AD, when the town most probably became overcrowded. There is also evidence of other ancient settlements around Mapungubwe referred to as Schroda, a Zhizo/Leokwe settlement and the K2 settlements. Some of these are also considered to have preceded the Mapungubwe settlement. Their structure and arrangement provide no evidence of Luvhimbi settling in the mentioned areas. On the contrary to Schroda and K2, there is evidence that the Mapungubwe site was set forth by the Luvhimbi people a while later given the existence of a rain making tabernacle or area inside as well as social classes architecture found on the site (Fig. 16) and the fact that the structure is closely similar to that of the earlier settlement at Mapela.

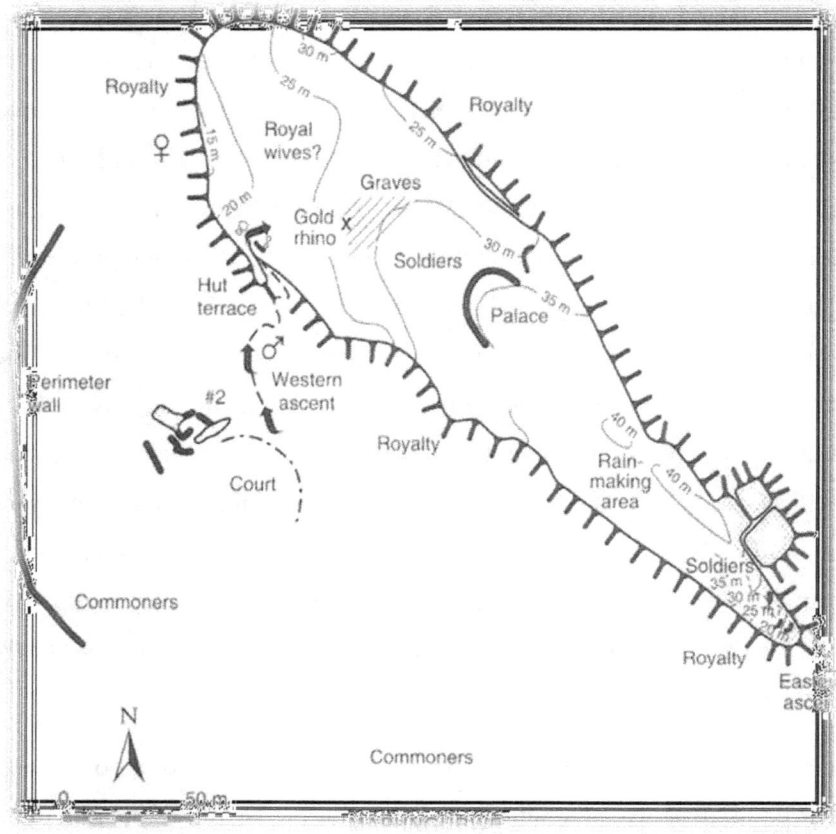

Figure 16. Map of Mapungubwe (CE1220–1290). Map courtesy of Huffman, (2007).

The previous existence of the rainmaking shrine is evidenced by the clue of a place where black cloth and *mikombe* (gourd cups) used in the symbolic manipulation of the environment to induce it to release the rains were stored. These included black or blue beads known as the Mapungubwe beads representing the two colours associated with rain (See Fig. 14). There is also evidence of a social stratification that involved those of the Mountain at the top, of the pool in the middle and those on the dry land at the bottom. According to the local culture, those of the mountain had both political power and power to perform rituals. Those in the middle could perform rituals but no political power. In the base of the social structure were the proletariats, known as those of the dry land. Fig. 17 highlights the power shift amongst the Ngona (Dzivhani), Luvhimbi (Mbedzi) and the Singo. In the Luvhimbi's iKalanga language there was a rendition that was used to express the existing hierarchy that went like, *"BoHe bagele dombo, zwilanda zwigele pasi kuBambandyanalo"* (Royalty reside on a hill, while the proletariats reside on the Bambandyanalo hill).

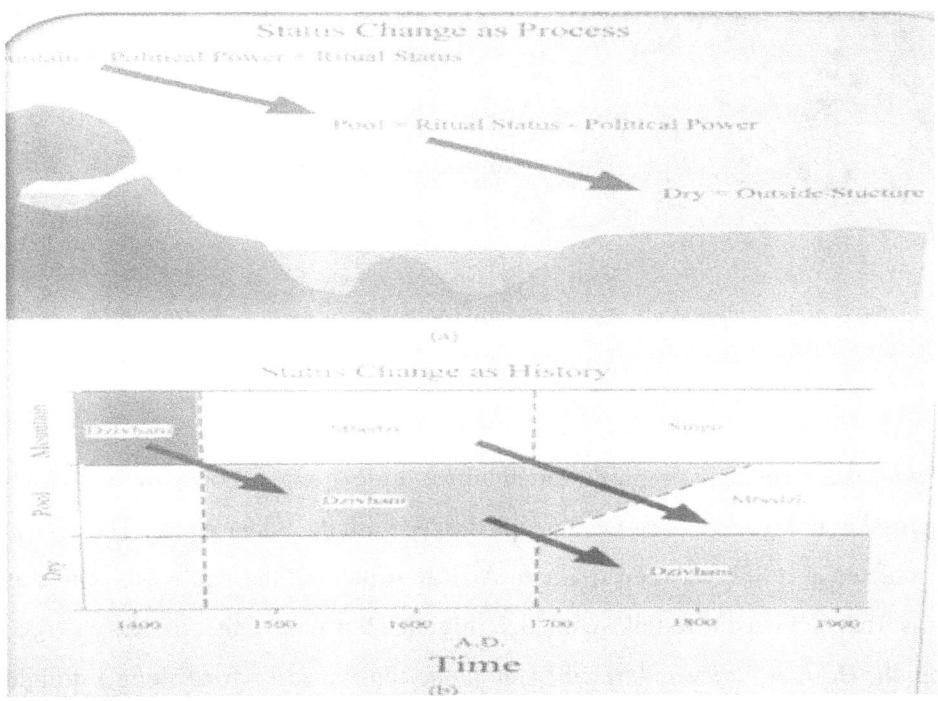

Figure 17. Status and Hierarchical Change in the Venda Society. courtesy of Loubster, 2008

Figure 18. Artist Impression of Mapungubwe Settlement - picture courtesy of PinInterest.com

Regardless, from the complex Mapungubwe trade Centre shown by an artist's impression in Figure 18, the local people traded with the wider world. The central point acted as a link between southern African tribes and the Arabs who came as far as from Yemen due to links with their migrated kinsmen. Other traders emerged from the Horn of Africa and travelled along the coast of east Africa along a straight line of trade points, from Ethiopia to the hill of Mapungubwe located in what is now known as the Limpopo Province. In the interview Continue Mhlanga (Conti Mhlanga, 2018) adds that trade peaked during the reign of Queen of Sheba who ruled Yemen and Ethiopia at that time.

This is mainly because she also had a good rapport with the local people who were originally from her land, such as the Luvhimbi clan who had originated from a place called Sena in the land of Yemen. The trade links between people of Mapungubwe and those along the route to Mombasa via Sofala is highlighted in the map as shown in figure 19 below. Probable trade routes that could have been followed are shown in the map.

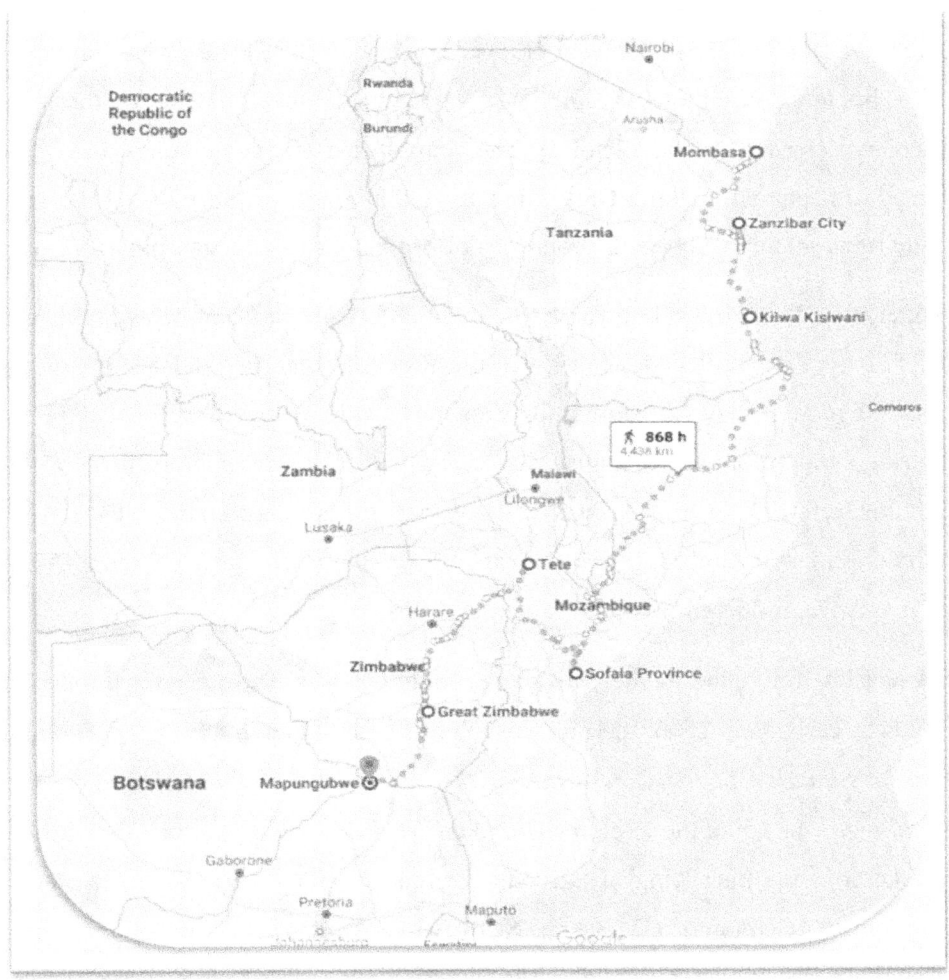

Figure 19. The main 11 to 12th Century trade route connecting Mapungubwe and the Arab North (Image drawn using Google maps)

Nonetheless, at some point in time, the distance from the north down to the south began to take its toll amongst the traders who were coming as far as Arabia. In addition, as the economy of the area began to expand, satellite trading points north of present day Mapungubwe began to emerge. Such areas gained status because they presented long distance traders with nearer trading alternatives. As a result, the centre of power and trade started to shift north to *Nzimabwe*, or the Great Zimbabwe Kingdom, and by 1290, the Mapungubwe Kingdom began to gradually collapse as the Great Zimbabwe took over as a trade centre. The Great Zimbabwe ruins lie in south- eastern Zimbabwe, about 19 miles (30 km) southeast of Masvingo (formerly Fort Victoria). The central area of ruins extends about 200 acres (80 hectares), making Great Zimbabwe the largest of more than 150 major stone ruins scattered across the countries of Zimbabwe and Mozambique.

Baxter, state that earliest known written mention of the Great Zimbabwe ruins was in 1531 by Vicente Pegado, captain of the Portuguese garrison of Sofala, on the coast of modern-day Mozambique. Vicente Pegado wrote of a fortress in the interior, built of stones, of unusual size and with a tower of more than twelve fathoms, referring to it as *Symbaoe*, likely out of his interpretation of the name *Nzimabwe*. Great Zimbabwe also appears on Abraham Ortelius' 1570 map *Africae Tabula Nova*, rendered "*Simbaoe*" (Baxter, 2018) (Fig. 20).

The earliest reference to the BuKalanga kingdom was also in association with Sofala as early as in 1506. In 1669, Joseph da Fonseca Coutinho's *"Report on the Present Situation of the Conquistas of the Rivers of Soffalla"* referred to it as '*Ucalanga*'. In 1506, the explorer Diogo de Alcáçova also described the edifices in a letter to the then King of Portugal, writing that they were part of the larger kingdom of '*Ucalanga*' (D. Beach, N, 1980). *Ucalanga* (pronounced *ukalanga*) might have been an attempt by the Portuguese to refer to *BuKalanga*.

As noted, historian Gwakuba Ndlovu also concludes that tjiKalanga was the proto or one of the proto- Bantu languages in pre-historic times especially in several regions south of the Great Lake's region. Kalanga is comprehensively associated with the Leopards Kopje culture first recorded by Robinson, (1959), a culture that was linked to material from both Mapungubwe and Hillside in Bulawayo. The analysis of the order and position of layers of archaeological remains of the Leopards Kopje culture, with the first phases of its occupation known as the Zhizo phase, shows that the earliest settlement was from the 9th century AD. Some scholars argue that the Leopards Kopje culture gave rise directly to the Kalanga culture but possibly indirectly or very differently to the Eastern Shona groups. The Leopards Kopje culture is largely linked to the ancient stone wall buildings, the *nzimabwes*. In the tjiKalanga language the prefix *Nzi-* means home and the suffix *-mabwe* means stones. *Nzimabwe* therefore refers to a settlement build in stones

It is also believed that people left Mapungubwe for Great Zimbabwe because the *Nzimabwe* (Great Zimbabwe) area was adjudged to have a more suitable climate. The Zimbabwe's Togwa and Rozwi empires later emerged, but the culture did not come to a standstill. In areas south of the Limpopo where the Venda-Kalanga tribes like the Luvhimbi lived, some novel pottery styles developed and maintained during the 14th and 15th Centuries.

Trade with the Middle and Far East at that time is evidenced by Chinese pottery and stoneware and a Persian bowl that were found in Mapungubwe and Great Zimbabwe. A similar species of grass was also found in all these coasts suggesting constant travelling between the coasts whereby traders would sensibly broadcast the seeds off their footwear. An Arabic inscribed coin from Kilwa, a Swahili trade city on the coast of East Africa, also confirm Great Zimbabwe's trade with the East.

Figure 20. Abraham Ortelius' 1570 map known as Africae Tabula Nova showing Great Zimbabwe as Simbaoe.

3,5. Luvhimbi-Mbedzi Alliance

At some unspecified period, two groups of relatives, the Luvhimbi and Mbedzi made a resolution on an integration and/or a formation of an alliance. These were alliances that were meant to recur many a times in the future. They were common informal, but strong agreements or treaties between clans to marry within each other with the aim of keeping cultural values intact, preserve family wealth, maintain geographic proximity, keep tradition, strengthen family ties, and maintain family structure. For the Luvhimbi clan, the intention was to try and maintain the ancient Malaba royal descent by attempting as much as it was possible to avoid diluting the original clan bloodline. As a result of the alliance, the Luvhimbi and Mbedzi began marrying within the alliance. It is important to note that the Luvhimbi-Mbedzi alliance was like none other because the mother of the Mbedzi family was a descendant of the Great Luvhimbi.

……………………………….

Although the first Luvhimbi (Lubimbi) had left his brothers Nyamukoko and Kaluba in the north while heading south, there was a constant connection and communication with other Mwali priests based in the Matopo shrines, especially the Shoko shrine custodians at the Wililani shrine. The connection endured the test of time until the Venda based shrines like Njelele were later moved to the Matopo hills, and ultimately the defeat of the Ndebele kingdom under King Lobengula by the British colonialists which dealt a major blow to the holistic Mwali religion. As Daneel noted, whenever the Luvhimbi failed to cause rain south of the of Vhembe, a messenger would be sent to the northern side of the river, where the Mbedzis based in Malungudzi would then send a messenger to the Matopos to contact

Mwali (Great God) on behalf of the South African vhaMbedzi (Daneel, 1970). The sphere of influence of the Mwali religion is highlighted in Figure 21 showing it stretching as far as Vendaland in present day South Africa.

At that time, the Matopo area was generally referred to as ku Mvumela, or place of meeting under a large indigenous (*Vumila/ivimila*) tree. The *Mvumela* tree was a symbol of fellowship, meetings, and a place of judgement. Matopo hills were generally also referred to as Mabwe-adziba meaning Dziba's rocks, in reference to Dzibagulu's initial establishment of the rainmaking shrine in the place, an indication that Dzibagulu levula is one of the founding fathers of the Mwali religion in the region.

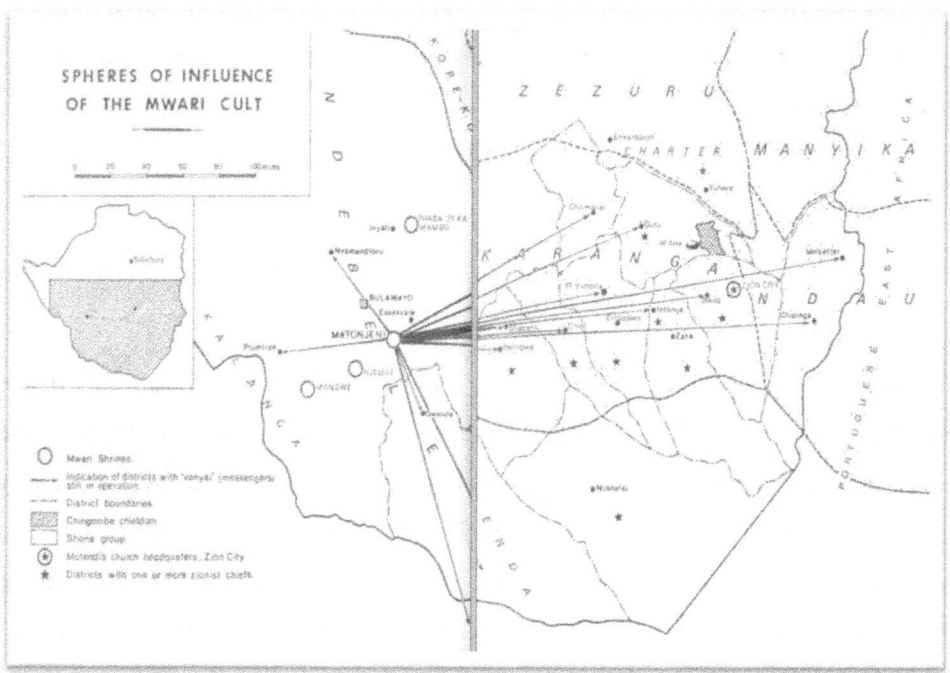

Figure 21. Map showing the spheres of influence of the Mwali religion – adapted from (Daneel, 1970)

When the descendants of the Tshivhase Singo dynasty in the eastern Soutpansberg eventually conquered the Mianzwi Mbedzi under the Luvhimbi dynasty of rainmakers in the nineteenth century (N. M. N. Ralushai, 1978), the Luvhimbi group had already been conquered by the Singo vhaSenzi people led by Dimbanyika before albeirt with either none or minimal resistance. In their oral traditions, the Lozwi even claim to have found the Ngona and Luvhimbi-Mbedzi group "a non-warlike rather disorganized people, who allowed the invaders to settle peacefully among them" (Stayt, 1968).

According to vhaVenda oral traditions, vhaSenzi, whose clans consisted of Masingo, vhaLaudzi, and Vhandalamo, had a magic drum known as Ngomalungundu. This was regarded as a sacred drum of Mwali, who was also the Great God of vhaSenzi. Ngomalungundu was the spear and shield of Vhasenzi. Their king is believed to have worked miracles with this drum which had magic and killing powers. In fear of Ngomalungundu, other groupings surrendered to or fled from the Singo killing powers. Through this conquest the vhaNgona came to revere and fear this greatest musical instrument. They regarded this drum as the Voice of their Great God, Mwali. Based on royal ancestry recalled in oral histories, the Singo Empire collapse around AD 1750.

Despite being victims of conquests, the vhaNgona had powerful and influential cultural norms because the vhaSenzi and all the other clans that settled in Venda were, with time, absorbed culturally and linguistically by vhaNgona, the clan they had conquered. It was generally accepted that any invading force in Southern Africa had to respect local customs and norms. Thus, the Venda language, its customs, and beliefs, is mainly rooted in the Ngona tribes that inhabited the area before the Mbedzi/Luvhimbi or the Singo clans (Luonde, 2021). The conquerors' descendants owe much of their present identity to the aborigines of Venda, the vhaNgona. It is believed that about 85 percent of present-day tshiVenda words and vocabulary come from the original tshiNgona. But the conquerors also transmitted a great number of tjiKalanga traits. Archaeological evidence indicates that vhaNgona were already in Venda and Southern Zimbabwe in 700 A.D. (Luonde, 2021). As the first group to settle in Venda, vhaNgona named most of the places, mountains, rivers, hills, and so on. However, names of several places and features in the present day Dzanani, in the Limpopo Province of South Africa bear the name Nzhelele, indicating the extent of the Luvhimbi clan influence and the significance of the second landing of the bateleur eagle in that area.

However, according to the *Nhlapo Commission* on *Traditional Leadership Disputes and Claims,* for three reasons, vhanNgona cannot claim seniority over the other traditional communities of Vhavenda firstly because there is no evidence that vhaNgona subjugated or conquered Masingo or any other traditional community. To the contrary, they concede that they were subjugated by Masingo. Secondly, there is no evidence that vhaNgona conquered, subjugated, assimilated, or exercised authority over vhaVenda at any stage in their history; and thirdly, even though vhaNgona were an independent traditional community, with their own cultural and linguistic elements, they lost their independence and identity when they were conquered, absorbed, and assimilated by Masingo and Bapedi (Nhlapho-Commission, 2010).

Kalanga-Lozwi clans such as vhaNyai, vhaLembethu, vhaLovhedzi and vhaSenzi also had conquered and settled in Venda (Luonde, 2021). These different clans were independent of one another until they were all conquered by Lambanyika (Dimbanyika) of the vhaSenzi to form one nation called vhaVenda. Their King's name Dambanyika or Lambanyika, meant 'he who refused to be the ruler of the land'. His name came after the death of the Lozwi king, Chiphaphami Shiriyedenga of the Singo dynasty in 1672 when a war of succession had ensued between his sons. It is believed that due to this war of succession Shiriyedenga's eldest son refused to be installed as the king (Luonde, 2021). Due to his refusal to take over as the king of Balozwi he was nicknamed Dambanyika or Lambanyika. He later agreed being king and is described as the paramount Chief of the vhaVenda, reigning from 1688-1720. He was originally from BuKalanga- Lozwi following the break-up of the Togwa state when he and his people moved into the present Limpopo area about 1688, settling in the Dzata region. King Lambanyika who died in the Nzhelele Valley about 1720 is regarded as the father of vhaVenda and vhaVenda's first king (Luonde, 2021).

Lambanyika was succeeded by Dlembeu or Djembeu who was known in Vendaland as Vele-la- Mbeu. Dlembeu had four children, one girl called Tshavhungwe, and three sons, Phophi (Thohoyandou) Tshisevhe and Raluswielo (Tshivhase). Data gathered by the Dutch at Delagoa Bay between 1723 and 1730 indicate that during Thohoyandou's time the VhuVhenda Kingdom stretched from Vhembe River (Limpopo) in the north to the Crocodile River in the south. The Singo domination of Venda was entrenched during King Thohoyandou's rule when during his reign, Thohoyandou deployed his son Munzhedzi Mpofu, to Luatame on Mount Songozwi, and his brothers Tshivhase and Tshisevhe to Dopeni. The Singo tradition has it that King Thohoyandou disappeared without a trace, probably murdered, in 1770 and it was believed that he had gone to BuKalanga (Zimbabwe), the land of his forefathers.

....

After the Mapungubwe settlement, Luvhimbi's residence had been first at Tshilavulu mountain where he befriended the vhaTavhatsindi in chief NeThengwe. From there he moved to Ha-Luvhimbi and before proceeding to Tswingoni. The continuous conquests of the vhaMbedzi clan by the people from the north had their socio- economic grade adversely effected. There were forced displacement of communities as a result. For example, the Singo conquests of the Nzhelele valley among others, led to a lot of suffering amongst the Luvhimbi and Thengwe clans. The rulers at Thengwe and Luvhimbi with his vhaMbedzi subjects were both suffering, however, the conversation recorded in the *Milayo* documents reveal that the conversations bordered around banter. The two clans would joke and sympathize with each other with the Thengwe clan largely expressing that Luvhimbi was not badly off since people were still coming and paying for rainmaking services. The Thengwe had a saying that, at the minimum, Luvhimbi still 'had a gourdful of rain' a phrase that implied a remnant of hope. The implication is that the rulers at Thengwe and Luvhimbi were both undergoing pain, distress, and hardship but the Luvhimbi-Mbedzis was not badly off because people were still coming to consult and paying for rainmaking services. The *milayo* recorded in the Oxford University UK anthropology confirm the magnitude of hard times experienced by the two clans then (Anthropology-UK, 2020). Thengwe would say,

"*Khalaru yo tiba Luvhimbi*," (The mist that covers the hill of Luvhimbi,)

"*Yo tiba -Thengwe a ....* (Covered the ruler of Thengwe.)

"*Vhatshinyali vha a seana*: (Those who suffer sympathize with each other (lit. laugh together)

"*Thengwe o sea Luvhimbi, ...* (The ruler of Thengwe sympathized with Luvhimbi,)

"*A tshi sea gumbu mvula. ....* "(But he at least had a gourdful of rain.)

In the journal, *Rhodesian History: The Journal of the Central Africa Historical Association, Volumes 8-9*, the Mbedzi khosi Luvhimbi is described as possessing "great magic powers, being able to make rain in times of drought" (Roberts & Warhurst, 1975). People came to him to beg for rain, they came in great numbers from all quarters and from many tribes. The old man Luvhimbi was able to converse in all the different languages of the lands around him…" (Garlake, 1978). He was also known as *Tshirumbula-Mikovha* (one whose rain turns gorges into rivulets). He was revered in the whole of Vendaland, and these magnificent skills were hereditarily passed down from descendant to descendant. His rain-making abilities have been enshrined in the saying: "*Mvula-mvula ndi ya Luvhimbi Ya Tshikambe i dina madumbu*" (Rain caused by Luvhimbi is excellent. Tshikambe's one is accompanied by storm) (Dube, 2015), leading to a line in the totem '*Batombo tshisipotelekwe Tshinopotelekewa kukaba mvimbi yoga*'.

Despite that, the impacts of these conquests were so significant they left the Great Luvhimbi a mere chief amongst his Mbedzi subjects and relatives. The disintegration of VhaMbedzi settlements led to the establishment of small self-governing groups spreading out in such places as Ha-Luvhimbi and Mianzwi, and other lesser-known units at Ha-Mukununde, Tshikweta, and Masetoni. As outlined above, despite all their social disintegration, Luvhimbi was still notable for being a great rainmaker.

………………………………

Following the disintegration of the Mapungubwe settlements and subsequent movement of people towards Great Zimbabwe as the new trade centre, it was almost the dark ages in Vendaland. Some argue that for the Luvhimbi and his Mbedzi people remaining tight at the Mapungubwe while the rest of the population migrated northwards towards to the new trading centre at Great Zimbabwe was a misjudgement. However, it was not principally an error of judgement because the Luvhimbi were shrine keepers and as a matter of fact, it was not easy for them to relocate without either the voice of Mwali sanctioning a move or them being casualties of a push factor or rather out of an utter desperate situation. Therefore, they stayed put in the south, mainly stationed on a settlement on Mount Tswingoni in the Nzhelele valley (Fig. 22).

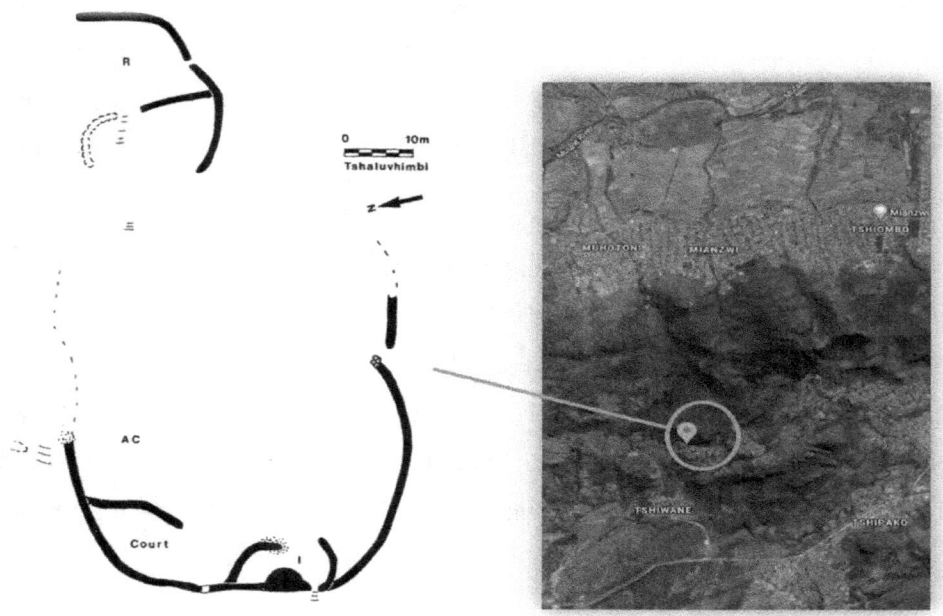

Figure 22. Showing a sketch of the layout of the Zimbabwe style Tshitaka tsha Makoleni located at the summit of Tswingoni Mountain. copied from Thomas Huffman Settlement Hierarchies in the Northern Transvaal: Zimbabwe Ruins and Venda History.

………………………………..

The Luvhimbi dynasty went on for centuries in Vendaland passing the legacy on from Luvhimbi generation to generation until the time of the last male Luvhimbi. His name was Khosi Bepe Luvhimbi. At one-point Bepe Luvhimbi had found himself without a surviving male offspring hence he is historically known as 'the last male Luvhimbi (N. M. N. V. Ralushai, 1977). Legend has it that Khosi Bepe

Luvhimbi could have lost his sons through a systematic killing by the invading Singo tribe who at some point had gone into a rampant killing spree that involved conducting the murder of all uncircumcised young males. The Luvhimbi clan still swore by the oath of Munyole of the ancient Bukusu tribe, and they did not practice circumcision. Actually, the Luvhimbi custom required that in the thanksgiving ceremony of *tebula* (*thevhula*), no-one who has undergone the circumcision was to be allowed to handle the royal artefacts (*nkombe*). This anomaly led to a near tragedy when at some point the male children were wiped out after being found to be uncircumcised. On the contrary, the Singo custom viewed uncircumcised young males as potentially heirs to the clan throne or just as reserves for any powerful future positions.

Besides the assumptions indicated above there is no clear explanation as to why Luvhimbi would not bear any more children at that point unless it was a question of not able to bear children through illness or other forms of misfortunes. What is nonetheless consistently emphasized by several scholars is that Bepe Luvhimbi who was also known as *Luvhimbi Gwa Gole* (Kole was the last male Luvhimbi in the history of the Great Luvhimbi Dynasty. In tjiKalanga the name Bepe is also a reference to wooden container in which Luvhimbi used to store and ferry his rainmaking kit. The specific container was later referred to as *Gobhodo lemiti* (medicine bag), either through a mere change of name or change of container type, most certainly from a wooden to a more portable skin-material one, or because extra contents were later added to it as it changed ownership.

………………………..

It was during the late 1760s that Bepe Luvhimbi is traced embarking on an exodus southward, heading towards Malungudzi. The trip is recorded in many scholar articles including Professor Ralushai's 1978 article entitled *Further traditions concerning Luvhimbi and the Mbedzi*, in the *Rhodesian History* journal. With benefit of hindsight, it was due to the dilemma of having no male offspring that Khosi Luvhimbi with his Mbedzi family made an all-important journey northward to Malungudzi. Although the time of the trip to Malungudzi is not specified by scholars, it is logical to pin it in the 1760s that Khosi Bepe Luvhimbi left Malungudzi after the meeting, heading back southwards with his wife Tshubalale and just-married daughter Tshiembe, and some of his Mbedzi family. Luvhimbi's other daughter Mbobvu was also a newly married to the popular NeTshiendeulu of the Ngona clan. The journey was of significance because noticeably, the reason for the trip was to attend to the issue of succession in the traditional leadership that included inheriting the rainmaking responsibilities that was looming large as Luvhimbi got more advanced in age. It is not known how long Luvhimbi and the Mbedzi stayed at Malungudzi but visibly the crisis of lack of male offspring was discussed and a resolution reached.

The decision reached at the Malungudzi meeting underscored an agreed arrangement that one of the Mbedzi people, Habedu of the Mianzwi Mbedzi clan and was a *Thovhele* or was called Thobela due to his relation to the Great Luvhimbi, would marry Luvhimbi and Tshubalale's first-born daughter Tshiembe. The far-reaching arrangement determined that the Luvhimbi cultural and religious legacy was able to be maintained through one of *Thovhele* Habedu Mianzwi Mbedzi and Tshiembe offspring. One offspring with both the Luvhimbi and Mbedzi DNA, would, after the death of the Great Luvhimbi, inherit the rainmaking responsibilities as well as the traditional leadership of the clan. Thobela (*Thovhele*) Habedu Mianzwi was a Mbedzi and Luvhimbi's maternal grandson born out of the existing Luvhimbi-Mbedzi marital alliance, making his mother to be a

MaLuvhimbi. Mbedzi had a brother called Masevhe (Masebe) who is the ancestor of the Ndou clan. As per Venda tradition Thobela Habedu Mianzwi Mbedzi was not only a deliberate but an appropriate rainmaker choice as he possessed a genetic linkage to the great Luvhimbi from both his father and mother's side. He was from the Mianzwi lineage too.

Accordingly, Thobela Habedu Mbedzi was genetically part of the Luvhimbi family and marrying Tshiembe implied marrying within the family not only for reasons of continuing the rainmaking inheritance, but also to protect the entire royal *Wele Malaba* legacy. Royal intermarriage was a practice commonly done in many clans as part of strategic diplomacy to enhance the prospect of territorial gain for a dynasty through acquiring legal claim to its sphere and through inheritance from an heiress whenever a monarch failed to leave an undisputed male heir. After marrying Tshiembe, Luvhimbi and Tshubalale's daughter, Habedu Mianzwi Mbedzi was assuming a new height and was no longer regarded as a commoner. He was from this time forth no longer going to be a sheer Mbedzi but henceforth be recognized with a new title of 'Mbedzinkulu'.

The newly acquired 'Mbedzinkulu' (Royal Mbedzi) title was meant to indicate the degree of Thobela's new position that, from here and after, distinguished him and his descendants from other Mbedzi clans. Mbedzinkulu's children with Tshiembe become the first in history to carry the Luvhimbi- Mbedzi or Mbedzi-Luvhimbi surname, thereby, heralding a new era, and a hybrid continuation of the Luvhimbi tribe, from which the Malaba clan would emerge and bestowed the Royal Malaba legacy. Judging by his title of Thovhele, it may imply that the Mbedzinkulu's VhaMbedzi clan previously enjoyed their own self-government. This is hinged on the fact that the Venda chieftainship was normally classified into categories or levels according to royal seniority. At the apex was the head, thovhele, which is translated as 'king', entailing that the Mbedzinkulu clan were themselves an autonomous clan reigning over their own state.

The Venda Royal Leadership Organogram:

Thovhele [*King*]

↓

Mahosimahulu (*Paramount Chiefs*)

↓

Mahosi (*Senior Traditional Leaders*)

↓

Mahosana (*The Headman*)

↓

Vhakoma (*Minor Headman*)

A possibility is that they could be the old Thovhela state mentioned by the Dutch diarists who were based at Delagoa Bay around 1730 (Dube, 2015). There is a recount that around the last half of the 18th century the Lozwi arrived at the Nzhelele valley of the Zoutpansberg Mountains where they found the Vhatavhatsindi, Twamamba and Lembetu ruling over the aboriginal inhabitants. These aboriginal inhabitants included the Ngona and Mbedzi whose Thovhela state had been in existence prior to the 1720's. Here too, according to the Dutch diarists, they found earlier Kalanga settlers ruling alongside and over the original Venda speakers, who were part of the 18th Thovhela sub state.

This is backed by the fact that research has always shown that not later than the 16th century, there had lived in the Buhwa Togwa kingdom of present-day Zimbabwe, a chief Tumbale-Thovhele of the Dziba or Mbedzi people. The record of the Dziba- Mbedzi correlation at this period highlights the pre-dating relationship between the Dziba and the Mbedzi clans, hence backing the conviction that the two were cousin clans who both naturally and systematically became a grouping. Maboko is clear that their most popular ruler at the time was Luvhimbi, a rainmaker and priest (Mabogo, 1990).

Mulaudzi (2014) also states that in connection with the Changamire conquest in the Kingdom of BuKalanga in about 1670, there lived some of the Mbedzis who later comprised one of Mbedzi groups heading to the south (Mulaudzi, 2015).

The group is reported to have stayed for a short time at Malungudzi hill before later settling south of the Limpopo-Vembe where they conquered the Lembethu and consequently adopting the Lembethu dialect. Another group under Tumbale remained in the Murehwa district of Zimbabwe and intermarried with the Lozwi, Nhowe and the Barwe. In east Vendaland the Mianzwi Mbedzi are recorded to have taken over from the Dzivhani Ngona.

As indicated before, the Mbedzi clan were maternal descendants of the Luvhimbi clan who further later on reached a marital alliance with the Luvhimbi clan in a bid to marrying within the family and protect the legacy. This is the Luvhimbi-Mbedzi clan who ruled from prominent stone ruins at Tshaluvhimbi and *Tshitaka-tsha-Makoleni* shown in Figure 23. One of them, Mianzwi settled a few kilometres to the North of Tswingoni Mountain and the place is named after him.

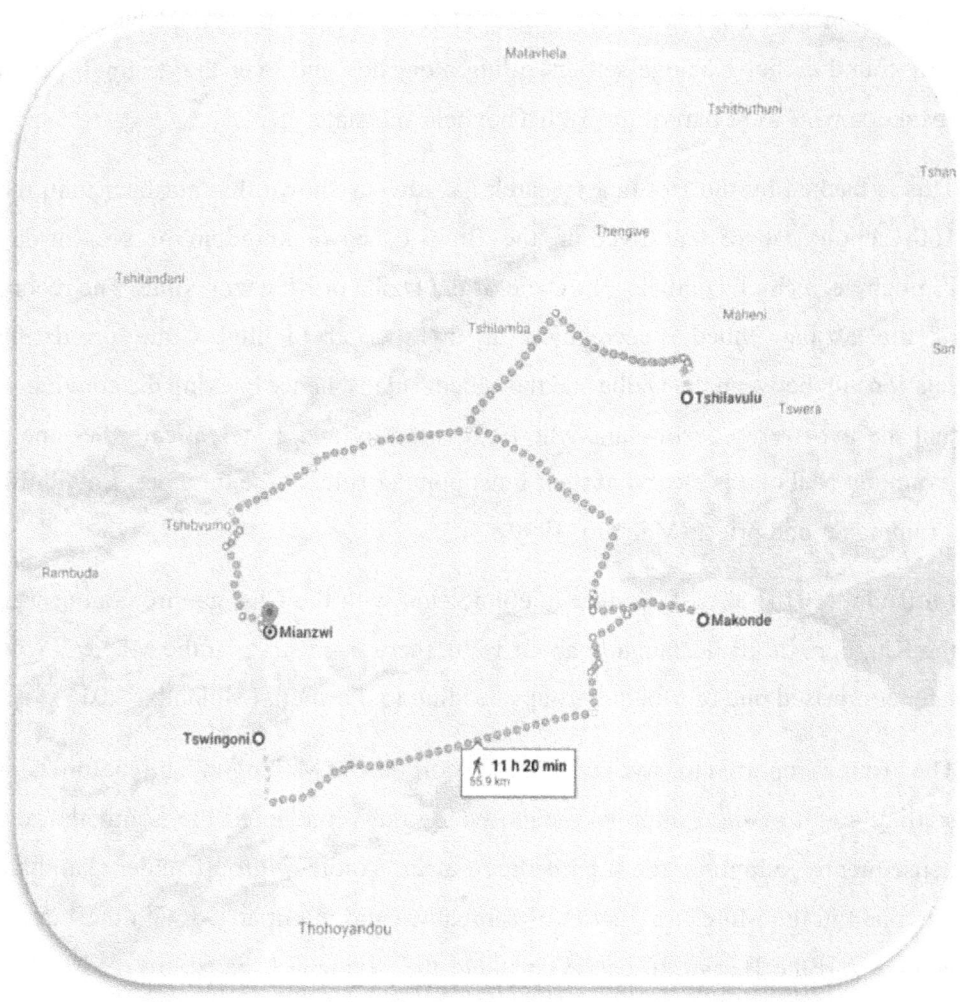

Figure 23. Show the areas settled by the Mbedzi Luvhimbi people as they arrived from Malungudzi, North of Limpopo.

3,6; The Children of Mbedzi-nkulu

In 1770, Dlembeu's youngest son Masindi or Phophi, known as King Thohoyandou, disappeared without trace. He had allegedly been killed but the people were made to believe that he had gone to vhuKalanga, (Zimbabwe) or *kamme*, the land of his maternal forefathers. Believing that Thohoyandou was going to come back, the people installed his brother Tshisevhe as acting king but even when the truth about the death of Thohoyandou finally came out Tshisevhe refused to step down as acting king, and this led to a conflict between him and Thohoyandou's son, Munzhedzi Mpofu. That same year the Mbedzinkulu family is blessed with a son, Mantsha. Mantsha was so loved by his grandfather Bepe Luvhimbi that he chose him from amongst other sons to become an apprentice for rainmaking, a traditional healing, and a clan leadership pupil.

From an early age, Mantsha started receiving intensified training on skills relating to leadership, rainmaking, custodianship, and traditional healing which were important characteristics of the ancient Malaba royalty. It was out of this apprenticeship that Mantsha was to blossom and become a well-known rainmaker and traditional healer, a practice that earned him the names Mpangana, Ngwali, Wonyedzapasi, Ngqamebukhali, Manikiniki and other praise names.

Mpangana basically became the first to be ordained with the ancient Malaba royal highness amongst the Malaba family in the southern hemisphere, but that presentation would not be considered complete without an individual undergoing and winning a pool contest. Winning a pool contest was a decision by Mwali and the winner was acknowledged to be Mwali's chosen one and was coronated. Like many others during his time, the names emanated mainly from his daily traditional healing activities and his routine appearances in traditional costume. He was also being referred to as *Malukanjita*, a name probably derived from the clan praises *"bakalunji gusipfume ngubo, gwakasimila pfuma lutombo"* (the needle that does not saw blankets but saw rocks) and partly because he was in the dominantly Mbedzi occupation of making leather, fur, wool, feathers, silk clothes and other materials out of animal skin. These items were traded with Arabia, China, and India through the East African harbours. According to the Malaba oral narrations, one of Mpangana's conserved stories was one about the so-called Kaffir Wars that took place when he was in his teens. The *Kaffir* wars or the Cape Frontier Wars a phrase that refers to a series of nine battles between the farmers known as the Boers and the Xhosa that lasted for nearly a hundred year from 1779 to 1879. These conflicts are still regarded as the longest-running military action in the history of African colonialism.

The word "*kaffir*," originally used by Arab slavers to denote unbelievers or heathens, came to be used in nineteenth- century South Africa to refer to any Bantu, particularly a member of the Xhosa tribe (Beck, 2000). The Boers gained significant ground against the Xhosas as they went on to create the Stellenbosch, Cape, Swellen dam, Graff Reinet, and the Zuuveld Districts. United, these Districts constituted was what was to be known as the Cape Colony. Slaves were brought from various parts of Africa and Asia as captives for forced labour in building the Colony.

At that time, Mpangana was already the next-in-line to Bepe, the last male Luvhimbi. Out of his marriage with Tshiembe, Mbedzinkulu had earlier on conceived two daughters named Mufanadzo Mbedzi and Tshawila Mbedzi. Between 1860 and 1868, she along conceives sons, Tshimba-Bhangwa Mbedzi, and Sabaswi Lubimbi-Mbedzi

....

Thereon, in his final days, the last male Luvhimbi resolved that it was the right time to pass on his leadership and rainmaking legacy to the next inheritor and this was to occur before his demise. As per the Kalanga-Venda culture, if a legacy had failed the natural inheritance process handover and was to be transferred to a different family member, family or clan, the inheritor was to be determined by Mwali the Creator, God the Almighty, through some ritual performances. Dzibagulu levula is assumed to have attained his name after going through the same process. In vhuVenda, the process involved a competition customarily undertaken at the sacred pool of Maneledzi in the Mutale River in Mianzwi. The contestants traditionally constituted heir apparent and/or first-born sons from various houses.

Under the watchful eyes of the elders, a group of contestants would receive instructions to dive in and swim across the pool. Each one of them would be holding and branding a burning stick. The ultimate objective of the task was that whoever emerged on the other end of the pool still clutching an unextinguished firebrand was declared the Mwali chosen champion and new leader of the clan. Such was a prevalent Kalanga-Venda tradition aimed at the determination of a transfer of power from one clan or family to the other being left at the discretion of Mwali the Almighty God. The Kalanga-Venda people so venerated the pool of Maneledzi that they described it as "so deep and black that you can see stars". The Maneledzi pool was itself Mwali's dziba gulu levula (Mwali's pool). A picture of the Maneledzi pool is shown in Figure 24 and the significance of the pool is captured in the Venda Domba dance songs as follows:

"Maneledzi maandatshena" - Maneledzi which is like a mirror,

"Midzimuni ya Vha ha Luvhimbi" - Where live the ancestor-spirits of the rainmakers of Luvhimbi.

"Vhumbedzi ndi hunakaho" - The country of the Mbedzi is beautiful.

Although some of these songs are now sung in public, these were originally sacrilegious songs sung in private or only during the worship of Mwali.

Figure 24. The Maneledzi Pool on River Mutale: where the "pool contest" took place. This site together with Tswingoni and Tshilavulu form a holy trinity of the sacred circuit of the Luvhimbi Thebula ritual (Courtesy of Manombe Luvhimbi – Venda)

It was early 1823 in Mianzwi, vhuVenda. In the south, the Khumalos of Mzilikazi were beating off the first Zulu attack heralding the emergence of a new Ndebele state in the process. In the north, Mambo Tjibundule Madabhale was ruling from the capital Khami (*Kame*), while his provincial chief lived at the Domboshaba or Luswingo. In VhuVenda, the genarian or possibly centenarian Luvhimbi's days on earth were numbered. This signified that the time had come for him to pass the baton to whoever was to be successor to the throne. An arrangement was hastily made for the undertaking of the momentous ceremony. On that particular day, with the assistance of Mwali the Creator, God the Almighty, a successor was to be chosen amongst a number of offspring. The chosen one was to carry forward the divine gift of the royal Malaba legacy, the Royal gift of *Wele* Malaba, the vestige of Dzibagulu levula and the spirit of the Great Luvhimbi which had been passed on from generation to generation with a high degree of precision.

Thus, one morning, as dawn sent shimmering rays over the placid Mutale River, bestowing a golden path from the riverbank to the horizon, a group of men, young an old, stood by queuing along the edges of the sacred Maneledzi pool, watched by communities from afar. The men were readying for an escapade of immense historic proportions. The Great Luvhimbi who was the traditional master of ceremony, stood there like a colossus, it is narrated, motionless as if cut from stone, his face with a fixed gaze like a statue of an angel of hope and glory. Like the usual natural, as darkness surrendered, every colour changed from tinges of charcoal to a vibrancy, making the contestants more visible otherwise in the prime of dawn. Their silhouettes reflected a group of individuals faced with uncertainty however, raring to go. Customarily, the Mbedzi people of VhuVenda were commonly known as the pool people. Therefore, this precise pool contest was not the first of its kind to be undertaken in this manner. However, on this distinct day, the entrants were derived only from the house that directly descended from Thobela Mbedzinkulu and his wife Tshiembe.

The sole aim of this technique was to avoid diluting the principally Luvhimbi bloodline. However, because of lack of numbers, the sons who had reached 'the age of herding cattle' were, as per custom, summoned to participate too. Therefore, in this group of aspirants, the contestants comprised Mpangana and his son Tshibi from his own first house. Bhangwa was accompanied by his sons Sekudza and Mbikwa, who was also known as Tawulo, while Sabaswi came in alongside Npininga his only son. The Mbedzi females Mufanadzo and Tshawwila could not be allowed to participate in this 'exclusive Luvhimbi ceremony' nonetheless, the Mbedzi culture granted female children to rule as *makhadzis* if they qualified as heiresses. The raring to go aspirants were armed each with burning sticks before plunging into the pool. As explained above, the rule was that whoever emerged at the other end of the pool with the firebrand still ablaze was the one chosen by Mwali, the God Almighty. The Invictus amongst the contestants was to immediately assume the extraordinary gift of rainmaker, conjoined with the corresponding leadership role of the clan.

With all the instructions inscribed on their hearts, the boys dived into the sacred Maneledzi pool under the watchful eye of the clan elders standing by. Before a cow could finish mowing, all the boys were resurfacing at the other end of the pool still clutching the firewood sticks in their hands as if their dear lives depended on it. However, in a dramatic form, from amongst all the competitors, only one, young Tshibi, emerged out clinging on to a firestick that was still aflame and blazing like a mighty sword. The spectators still fixed adjacent the pool, were left in awe by the peculiarly burning of the stick which was, at that instant, glowing with an even more luminous intensity.

....

From the unspoiled picturesque of the land of VhuVenda that lay facing the mighty river of Vhembe, to the mountains of Malungudzi that thrust its spires of naked rock into the heavens, and yonder to the distant panoramic hills of the Matopos in the land of Bukalanga, Tshibi's triumph was heralding a new phase and a new epoch in the Malaba legacy. The victor of both the rainmaking and the traditional leadership experience had been determined. For the clan elders standing by, Mwali had pronounced it in a way that was as clear as daylight. A new dawn had emerged with new possibilities, and a fresh page had been launched but to be written on. From the abstract world, the jubilee sound of the new hero song was piercing through the atmosphere like the Biblical arrows of the tribe of Benjamin, announcing the arrival of a new historical period. Cutting a long story short, it was a day an heir to the throne had been chosen by Mwali to assume and carry the Malaba cultural and religious legacy. Tshibi had been bestowed with the endowment of *Wele* Malaba's royalty and like Dzibalevula who also had inherited the legacy through the same homogeneous design, he was essentially assuming a Malaba-*zinda/linga* act. Legend mentions that the Great Luvhimbi stood there transfixed, watching, and smiling triumphantly like one who had discovered a cure for duty.

Nevertheless, tradition states that the great Khosi Luvhimbi, upon realizing Tshibi's adolescent status, consequently made a far-reaching decision that led to the father figure, Mpangana being handed over the medicine bag, '*bepe*' or the "*gobhodo lemiti*". The job was made easy by the fact that Mpangana had not just been Luvhimbi's right hand man but was an apprentice. The package involved Mpangana being a place holder while young Tshibi grows to the age of maturity fit enough to assume the cultural, political, and religious leadership of the clan together with the associated responsibilities. The meaning of the whole process was that, like his ancestor Dzivagulu levula, Tshibi had been selected by Mwali to inherit the great Malaba's *linga* or *izinda* as per the ancient Malaba tradition.

As expressed, beforehand, the *linga/izinda* was not only a legacy, but a cultural and spiritual power of a supreme and paramount ancestor that was being thrust upon Tshibi, to enable him to assume the role of the Great *Wele* Malaba, who was part of the ancient Bukusu Divine Trinity together with all his responsibilities. The process was made easy by the fact that Mpangana was already an expert on issues relating to leadership, rainmaking custodianship, and traditional leadership through a lifetime training by the Great Luvhimbi.

Rituals were thereafter undertaken, and a process of coronation conducted which meant Tshibi's life was to significantly change from this time forth and looking toward as he assumed the all- important role of representing the clan. From that point in time, the entrusted Tshibi was recognized and acknowledged as the custodian and epitome of customs, values, and traditions of the Malaba clan and beyond. From that point Tshibi Malaba was to have a responsibility of providing traditional, political, cultural, and religious guidance to the clan, which included a diversity of functions ranging from administrative and religious to much more extensive judicial and development duties. Just like in the history of the Bukusu people when Sioka's brother Malaba died, Sioka recreated the legacy through his son Malaba.

The occurrence meant that Malaba son of Sioka, became a clan father and be a 'father figure' even to his own father. However, Malaba son of Sioka became more significant as he became perceived as a demigod (*Wele*), making his legacy to carry even more authority, influence, and responsibilities. Through Tshibi, the Malaba legacy was re-created once more and Tshibi was now a beneficiary of a great inheritance and a special destiny. Now, therefore, at that point Tshibi was enacting the legacy and becoming not only a father figure to his father, but the entire clan. Since the Malaba *zinda/linga* was supernaturally passed on to Tshibi, that implied thereupon, that the entire house of Mpangana was automatically falling under the assumption of the Malaba title, with the role and responsibilities that went with it included. More so, it is of paramount importance to note that Mpangana's brothers, and sisters, Sabaswi, Bhangwa, Mufanadzo, Tshawwila and anyone else's families were excluded from the new Malaba clan. Imperatively, Tshibi, with all his brothers and sisters and father figure included therefore, become the creator (*bhaluli/umdabuli*) of the newly established Malaba clan.

Oral traditions complement with the benefit of hindsight that whoever had assumed the Malaba legacy through means of a pool contest had the name *Mwali/uNgwali* systematically attached to him. As also noted by other history writers like Hole, the name Ngwali was not a personal, but an official and traditional name assumed by the head *wizard* on succeeding to the post (Hole, 1968). Dzibagulu levula evidently assumed the legacy through a pool contest and was also called by the Mwali name because he was chosen by Mwali at the *dzibalevulu*. As observed earlier on, Dzibagulu levula was also known by the name Mwali (*uNgwali*), denoting, through observation, hindsight, and analysis, that he had assumed the rainmaking legacy through a similar custom of being chosen by Mwali in a pool (*dzibalevula*). By the same token the newly established Malaba clan was to have the titles of '*dzibalevula*' and Mwali (*uNgwali*) assuredly affixed onto their totem. Equivalently, as taking over the religious rainmaking legacy, Tshibi was to assume the title of Mwali (*uNgwali*) or the son of Mwali. The concept was adopted from their Hebrew originality. However, for the reasons yet to be highlighted, it was, in lieu, Mpangana who became synonymous with the title of *uNgwali* in most history narrations.

As maintained before, the Malaba *zinda/linga* involved quite a huge responsibility of both traditional leadership and the authority to oversee over the rainmaking process. It was a role that was to affect not only the Malaba clan but all those whose livelihood depended on agriculture for survival. Some oral narratives refer to Tshibi as Nsenya a nickname he, likely, got after emerging victorious in the pool contest, and he was also nicknamed Mmalahaba because of his light complexion and because as a young man, he was smart and intelligent like an impala (Wentzel & Kumile, 1983). The pool incident was an era of utmost importance in the history of the Malaba clan as the important leadership baton was being passed down from the great Luvhimbi to his descendants, the new Malaba clan. From that point forth the Mpangana family was going to be duty-bound for a critical role of rainmaking and traditional counsel.

Water was a symbol of life, and as a result, rainmaking ceremonies grew in popularity as an effective strategy to overcome the negative consequences of climate change like drought, hunger, and diseases. However, amongst the people of the Great Luvhimbi, rainmaking was not only an intrinsic part of their culture and religion, but they had an inevitable answerability to both rainfall and/or lack of it. Therefore, for Mpangana Malaba, being trained into a rainmaker and being Tshibi's placeholder, was a demanding responsibility because the rainmaking leadership role constituted two interrelated components: the material and the spiritual. Although the Luvhimbi were descending from the ancient Malaba, it was through the hereditary nature of their family that the Luvhimbi title was passed on from generation to generation, creating a Luvhimbi dynasty that was sustained for centuries. However, they were in fact carrying and advancing the ancient Malaba legacy of traditional leadership and the religion of rainmaking.

Mpangana and ultimately, Tshibi Malaba, were not only going to just assume the traditional leadership of the new clan but as rainmaker successors, were also responsible for the wealth and health of the people by controlling and providing life-giving waters. Nevertheless, because Mpangana was being trained and incorporated into this role just as a placeholder for the young Tshibi, he therefore, was prepared not only to hold that rank with dignity but was also inclined to appeal to every available resource in the fight to protect the heir apparent Tshibi as well as defending the Malaba legacy. After the pool incident, Mpangana became the de facto traditional leader of the Malaba contingent. In this book, the Malaba contingent will be a reference to the entire journeying Mbedzi-Luvhimbi clan of sister Tshawwila and brothers Bhangwa and Sabaswi, while the Malaba clan is reference to the Mpangana family. Although age wise, the three were older than Mpangana, the Malaba leadership authority automatically fell on Mpangana's shoulders because Mpangana was, conversely, a Tshibi purebred while the others were not. This is the reason why both the Malaba title and authority exceptionally fell only under Mpangana household and discounting that of Mufanadzo, Tshawwila, Sabaswi and Bhangwa. Mpangana also became a monumental individual amongst the integrated Malaba clan, past and present, on the grounds that he rose as the oldest Malaba figure in this newly constituted Malaba clan at any time. However, these circumstances were not without drama.

When all was said and done, other Mbedzi family members, particularly Mpangana's sister Mufanadzo, were not pleased with the legacy being transferred to the young Tshibi. Mufanadzo believed, perhaps rightly so, that both the Luvhimbi and Mbedzi legacies were legitimately her own inheritance and were being scandalously transferred to the young Tshibi. Actually, Mufanadzo, by virtue of being the first-born girl to Thobela Mbedzinkulu, she, or her children, were granted by the Venda cultural laws to take over from the Great Luvhimbi, both the traditional leadership as well as the responsibilities associated with rainmaking. However, Luvhimbi illustrated to her that the custom being observed at the time was an exceptional Luvhimbi practice and that if she so wanted to inherit a legacy, she should depart Tswingoni and relocate to her father's kraal in Mianzwi, on the northern side of the mount Tswingoni where the Mbedzi kraal was. Besides the apparent fact that Luvhimbi subscribed to the old Malaba notion of a male rainmaker, he also believed the whole undertaking was solely a Luvhimbi arrangement guided by Mwali, therefore, intrinsically an exclusive Luvhimbi family matter.

However, Mufanadzo was uncompromising in her belief that she was the rightful heir to the Luvhimbi legacy moreover. The people of Mufanadzo, who in the meanwhile, had gone on to marry to the battle-hardened Tshivhase family, devised a plot. The conspiracy was to thwart the new establishment and eliminate Tshibi and those associated with his assumption of leadership especially Mpangana. The rationale behind having Mpangana as a target was on the backdrop that he had been trained as a rainmaker by Luvhimbi at the same time Tshiembe was training Mufanadzo. Although Mufanadzo's training could have been for the Mbedzi *makhadzi* leadership in Mianzwi, the pool circumstances created a fierce rivalry. The makhadzi role is also regarded highly among the Vhavenda as they hold authority for sustaining and preserving custom in the conduct of marriages as well as in resolving family disputes.

By getting married to the Tshivhase family, Mufanadzo was creating an argument that she was 'marrying within the family' as a way of strengthening her resolve to inherit Luvhimbi's legacy. Tshivhase was the brother of Thohoyandou son of Dlembeu, who himself was a descendant of Mambire and Mambire being a cousin to the Great Luvhimbi (See table 1 below).

Table 1. Singo leadership lineage, compiled by Dr Matiwaza Ncube from various sources.

Mambire	Son to Luvhimbi's daughter Like the Mbedzis, the Shokos were incorporated into the Mwali priesthood. The tribe was transferred from Mapungubwe to Great Zimbabwe then tothe Matopos.
Tshilume	Son to Mambire. Great Rozvi king - His royal kraal was known asMatongoni (Great Lakes). He is said to have been instructed by Mwali to move southwards.
Tshikalanga	Also died in Mvumela/Matopo
Hwami	Good character cautious Senzi leader
Ntindima	Low key leader
Dimbanyika	Arrives in Venda from Danangombe (via Mvumela) after refusing to rulein Zimbabwe - he was following his uncle who had settled in Vendaland. His brother heads to Zambia or Hwange areas

Dyambeu	1722-1760
Thohoyandou(Phophi-Tshikalang)	1760-1791 Had three sons, Munzhedzi Mpofu, Mandiwana and Ratombo Tshivhase married Mbedzinkulu's daughter Mufanadzo. Mpangana is born 1770
Munzhedzi Mpofu	1793-1829 ca.1800 The Great Luvhimbi - Khosi Bepe visits Malungudzica.1823 The Great Luvhimbi dies: 1823-28 Mpangana contingent leave Venda
Ramabulana (Rusithu)	1829-1864
Makhado	1864-1895
Alilali Tshilamulela(Mphephu I)	1895-1924
Mbulaheni (Mphephu II)	1925 - 1948

After his father's death, Tshivhase had fled east to Dopeni, on the way pillaging and torching villages. These actions earned him the name *Midiyavhathu* Tshivhase which meant 'the one who burnt everybody's house' (Mcnell, 2011). Under the circumstances, a fight with the hostile Tshivhase clan was always going to be an uphill task for Mpangana and family. However, by accepting the responsibility thrust upon him by the Great Luvhimbi, Mpangana trusted not only his instinct but his supranatural prowess too. Author Ralushai (1978), also narrates in his findings that the Mbedzinkulu family split because Mufanadzo, also known as Tshisinavhute, wanted to be chief but the Great Bepe Luvhimbi would not allow her to be one. Luvhimbi had evidently decided on how his legacy was to be continued.

It was after the internal conflict that Mufanadzo, indeed left Tswingoni to become chief at Mianzwi, a few kilometres North of Tswingoni. Several Venda researchers including the likes of Ralushai (1978) point up that she certainly went on and became a rainmaker in Mianzwi with the blessing of her father Mbedzinkulu. Nevertheless, she was to never let go the question of the Luvhimbi succession in Tswingoni, and therefore the conspiracy plot to eliminate the young Tshibi deepened and, it was then that Mufanadzo had to request the help of Ligegise Tshivhase, to chase out and kill her brother, the powerful rainmaker Mpangana Manikiniki Mantsha, as well as the successor to the throne Tshibi Malaba. The Tshivhase clan are also the ancestors to the South African president Matamela Cyril Ramaphosa.

As had been suggested by the great Luvhmbi, Mufanadzo, had been given the greenlight to assume the rainmaking role by her father Mbedzinkulu at Mianzwi and succession at Mianzwi became matrilineal and rulers used the title of Tshisinavhute and/or Dzhenzhele Ramiholi (Roberts, 1977). According to The Special Milayo of the Rainmaking Clan, Mianzwi then became synonymous with the attribute '*Hafha hayani: wa ha Tshisinavhute*' meaning 'there at home, a homestead at Tshisinavhute's'. However, oral traditions indicate that still was not enough for Mufanadzo. Therefore, sensing grave danger, oral traditions account that one of Mpangana's brothers Bhangwa, advised that Mpangana and the rest of his family take off and escape. After much deliberation, began the preparations to embark on a historically significant journey northward across the Vhembe (Limpopo) river. The aim was to seek refuge closer to the Mwali shrines at Matopo hills where other Mwali religious custodians were mostly concentrated.

Nevertheless, Mufanadzo and her people's conspiracy was inadequate. Luvhimbi had relinquished the medicine bag '*Gobhodo lemiti*' or the bepe, to Mpangana as a stopgap for the young Tshibi. Oral traditions also indicate that the contents of the medicine bag consisted, among other things, the symbolic two knobkerries. The two knobkerries were a set of gadgets that believably possessed an ability to give virtual powers to whoever was assuming the clan leadership role. The two knobkerries were an emblem of power and authority. According to legend, these knobkerries resembled Moses' stuff of God and were of great importance in all their journeys, heritage, and legacies. Like in the Biblical stories of Moses, the knobkerries were hitherto useful in crossing places like the Red Sea into Egypt, then the River Nile and both the Zambezi and the Limpopo rivers as well as in all their settlements.

The apparatus could be transported by any authorized individual, but more importantly, they could only be essentially put into practical use by a clan leader chosen by Mwali. Therefore, in this case, Mpangana's role involved just holding on to the apparatus as an emergency but had no legitimacy in putting the appliances into practical use or more so, use them to perform a ritual, further implying that Mpangana's position was on interim basis. After the Malaba contingent had departed from VhuVenda, tradition tells a story of Magwabeni, a renowned messenger of Mwali to 'Malungudzi', who at that time, brought instructions from the Mwali shrine to the local traditional leadership in Vendaland.

In a typical Mosaic fashion, Mwali had appeared to Magwabeni at Makonde in a great light which lit up the whole mountain. Makonde was a shrine established by both the Ngonas and the Mbedzis of Luvhimbi and was well known as the place visited periodically by Mwali. Magwabeni was a Ngona who also spoke tjiKalanga, the language of Mwali (Shutte, 1977). According to tradition, the light arrived with a thud and was accompanied by a great wind that flattened huge trees. As the light grew dimmer it either went into the mouth of a cave on the mountain or hovered near the house of Magwabeni the medium. He received a message and the messages given to him was exclusively concerned with agricultural matters. The message that Wednesday and the first day of the new moon should be a day of rest was to be delivered to all religious leaders. No tilling should be done on

Wednesdays. One chief, Ravhura maintained that the people at Mianzvi, Luvhimbi and Thengwe areas were subject to these instructions which they had to receive at Ravhura's place. One other important issue to note was that, after the departure of the Mpangana family, despite Tshisinavhute' claim as a rainmaker, Ravhura and his people never went to Tshisinavute, at Mianzwi in order to ask for rain. In fact, even her relative, the headman of HaLuvhimbi, had to bring a black sheep to Ravhura to obtain *phamba* (medicine) for making rain. After Tshisevhe's assassination, Ravhura had fled from Dzata on way to become the new Khosi of Makonde, in the process conquering Makonde which was under Khosi Muthivhion. The Mwali shrine had already been established when Ravhura settled at Makonde and Mwali continued to visit Makonde to communicate with vhaVenda from the peak of Mount Makonde, even after when Makonde was conquered by Ravhura (Luonde.com, (2020).

For Magwabeni to deliver such paramount prophecy to all leaders except those at Tswingoni, meant that Mwali was thereby endorsing Tshibi Malaba as the emerging legitimate traditional leader and heir to the rainmaking religion as well as the culture leadership. According to oral narrations backed by researcher Cobbing (1978), after the departure of Malaba contingency, Mwali ultimately ceased to appear in Venda country during so that his worshippers had to come to the Matopos to find him. The Venda people accepted the fact that the rainmaking responsibilities had been duly transferred to the Mpangana's Malaba clan as they started to send emissaries to Njelele whenever they were being ravaged by some drought spells.

By the early twentieth century Venda messengers were crossing the Limpopo to visit Mwali at his place of revelation at Njelele at the Matopo Hills. For example, one famous leader, chief khosi Mbulayeni Mphephu of Nzhelele had to send messengers all the way to BuKalanga in Zimbabwe in search of Mwali so that he could approach him for rain for his drought-stricken country. The Nzhelele area of

Limpopo was named after the Malaba rainmaking bateleur eagle, revealing the influence of the Luvhimbi/Malaba legacy in the area. Stayt writes that, "since then in years of drought and plenty alike Mphephu, and after his death, his son, always sent an emissary to Mwali at Mbvumela (Matopo). I was informed that last year Mbulayeni sent 100 sterling in cash, his emissaries returned more satisfied that god had accepted their offering and would send the required rain" (Stayt, 1931). It is certainly no coincidence that one of the main rivers of the Zoutpansberg is the Njelele River.

3,7. Migration from Venda; The Journey

After the momentous resolution to leave Venda was finalized, the Malaba fugitives began the uncertain northbound journey. The Malaba oral traditions emphasize that the mission was led by the elders that included Mpangana who was interim leader in the place of the young Tshibi, his brothers Bhangwa and Sabaswi and sister Tshawwila. Of most significance is that the Mpangana Malaba group carried the all-important rainmaking medicine bag *'Gobhodo lemiti'* with them in the custodianship of Mpangana as the figurehead of the newly established clan. It is noticeable that their northbound journey was ironically a typical reverse journey reminiscent of the original Luvhimbi's journey southwards. In reference to the medicine bag-*Gobhodo lemiti,* historian Beach (1980), points out in his account of the incident, that the Mpangana group took with them a rain-*cult* which was derived from the Raluvhimba (Mwali) *cult* of that area. Oral traditions states that the Mpangana Malaba people left Venda in the middle of the period when some of Mpangana's sons were born, which based on scientific theory, was in 1823. Based on the oral narration of Mpangana's Mosaic crossing of the troubled waters of the Vhembe River, it was between the rainy months of January and February.

This was not a journey like any other and it was going to be more than just a jaunt, but predictably an arduous long haul and a taxing trip. Nevertheless, according to old Tshemane Malaba's narration, the journey began in earnest, with each member of the entourage very much aware of the consequences in case the enemy caught up with them. Just ahead of them, trickling through the trees heading for the Indian Ocean far ahead, and like a lost child, appearing to playfully jump over the timeworn rocks as if to entertain itself on its journey to the sea, was the river Mutale. The river winded like a solitary tear suspended on the cheek of time, oozing, and dribbling nimbly through the forest. Sparkling like tinsel, with some festooned butterflies drifted lazily over its steep banks, the three distinct brothers

Bhangwa, Sabaswi, Mpangana and sister Tshawwila were feeling more than before, the urge to lead the clan to sanctuary. The four were a shield and an armour to the heir at law, Tshibi Malaba, the man who had just achieved greatness to be the successor to the clan throne. Mpangana, as old Tshemane would describe him, was a man of fine figure and stern in aspect, constantly walking with some measured springless walk of a skilled countryman as opposed to an ordinary person who is a member of neither the nobility nor the priesthood.

Legend has it that, directed by the Njelele bird of the sky, the bateleur eagle, and with the intended destination as the Mwali shrine of the Matombo (Matopo) hills or Mabweadziba, the Malaba company's historical reverse journey followed the mountain range curving with it up until they made the first stopover at Malungudzi. This part of Malungudzi was later called Beitbridge, named after Alfred Beit's Bridge, that was built over the Limpopo River. The mountain range pathway was religiously symbolic. The concept of God living on a holy mountain was a significant theme in the religion of Mwali. The previous journeys of the Malaba people, right from the Arabian Peninsula of Yemen via the mountain of Sinai, the Mavuladona mountains, the Matopos, the hills of Mapela and the Mapungubwe hills, were specifically associated with the God of the Mountain. The Malungudzi stopover was imperative because it provided an opportunity for the Mpangana Malaba entourage to deliberate on the novel developments and probable brainstorm with the Malungudzi vhaMbedzi on the way forward, vis-a-vis the new rainmaking commission.

The opportunity also provided the Malungudzi vhaMbedzi with some sufficient time to send a foreword to the other Mwali shrine custodians at Matopo ahead of the arrival of the Malaba group. The vhaMbedzi kingdom's royal kraal was in Malungudzi, Zimbabwe and was customarily the headquarters of the kingdom of the rainmaking vhaMbedzi, who were relatively part of the Luvhimbi family. An investigation into the nature of Malungudzi highlighted the area as stretching from

Masvingo way up to the north-eastern Vendaland. The Vhembe River (Limpopo River) was never a barrier between the people living on either side of the river. It is cited that the two vhaMbedzi groups originally paid tribute to the King in Malungudzi. But later great distances and the disintegration of vhaMbedzi settlements led to the establishment of small autonomous groups at Ha-Luvhimbi and Mianzwi, and other lesser-known units at Ha-Mukununde, Tshikweta, and Masetoni. But whenever the South African vhaMbedzi failed to cause rain to fall, they would send their messengers to Malungudzi where the Malungudzi Mbedzi would proceed to the Matopos to contact Mwali on behalf of vhaMbedzi south of Vhembe (Luonde.com, 2020).

There is also a myth that went, like the Biblical Moses, upon approaching the river, Mpangana held out one of the revered two knobkerries and the waters of the mighty Vhembe (Limpopo) river were parted by Mwali and giving a freeway to the entourage to walk on the exposed dry ground and crossing the great river. It is also essential to be cognizant of the fact that most of the Malaba people history, legends, myths, and fairy tales are commonly intertwined with those of the Jews, further explaining the linkage in origin and cultural backgrounds. As new leaders in Mwali's rainmaking religion, the group's intended destination was the Mwali shrine of the Matopo hills, with not only the objective of leading a nation, but also to protect the Mwali chosen figure of Tshibi. Their longing of the proximity to the Mwali shrine was being driven by the need for protection from the enemy as well as performing the duties and the custodianship of the rainmaking practice.

The Mpangana Malaba contingent crosses the Vhembe (Limpopo) river in about 1823 heading straight northbound making their second stopover at Tshizeze, which is the present-day Zezane in Beitbridge. The Malaba people are at the Zezane (Tshizeze) area of Beitbridge area on transit from VhuVenda, a historical event corroborated by several informants from the Mianzwi area of Limpopo Province of South Africa. Through literature and oral narrations, research findings also determine the Malaba residence at Tshizeze as not pre 1823 and certainly not post 1827. The interviews with some informants both in Mianzwi and Tshizeze (Zezane) also substantiated that the contingent was on way to the Matopo hill, the epicentre of the Mwali religion. The hindsight, furthermore, testify that in the Matopos, the clan was to re- establish a rainmaking shrine on the ancient Mabweadziba site. The shrine was to be known as the Njelele shrine, a rainmaking component of the holistic Mwali religion. It is worth mentioning that the Mabweadziba site had previously been established as an epicentre of the Mwali religion by Dzibagulu levula, an ancestor of the Malaba clan, some long time before, at about 1210 BC.

It is from the Tshizeze settlement that the group is recorded making a procession *en route* to visiting a place called Sioka or Siyoka located near the present day Zezane. When the Mpangana Malaba contingence made a settlement in this locality, apparently the place was residence to a clan led by a man called Siyoka. According to the Siyoka clan account (Muleya, 2018), the place was named after Siyoka the man. It is alleged that some of the Muleya people around that area are descendants of Siyoka. According to their account, it was in the early 1800s that two hunters from the Phuthi family had come from the land of the Batswana, eventually settling in the area. Immediately after settling in the area, one of the hunters, Siyoka, got a local woman pregnant. The woman was from the vhaLea clan which were one of the original inhabitants of the northern VhuVhenda.

For some reasons, the Muleya woman fled the area before she could conceive, only to settle in a place called HaMatsa located along towards the small town of Musina down south of the river Vhembe. The woman eventually gave birth to a son who adopted her Muleya surname instead of his father's surname of Phuthi. A 2018 interview with Soneni Muleya also revealed that instead of the Phuthi surname, most of the Siyoka still use Muleya as surname to this day. The Muleya were a cluster of the Tonga-Leya who originated from Namwala in Zambia. The Tonga-

Leya clusters include the Mwendabeli in Karoi, the Nleya in Plumtree and the Muleya in Beitbridge. Interestingly, deeper research revealed the Siyoka Phuthi and the Malaba clan were likely descendants of the same ancient Bukusu ancestor known as Sioka. If the findings possess some degree of accuracy, then the circumstances around the issue assist in explaining the reason of the Mpangana Malaba people making a stopover at Tshizeze (Zezane), which was most likely for a briefing with their cousin clan. Although the Mpangana Malaba contingent had had a brief stopover at Malungudzi before, they built the first Mwali shrine at Tshizeze before proceeding with the journey to the main Mwali shrine in the Matopo hills.

....

It was at Siyoka where oral tradition alludes to the occurrence of three key incidents that were to define the future of the Malaba clan. Because oral narrations have floundered to explain, this is where and when the speculated untimely death of the Mwali chosen young Tshibi Malaba transpired. The assertion that Tshibi could have met his death at the Siyoka-Tshizeze settlement is based on the grounds that, while it is evident that the Malaba family in essence, arrived at Tshizeze with all significant members of the larger Malaba contingent family still alive and active, however, in physical form, Tshibi is only traceable to the Tshizeze however, not traceable beyond the settlement. As the journey proceeds, Tshibi is neither visible nor detectable in physical form beyond the Tshizeze settlement, denoting that his existence terminates at that specific time and space.

There is also an indication that from that point Hhobhodo/Hhoba begins the role of being Mpangana's righthand man and further trainee for future leadership. Nsala Malaba attested that at some point Hhobhodo accompanied Lobengula on a trip

(Dube, 2015) identifying to him all former Mpangana's tabernacles, from Siyoka, Mtshabezi-Kumbudzi, Pangani (Mpangana Mine), Mpangana dam and Mpangana river in Matopo. Hhobhodo/Hhoba's knowledge of the existence of all Mpangana's revered points is evidence that he became an apprentice of Mpangana by the time of the Tshizeze settlement, thus, in addition, confirming Tshibi's death having occurred at the Tshizeze settlement and not before or after. Oral traditional accounts highlight that the Mpangana family was residing at Siyoka at the period when some of the sons of Mpangana were reaching adolescence. This, therefore, implies the events at Siyoka transpired during the period around 1825. The account hence insinuate that Tshibi died in his twenties or younger.

Legend has it that the Mpangana Malaba clan was devastated by Tshibi's untimely death however, no comprehensive explanation nor meaningful account is provided through both oral traditions and literature as to the reason or how the young Tshibi finally met his death. The conspiracy theories emanating from both family and circles outside of the family on the issue range from unsubstantiated allegations of murder, death by accident to natural causes of death. However, the data limited as it is, the paltry clues signalled a tragic death. Pointers highlight that, gathered at a place close to Siyoka the clan elders comprising Mpangana, Bhangwa, Sabaswi together with their sister Tshawwila, decided to make the final sending-off for Tshibi, summoning the spirit of his great ancestor, Sioka of the ancient Malaba legacy, to take care of the departed great son. The place was named Vhutulula (Tulula).

An attempt to investigate the origin of the name Vhutulula yielded more than one explanation. The Some Malaba informants contended that the name came about when they were 'surrendering or offloading' Tshibi to his ancestors and to Mwali while they are those who attested that the name referred to the offloading of goods during the journey break. In one of his articles, historian Phathisa Nyathi also alludes to the incident and name as he writes that, "I began enquiring about the name Zezane. My informant indicated to me that Zezane was a Mbedzi man who lived in the area. He pointed out that the Sitaudzi chieftainship is Mbedzi just like the Matibe further east, near Malungudzi Mountain. He indicated the Mbedzi in the western part of the district travelled from the east. A hill in the area bears a name that points to that migration. A hill to the north bears the name Vhutulula. My informant said some time ago there lived a Mbedzi man not far from Zezane. He pointed out that during their north-westward migration the VhaMbedzi rested near the said hill. Goods were offloaded as the migrants took a rest. The hill was accordingly named Vhutulula" (Nyathi, 2019). Nyathi's informants are also useful in demonstrating that the clan was still employing the Mbedzi surname at this juncture.

Now that Tshibi was gone, there was a leadership vacuum that needed to be filled. This led to the second large-scale decision being taken at the Siyoka-Tshizeze settlement. The fact that Tshibi had been chosen by Mwali at the Maneledzi pool contest meant that his position was not conferred by or based on inheritance. That being the case, the vacuum could only be filled by a deliberate and systemic recreation of the house of Tshibi. It was in that respect that the Malaba made an alliance with their anticipated cousins, the Siyoka Phuthi, on the way the house of Tshibi was to be revived or recreated. The important part of the alliance could have been to protect the clan genetic linkage because of the conceivable ancient links between the Siyokas and the Malabas showing that they largely came from the same stock or share an ancient ancestor. The Siyoka-Tshizeze Convention agreed and made a resolution that Tshibi's maternal inheritance was to emerge from the Phuthi family.

The third major decision was regarding the rearrangement of the Mbedzi-Luvhimbi contingent. Like every journey the Malaba clan journey was occasionally a brutality one because of the loss of all the familiar comfort of home, friends and close relatives and being constantly off balance. Nothing became theirs except the air, sleep, dreams, the rivers, and the sky. More so, things became more complicated. Among other things, boys and girls reaching adolescence and the natural desires of the body and the mind that go with it. Normally, this natural transition from childhood to adulthood is marked by an increasing need for independence combined with personal and group responsibility. Such was the case with the Malaba traveller's offspring. For boys like Hhobhodo, Mbikwa, Sekudza and Npininga, adolescence development naturally reached the stage of human sexuality.

Unlike in the present century when the population has increased significantly, the population in Southern Africa during the era was low. People could travel for days without sighting a soul. As such, tradition has it that the older boys actively began considering making a surprise backtracking, attempting to head back to VhuVenda. If their plans had succeeded, the move would have had potentially far-reaching ramifications because it would be synonymous to surrendering the group back to the enemy. After the probable sacred burial of Tshibi, the clan elders gathered, where another significant and historic verdict was arrived at. The three families of Mpangana, Bhangwa and Sabaswi were to break off from each other as siblings. They were biologically blood relatives; however, they were synthetically no longer going to be thusly. The decision on the tripartite division of the family was far-reaching in that the trilateral generation was on that account going to intermarry not only for purposes of defence, but, like the Biblical clans of Manasseh son of Joseph, also for its legacy and inheritance to remain in their Malaba contingency. A trinity that was typical of the Bukusu Divine Trinity of *Wele* Khakaba, *Wele* Mukhobe and *Wele* Malaba and that of Dzibagulu levula sons, Luvhimbi, Kaluba and Nyamukoko was to be assumed once again, and this time the triagonal family comprising that of Mpangana, Bhangwa and Sabaswi.

It was then at that moment that duties and other varying responsibilities were distributed and apportioned to the three brothers and their respect families. The first obligations included custodianship, traditional healing, and leadership, the second involved the Hosanna priesthood and least but not last were the rainmaking shrines priesthood. Again, in all this, as per the ancient Malaba custom, the number three was once more being observed and maintained as supreme. In addition, the observing of Wednesday the third day of the week as holy and as a day of rest was further advanced and strengthened. Biblically, the number three represented divine wholeness, completeness, and perfection and therefore, making the Semitic elements clear in the Malaba clan through religious practices.

If ever there was a desire to highlight an idea, thought, event or noteworthy figure in the Bible for their prominence, the number three was used to put a divine stamp of completion or fulfilment on the subject. The observation of Wednesday the third day of the week, the Bukusu Divine Trinity of *Wele* Khakaba, Mukhobe and *Wele* Malaba, the three sons of Dzibagulu levula, Luvhimbi, Kaluba and Nyamukoko and the distribution of duties among the new three, Mpangana, Bhangwa and Sabaswi, were all representatives of the divine stamp of completion, divine wholeness, completeness as well as the perfection of the clan. Furthermore, another momentous decision arrived at the Siyoka-Tshizeze Convention was that the Mbedzi surname, which comprised the Ndou/Ndlovu/Hhowu) totem, was to be dropped and the Wudo/Ncube surname adopted and thereby being promptly incorporated in the Malaba token.

It is essential to note that some of the interviewees approached during the conducting of the research constantly referred to the Malaba entourage as the Ndou/Hhowu/Ndlovu group. The general explanation was that, in Venda the Mbedzis were divided into different Ndous/Ndlovu/Hhowu. Dzindou dza Vharundwa / Dza Mitshetoni /Dza Manenzhe. The Mbedzinkulu cluster also belonged to the Ndous/Ndlovu/Hhowu section of the Mbedzis which was associated with the Dombo-la-ndou rocks of the Soutpansberg mountains, and they also used the Ndou/Howu/Ndlovu surname dating back.

Therefore, Ndous/Ndlovu/Hhowu was, without any elaboration, a collective motto generally adopted by some Venda tribes into their surnames, the Mbedzis also falling under that grouping. In an interview conducted by the author, several informants were in consensus in that the Ndlovu or elephant clan were the original Mwali clan located in the Matopos before the arrival of the Ncube Nyubi settlers. Observations also reveal that the elephant totem was the main Lemba/Sena totem in Vendaland. Therefore, in conclusion, it is important to note that in this context, Ndou was an address used to cover a broad category of groupings rather than a single specific group of people. The Luvhimbi dynasty fell under that category.

In this development, a new phenomenon was being born. The three Mbedzi siblings of Mpangana, Sabaswi and Tshimba, were here forth going to be regarded as unrelated, unconnected, and detached through a process of *tubula bukamu* or *ukuquma ubuhlobo* ('washing off' the relation or ties) in TjiKalanga and isiNdebele, respectively. In this new arrangement, the three families were to be classified under different groupings as a way of splitting them for purposes of intermarrying.

Mpangana and his family were to assume the Malaba signature leading to what is now known as the *Ncube yakaMalaba* (Malaba Ncube). This is because they had taken over the ancient Malaba traditional, cultural, and religious legacy, therefore, fundamentally becoming seniors and leaders of the clan through the Mwali chosen son Tshibi. The Sabaswi family were to be recognized as the Lubimbi,clan or be recognised with what is now called *Ncube yakaLuvhimbi* (Lubimbi Ncube). This is because they were assuming the priesthood, but not custodianship, of the rainmaking shrines. Bhangwa and his family were to adopt the Tshimba title or what is currently known as the *Ncube yakaTshimba* (Tshimba Ncube), reasn being that they would be priest of the *amaHosannas*. In the particular arrangement, Tshimba-Bhangwa and Sabaswi Lubimbi do not become Malaba because, conversely, Tshibi does not become their father. Their involvement in the rainmaking process is subsequently in respect to being family in general and their Luvhimbi descent in particular. Therefore, since Mpangana and his family were succeeding onto the Malaba legacy, it is also essential to note that both the rainmaking and the Hosanna priesthoods fell directly under the tutelage and custodianship of the Malaba family who had a responsibility for taking care of or protecting the integrated and holistic Malaba legacy.

Although the regular changing of clan names and totems was a common feature among pre- colonial African societies, the choice of Gudo/Wudo/Ncube as surname by this otherwise Mbedzi-Luvhimbi clan is vaguely explained both in literature and oral traditions. While a proper or reasonable way of thinking would deduce that the Gudo/Wudo/Ncube name was befitting because it was associated with the mountains, the group resorted to the Gudo/Wudo/Ncube name not only to gel in with the Soko/Shoko clan who were already priests of the Wililani Mwali shrines in Matopo but were simply adopting the name of one of their cousin clans. According to several scholars, the Luvhimbi were since time immemorial, constantly in contact with the Shoko who had been prominent priests at the Wililani shrine in the Matopo through some religious consultations.

The three groups, Ncube yakaMalaba (Malaba's Ncubes), Ncube yakaTshimba-Bhangwa (Tshimba-Bhangwa's Ncubes) and the Ncube yakaLubimbi-Sabaswi (Lubimbi-Sabaswi's Ncubes), up to this day remain 'unrelated' through a man-made arrangement rather than occurring naturally. However, the evidence that they are blood relatives is clear as a profile of the Goddesses. A totem, or Ojibwe doodem, is defined as a representation of an animal, object, or symbol that serves as an emblem of a group of people, such as a family, clan, lineage, or tribe. The reason for the creation of totems was to ensure that there was no identity confusion amongst clans. Those who shared totems were known to be blood relatives who came from the same family or shared the same ancestry. The Malaba, Lubimbi and

Tshimba totem are strikingly similar implying not only a strong blood relation but also a blood brotherhood.

The Mpangana/Malaba totem goes:

Ncube (the Ncubes)

Kumbudzi (the king's special advisors) Malaba (the royal Malaba family) Mbedzi (of Mbedzi Clan)

Thobela (the descendants of Thobela)

Mbedzinkulu (the descendants of Mbedzinkulu) Dzibalevula (descendants of Dzibagulu levula)

Matanna nti netiko (those who climb the tree with the back of their heads)

Zebe dzakakwakwatila (while holding on with their ears)

Imwi bakaMwali nkulu (those of the Great God)

Imwi munahhamu lingompela (travelling with their one breasted sister)

Babvumbi bevula (the rainmakers)

Mbibhanyi wahongwe (the breakers of tough rocks)

Bankukutu selutombo (those strong as a rock)

Tombo Tshisipotelekwe (the volatile hill that must never be messed with)

Tshopotelekwa ikabe mibvimbi (once messed with, shall as a result, cause thunderstorms)

Baka lunji gusipfume ngubo (those of the needle not meant for cloth knitting)

Gosimila pfuma lutombo (but meant for breaking rocks)

Bankwakwa usiwome (the ever green, green monkey orange tree)

Unodliwa nebana muhhiha neTshilimo (that provides food for the children all-season)

Imwi gumbo ivula (those whose dances bring the rains)

Bantandabale (the ritually relaxed one)

Banotandabala ikabe mibvimbi (whose stretching of legs ceremonies brings the rains)

Mazana zwibuya (the epic dancers)

Banozana vula ikana (whose epic dances brings the rains)

Bagudu ba Njelele (the custodians of the Njelele shrine)

Bompani usina mmako (the Mopane tree without a hole)

WakaTshidza sindi yanyala (yet still provided refuge to a desperate squirrel)

Mbuluki wedzilikadzi nesiyan'wa. (The saviour of both the rich and the poor)

The Lubimbi Totem…

BakaLubimbi, (the descendents of the Great Lubimbi)

Bakampani usina mmako, (the mopane tree without a curve)

WakanoTshidza sindi yanyala, (yet still provided refuge to a desperate squirrel)

Bhabanyi wahongwe, (the breakers of tough rocks)

Ndawu yaThobela, (the descendants of Thobela)

Ndawu yaMaseka, (the descendants of Maseka)

BaMbedzi bakulu (the descendants of Mbedzinkulu)

Mwali unahhamu lin'ompela (those with a one breasted rainmaker sister)

Linomwiwa ngenjhaba dzose (the one breast that feeds the nations)

BakaMwali unkulu (those of Mwali the Almighty God)

BaMbedzi bakulu. (The royal Mbedzis)

Thobela! (Those of Thobela)

Swimbwana yangu, (owners of the knobkerry)

Mposela kule (the long-distance throwers)

Inobona nezwikaTawana, (the receivers of Twana's instructions)

Njelela kule, (the Njelele from faraway)

Inobuya bana bahuba (the shrine that brings the rains upon a song)

Imwi gumbo ivula (those whose dances bring the rains)

Motandabala ikabe mibvumbi. (Those whose rituals also bring the rains)

The Tshimba totem.

Tshimba (Descendants of Tshimba)

Thobela (the descendants of Thobela)

Mbedzinkulu (the descendants of Mbedzinkulu)

Dzibalevula (descendants of Dzibagulu levula)

TomboTshisikuyiwe (the volatile hill that must never be messed with)

Tshika kuyiwa kukabe mvimbi (once messed with, will cause thunderstorms)

Mpaninkulu usina mmako (a Mopane tree without a curve)

Wakatshidza sindi yanyala. (Yet still provided refugee to a desperate squirrel)

Iswi bebango taka tana nti ndetiko (those who climb trees with the back of their heads)

Zebe dzakakwakwatila (while holding on with their ears).

Owing to the fact that the Malaba people had changed and adopted the Ncube/Wudo surname, it became reasonable to also investigate the Soko/Shoko totems. The investigations revealed that the Soko/Shoko people totems also contain traits, outwardly indicating evidence of some distant relationship with the Malaba people specifically indicating a linkage to two common denominators, Luvhimbi and Dzibagulu levula. In the local Karanga language, some part of the Soko/Shoko totems go like,

Ewoi Soko, (Thank you Soko)

Vakaera mutupo umwe nashe, (Those who have the same totem as the chief)

Vana VaPfumojena (The descendants of Pfumojena)

Vakabva Guruuswa (Those who came from Guruuswa)

Soko Mbire yaSvosve (Soko Mbire of Svosve)

Vapfuri vemhangura (The iron-smelters)

VekuMatonjeni vanaisi vemvura (The rainmakers of Matopo)

Zvaitwa matarira vari mumabwe (Those on the steep rocks and cliffs, one-who-rests-only-when- he-is-full).

3,8. Ncube YakaMalaba

Inter alia, the responsibilities of the Mpangana's *Ncube yakaMalaba* people included the medical welfare of not only the clan but beyond. As indicated prior, the *Ncube yakaMalaba* (Malaba's Ncube) led by Mpangana (Fig. 25), is the family that assumed the guardianship of the *Gobhodo lemiti* (the medicine bag) which contained the all-important traditional medicine, herbs and charms literally becoming the head priest or custodians of Mwali the 'Great Spirit.'

Figure 25. An Artistic Impression of Mpangana Malaba: Courtesy of author Lynn Bedford Hall

3,9. The Ncube YakaLubimbi/Sabaswi/Kole

The Sabaswi Koletshevula Lubimbi people were afforded the responsibility for the spiritual welfare of the clan and were entrusted with the upkeeping of the religious affairs of the Njelele shrine. It was because of this role that they adopted Bepe Luvhimbi's Koletshevula name, hence they were to be known as the Sabaswi Kole tshevula Lubimbi. Sabaswi, a Mbedzi before a Ncube, adopted the Lubimbi name after assuming the rainmaking responsibility. His family was to assume the custodianship of the newly established rainmaking shrines at Tshizeze, Nhawebezi (Mtshabezi), Makwe and Njelele, a role that was incorporated in the Mpangana Malaba family custodianship.

3,10. The Ncube YakaTshimba-Bhangwa

The Ncube yakaTshimba-Bhangwa (the Ncube of Tshimba-Bhangwa) people were allocated the duty of organizing the Hosanna ceremonies and being priests of the Hosanna institution. The word Hosanna by its very nature is Jewish, meaning (especially in Biblical, Judaic, and Christian use) "Please Save Us." "It is a Greek word "ὡσαννά" that most scholars believe is the transliteration of two Hebrew words- יָשַׁע - "yasha" which means "to save or deliver" and אנא – "anna" which means "please, I beseech." Other scholars believe its Hebrew roots come from a different verb tense of "yasha" הוֹשַׁע which means to cause or to bring about salvation.

In this tense, hosanna becomes a command to bring about or cause salvation" (Noyes, 2019). In Judaism hosanna the complete cycle is sung on the seventh day of the festival, which is called Hoshana Rabbah and similarly, the Njelele hosanna ceremony took place on the seventh day of the week and its overall function was to dance for the rains to come and 'save' or 'bring about or cause salvation to the people from drought and famine. Some informants argued that Bhangwa got the name Tshimba, which meant singing for the rains later in life. The Tshibale Ncubes descends from the Ncube yaka Tshimba.

The Mwali religion constituted an annual pilgrimage to the shrine through a calling by the Lubimbi family. The mission trip year start towards end of August and beginning of September after the harvest. The Hosanna would ululate and dance in a number of places before members of the community would follow them with gifts and requests for the coming rain season. They would then gather together close to the rainmaking shrine where skilled woso dancers would showcase their nimble-footed dancing skills

These *Hosanna* dancers of Njelele dressed in black clothes, decorated with some Mapungubwe type green plastic beads, and a dress code that has a striking resemblance to the Middle Eastern religious dress. A typical Njelele dress is shown as demonstrated by actors in Figure 26. Some of the Hosanna dancers' behavioural traits and mannerisms mirror that of the Torah which enjoins Jewish people to eat only certain animals. The *Hosannas* of Njelele were also prohibited to eat certain foods if their ancestral spirits had animals that were a taboo.

Figure 26. A depiction of the Hosanna at Njelele: Courtesy of weekendpost.bw

After the introduction of Njelele by the Malaba clan in 1836, a lot of activities related to the rainmaking process became more pronounced, especially the process of what was referred to as '*tenela*'. Tenela refers to a series of actions taken to mitigate against any factors thought to be affecting the way rain clouds are developed. For example, trees that have been struck by lightning the previous season, bird nests as well as some types of fledglings are believed to be by nature obstacles to rain falling. Men who have gone through a process of cleansing would embark on a hunting spree. Bare breasted women clad in black and white gear would march around beating drums. The month of September was considered as the 'head of the year' when every dirt was cleared in preparation of the new season of production and creation.

Hosanna spirit mediums would act as middle people between the public and Mwali anywhere in the region. Such was the functionality run by the Tshimba-Bhangwa priesthood, nevertheless, falling under the guidance and custodianship of the Mpangana Malaba family. While the Tshimba-Bhangwa were *Hosanna* priests and the Sabaswi- Lubimbi being the Njelele shrine priests, the Mpangana Malaba were overall custodians, overseers, and guardians of these two institutions. Those were the fundamentals and essential facts of this detachment of the two priestly families, the Tshimba-Bhangwa and Sabaswi- Lubimbi, under an administration or custodianship of the Mpangana Malaba family.

3,11. The Journey Continues

Figure 27. Bakalanga of Botswana and Zimbabwe doing Hosanna dance; Picture Courtesy of papers.ssrn.com

It was 1827 when the Mpangana contingent made a resolution to depart the Siyoka-Tshizeze settlement with the exodus proceeding northbound. An illustration of the journey is shown by the map in Figure 27. Considering, this was broadly a remarkable era of upheavals, during the winter of 1827, in the south Mzilikazi too was choosing to migrate northwards, in the process attacking the Pedi and sweeping through the Magaliesberg via Kommandonek near the present-day Hartbeespoort Dam. Through his well-coordinated military prowess, Mzilikazi was able to control the territory covering about two hundred miles in extent from west to east with an apex about half-way between modern Ermelo and Volksrust.

At about the same time his Ndebele army was making an advancement towards the north to attack the Pedi of the Mlulu mountains (Rasmussen, 1976). Meanwhile in the further world of BaKalanga, Tjilisammuli's army was fending off an attack by chief Kgari, resulting in the Ngwato chief Kgari's defeat by the BaKalanga of Tjangamire Dombo Mambo Tjilisammulu who was known as *Dombolakona-Tjing'wango*. What had motivated the BaNgwato to decide to attack the Mambo kingdom of Tjilisammulu was that they had become landless since a large tract of their land had been occupied by the Kololo of Sebetwane. Kgari was finally killed through seduction by a beautiful woman (Malikongwa, 1979). Using beautiful women as weapon of war through seduction seems to have been a strategy consistently applied by Tjilisammulu. It had happened before that after several failed attempts to overthrow Tjibundule, Tjilisammulu finally succeeded in mission by using the instrument of his daughter, Bagedze Moyo, who he gave to Tjibundule as wife (Moyo, 2012).

From Tjizeze/Chizeze the Malaba group proceeded assuming a temporary settlement in a place they named Mpangana, located in the present-day area of Filabusi. By virtue of being regular craftsmen inspired by the Mapungubwe trade, they had targeted this area because of its richness in copper. The place's name was later corrupted to Pangani, and it is currently a copper mine known as Pangani Mine. Mpangana also operated in this area healing and performing the traditional medicinal escapades that made him famous. It is assumed that their Mbedzi sister Tshawwila separated from the rest of the group at around this place where she travelled further on towards the Masvingo area then to the upper Kwekwe region and become part of a section of the current Karanga people referred to as the Mhari. According to Karanga history, there is a section of the Mhari people who are descendants of a woman known as Chifedza. Like Tshawwila, this woman was associated with rainmaking and again, like Tshawwila, the woman is described as had one breast where the warriors would suckle when they were going to war, and they would all come back alive. The description squarely matches that of Tshawwila who is reported to have had one breast as well as advanced rainmaking knowhow. The Mhari people had a chief whose name was Tshibi or Chivi who dwelt across the Lundi river in the present-day Chibi district of the Masvingo Province of Zimbabwe. The name Tshibi/Chivi also possess some striking resemblance to Tshibi Malaba, who was Tshawwila's nephew and had mysteriously disappeared before reaching the Matopos. Agreeably, the episode needs further researching on, nevertheless, in the document entitled *The Ndebele State*, historian Cobbing also confirms that Chivi/Tshibi was a Mhari.

Guided and following the Togwa route, the Malaba group proceeded further on by the Tjingwangwe (currently known as Singwango) route, Lummene (place of the buck), Gwabanyemba (now known as Gwaranyemba) in Filabusi and further down to Tjilalabuhwa (Silalabuhwa or Silalatshani) in the Insiza district and past Gwanda ('one who is gone). These Kalanga named places depicts a straight route from Great Zimbabwe through to Khami ruins which can only logically explain or be accredited to the earlier exodus by the Togwa of Tjibundule the 1450-1650. While the people in the Great Zimbabwe area spoke proto-Karanga (Huffman 2007), the distribution of Khami markers and the linguistic history of the Zimbabwe culture area show that the Khami phase marks the distribution of Kalanga-speaking polities (Huffman, 2011). Nsala Mili Malaba, former chairman of the Kalanga Cultural Promotion Society in the 1980s, argued that it was Hhobhodo/Hhoba together with Lobengula who named most of these places (Dube, 2015).

A place named Mpangana Dam in the Matopo river is assumed to have been one of Mpangana's secret tabernacles when the clan settled at Marula. It was a norm that Mpangana established a tabernacle or a mini shrine at every of their settlements. Upon their temporarily settlement at Nhawebezi (home of the newcomers), currently known nowadays as Mtshabezi, his mini shrine was at a place called Kumbudzi (special advisor to the king), where the present-day

Kumbudzi Primary School is located. Later being run by Siginyamatshe, Dapa and Vudze, the Nhawebezi (Mtshabezi) tabernacle became powerful for a long time. After making an extended settlement in the Mmakwe area of Gwanda, in 1835, Mpangana's tabernacle is considered to have been located at a river currently known as Mpangana river, a tributary of the Matopo river. The same system had occurred at the Tjizeze/Chizeze settlement where a mini shrine was established at Siyoka, which is currently a ward in Beitbridge District.

Upon leaving the Mmakwe area, the Sabaswi Lubimbi -Koletjevula, Tshimba-Bhangwa and Mpangana Malaba procession arrived in the Matopo region of Bukalanga by early 1836, just before the Matabele led by Khondwane Ndiweni, known as Gundwane, also established a settlement near the Malungwane hills east of the Matopo Mountains in Zimbabwe in 1837. In many ways the arrival of the Matabele differed from that of Zwangendaba and Nyamazana. While the Ngoni arrival was characterized by violence and pillaged, Mzilikazi's people made no attempt to attack the central part of the Changamire state (Beach, 2009). For the Malaba, it is believed that the bateleur eagle made its third ever landing as it signalled the Mabweadziba site as the new rainmaking shrine. It was a symbolic second coming for the Malaba people as they ultimately arrived in the land of their forefather Dzibagulu levula. They had hoped for a BuKalanga kingdom that was intact however, lamentably they arrived in the same year the Mambo dynasty under Mambo Nichasike Tjilisammulu was disintegrating.

Tjilisammulu had ruled the Mambo Kingdom for a long time. Before him, the Togwa/Tolwa of the Mukwati-Tjibundule of Howu totem who was accompanied by priests Ncube/Shoko/Soko totem, had ruled a Bukalanga kingdom which was centred at Khami or Kame until 1685 (D. N. Beach, 1980). The kingdom covered Western parts of Zimbabwe and Northern parts of Botswana. Tjibundule's real name was Madabhani or Madabhale. Apparently, he earned himself the name Tjibundule when he would boast (*bundula*) 'sounding of the war horn' or 'roaring like a bull' whenever he was victorious in battles (Kumile Masola in Wentzel 1983). Tjibundule was ultimately toppled by Nichasike Tjilisammulu of the Moyo Lozwi Mambos. He was a Nyayi who hailed from a military background, being one of the commanders of the Mutapa army and whose dynasty ruled for a long time across Zimbabwe, Southern Mozambique and Northern South Africa. The Tjilisammulu people had come from the Mwenemutapa (Monomotapa) state and had their dominance stretching until 1836. The Tjilisammulu Ninchasike Lozwi succession went on until when the Zwangendaba and Queen Nyamazana armies arrived in the vicinities of the BuKalanga Kingdom in 1835.

As briefly referenced prior, at some point in time Nichasike Tjilisammulu had a powerful army which in 1827 fought and defeated king Kgari's army that had invaded the Mambo kingdom. King Kgari was leader of the BaNgwato people from Botswana. It was in the early 1835 that African warrior queen Nyamazana Dlamini defeated Mambo Tjilisammulu and established a Nguni state. The events had ensued when a remnant of Zwangendaba's Nguni led by his female Nyamazana (Nyamatane) Dlamini, had remained behind on the Zimbabwe plateau. Nyamazana capitalized on the Lozwi whose Empire was rather nearing its collapse due to power struggles between Tjilisammulu and Ntinnima as well as weak leadership attributed to Nichasike's disrespect of Mwali the Creator. Also, Zwangendaba's attacks and raids before had by then destroyed the structures and settlements at both Great Zimbabwe and Danangombe-Dhlodhlo. Nyamazana Dlamini was therefore left in charge just to reinforce the otherwise newly founded Zwangendaba kingdom in the Zimbabwe plateau whilst Zwangendaba himself was crossing into the Zambian side, then Malawi and as far as Tanzania. Nevertheless, as highlighted by historian Wan Waarden, it was unfamiliar to have a female leader in southern Africa, let alone one who leads an army, therefore maybe she may have been a *regentess* or a person who was appointed to administer a state because Zwangendaba was absent.

She was nicknamed "The antelope and began by attacking the Buhwa state but was pushed away, however, she struck again attacking Mambo Nichasike Tjilisammulu, this time coming off victorious. There are varying versions of how Tjilisammulu died but some versions state he was skinned alive by the Swati army while some argue that he committed suicide under military pressure at his Dhlodhlo-Danangombe place of residence. Either way, this was not only a defining moment of the land of the BaKalanga, but also an event of a national destruction magnitude. A dynastic empire that has been systematically constructed right from the ancient times of the arrivals of the people of Dzibagulu levula, to their Dziva-Hungwe marital alliances, to the Balilima of Mengwe and to the Togwa state of Tjibundule, was hereby witnessing a proud long history being decimated under the leadership of the Lozwis of Mambo Nichasike. The BaKalanga who for years, using spears and shields, had scored telling victories against the marauding Portuguese and other Europeans, were having their kingdom under a deadly attack.

The BaKalanga kingdom that under Tjilisammulu had become independent from the Mutapa, and for years had managed to maintain their control of the land and gold mines, was witnessing the collapse of their empire. However, there is no evidence that his Danangombe residence was demolished through a suicidal act. A number of informants attests that Mambo Tjilisammulu's defeat was as a result of his defiance to the Mwali oracle. It is said that Ntinnima had tried in vain to convince Tjilisammulu to offer some of the cattle gotten after the defeat of Kgari the king of Bangwato. It was after the refusal that the voice of Mwali was heard out of nowhere cursing the Mambo, speaking first from a house and then from a tree. The Mambo had the house burned down and the tree chopped and burned, but the voice remained, cursing through the wind (Ramsey, 2020). The miracle signalled the defeat of Tjilisammulu.

Mambo Tjilisammulu was survived by his son Tjigadzike/Chigadzike, who led the remainder of the BaLozwi army against the Nguni at Khami, but was also killed in the battles (Kumile Masola,1983). The Mengwe people who were under Mambo Tjilisammulu escaped and went down to live by the Shashe River. The Shashe river was named when the people of Mengwe who had lived in the area after the demise of the Mambo kingdom. The Mengwe people were complaining that they "shaya she or Haya Hhe" meaning that they did not have a King. Later, the powerful Queen Nyamazana Dlamini ironically, became one of King Mzilikazi's queens. Campbell, records that the king took Nyamazana into the *'isigodlo'*, and she became his wife" (Campbell, 1926). Although argue that there is no evidence that their marital union produced any offspring, some scholars and oral narrators say that the union indeed produced some offspring.

Prince Nyanda has assumedly been the son of Mzilikazi and Nyamazana and the Mzingwane area, (*umuzi wamaNgwane*), is stated to have been the homestead where Nyamazana Dlamini's people were based. Through the marriage to Queen Nyamazana, King Mzilikazi took over the nation. Some writers mention that with the objective of building one nation from the nations of AbaThwa, BaKalanga, Swati and the Ndebele, in an 1840 meeting king Mzilikazi is said to have asked a traditional healer Mphubane Mzizi, "to go and bring some potsherd, *udengele*, and a sharp (*insingo*) razor. Into the container, the celebrated doctor collected his own blood, that of Queens Nyamazana Dlamini, Mwaka Nxumalo, Fulatha kaMabindela and Umthwakazi. Off went healer Mphubane Mzizi to work on the blood with the aim of welding three disparate nations into one" (Cont Mhlanga, 2017).

According to Nyathi, "the king then addressed the people. "*Lina Mahlabezulu* (*abahlaba uZulu*-stabbers of the Zulu people), *lani bakaMthwakazi* . . .". For the first time the king uttered the name Mthwakazi or Mbuthwakazi in public and the name stuck. It became a reference to the Ndebele nation from then on" (Cont Mhlanga, 2017).

At around 1836, as the Malaba contingent approached the Matopo hills they encountered the people of Mambo Nichasike Tjilisammulu. Not much is recorded on this encounter, but Saul Gwakuba refers to the incident, as he writes in *The Patriot*, that "a very important thing that occurred during Mambo Tjilisamhulu's time was the arrival of some people of Venda extraction who worshipped a god called Mwali" (Gwakuba-Ndlovu, 2017). In allusion to the Malaba contingence of Mpangana Malaba, Sabaswi Lubimbi and Tshimba Bhangwa, Gwakuba, mentions that those people belonged to the Malaba clan and comprised three main families that shall be discussed broadly in the next chapters.

CHAPTER 4

THE MALABA FINAL SETTLEMENT.

4,1. Chieftaincy and Chiefdom

Although in pursuit of Mwali the Almighty God, by design, upon arrival, Mpangana and his Malaba people bypassed the Matopo hills where the *Njelele* hill is located. In the fore, being led by the njelele bateleur eagle, the contingent checked in to the Mabweadziba site when the bateleur eagle is said to have executed its third ever landing, signifying that the Mabweadziba site was to become the rainmaking shrine. The third landing is believed to have symbolized the final and permanent epicentre for the Mwali religion.

Just like any other average traveller before them, the Malaba contingent were stunned by the beauty of the Matopo hills and the warm breeze that accompanied that beauty. The thick dense shrubs predominated by the blossoming mopane trees and filled with the symphonists singing of the invisible birds of the air. Such are some of the superlatives fit enough to describe the beauty of the land of the BaKalanga people. Hence, after a routine observation of this metaphysical site of Mabweadziba, the new rainmaking shrine was named after the Njelele bird and was called Njelele.

Solemnity accomplished, the Malaba strutted on the hill foot, meandering further on until, they at the close, settled at a place called Nkalange. Nkalange is a place located south easterly of the hills, and next to Gurumane in the present-day Marula and according to Cobbing Malaba "becoming one such Kalanga chief who had secured local independence" outside of both the Mambo and the Matabele (Cobbing, 1977). Thereby, the clan built a giant homestead exactly where Mangwe Police station is currently situated. The Malaba contingent arrived at the Marula area in the beginning of the year 1836 because tradition attests that, upon reaching the Matopo hills, the travellers had an encounter with the remnants of the Mambo dynasty. After the death of Mambo Tjilisammulu in 1835, some of the Mambo administrators like Ntinnima, Lukuluba, Tjowetsipi, Mahayangombe and others were still alive and kicking up until early 1836. It is also reported that upon arrival in the Marula area, the Malaba people quickly involved themselves in the tillage of the land indicating an early 1836 settlement.

Just as the Malaba contingent were settling in Marula, the prematurely greyed hair Mpangana Malaba was to embark on a special journey, heading towards the present day Jotsholo area. His intended journey's end was a special mission at dombo laMengwe. *Dombo la Mengwe*/Ntjongogwe (Ntjongogwe's mountain) is in the present day Jotsholo in the Lupane area. It was also known as *dombo lobunganga* (mountain of the witch doctors) because it was where traditional healers would gather for a trance-inducing competition known as *ukulibhana* (teasing) where it was mandatory for each *n'anga/inyanga* to showcase their own individual 'witch doctorate' skills. The gathering was an opportunity when traditional healers would not only test but also sharpen their skills as well as learn and acquire new artistry in traditional medicine, power, and magic. For Mpangana as a migrant, this was to be a special destination place because it was where he was to prove his ultimate traditional healing power before settling as a powerful traditional healer in the Kingdom of Bukalanga.

The mention of dombo la Mengwe provides an opportunity to time travel back to the dramatic events of the decline of the Great Zimbabwe in the 15th century. Mengwe, who was also known as Ntjongogwe (Ntshongogwe) was Tjilisammulu's general, chief councillor and governor commanding the Balilima from 1685 through 1700 while stationed at Domboshaba or Maitengwe (Mabuse, 2012). He was of the Moyo totem and was son of Nnale, who was also a descendant of Tjingwango (Chingwango). Tjingwango was also a brother to Kutamadzoka.

Indication is that Tjingwango or perhaps his father had moved from Mapungubwe to Great Zimbabwe during the northwards exodus and became known as Luswingo which means "Stone Mason" or "Builder of Stone Walls. This is because there is no evidence that Mengwe came with the Changamire Dombo people. Which implies that Tjingwango or his descendant most likely had left Great Zimbabwe before the Mutapa - Togwa conflicts of the 1450s, consequently settling in the Buhwa (Butua) land where he reigned until he was neutralized by the arrival of the Togwa of Tjibundule and his Togwa people who were a break away section from Great Zmbabwe. The other faction moved towards the Dande valley creating the Mutapa state after a fearsome battle that involved the Portuguese settlers in the Great Zimbabwe (*Nzimabwe*) area.

When Tjilisammulu defeated the Togwa people of Tjibundule with his Lozwi army, Mengwe was Tibundule's governor at the time. As a result, Tjilisammulu Nitjasike is said to have praised his gun calling it "*Dombo Lakona Tjin'wango . . . wabulaya mabwe dumulo lingatani*?" (A rock that defeated the son of Mengwe the son of Tjingwango) (Gwakuba-Ndlovu, 2012) because Mengwe was a descendant of Tjingwango. As part of the integration process, Mengwe was then sent by Mambo Ninchasike Tjilisammulu towards the west to govern over a Balilima area (present-day Plumtree) on behalf of the newly crowned Tjangamire or Lozwi state. The area became known as *Bulilima gwaMengwe*, (Mengwe's jurisdiction) later corrupted to Bulilima-Mangwe (Van Waarden 1988). Based on his Tjangamire Dombo ancestry, Mengwe gave Domboshaba a new name, Luswingo.

According to Moyo in his book, *The Rebirth of BuKalanga: A Manifesto for the Liberation of a Great People with a Proud History*, Tjangamire is a combination of two words, *tjanga*, a Kalanga and *emir/amir*, an Arabic word. Both words mean 'justice' or Governor. As was stressed beforehand, the Arabs were trading with the African locals, with Mapungubwe and then Great Zimbabwe as trading centres, and they are likely to have carried the emir (for example United Arab Emirates) title from their homeland to Bukalanga as an address to *Tjanga* (the Justice/Governor) of Bukalanga (Moyo, 2012).

Between 1300 to 1500AD Great Zimbabwe had taken over Mapungubwe to become the largest settlement and trade centre in sub-Saharan Africa. Mapungubwe became the economic hub of southern Africa with the main source of prosperity being cattle and gold trade with Swahili merchants based at the Sofala coast of the present-day Mozambique as well as the Arabs from the Ancient Near East. But by 1450 land exhaustion due overpopulation and succession disputes weakened the ruling elite at Great Zimbabwe which split into two successor states (Parker, 2010).

At Mapungubwe, the Great Thobela Luvhimbi was the leader, but he stayed put there and could not join the northwards exodus because of the rainmaking shrine keeping responsibilities at vhuVenda. So, when the group was leaving Mapungubwe for Great Zimbabwe it is outlined that Luvhimbi instructed Shamuyenanzwa and Mambire with his Shoko/Hoko/Ncube priests to take the leadership responsibilities, amid on temporary basis. Mambire is the founding father and creator of the Lozwi/Lozvi nation. Some argue that the way Great Zimbabwe is structured highlights a power struggle that ensued from the beginning of the settlement. The place could have three royal places, two hill complexes and the famous Great Enclosure.

The two hill complexes could have been occupied by Shamuyenanzwa and Princess Dzugudini's father who abided by their rainmaking culture and the traditional hill hierarchy, while Chibatamatosi Mutota could have occupied the Great Enclosure because it served as a royal compound. Oral traditions state that regardless of that fact, when it was Mutota's turn to rule *Nzimabwe*, Shamuyenanzwa's maternal descendant Mukwati of the Tjibundule dynasty refused him. Some analysts attest that the defiance was mainly as a result of

Mutota's close relationship with the Portuguese as well as his apparent disregard of the rainmaking customs. As a leader associated with rainmaking the prerequisite may have been that he resides on a mountain or higher ground.

After a fierce power struggle, the faction under Mutota Chibatamatosi's son Nyatsimba, went north, establishing themselves in the southeast of the plateau and founded the Mutapa State (Roufe, 2015) (Baxter, 2018). It was from here that the Monomotapa state constantly shifted its capitals between the Dande and Zambezi Valley in the Northern part of the Zimbabwean plateau. It is worth mentioning that in contrast to their Shona counterparts, the Kalanga traditions do not mention Mukwati but rather put emphasis on the name Tjibundule. This assertion can be backed by two properties named Mutapa and Mukwati respectively, that were constructed in Harare in honour of the two historical figures.

It appears Tjibundule (Chibundule/Chiwundure) who was also called Madabhane or Madabhale, travelled west alongside the Shoko priests and he was a maternal relative of the Dzibagulu levula people. The mother of Mambire was a daughter of the Great Luvhimbi and therefore, like Tjibundule regarded the Mabweadziba area of Matopo as their mother's homeland. It is purported that when asked where the Tjibundule/Shoko crew were heading to, they replied and said *"tonda kame"* (we are going to the land of our mother). When further questioned what had happened, they again answered and said that it was because *"togwa"* (we are fighting with our kinsmen). Therefore, the Togwa State, sometimes called Torwa or Tolwa, was born, with its capital at *Kame*, which was later corrupted to Khami (Alpers, 1970) and evidence points to its people speaking TjiKalanga (Rodewald, 2010). In the 1506 documents, Alcáçova refers to it as 'Toloa' (Randles, 1975) while the Portuguese documented it as 'Torwa', 'Toroa' or 'Thoroe' most likely because their Karanga-speaking informants later would have pronounced it that way.

When Madabhale arrived in Buhwa (Butua) and conquered the local people it is claimed that he went on top of a hill and boasted saying "*ndobundula hango yangu ndiyani ungandi piya poni, ndobundula ndikhonya*" literally meaning that 'I am the one who roars here, and no one can rule me I am the ruler the one that roars' (Gwakuba, 2008).

He began to be known as Tjibundule meaning the one that roars. The Bakalanga people found in the state of Buhwa (Butua) during the Tjibundule days called themselves Balilima (Van Waarden, 1988). Mbire's Shoko/Soko priests became the pioneer Mwali priests in the Matopos, specifically based at the Wililani shrine. The Togwa state was later destroyed by Tjilisammulu Ninchasike who had migrated from the Monomotapa state with his Lozwi army. Tjilisammulu was hailing from a place called Zwengombe (Zvongombe), and after the conquest in 1670, he transferred from Khami and made Danangombe (Dhlodhlo) his headquarters, naming it after his old home Zwengombe (Randles, 1981). The Danangombe-Dhlodhlo ruins (Fig 28) are located about eighty kilometres from Gweru in the direction of Bulawayo and about 35 kilometres south of the highway.

There is another place in Nkayi, Matabeleland North, named Singwangombe (Tjingwangombe). According to Posselt, the Lozwi (Rozvi) identity emerged chiefly from a warrior/client class known as the Nyayi, a term initially used to refer to soldiers of the Mutapa army but that was gradually used interchangeably with the term Rozvi itself (Posselt, 1978). According to Mazarire the term Lozwi/Rozvi was used to refer to the soldiers of the Mutapa state who were sometimes known as BaNyai. Because they accepted into their nation other groups who belonged to other totems this then means that all Lozwi were *Banyai* but not all *Banyai* were Lozwi.

Figure 28. The main retaining wall at Danangombe showing the patterned walling. Picture courtesy of Zimfieldguide

As Mutota headed north to form the Mwenemutapa kingdom and Madabhale travelling west to establish the Togwa state, a third force, Princess Dzugudini, also from Great Zimbabwe returned to the modern-day South Africa where her people became known as the Lobedu. Archaeological evidence from 1993 showed that the Lobedu had built another *nzimabwe* (place of stone), known as Thulamela, which is tjiKalanga for a 'hill with no vegetation or' the place of giving birth' (*Submission of the VaNgona nation to the south Africa parliament, 2018*). Thulamela a stone-walled fortress which carbon dates reveal to have been constructed between 1250 and 1700 was a continuation of the Leopard's Kopje Culture and is located 200 miles to the east in Kruger National Park.

According to archaeologists the high place doubled as a burial mound for its rulers. This implies that by this time the local settlers were already converting iron to carbon steel and doing barter trade. The Lobedu people use the Thobela praise name revealing their relation to the Great Luvhimbi and have amongst them, a rainmaking queen, Modjadji. Years after princess Dzugudini, there had been another sacred rainmaking queen, Maselekwane Modjadji who reigned from 1800 to 1854 before being succeeded by Masalanabo who reigned until she died in 1894.

Around the same time Khami was built, the Portuguese had succeeded in penetrating the Indian Ocean in an event known today as the 'Age of Discovery' or the Age of Exploration. Upon settling in the area, the Mutapa began having unavoidable interactions with the Portuguese. In the area also lived the Kaluba people who they called the Karuva. Their leader Kaluba was a descendant of the original Kaluba son of Dzibagulu levula and a brother to Lubimbi and Nyamukoko. He ruled his baTonga and Tavara people in Binga and the Dande Valley, because after the death of their father Dzibagulu levula, the three brothers had separated with their elder brother Lubimbi heading south to vhuVenda which was also known as Lukungulubwe. Kaluba remained north and later trekking down towards the uMsengezi river and establishing the Tavara and the Tonga people of Lubimbi in Binga, while Nyamukoko's descendants assumed the Gunguwo totem.

As a result of the fight between the Mutapa and the Togwa people at Great Zimbabwe, Kaluba's people instantly regarded the Mutapa as arch enemies upon arrival at the Dande area. This mistrust made the Mutapa suspicious of Kaluba and his subjects who they suspected could attempt revenge through witchcraft for the previous Mutapa – Togwa battles. As a result, Mutota directed his intelligence to keep an eye on the movements of Kaluba and his people, a deed that resulted in one of the most infamous murders of the times. The murder of Dom Gonçalo da Silveira, a Portuguese citizen.

The Dom Gonçalo da Silveira murder was a case that rocked not only the settler Portuguese, but the whole nation of Portugal also regarded it as a Shakespearean murder most foul. According to Nickel, Dom Gonçalo da Silveira, a Jesuit missionary was born in Portugal on 23 February 1526 at a place called Almeirim.

He was the tenth child of Dom Luís da Silveira, Marshal of the Kingdom of Portugal (Nickel, 2015; Roufe, 2015). He lost his parents when he was a juvenile and was brought up by his sister Filipa de Vilhena and her husband, the Marquis of Távora (Nickel, 2015). He was received into the Society of Jesus by Father Miron, the Rector of the Jesuit college at Coimbra before he was sent to the unexplored mission field of south-east Africa. He arrived at Sofala on 11 March1560, and on the 26 December 1560, he arrived at the capital of the Monomotapa kingdom that was based on the basin of the uMsengezi river (Roufe, 2015).

At some point in time rumours started circulating around the Monomotapa kingdom with spreading claims that Silveira was in fact a spy for Kaluba and his baTonga and the Tavara people. The rumours began associating and linking many of Silveira's behavioural traits to those of either Kaluba himself or his subjects. For example, Silveira was accused of being seen near the precinct of the Monomotapa king's palace walking naked from the waist up, and in his possession were barks of wood tied to his shirt. This appearance was blamed for the lightning that later descended from the sky and breaking a pole from the king's doorway (Caiado, 1898). The description of a half-naked Silveira is also related to Kaluba's forefathers, the Dzivaguru and their mediums (Von- Sicard, 1946). Kaluba had also been accused of the same offence at some point before (Bourdillon, 1972).

Silveira was also accused of being possessed by a foreign spirit, and the cult that was known as possessing a foreign spirit was that of the Dzivaguru-Karuva (*Dzibagulu levula and Kaluba*) (Mudenge, 1988) and during the Monomotapa dynasty this foreign spirit was said to be belonging to the Lower Zambezi Tonga and Tavara. Local *n'angas* were consulted and they fanned the flames by confirming that Silveira was indeed a Kaluba spy and a witch. If he were not killed and his body thrown into the river, he would soon cause the Monomotapa people to begin killing each other without any reason in a state of a civil war. Thus, Mutota sanctioning the elimination of Silveira. Some of the Moyo Chirandus who were also called the Bvumavaranda/Vumabalanda because of their leniency towards the captured Portuguese prisoners of war would normally demand that war prisoners be treated humanely and not with a heavy hand, so *bvuma-* meaning accept positively, and veranda, referring to war captives. But their influence did not stop one of the most infamous murders of the time.

According to a letter by Antonio Caiado (1898), a Portuguese translator, on the night of the 6th of March 1561 (Baxter, 2018), a very high-ranking official at the court of the Monomotapa, together with eighty other men, brought Silveira into a hut where the high-ranking official laid him on his chest. Four men seized father Silveira "by his arms and legs, while two other men tied a ribbon around his neck, each one pulling to the opposite side. After Silveira died from suffocation, a rope was tied around his neck and his body was dragged on its back and thrown into the uMsengezi River (Caiado, 1898).

There are some scholars who argue that Silveira (Musengezi) was killed because he had sinister intentions of destroying Mutota and his people by persuading them to become Christians and ultimately becoming subjects under his control. But researchers like Roufe (2015), back the argument that Silveira was killed because he was regarded as a traitor and believed to be possessed by the spirit of the Dzivaguru-Karuva, who was sent by a *fumo* named Capote. Moreover, after the murder, there were no repercussions for the general Portuguese population in the Zimbabwe of the Monomotapa in particular or in the region in general, implying that in the local perception, the act against Silveira was not associated with the Portuguese as a group (Roufe, 2015). The murder of Dom Gonçalo da Silveira is regarded as a key moment in the history of the Portuguese presence in Africa and of the political and social systems along the Southern bank of the Zambesi. Angered partially, by Silveira's murder, the Portuguese public was galvanized into a frenzied demand for a crusade (Baxter, 2018). The Portuguese had settled at the

Sofala coast and established a fortress which rendered the Swahili and Arab trade with the Togwa state at Khami virtually unmanageable.

The historically flourishing Arab-Swahili trade system that had dominated the coast leading to the gold trade, significantly diminished, and bringing the Togwa state economically to its knees. Kaluba descendants, Biri and Ganyire, later became especially important *nkumbudzis* (advisors) to the Mwenemutapa leaders and their spirit of Dzibagulu levula is still esteemed amongst the Korekore people of Mutapa. Biri and Ganyire originated the Nyandoro clan when they assumed the *Nhari Unendoro* totem after continuing the Dzibagulu-levula customary practice of marrying within the family.

Now, practically 200 years after the collapse of Great Zimbabwe, as the events unfolded, oral traditions have it that Mpangana was guided to *Dombo lobunganga* by a man, whom he had met on arrival at the Matopo hills. His name was Bangojena, which meant 'dry wood' and he was of the zebra totem of Dube. He was from the leading family of the BaNyubi clan and is believed to have been a direct descendant of Mambo Tjilisammulu, but it is not clear if it was a paternal or maternal descent. Bangojena is considered to have been a bright, sharp, and clever young man who had become the eye of the king during Mambo Tjilisammulu's reign. He was given a higher position of advisor because of his sharp-wittedness, hence, like the Malaba clan who also became advisors (*Nkumbudzi*) to King Mzilikazi and later Lobengula, the Bango clan also uses the title of Kumbudzi (*nkumbudzi*) because of their role as advisor to their relative Mambo Tjilisammulu. The Ndlovu Lumehwe are a clan that uses the title of Kumbudzi implying that they may have been advisors of one of the Mambo Kings at some point in time.

At some point Bangojena had become a chief in areas towards the present day Lupane where he had settled in the area long before the arrival of the Matabele. Lupane is argued to have been comprehensively a Kalanga area during the Mambo dynasty and was also a trade centre, hence its name *lupana*, referring to exchange of goods in tjiKalanga. Since the central Lozwi rule was dwindling during that period, most chieftaincy including the Bango assumed total independence. After the arrival of the Matabele, Lupane began to be dominated by the Ndebele speakers and fearing that they may lose their chieftaincy, the Bango moved from the Lupane area and ultimately settling in the Matopo Hills.

Although the Malaba had built a strong working relationship with the Matabele in general and the Khumalo clan, the Bango seemed to have been more sceptical of the Matabele presence in Bukalanga. Like many other Kalanga speaking people, the Bango generally viewed and regarded the Matabele of Mzilikazi and the Ngunis of Nyamazane as responsible for the collapse of the Mambo kingdom. The Bango people therefore, created and maintained their distance from the businesses of the Matabele, except in instances of army conscriptions where they would at times come in by the way of the Malaba clan. As author Webner notes, the Bango people had shown a strong and practical disapproval of the Matabele rule from its beginning and were strong advocates of the revival of the Mambo dynasty. Therefore, unlike the Malaba people, the closer the Bango people's acquaintance with the Matabele establishment was, the greater their sense of alienation became.

The Bango totems mainly express their way of life.

Bango (Bango people)

Nyubi (the Nyubi)

Nkwakwa. (Green monkey orange)

Banu baSemukwi (people of the Semukwe river)

Semukwi agunahanga (the Semukwe river does not own the reeds)

hanga bana baBango. (Because the reeds are the people of Bango)

Banu baDzilobwe (people of Dzilobwe)

Dzilobwe idulamilo (Dzilobwe is a high mountain)

Notulamila ukabona Shashe (where from above it one can view the Shashe river)

Shashe lukoba. (Shashe being a great river)

Banosena Ntjingidzi, (those who crawl under the Red Bushwillow tree)

Unolamba sena unofa. (Death to the one who refuses to crawl under)

Banongula nenkaka (those who bath in milk)

Beti vula inanyubwila (Because they believe water contains some tadpoles)

Bana meho anonga nyimo (those with eyes like round-nuts)

Makope engadzilo. (Those with bushy eyebrows)

Bango wakonaMambo. (The great Bango who won Mambo's admiration)

Wangina mudziba (the one who entered the pool)

Ekabuya akabhataNgwena ndume. (And came out holding a male crocodile)

Kunitjipfuta (and a firebrand in hand)

Mambo tjadzima wabuya nehadzi. (The Mambo who came with a wife)

Wundanyika yaBango (Bango's nation)

Yatulula nyanga dzemmofu kaMbeba. (The nation that took the eland horns at Mbeba's)

NdiNkumbudzi wangombe (the advisors who rear cattle)

Usina ngombe atewedu (the one without cattle is not a Bango)

Bango jena labakanzi baTjillisa (the dry white bark that belongs to Tjilisa's wives)

Bekabaka nelinamakwati. (Who built using a dry bark)

Nyubi unongwa mmanga (the male Nyubis who drink matured beer)

Bakadzi bengwa bhilima. (While the females drink the immature one)

Botela (of Botela)

Dulibwe (of Dulibwe)

……………………..

When the Malaba contingent settled at the Nkalange area of Marula in the 1836, their three elders, Mpangana Malaba, Sabaswi Lubimbi Koletjevula and Tshimba Bhangwa were reaching advanced ages. These were men who had displayed unparalleled astute leadership in their various roles and responsibilities, but the 1836- 40 period was certainly a transitional period in the clan history, heritage, and legacy. Immediately after settling in the area, Hhobhodo/Hhoba often was being sent to convey to Mzilikazi and his people, some directives from his father Mpangana and Luvhimbi the rainmaker, that, the people in this part of the Bakalanga world worshipped Mwali the Almighty whose voice could be heard from the Njelele shrine. That is where they got instructions on what to do at any given times and occasions and seasons of the year.

Although it is generally cited by different scholars that Lubimbi Kole was the chief priest of Mwali at the time of arrival in the Kingdom of BuKalanga, it was from fact, his son Npininga who became the first priest at the Njelele rainmaking shrine. This fact is also backed by researcher Cobbing who attests that the first Njelele priests were "Npininga and Jenje of the Mbedzi Venda who had fought with their tribe in the Transvaal (Venda)" (Cobbing, 1976). Nothing of big significance is recorded about Tshimba Bhangwa particularly during this time. This could be mainly because their Hosanna role presented less interaction with diary enthusiasts. However, most literature cite Mbikwa who was son of Tshimba, who author Hole describes as was one of the known satellites for the great Mpangana Malaba (Hole, 1929).

An interview with Mbangiwa Tshimba reveals that even so, Mbikwa was father to Nswene who in turn was father to Nlumbe. The activities of these three adults, Mpangana, Lubimbi and Tshimba, paints a picture of elders who upon arrival in Bukalanga, were retiring from active political, religious, and social roles and currently, serving only like many community elders, as directors of operations and fountains of wisdom to both the nation of BaKalanga and later that of the Matabele.

Despite the existence of varying narratives, historians from different perspectives each time establish the fact that Mpangana Malaba was a figure of paramount importance in history. Besides having taken over the ancient Luvhimbi command and its rainmaking legacy on behalf of the young Tshibi, and ultimately leading the new clan to the 'promised land', several records agree regarding the fact that Mpangana Malaba was a powerful traditional healer whose reign in magic exploits were noticeable right up to the time of Mzilikazi's rule.

In dealing with the chosen people, the Biblical Moses periodically acted as an intercessor with God, so as to avert divine displeasure with Israel. Mpangana was a classic Biblical Moses. He was both a religious and traditional leader who delivered his people from endangerment and fundamentally founded the religious family known as the Malaba people. As the leader of the Mwali stipulations, he was head priest of the 'Great Spirit' and the organizer of the vhaVhenda- Kalanga communities' religious and civil traditions.

In the Malaba tradition, he is revered as the greatest traditional medicine man ever to emerge from the clan and from the nation. His influence continues to be felt in the Malaba religious and traditional life, moral concerns, and social ethics of the Mwali religion, and therein lies his undying significance. Due to his exploits, the Ndebele of Mzilikazi called him *Nqamu-ebukhali* (sharp knife), because it perfectly suited their language. There are also magnified claims that he was once ruler before Nichasike Mambo, but these claims only serve to mask his social, political significance and religious noteworthiness in both the BuKalanga and the Mthwakazi kingdom but not representing real events.

It all began with Bangojena's companionship that got Mpangana set for the *ukulibhana* commission. On arrival at the Ntjongogwe's mountain, it was all-systems go for Mpangana. Tradition has it that he was pitted against a number of traditional doctors and outperformed all his competitors. Yet, he was mesmerized by three traditional doctors.

According to oral narration, Mpangana was first pitted against one of Mengwe's relatives from the Ntjongogwe Moyo clan who went by the name Bhule and was of the Moyo totem, in a high-stake clash whereby a defeat entailed one not advancing to the next stage. Mpangana resorted to his trademark incantation straightaway, *"wafa wafa"* (Whoever dies, dies). It is avowed that Mpangana managed to score success against his competitor who was so impressed he offered Mpangana a wife in exchange of being apportioned some of Mpangana's medicinal brew. It was through this wife that Mpangana had one of his youngest houses consisting of Bhule Malaba and his brother Manyele. Bhule the son of Mpangana hence got the name from his maternal grandfather.

Mpangana's penultimate opponent was another esteemed inyanga by the name Hukwi Nkomo.

"Wafa wafa".

It was a show that generated a fierce battle of bewitchment, mumbo jumbo as well as spell-to- spell firing from both sides. Oral tradition has it that Hukwi demonstrated a high degree of skill and exhibited something Mpangana Malaba had never witnessed before. It was Hukwi's use of a special concoction referred to as *tjathiyane/isathiyane* that caught Mpangana by surprise. *Tjathiyane/isathiyane* was a type of a viciously boiling porridge originated by Hukwi Nkomo himself. According to oral tradition, the porridge could boil at blast furnace conditions, rippling with heat and throwing some vicious red-hot drops equivalent at one hundred degrees Celsius. Although Mpangana was feeling the utmost heat, he was known to be a character who naturally believed that success lie on not giving up.

By and by, against the run of play Mpangana edged Hukwi and won the contest. After being mesmerized by Hukwi's performance, Mpangana offered Hukwi a wife from amongst his people, the house of Tshedu, in exchange of the adoption of the *tjathiyane/isathiyane* concoction. This was not before Hukwi had refused an offer of land otherwise settling for a wife and a marriage alliance between the two clans. Mpangana later passed the *tjathiyane/isathiyane* legacy down to his apprentice son Hhobhodo/Hhoba. Hhobhodo/Hhoba perfected its use and further transforming it into both a weapon for defence and attack when he later became a fully-fledged inyanga. Hukwi Nkomo was succeeded as inyanga by his son Mawwila Nkomo.

Mpangana's third and final *ukulibhana* show is argued to have been a too close to call encounter against none other than Ninchasike Tjilisamhulu's medicine man, Ngomane Gumbo. The Malaba oral tradition humbles itself by admitting that the hypercompetitive encounter was a deadlock that earned a lifetime respect between the two opponents. Ngomane Gumbo and Mpangana Malaba later worked together as traditional medicine men of great repute. Gumbo even adopted the nickname Bepe which referred to bepe or *gobhodo lemiti* that he later shared with Mpangana. Some descendants of Ngomane Gumbo still live amongst the Malaba people in the

Sigangatsha area of Kezi. Although Ngomana was more of an inyanga (traditional healer), the current Gumbo family in Kezi are well known for being *izangoma* or *izanuse* (diviners). As a token of gratitude to Bangojena, Mpangana gave a wife from the Malaba clan to Bangojena's son, Nimahamingo Tshilise and a marital alliance was reached between Malaba and Bangojena clans.

Mpangana returned home to Nkalange to witness his first ever encounter with the Matabele of Mzilikazi Khumalo. It was in the end of 1839 or the beginning of the year 1840 when the first practical encounter with the Ndebeles of Mzilikazi occurred. On way from Zululand, Mzilikazi had come through Bulilima and making a temporary stopover at a place they called Mkuwa (Marula tree) which was about 15 kilometres north of Nkalange where the Malaba people were settled. After the Mkuwa stopover, the Matabele vigilantes were patrolling on the south of the Mkuwa area before approaching the Malaba homestead located in the Gurumane area of Nkalange.

As old Tshemane Malaba would narrate, it was at Nkalange in Marula that one morning dawned, bright and sweet, like ribbon candy. It was the typical unending bright sky, glorious luminous blue and pink heralding the tropical savanna climate, which, normally, is characterized by a dry season with a noticeable amount of rainfall followed by a rainy wet season. In essence, the tropical savanna climate mimics the precipitation patterns more commonly found in a tropical monsoon climate, but do not receive enough precipitation during either the dry season or the year to be classified as such. And it was such weather patterns that King Mzilikazi's guards and runners (*Izithunywa lezigijimi zenkosi*), would do their routine patrols. And it was during one of the daily routine patrols by Mzilikazi's local guards that the new unknown establishment was discovered.

As they approached the Nkalange area, they could not believe the evidence of their eyes, as suddenly they came upon a self-sufficient serene homestead, a sight of children of all ages playing within and without the homestead grounds with some noise of laughter signifying freedom and reflecting a happy family. The village layout was a typical Venda-Kalanga homestead, resembling the *tshitaka-tshemakoleni* settlement structure proscribing a central circular cattle-fold with the pole-and-thatch round mud huts arranged in a crescent at the higher end of a gradually sloping piece of land. Houses were traditionally wattle-and-daub constructions with thatched roofs.

The Malaba homestead in Gurumane was one big family, comprising several shelter huts, (*nzi nkulu/inxuluma yomuzi*), representative of the eight family houses of Malaba, linked together with mud-brick walls and like the traditional Mbedzi format, arranged around an open central courtyard with a central fireplace where the family sits in good weather. The hut floors comprised a densely compacted mixture of ant-hill sand and cow-dung, polished to resemble a dark green marble. Small, irregularly shaped fields for planting grains and vegetables were nearby and protected from animals with interlaced thorn- branch hedges. Like the *Tshitaka tshamakoleni* format, the huts in the homestead were in a linear formation arranged in order of seniority with Mpangana as its figurehead. Furthermore, it should be pointed out that the reason hereby, of referencing the Malaba offspring as houses of Mpangana instead of his sons, stems from the fact that in some circles there exist a couple of oral narrations presenting forth some names such as Nkumbalala, Malukanjita, Malabazinda, Nkubi, along with others, as some of the Malaba father figures. Bar the fact that the names are mentioned by less than one hundredth of the entire Malaba oral narrators, research efforts could neither locate, detect, attach nor relate the names to any form, time, or space. Therefore, in the book the bodiless names are either attached to the figure of Mpangana or absolutely discounted.

Amongst the Malaba's eight houses, Tshibi, born 1805, was the first son from the first and leading house. As reflected before, Tshibi's headship was not only because he was the oldest of the boys but had assumed the successor to the throne role after having been chosen by Mwali at the Maneledzi pool contest. Again, as mentioned beforehand, unfortunately Tshibi had succumbed to death earlier during the gruesome trek from Vendaland to BuKalanga, in the event, leaving behind "no born son". Thereupon, as the clan reached this part of the world, they were still mourning the loss of their eldest house. In this homestead it is known that the Tshibi house was just an uninhabited but symbolic house. Therefore, amongst the clan, Tshibi may not have existed physically but in spirit he did.

The second house was that of Kuyani who was born at around 1815 while the third house was that of Hhoba who had been born in 1810. Hhoba was later called Gobhodo after receiving the medicine bag *'gobhodo lemiti'* from his father Mpangana. The name was later corrupted to Hhobhodo, a name that he was to be known by till the present era. The name Hhobhodo or Gobhodo was synonymous with each member of the clan in possession of the Gobhodo lemiti (Medicine bag) at a given time. Therefore, Bepe Luvhimbi, and Mpangana Manikiniki Mantsha could also be referred to as Gobhodo or Hhobhodo. In effect, the name Bepe was a reference to the *gobhodo-lemiti* medicine bag. Hhobhodo/Hhoba had maternal brother, Mkhubazi.

The fourth house had Hadledzi who was born around 1813. Other houses of Mpangana included Tshada, Tshedu, Lungombe (N'ombe/Phondo) and Bhule Muruthe. Tshada and Hhobhodo/Hhoba's mothers were sisters. Tshada's mother was a younger sister to Hhobhodo/Hhoba's mother. She was also Mpangana's favourite wife, *bawosi/intandokazi (*the beloved one). Tshada had a maternal brother called Manusa. Oral traditions also highlight that Bhule was one of the youngest houses of Mpangana, if not the youngest. Bhule son of Mpangana is therefore born in or just after 1837, becoming the youngest house of Malaba. Bhule had a maternal brother called Manyele.

After encountering the new arrivals, it was conforming to standard ways that Mzilikaz's patrolling men found themselves interrogating the Mpangana contingent.

"*Who are you?*" They asked.

"*We belong to one Hhonyedzapasi*", they replied.

Although the Hhonyedzapasi name later became synonymous with Mpangana, as a matter of fact, it was originally a name of an imaginary being rather than a name of any specific individual. No individual ever bore the name Hhonyedzapasi amongst the Malaba people until it was mentioned as a diversionary tactic at that point. Legend has it that the mention of the name Hhonyedzapasi did not go down well with the Matabele people of Mzilikazi as they interpreted it as a mockery. A devastating drought that was ravaging Matabeleland in the 1830s is mentioned by Thenjiwe Lesabe in *Ranger's Voices from the Rocks*. Lesabe relates about the ravaging drought of that time when she said, "he (Mzilikazi) had trouble, his cattle were dying, people were running short of water" (Terence O. Ranger, 1999). Thomas also refers to occasions when the Matabele, in times of famine and scarcity of rain, would contract "diseases which resulted in death from eating improper food" (Thomas, 1986). Some Malaba oral informants argued that the drought period was a deliberate and strategical plan by Mwali to have the Matabele fundamentally endorsing and acknowledging the rain making powers of the Njelele shrine.

As a result of that, the Matabeles misinterpreted the name Hhonyedzapasi as a mockery of their misfortunes, whereby they are said to have been feeding on badly spoiled meat sometimes full of maggots (*Hhonyedzapasi*). Mzilikazi's guards were displeased by the response. Surely it was a necessity that the Matabele *amabutho* (runners) took some form of action against the strangers and oral traditions has it that Mzilikazi's army commanders suggested that the new Malaba settlers be killed. It was upon making a swift move to raid the whole clan that Mzilikazi's raiders were met with Mpangana Malaba's pot of viciously boiling porridge, called *tjathiyane/isathiyane*.

In the Malaba oral traditions, the *tjathiyane/isathiyane* is narrated as a deliberately made concoction that boiled like a blast furnace, sometimes throwing some vicious clumps of coagulated bovine colostrum (calf milk from recently delivered cows) at more than one hundred degrees Celsius. The composition of bovine colostrum (calf milk) meant that the concoction had an extremely poor heat stability at high temperatures implying that if some catalysts were added to it, and the contents enclosed in a weak ceramic or metal pot, it would erupt into a quite deadly substance. In addition to that, it was the mystical knowhow of the Malaba elders that led to the alchemistic *tjathiyane/isathiyane* concoction having deadly physical and parapsychological effects. The mind games associated with setting the *tjathiyane/isathiyane* trap made it into a weapon of surprise against unsuspecting invaders. The *tjathiyane/isathiyane* had become, not only part of the medicine bag '*gobhodo lemiti*, but a reliable weapon that Mpangana used to defeat the enemies in times of attack. Petrified and terror stricken, it is stated that the amabutho turned around and ran as fast as their legs could carry them resulting in the Malaba settlers somehow surviving what could otherwise have been an offence punishable by death.

Some mention that the raiders consisted of the Amagogo regiment led by Maqhekeni Sithole. Ironically, later on the Malaba people militarily served under Maqhekeni's son, Gampu Sithole's jurisdiction who in 1871 had become 'a kind of lieutenant governor of a large district' extending mainly to the west where the Kalanga of Usaba and Lulwana also lived. Besides being dominated by the Kalanga of Usaba and Lulwana, it became a norm that the Malaba young men would make joining the Amagogo Regiment a clan tradition. Mzilikazi's temporary stay in Mkuwa is currently evidenced by some members of Mzilikazi's contingency like the Mlilos and some Sitholes who remained and made Mkuwa their permanent place of residence.

However, the Mlilos led by Mtotobi later spread further yonder to the nearby Emncwazini homestead. The Mlilo people were travelling with Mzilikazi because since they descended from Mabaso, son of Mntungwa, who was son of Mbulazi, they were Khumalo cousins (S. Nkala, 2017). The Sithole people were also intricately linked to Mzilikazi because Sithole's son, Kuhliwe, had, at some point, became involved with the Matshobana Khumalos. It is outlined that Kuhliwe had married Maqekeni, the daughter of Mpindo Thebe, and they produced twin sons, Maqhekeni and Ngqephu whom Matshobane had brought up as his own children. Maqhekeni later got married to Mtshakazana who was Matshobana's daughter (Cobbing, 1976)). Accordingly, Maqhekeni became one of Mzilikazi's outstanding generals and subsequently leading the Igabha regiment in the 1830s. As per protocol, a messenger was sent to King Mzilikazi at Mkuwa, to convey the unpleasant tidings regarding the *tjathiyane/isathiyane* attack by the people of Mpangana Malaba. Nonetheless, it was these circumstances that were to result in the forging a new relationship between the Khumalo and the Malaba clans. Recalling that moving north and northwest from Zululand, Mzilikazi was on a nation building mission, and he rounded up the strong men and women, turning the men into army recruits for his warriors, his possessions increasing his power and prestige, and his followers numbering.

Hence, it followed with obviosity that a report on sightings of a new kind of people in the vicinity implied a raiding. Duly, when Mzilikazi learnt of the mysterious way his foot soldiers were sent scaring for cover by the new settlers, he formally gave a directive that the leaders and all the able-bodied men of the Malaba clan be captured and be brought before him, not dead, but alive, and that he ostensibly wanted to attend to them at a personal level.

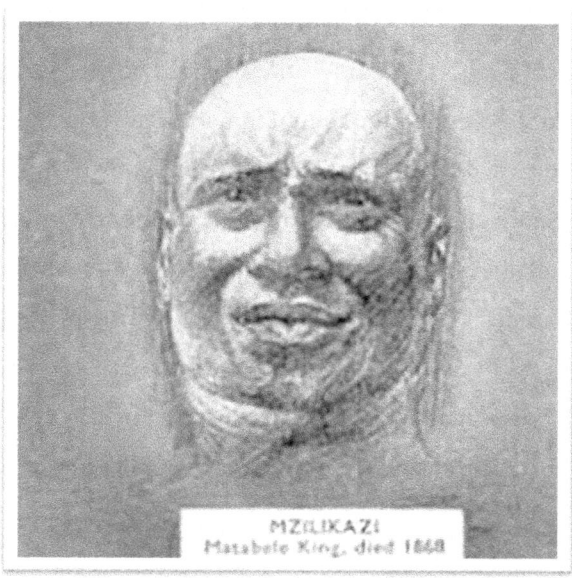

Figure 29. An unknown artist's impression of King Mzilikazi Khumalo the king of Matebele, died 1868 – picture courtesy of South African History online, (2020).

As per Maheleni's account Mzilikazi said "I want those people to be brought before me, not dead, but alive", commanded King Mzilikazi. "I am going to deal with their fate myself" (Maheleni, 2015). Before a cow could finish mowing, most of the Malaba able bodied men had been brought before Mzilikazi. They were piled inside a tiny beehive-style construction thatched with grass and a floor made from a mixture of anthill clay and cow-dung. Despite having been informed prior that they were to meet King Mzilikazi in his personal capacity, after a while, the door flew open and two strong broad-shouldered men lingered in the brightly lit outside for a second before entering the hut. Fear and uncertainty are said to have gripped the Malaba inmates.

As the two figures drew closer, their instincts were telling them that they certainly were not going to enjoy the day's experiences. According to a narration by one of them, they got a good look at one of the men, a bulky man with eyes made to frighten than to inspire. They may have known straight off that it was Mzilikazi. Robert Moffatt described Mzilikazi as short, as did Andrew Smith however, the likes of French missionary Jean- Paul Pellissier, thought of him as of average built. Captain W. Cornwallis Harris regarded Mzilikazi as being tall with a round forehead and a pleasant smile, a gentle countenance, and a soft, effeminate voice. "He tended to corpulence and had the scars of war. He appeared shrewd and observant, cheerful, even-tempered, dignified, reserved, wily, suspicious, avaricious, robust and virile to various of those who met him" (Cobbing, 1976). So far, the closest resemblance to him is a sketch by an unknown artist (Fig. 29). With a voice imbued with the bass of a rockslide and the pride of a lion, he, began to speak.

"Who amongst you is responsible for the deed?"

Together in unison the Malaba men answered in chorus, like they had rehearsed it.

"We don't know what you are talking about nkosi".

The man spoke again. "*It's either you tell me, or something worse is going to happen.*"

Before they came out with the answer, the second man in the room, who they later not only knew, but befriended as Mncumbatha son of Kholo Khumalo, now calmly interrupted with a melodious whisper.

"Look here young men, we are busy men who need to go on and do our jobs for the day, but we can't do our job without you telling us what or who exactly did the deed. So just help us out, and we can let you go."

Sensing the smell of immediate death one of the Malaba inmates, in a state of betrayal, is presumed to have pointed to Hhobhodo.

"*It is him.*"

Hhobhodo/Hhoba the man who had been Mpangana's apprentice, had by now matured into a fully-fledged traditional magician involved in practically every performance Mpangana partook. Mncumbatha stepped forward, as if to strike but hesitated and came to a halt.

"I am going to do it myself. May everyone leave the hut. And you Mncumbatha"

Mzilikazi is believed to have uttered the words. The other Malaba men disappeared into thin air like a daydream. Old Mncumbatha followed, albeit in an extremely sluggish pace. Left in the room was Mzilikazi and Hhobhodo/Hhoba standing eyeball to eyeball. Man, to man, they conversed. It is said that it was at that point in time that Mzilikazi learnt that the leader of the Malaba contingent was not Hhobhodo/Hhoba but one, old Mpangana, after which an *isigijimi* was sent to summon and bring his old self to *eSigodlweni* for a one-to-one meeting with the king of the Matabele people.

This decision would have left many of his generals taken aback, but it was, on the face of it, a strategy by king Mzilikazi. Although traditional norms required the King to seek the guidance from his cabinet of advisors before making important decisions, the final decision was always the king's.

Momentarily, Mpangana, as leader of the Malaba clan was finally brought before king Mzilikazi. In his book *Lobengula*, writer Marshall Hole, presents his own description of Mpangana as he details that "from a recess in the rocks, two of the Matabele soldiers appeared, dragging by the wrists the strange figure of a gaunt native, whose short, grizzled chin beard, bald head and parched and wrinkled skin showed him to be well on in years" (Hole, 1929).

The author, Lieutenant-Colonel Hugh Marshall Hole, was an especially important figure during the Rhodesian era. He was also an English pioneer who became a Civil Commissioner of Bulawayo and Chief Native Title Commissioner for Matabeleland, which fell under the Ministry of Native Affairs. He had initially acted as Clerk of the British South African Company in Kimberley before being transferred to Administrators Office Salisbury as Secretary where he served as a Lieutenant with the Salisbury Horse during the Mashona Rebellion and was awarded the BSA Company medal 1896. In 1901 he was sent in a special government service in Arabia 1901 concerning native labour before ultimately receiving an appointment as an Acting Chief Native Commissioner of Matabeleland in June 1907. Marshall Hole is best known for issuing "Marshall Hole currency" in Bulawayo in 1900 (Fig 30) and is one of the best diarists of the Mzilikazi-Lobengula times.

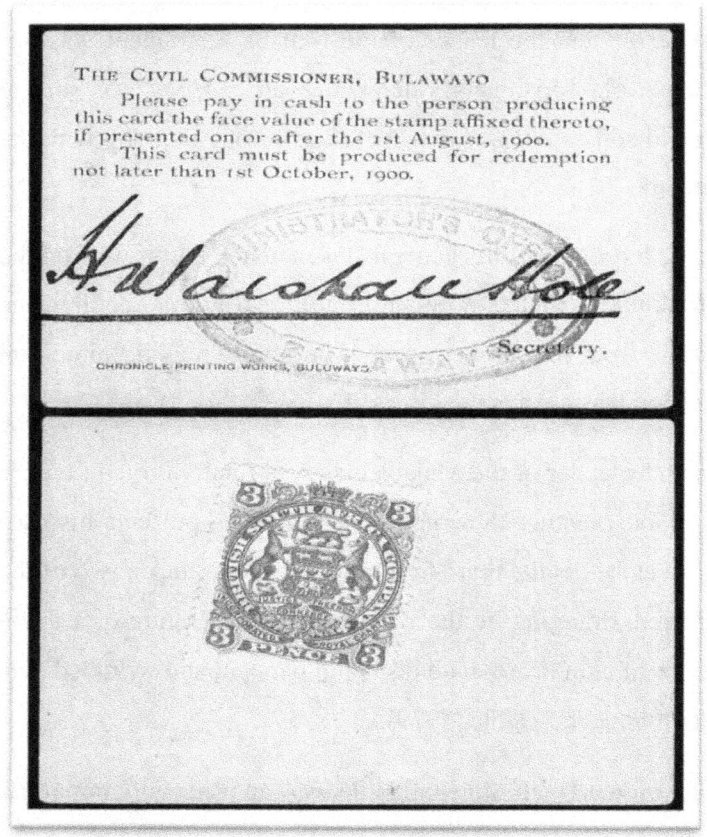

Figure 30. The Marshall Hole Currency of 1900 in Bulawayo, Courtesy of http://www.rhodesianstudycircle.org.uk/

Basing his account on eyewitness narrations, Hole (1926) continues to describe the ordeal when he writes that "from a thong round his neck hung four oblong ivory tablets carved with grotesque symbolic patterns, the inflated bladder of some small animal and an assortment of birds' beaks, leopards' claws, small tortoise-shells and other `amulets.' Marshall Hole's narration further gives an accomplished picture of Mpangana of whom he mostly referenced with the rainmaking crown of *Ngwali*, as he accounts that "his only garment was a long strip of filthy hide, soft with age and use, hanging from a waistbelt of snake-skin, and in one hand he clutched a staff, on the top of which was fixed of all strange ornaments, the cut glass stopper of an old-fashioned decanter".

It is known with benefit of hindsight that it was this physical appearance of Mpangana that led to him earning such names as '*Manikiniki*', '*Malukanjita*', *Ngqamu ebukhali* and other definitive names. In his narration, Hole continues to recount that, "with such strength as if he were possessed, he strove to break away, screaming out what sounded like horrible curses. He was brought up to the King and forced down on his knees. His struggles subsided but he poured a stream of unfamiliar words. "*Mlimo! Mlimo! Ngwali! Ngwali!*" he kept on repeating" (Hole, 1929).

Eventually, Mzilikazi had a one-to-one encounter with Mpangana, with the aim of clarifying issues with the perfect stranger, however, there was communication breakdown because although a Venda by background, for religious reasons Mpangana spoke the tjiKalanga language, the language of Mwali, and to all appearances, king Mzilikazi got lost in translation. Mpangana was taken out to be questioned in a public forum in case someone from the multitudes was able to understand and interpret his words. It was thereupon when, a Kalanga-Tswana woman who constituted the Basotho people raided by Mzilikazi on his way to Bukalanga, made herself available to translate. The writing that come closest to providing a vivid picture of the events is by history novelist Hole who outlined and summarized the core fundamental mission of the Malaba clan in a single description.

"*I understand him a little, Great One,*" she proclaimed.

"His words are like the words of my own people, the Basotho. He says he is a man from (Mwali) God. Nkosi! He says the people of this country are the Makalanga, the children of the Sun, and this hill is called Malindandzimu. But none of the tribe live near it except himself and his family, for they are afraid of the ghosts of their chiefs, who are all buried round this spot. Only the great ones of the nation lie here, Nkosi, those that have deserved well of their country. The spirits will not molest him, Nkosi, for he is a Mwali priest, their friend. But others only come here when they want the spirits to help them, and then they bring gifts; and they cannot talk to the spirits themselves, Nkosi, but only through Mwali; and the voice of the spirits speaks to them out of the caverns in the rocks. Yes, Nkosi" (Hole, 1929).

It was in that brief consultation that the principle and objective of the Malaba clan in that part of the world, was construed not only by king Mzilikazi, but by the whole nation.

In keeping with Marshall Hole's written account, Mzilikazi and the Matabele people were never the kind of people who concerned themselves much about things pertaining to spiritual office. In preference they were extremely uptight with material possessions to an extent they had less regard of the supernatural realm and therefore, but although they shirked such questions, and avoided discussing them, they were profoundly credulous on subjects connected with magic and sorcery. Although the likes of researcher Cobbing argues that the Nguni communicated with *Unkulunkulu* and *uSomandla* (Cobbing, 1976), they were Zulus and, "there is no evidence of belief in a heavenly deity or sky-god in Zulu religion before the advent of Europeans" (Hexham, 1981). Belief in a creator God (uNkulunkulu) appears to have originated from efforts by early Christian missionaries to frame the idea of the Christian God in Zulu terms.

Traditionally, the more strongly held Zulu belief was in ancestor spirits (*amathongo* or *amadlozi*), who had the power to intervene in people's lives, for good or ill. The Zulu believe that the *isithunzi* (shadow) becomes the ancestral spirit after death, but only after the *ukubuyisa* ceremony has been performed, during which the spirit is 'brought back home'. Sacrifice played an important role in maintaining contact with the ancestral spirits, providing a 'bridge' which enabled the individual to ask for favours or to thank the ancestral spirits for their blessings. Amongst both the Zulu and the Matabele, ancestral spirits are still believed to have the power to regulate the forces of nature and are approached before all important events.

……………………………………

Despite still having an unfinished business with the Malaba elders, it is said that Mzilikazi moved further up instructing to meet up with Gundwane at '*umfula olamanzi amnyama*' (the river with dark waters) later hailed as Amanzamnyama river. The *Amanzamnyama* river was originally known by the indigenous BaKalanga people as river *Nata*. He then was taken by Gundwane even further to Ntabazinduna and then to what became his first capital at Inyathi before coming back to the Matopos where he had a repeat encounter with the Malaba clan as he challenged them to *ukulibha* (experimenting) test.

At the earliest convenience, old Mpangana commenced brewing his concoction. The people gathered around, comprising mostly the Matabele, were apprehensive in anticipation of a deed to be done. Before one could pronounce the word

Mahlabezulu, their fears were confirmed because, out of the blue, there was a "terrific clap of thunder that burst over them and echoed and reverberated through the granite kopjes", (Hole, 1929). As it died away, he continues, a hollow unearthly voice issued from the rocks just behind Mpangana where no man stood. "*Wafa Wafa! Baleka* (Whoever dies, dies! Run!)". *Wafa wafa* was Mpangana's trademark incantation. Like bats out of hell, the gathering ran down the skinny menacing hill in fear and trepidation. Even Mzilikazi, who (J. P. R. Wallis, 1946), describes as "would never be disturbed by any noise be it of men or dog", momentarily lost his usual calm. Nonetheless, with baffling speed, the ordeal had been put to bed.

Although it was not the first and last time Mpangana had exercised his artistic gifts involving the vicious concoction now certified as *isathiyane sakoMalaba*, he had earned his respect from Mzilikazi and his whole Matabele nation. After the trial, it is maintained that King Mzilikazi wished to have a private audience with Mpangana as the leader of the Malaba people (and whom the Ndebele referred to as *Mpethuyaphans*i (Honyedzapasi) one more time. Mzilikazi was almost certain that Mpangana was a great magician nevertheless, as per custom, he needed to prove that beyond reasonable doubt. As he was taken away, Mpangana was ridiculed and accused, of being a fake medicine man. It was just intimidation aimed at proving his genuineness and resilience.

"We are not bogus medicine men. We are a family of traditional doctors", Mpangana argued.

Legend has it that Mzilikazi called to have the Malaba medicine men's ingenuity tested. But Mpangana pleaded that he "could not do the miracle except in the actual presence of the spirits. Therefore, finally, with some trepidation, a few of the leaders consented to accompany him to his old retreat amid the mysterious fastnesses which were said to be haunted by the shades of the departed" (Hole, 1929). He was dragged straight to the hills where his medicine skills were to be put into test against other locally tried and tested *nyangas* (medicine men), through a process known as "*ukulibha*". It was a glorious chance for Mpangana to demonstrate his powers, one that he had long been hoping for. His confidence relied on the skills that were not only tried and trusted but recently been sharpened at the *Dombo laNtjongogwe* contest. In conjunction with that, according to one informer, it seemed to provide him with another further opportunity to clear the country of the Matabele whom he considered to be odious intruders.

To keep up with Lynn Hall's narration in the book, *Return to Corriebush*, Mpangana chose the location of Malindandzimu the sacred hill of the spirits where he drew on all his resources to make the most of it. Arriving at Malindandzimu in the climax of the spiritual Matopo hills, Mpangana is reported to have given a full demonstration of his magic chants, that kept the observant indunas on tenterhooks of suspense for some hours while he engaged himself in the ancient divination technique of throwing 'bones'. They stood there like hummingbirds, watching as old Mpangana muttered incantations, and burning strange objects in a fire (Hall, 2013).

Attributed to some divine agency, on that day Mpangana executed extraordinary performances that were explicable by nature. For those reasons, Mpangana's performance at the *ukulibha* contest was unequalled. His miracles outclassed the local *nyangas* and according to legend, the performance included "nailing a cow skin on a hard rock with wooden nails". The Malaba people were already well known for this performance, earning themselves the praises '*bakalunji gusazosimila pfuma koga gwakasimila bhaya pasi*' (those with the needle not meant for cloth knitting, but meant for digging).

As if that was not enough, towards sunset, Mpangana announced that the oracle was about to speak, and sure enough the same dread voice issued from the mouth of a cave and everybody who was present understood the voice.

"Your King calls you. He has eaten up the River King and seized his country. All must join him, and death will come to those who hold back."

Legend has it that King Mzilikazi and his indunas were all left in an amazed consternation, and the Ndebeles who were ordinarily a hardened group of warriors, who typically would gaze unmoved at the most revolting butcheries, in that occasion quaked like young children at contact with the supernatural. More so, Mpangana's performance is alleged to have had some of them jumping to their feet, starring into the darkness with fear as "the air seemed full of whispers, and when the unearthly laugh of a hyena suddenly sounded just behind them" and as one author described, what they could hear was just a sound of a "ghostly hyena, whose mocking roar was heard again, dying away into the distance, and when they reached home and related their experiences, they found that no one paid heed to them".

The King Mzilikazi was left convinced that indeed, Mpangana was a man gifted with amazing magic powers! Henceforward, tradition has it that it is when Mzilikazi immediately summoned and convened a private man to man meeting with Mpangana in his kraal. According to the Malaba oral traditions Mzilikazi commanded, "take him behind the granaries. I shall meet him there. I am seemingly going to kill him myself" (Maheleni, 2015). Therefore, Mpangana was dragged out of the confinement and taken for Mzilikazi's further interrogation.

In private, the meeting between Mzilikazi Khumalo and Mpangana Malaba was done in accordance with convention suitable and constituting an official and important occasion. Creating alliances with other clans was a Malaba tried and tested approach to creating valuable friendship and therefore, strengthening the clan's collective steadfastness. As trust was being earned between them, it was now time for Mpangana to explain his background to the curious Matabele King.

Mpangana, an eloquent and skilled orator, went on to give an incredible narration of the background of his own clan. The chosen royal clan of Mwali.

After the private meeting of the two, King Mzilikazi began by expressing his conviction and admiration of Mpangana's prowess in African traditional medicine. A 2018 interview with Maheleni Madla Malaba reveals that, Mzilikazi, with a voice that carried an edge of alpha male aggression, went on to narrate to old Mpangana, his own encounters with Shaka the King of the Zulus, and the reasons that led to his up migration to this part of the world. He narrated that on the death of his father Chief Mashobane, who had been murdered by the Ndwandwe Chief Zwide, he, as Crown Prince was duly installed as the new chief of the Northern Khumalo clan. However, after chief Dingiswayo's death, instead of siding with chief Zwide, in exchange for the protection of his people, chief Mzilikazi swore allegiance to King Shaka who had risen to power as a commander of chief Dingiswayo's army and had usurped the Zulu chieftainship and taken over the Mthethwa confederacy after Chief Dingiswayo's death.

Proving himself a fearless warrior, Chief Mzilikazi soon became one of King Shaka's advisers. King Shaka trusted Chief Mzilikazi but secretly Mzilikazi dreamed of being a king himself. At a later stage, dissatisfied with a life of subservience, Mzilikazi plotted to free himself and his people from King Shaka's influence. In June 1822, King Shaka sent Chief Mzilikazi's regiments to attack the Sotho chief Ranisi (Somnisi). They pounced on the Sotho chief's defenceless flock and drove away their herds. It was as per custom in Zululand that after a chief and his subjects raided and captured some herds, they would tender the cattle to the king. As a token of appreciation to the chief's efforts, *umlenze* (a round), would be prepared for the chief's family, especially the wives, to consume in KwaBulawayo. Instead, defying King Shaka, Chief Mzilikazi refused to give up the spoils of battle, hence earning the praise, *"wena owala ukudla umlenze kwaBulawayo"* (one who refused to eat the round in Bulawayo), a phrase that, generally, was used to refer to a refusal to take instructions from a leader. In the winter of June 1822, Mzilikazi gathered his followers and headed north to become a powerful King through his conquests and protective powers.

Dingane's Zulu army led by a renegade Mzilikazi induna from Inxa called Nhlanganiso attacked the Matabele in July 1832 but was defeated. Dingaan killed some of his indunas for the failure, and in November 1832 a group of Zulus fled to join Mzilikazi's Matabele (Cobbing, 1976). King Mzilikazi expressed that, knowing Dingane's determination, he would not be shocked if he was still being pursued by Dingane's agents. Despite the 1832 victory they remained an ever-present threat to Mzilikazi. Therefore, he, King Mzilikazi, was happy engaging Mpangana's medicinal skills to act as part of the deterrent against a potential Zulu pursuit. A house of the Khumalo-Malaba bilateral relationship was forged and was an alliance that was to manifest itself for years to come especially in both matters relating to king Mzilikazi's notion of nation building and the Malaba religious pursuits. Under the Royal House of Khumalo and using considerable statesmanship, Mzilikazi was able to meld the many tribes he conquered with his own people into an ethnically diverse but centralized kingdom (Coltart, 2016). In his 1857 letter to his wife Mary, (E. W. S. Wallis, 1946) notes, Mzilikazi's strongest intentions was forever to increase the number of his people instead of diminishing them.

……………………………

The Matabele led by Mzilikazi finally had settled at a town they named Umhlahlandlela. Mpangana, whose cunning had enabled him to quickly discern what was in the King's mind had decided 'to paint an attractive picture to tempt Mzilikazi and the Matabele to move on and leave the Makalanga tribes in peace in their land'. Mpangana and his Malaba people were still disheartened that their hopes and expectations of a reinforced and prosperous Kingdom of Mambo were prevented from being realized.

To use writer Hole's narration, Mpangana then told Mzilikazi, "*On the embankment of the Vhembe, there are villages so numerous that they cannot be counted. In every village there is a herd of fat cattle. The men do nothing but hunt and fish. They have no need to kill oxen for they always have the meat of buffaloes. They have many wives to make beer for them. The corn grows there without being tended. Their King has a great store of ivory, for elephants are as plentiful as hares. Yes, my master, it is a good country*."

"*Does it follow that these people you are talking about have a King?*" Mzilikazi inquired.

"*Certainly, they have a king. His name is Sebetwane, and his tribe are the Sotho who now call themselves the Makololo. These people had come from Kuruman many moons ago, and he has eaten up all the chiefs near the river.*"

Mzilikazi is said to have chuckled and slapped his naked thighs in excitement.

"*That is the man who gave us the slip once before in the Bechuana country and took some of my cattle. Good! This time he shall not escape. I will follow him and get back the cattle. I will teach him who is the greater, he or I*" (Hole, 1926).

Turning to Mncumbatha, Mzilikazi inquired,

"*What say you?*". Mncumbatha is alleged to have expressed his reservations without saying a word. Nonetheless, without wasting much time, Mzilikazi set off southbound in pursuit of Chief Sebetwane of the Kololo tribe. After a few days of Mzilikazi's spontaneous journey, rumours started to swirl that he had vanished for good.

4,2. Hhobhodo/Hhoba Malaba and the Clan Chieftaincy

After the departure of Tshibi from the earth, Hhobhodo was the oldest of the remaining Malaba sons. Although he was from the third house, he had been chosen and trained as the most appropriate apprentice of his father. As a result, although the ageing Mpangana Malaba was a respected medicine man amongst his clan and beyond, his older son, Hhobhodo/Hhoba, did not only inherit the skills, but he also became a more ardent and more accomplished *n'anga/inyanga* (medicine man). With constant instructions and schooling from his father, Hhobhodo/Hhoba in the long run inherited not only the traditional leadership of the clan but over and above became a comprehensive magician credited with powers of healing, divination, and protection against the magic of others.

By reason of king Mzilikazi having been awed by the Malaba people's wisdom, command, and divination, it was unmistakable that a reward was ensuing. Sequentially, other than the view that Mpangana Malaba had reached an advanced age, it was for those reasons that by 1841 Hhobhodo/Hhoba had ultimately been appointed a chief. This was a distinguished decoration as Hhobhodo/Hhoba became the first non-Nguni individual to be accorded such a distinction by King Mzilikazi in Bukalanga. The absolute implications of this appointment were that Hhobhodo/Hhoba was, on top of being a chief, be a chief advisor (*Nkumbudzi*) in conjunction with being a paramount religious leader and a personal traditional healer within King Mzilikazi's kraal.

He, as a matter of course, became an important advisor to members of the King's Advisory Council otherwise known as *umphakath*i in Sindebele or *lubahhe/phutheho* in tjiKalanga, a term that referred to the inner circle of chiefs that both King Mzilikazi and Lobengula consulted on important issues.

During Mzilikazi's reign the prominent members of *umphakathi* included his brother-in-law, Maqhekeni Sithole and his cousin, Mncumbatha Khumalo. During Lobengula's times the *umphakathi* comprised the likes of Ngubongubo, Sibambamu, Nyanda, Muntu, Silwane, Fezela and Mahlahleni.

The details of how the Malaba chieftaincy came about in this part of the world was clarified in the Hhobhodo Delineation Report, where Mpangana's son, Hhobhodo/Hhoba is said to have emerged as the first ever Malaba chief after the assignation by King Mzilikazi. The *umphakathi* played a crucial role in the determination of national policy since they sat in judgement. Mpangana himself continued in his individual role as a nkumbudzi (special advisor) and African traditional doctor in King Mzilikazi's kraal.

The April 1965 *Delineation Report* entitled *'the Delineation Report of Obodo Community'* substantiate the fact that Mpangana and his people were chief practitioners to the Ndebele kings, with a figure referred to as *'Obodo'* (Hhobhodo/Hhoba) the first individual in the Mpangana family to be accorded the chieftaincy by king Mzilikazi.

The Delineation report on the Mpimbila, Nata, Sanzukwe, Raditladi, Mphoeng's, Nata North and Nata South Tribal Trust lands and Brunapeg Purchase Area, compiled by A.D. Elliott, the District Delineation Officer, Bulilima District found in Zimbabwe's National Archives, also gives the background information for chiefs and headmen. The Malaba people are still referred to as the Kumbudzi (advisor) due to their commission and authority in the king's kraal.

4;3. Lobengula Khumalo and Sara Liebenberg at The Malaba Kraal

It was the dramatic events that took place within the Ndebele royal family in 1840 that led to Lobengula going to live with the Mpangana Malaba people for a considerable period. According to Ndebele law of succession, the Great House (*uNdlunkulu*) is the most senior and respectable Queen because she is expected to give birth to the Crown Prince. When she comes into a marriage, she is accompanied by a female relative who will assist her in daily chores. This female helper is called *umthanyelo or usomthanyelwana* (sweeper or female helper). The female helper also becomes the King's wife, and she helps with giving birth for the Great House in case the Great House is barren or cannot conceive a son.

In the case of King Mzilikazi, the Great House was Queen Mwaka Nxumalo, the daughter of King Zwide Nxumalo and her *usomthanyelwana* (female helper) was her cousin Queen Fulatha Tshabalala, daughter of Malindela, a ' brother ' of the Swazi King, Sobhuza (Cobbing, 1976). Tshabalala, a Swazi, though noble, but not of Royal blood, was given that name after being born feet first (Young, 2015). Queen Mwaka gave birth to sons Crown Prince Nkulumana who was born when his father King Mzilikazi and his Ndebele nation were resident in present day Gauteng Province of South Africa. Nkulumana was born when London Missionary Society (LMS) missionary Reverend Dr Robert Moffatt was visiting from Kuruman in the land of the Bathlaping, hence the name of the prince. Prince Buhlelo was Mwaka's other son while Fulatha, the helper gave birth to Prince Lobengula in 1836 and daughter Princess Mncengence Khumalo thereafter. Lobengula was born in 1836, the year the Matabele first clashed with the Boers at a place called Mosega, otherwise known as Mkhwahla in Transvaal in South Africa.

An incident which involved the Great House led to its punishment. During the Journey from Zululand, Mzilikazi had become separated from the bulk of the tribe.

They gave him up for dead and hailed his young heir Nkulumane as his successor. All the chiefs who had chosen him were put to death on Mzilikazi's orders at Ntabazinduna. Crown Prince Nkulumana never came back after being taken out of the Kingdom, Princes Buhlelo and Lobhengula were to be "executed" at their father's order (M. Nkala, 2018). Prince Buhlelo was unfortunate because he was executed while Prince Lobengula survived death and was sent away by Mncumbatha Khumalo and Gwabalanda Mathe accompanied by a white Dutch girl named Sara Liebenberg, who had become his foster mother.

The life story of the Dutch girl Sara Liebenberg is an engrossing and fascinating one. Sara was one of the three Dutch children who had been captured during one of Mzilikazi's raids that took place near the Zoutpansberg Mountains. It is recorded that in 1835, there were two small groups of travelling settler parties that comprised the first groups ever to leave Cape Town and heading north. The two groups were under Louis Trigardt and Janse van Rensburg respectively and are said to have been accompanied by their wives and approximately thirty children. In like manner, on the 24th of May 1836, the great Boer trek period, two groups under Andries Hendrik Potgieter and Sarel Cilliers also set off from the Sand River and followed northwards. Potgieter's group included forty armed men (Hall, 2013). Collectively, these were groups of Boers leaving Cape Town because they were discontent with British rule in the Cape of Good Hope area believing that they were never going to have security under the Government of the Cape. According to them, there was no law, no protection, and no fair judicial system and therefore, believed that it was the time for the Afrikaner nation to rise and go. And because they no longer had any ties with their previous countries, South Africa was their country.

Potgieter and Celliers who was from the ward *Nu-Hantam*, in the later district of Colesberg, called themselves the 'Emigranten' (emigrants). As a veteran of the 1811-1812 as well as the 1818- 1819 Frontier Wars, Potgieter was elected as leader of the combined trek, with the title of *commandant*. Amongst them were also teenage boys who carried weapons. Along the journey Potgieter and Cilliers were joined by other travellers comprising people of various nationalities (Hall, 2013). Also incorporated in the travellers was a group that belonged to one Barend Godlieb Liebenberg, with his wife Estella and three children. Liebenberg is announced to have been a challenging and difficult man who kept himself and his immediate family aloof from the others. He had decided to travel separately with his family and workers, a move that was to prove costly for him, his family, and his group (Hall, 2013).

One day, on the 22nd of August 1836, at a misleadingly rosy dawn on the foot of the Zoutpansberg mountains, a group of Matabele led by Mzilikazi, who in 1832 had established a military capital at Mosega 15 km south of the modern town of Zeerust, ambushed and pounced on the group. The war is recorded to have been a bloody one. While the Voortrekkers made use of a *laager* to ward off the assault at Kopjeskraal, the Liebenberg group had no chance against the Matabele warriors and most of them were killed in the clash. The battle hill is today known as the Liebenbergskoppie. When the dust had settled the Matabele caught sight of three white children curling themselves in a corner like heaps of sand. The children had hidden themselves under a sail in one of the wagons as the battle raged on. The three children comprised two little girls, Sara and Anna Maria, and their little brother Christiaan, and were all Liebenbergs (Hall, 2013). The three children together with the wagons and cattle belonging to the Liebenberg, and some Black servants who had survived the onslaught were routinely captured and immediately incorporated into the Matabele group.

According to oral narrations, upon presenting the children, Mzilikazi insisted that his warriors should never have captured the children after all as it was against protocol to hold minors as prisoners of war. He ordered the warriors to take effect immediately and reunite the children with their parents. But returning the children at that time proved impossible as veld fire emanating from the battles raged on in the grassland (Hall, 2005). Finding themselves between a rock and a hard place, Sara and her two siblings, Anna Maria, and Christiaan, were consequently incorporated into the Matabele group. For purposes of easy communication, the white Dutch children were awarded Ndebele or Zulu names. Christiaan became known as Velaphi meaning "Where do you come from?". Anna Maria who had been crying inconsolably since their capture, was called Mswanyana, which meant "why are you always crying?". Sara was called Toloyi. It is unclear what the name Toloyi referred to, except that there was a Tolani River in the vicinity of the Zoutpansberg mountains which could explain the name (Walter, 2017).

Sara is believed to have been a friendly little girl who was always willing to talk, socialize and engage in activities with other peoples, and though she only knew yet a smattering of their language, she was well liked by the Matabele women, for she was always ready to assist in taking care of all the kids as well as performing some extra domestic chores. As Hall (2005) records, in truth her own people were somehow vanishing from her young memory at any rate she had ceased to mourn for them. Anna Maria and Christiaan's weak bodies found it tough to manage to persevere the arduous Matabele journeys. Anna Maria finally dejectedly succumbed to dysentery and other diseases and died. Sara and poorly Christiaan, nevertheless, survived the crushing journey. In 1836, the two children were separated as Christian Velaphi was incorporated into the major section of the Matabele group, which was under Majijili Gwebu, Mkhaliphi Khumalo and Khondwane (Gundwane) Ndiweni that had become detached and pursuing a separate path to the north-east and ultimately reaching the present-day Zimbabwe by end of 1837 and settling at Ntabaende near to where the present-day Falcon College is situated. In this place they established the villages of Gibixhegu (Khondwane's new capital), Godlwayo (Dambisamahubo Mafu's capital), Mzinyathi (Majijili Gwebu's capital), Intunta (Mhabahaba Mkhwananzi' capital),

Siphezini (Ngwadi Sigola's capital), Ngwegwe (Mkhanyeli Masuku's capital), Matshetshe (Sifo Masuku's capital), Makhandeni (Dludluluza Zikhali's capital) and others. Sarah remained with the other group travelling with King Mzilikazi, cutting across Sekgoma's country into the Kalahari Desert.

The presence of the Dutch children is said to have been evidenced by travellers to Matabeleland who for years would speak of occasional sights of several whites who seemed to be part of the Matabele nation. There was also talk of a young man who had a senior position in one of the regiments and a teenage girl had taken on the role of nursemaid to Mzilikazi's youngest son, Lobengula. Author Walter (2017) was a distant relative of the Liebenberg and wrote that Christiaan Velaphi Liebenberg indeed survived the Matabele journeys and grew up to acquire all the characteristics of a Matabele boyhood including becoming a fully-fledged warrior. It appears though, that the young man had inherited most of his father's challenging behavioural traits which literally converted into a recipe for his downfall. Like his father he became a near impossible man to deal with and was "difficult and continually fighting with his fellows" (Walter, 2017). Nevertheless, Mzilikazi admired that hostility in Christiaan 'Velaphi''s nature that he thereupon, promoted him into a leader of a regiment. Velaphi performed and carried his duties with flying colours until one fateful day.

According to Walter, Mzilikazi's military law required that "individual regiments carried shields made of cattle hide in distinctive colour and pattern" (Walter, 2017). For example, the eZimnyama Regiment which incorporated a number of the Malaba clan were known as 'those with the black shields. Velaphi was given all the instructions as per what colour was a requisite for his regiment, or he was purported to have been given those instructions and rightly followed them. By all appearance, it was just a booby trap designed to be a punitive measure for the young man who, according to some Matabele *indunas*, had constantly displayed a strong desire, ambition, and determination to reach the top. One day post the

Inxwala dance Christiaan Velaphi was summoned to deliver a military presentation to king Mzilikazi. According to Gatsheni, the inxwala ceremony was partly a festival of unity serving as a means of maintaining the power of the king over his people. The numerous men and women who assembled around the capital for *inxwala* ceremonies also came partly to renew their allegiance to the kingship, politically to the person of the king, and spiritually to the memory of the royal amadlozi as national ancestral spirits (Gatsheni, 2008).

According to oral tradition, on arrival, Mzilikazi turned to Velaphi, stood eyeball to eyeball before him and coldly, he said to Christiaan Velaphi Liebenberg,

"Those shields are not of the colour I instructed".

"The colour is exactly as you instructed Nkosi" replied Velaphi.

"I said those shields are not of the colour I instructed",

Mzilikazi repeated yet likewise, Velaphi stood firm on his insistence that he had followed the king's instructions to the letter. It was at that stage that Mzilikazi beckoned, and Christiaan Velaphi Liebenberg was executed right off the bat ostensibly for treason and the taboo of defying the king's orders. Even so, his name was not erased from the history books as it was later resurrected in the Malaba house of Lungombe. As a reminder of their noteworthy life with Sara the Dutch girl, Lungombe Malaba gave his first son the name Velaphi. Velaphi went on to have gallant men like Misheck Ntundu Velaphi as descendants. Misheck Ntundu Velaphi was a Zimbabwe African People's Union (ZAPU) cadre whose contribution to the liberation and independence of Zimbabwe is well documented. Misheck Ntundu Velaphi died on 29 April 2019 and was laid to rest on May 9, 2019, at the National Heroes Acre in Harare, Zimbabwe.

………………………

There is consensus amongst certain scholars and history writers that it was during Mzilikazi's moment of frenzy that Lobengula left the Royal palace. However, the orality of the Malaba clan provide an intriguing narrative on the same autobiography. In consonance with their oral narration, it was through his extraordinary miracle execution that Mpangana managed to earn Mzilikazi's respect and trust. The artistic exercise involving the vicious *tjathiyane*/isathiyane concoction had left Mzilikazi acclaiming that Mpangana was naturally an African traditional medicine man of note and that the Malaba people were indeed a noteworthy clan that would be beneficial to his ambitious nation building policy. Writer Marshall Hole (1926), notes that there are no English superlatives that could precisely describe the essence and being of the Malaba people however, their role as the *Hosanna* men of "exceptional ability and intelligence" left Mzilikazi singing *Ngwali's* (Mpangana) praises (Hole, 1929).

He further notes that as skilful artists and jugglers who had an intimate knowledge of medicinal herbs, poisons, and remedies, as well as being shrewd observers of the weather, the Malaba people had the Matabele not only appreciating but also respecting their magical power performances. Aside from that, Mpangana himself was viewed and regarded by the whole nation as a puzzling person known to many yet difficult to decipher or comprehend, leading to him earning names such as Malukanjita, Manikiniki and Mpangana (*ngqamebukhali*) the sharp knife. His life is reported to have been unpredictable, and often left people in awe and speculation. In the collections entitled *The Matabele journals of Robert Moffatt, 1829-1860, Robert Moffatt (1795-1883),* a Scottish pioneer missionary to Southern Africa also wrote about his first-hand encounter with the Malaba people (J. P. R. Wallis, 1946).

Of significance, he noticed some striking Semitic characteristics in both their physical appearance and general behavioural traits. In reference to the Malaba people Moffatt mentions the people from what he calls the Sena hills. The Sena name originated from an abandoned ancient town in Yemen. Coincidentally, research explorations reveal that the Malaba people had their origin in Senna, Yemen, before migrating further into southern Africa. In probably a reference to the *tjathiyane/isathiyane* incident, Moffatt writes that, these people dared Mzilikazi's raids and were strong enough to put one of his commandos to flight. Moffatt was awed into describing those people as a superior people to the Matabele, evidently a civilized and industrious people. Their dress is much more decent, than that of the Matabele, he wrote. More importantly the Malaba people had introduced Mzilikazi to Njelele, a shrine that was to be invoked in times of illness and death, domesticated animal diseases, during agricultural seasons of sowing and reaping, succession disputes, personal and ethnic groups, natural phenomenon such as rainfall failure, and even times of politics and war.

It was on the backdrop of all these distinctions and attributes that, with the objective of reinforcing his powers and fortify his kingdom against his enemies, Mzilikazi sought to acquire Mpangana's expertise. However, it is told that Mpangana gave a directive to Mzilikazi that since he, (Mzilikazi), was then at an advanced age it was preferable if the mystic powers were performed to whoever was heir to the throne. Apparently, for Mpangana it was the future of the kingdom that was more important than the present. All at once, after the disappearance of Nkulumana the Ndebele order of succession had become top secret information serve for the few trusted insiders. Therefore, for Mpangana Malaba to be granted security clearance to such classified information served to highlight his acquired status in the hierarchy of the Ndebele nation. Upon that, Mpangana's appeal to have Lobengula under his protective care was granted albeit in secretive and circumstances that were shrouded in mystery.

According to the Malaba traditions, it was Mbikwa Tawulo Tshimba's rendition that they learnt of the events of that momentous night. Accompanied by Mbikwa himself, Mpangana had arrived at the Ingama village in the dead of the night.

According to Mbikwa's narration of the events, "in one part of the village, Mpangana drooped kneeling down to perform a ritual. He nailed an eland's horn deep on the ground and at the same time hymning a line out of his totem, "*bakalunji gusipfume ngubo, gosimila pfuma pasi*" (the needle that does not sew blankets but sew rocks). Still in those small hours of the night silhouetted human being figures could be seen withdrawing out of Ingama village. At the head of the queue was the figure of Mncumbatha son of Kholo kaManzamnyama Khumalo". Mbikwa, the centurion of the Malaba clan hovered on the side lines while old Mpangana strode confidently in the middle of the park. Alongside his towering body were small figures of two children, Lobengula Khumalo and Sara Liebenberg. Such was Mbikwa's recount according to the Tshimba orality.

Young Prince Lobengula and Sara Liebenberg's relocation finally led them to a newly found refuge in the Gurumane-Nkalange Malaba homestead. As for Mncumbatha, he was not only accompanying Lobengula and Sara off to the Malaba homestead, but, moving with them, subsequently building his own new homestead to be known as Enkantolo situated adjacent to the Malaba people, but towards the Matopo hills. The Enkantolo homestead epitomized a watchtower built to create an elevated observation point throughout Lobengula's stay here. In a chain reaction generated by Lobengula and Sara's relocation from their home into the Malaba homestead, oral tradition states that one of Mpangana's sons, Tshada Malaba who was also known as Mmandu, was aptly conscripted into the Amahlokohloko regiment as collateral. This was a way of holding on to him as surety unless something worse happened to prince Lobengula during his remain at the Malaba homestead. The Amahlokohloko regiment under Mbambelele Hlabangana were based just west of Isiphongo Hill off the Bulawayo-Inyathi Road where a place known as Esiphikeni is situated today.

In the book *Return to Corriebush*, this historical episode is profoundly outlined by Lynn Hall (2005), as she writes about the first encounter between Lobengula and the Malaba people. She describes when young prince Lobengula and Sara were taken from down the mountains to the Malaba's Nkalange homestead and upon their arrival at the kraal they were given strict instructions by Mbikwa (Hall, 2013).

"You are little bucks that have jumped out of a trap. If you return Mwaka will kill you, but if you stop with me in these hills, you will be safe, for you will belong to the Great Spirit. Place yourselves in my hands and obey my orders and you shall be unharmed" (Hole, 1929).

To this end, Lobengula on whom so much depended, found a home among the Malaba people, a clan renowned for traditional magic and healer ship, Hosanna priesthood and the custodianship of the Njelele rainmaking shrine. Judging by author Walter's assertion that Lobengula was six years old when he turned up to stay with the Malaba people, and with Hall's mention that on arrival, the Malaba had prepared the two hungry children some delicious 'pumpkins and plenty of cow milk' (Hall, 2013), determinately, then Lobengula and Sara arrived at the Malaba kraal between the month of January and February 1841. This reciprocates the Malaba oral narrations affirming that, Lobengula and Sara showed up during a season of plenty of food which is the season of harvest.

For prince Lobengula and Sara, living in the Malaba kraal was not only affording a different kind of life but it was also a culture shock! Nevertheless, as their residence prolonged, legend has it that young Lobengula began picking up a few words of the Kalanga language as well as grasping the ideas, customs, and social behaviour of the BaKalanga in general and the Malaba people. At the Mpangana Malaba homestead, it is narrated that the famished children at first thought of nothing but the food. A little later they accepted the reality of the situation with complete confidence and without a second thought of the life which they had left behind them at the great kraal. The Malaba people had gone out of their way to make the two stayers feel at home, providing them with whatever creature comforts they could afford. They awarded them royal treatment and served them as one of their own.

The staying children were under a constantly watchful eye of Mbikwa, the son of Tshimba- Bhangwa, whose responsibility was being one of the Malaba satellite detectives. Hole captures the overly amplified surveillance as he writes, "she was just in time to see the head of a native bob down behind a bush. In the brief glance she thought she had recognized him—Mbikwa, one of *Ngwali's* satellites. Could he be spying on her? She darted to one side, left the path, and struck through the bushes towards a small bare patch of granite. And now there could be no mistake, for as she reached its edge, she caught sight of another figure which immediately retreated" (Hole, 1929).

Of course, another influence was at work upon the young Lobengula. His daily relationship with the Malaba people and observation of the medicinal escapades filled him with a profound respect for traditional medicine. Lobengula watched the Malaba people foretelling the weather by pouring over the insides of disembowelled goats, and, in seasons of drought, extracting heavy payments from those who came to consult them for interceding with the Mwali to send rain. He saw them selling charms to their customers to bring fertility to their wives and their cattle, to render them proof against disease and to avert the evil eye.

Again, Lobengula learnt what a valuable tool this religious knowledge might be made in the hands of those who knew how to turn it to account and by these two influences the fates were shaping the character of Lobengula for their own ends (Hall, 2013). To some, Lobengula was effectively being trained, among other things, to the effect of being a rainmaker. On the other hand, Sara, the Dutch girl, could not figure out why they ended up in the Malaba kraal nevertheless, the hospitality made her feel at ease. No photo of Sarah Liebenberg has been found, but an artist's impression of the young lady was drawn by Lynn Bedford Hall (Figure 31).

The Malaba oral traditions has it that by living in the Malaba kraal, Lobengula escaped among other activities, the hard exercises by which other Matabele young males were trained for the profession of warfare, but nevertheless he grew rapidly in stature, bodily vigour, and physique. He acquired new skills and became a daring and skilful hunter of game, fleet of foot and expert with the assegai and knobkerrie. And, as Hole captures it, "at the same time his mental faculties were developing in a way which would not have been possible had he remained with his tribe" (Hole, 1926). From infancy Lobengula's naturally receptive mind had been moulded by constant association with Mbikwa Tshimba and Sara who had taken the role of a foster mother. There were frequent visits from Mncumbatha who had kept a vigilant eye on the boarders and constantly reminded Lobengula of his royal birth since he had entirely cut off from his own tribe. "You are safest here," a visiting Mncumbatha would reassure the two children (Hall, 2013).

Mncumbatha Khumalo and chief Gwabalanda Mathe did not exclusively keep the secret of the prince's whereabout under wraps as it is believed they informed others like, Chief Mnengeza Fuyane who resided adjacent to the Malaba homestead towards the Matopo hills, who also kept it under wraps. For Lobengula, there were also just few circumscribed visitations to and from one, Fakafaka Mabhena, who so liked Lobengula that he later became his staunchest supporter. It is considered that these men would ordinarily take turns in escorting Lobengula to his regular schooling with the *Imbovane* brigade, a special detachment of men who comprised the trusted king's guard. Their ages normally ranged from ten to around fifteen years and could not marry or consort with women for reasons of, despite being too young, self-discipline and control.

Mpangana had vowed from the beginning that when he was done with the young prince Lobengula, not only was the young man going to be an invincible figure, so powerful it was impractical to harm or destroy his physical person but was going to be an insurmountable task for his enemies to pursue and apprehend him, just like the Malaba people whose enemies could not locate them during their arduous journey from VhuVenda. Oral traditions have it that Mpangana also had acquainted Lobengula to shrewdly plant trusted people in various strategic places in various locations in case he would be fleeing from an enemy. These people would provide refuge and assist him in case he needed escaping.

This was the same master plan that the Malaba people used to evade their pursuers when they fled from VhuVhenda. Besides the many villages under various Ndiweni chieftaincies, one of the most important strategic points in case of emergence was to be at Lobengula's cousin, King Mpezeni's capital in Mtengeluni, in the present-day Zambia.

The Malaba-Khumalo relations were not just a mere organization but a significant and indispensable association. As Prince Zwide Peter Khumalo also wrote in an article, "there is hardly any history of battles between the Mambo people or the BaKalanga, for that matter that any person worth his honest salt can speak of, and King Mzilikazi people, most of whom were Nguni. King Lobengula, for instance grew up in the Malaba family. Chief Malaba ranked remarkably high in King Lobengula's rule. There are Chiefs in the Kalanga region, not necessarily of Nguni origin who were given that status in recognition of their leadership prowess among their own by King Lobengula". Khumalo further confirms assertion in an interview when he said, *"uLobengula wondliwa koMalaba. UMalaba wayeyinduna ephezulu"* (Lobengula was brought up amongst the Malaba people. Malaba was a supreme chief) (Khumalo, 2020).

4,4. The Potgieter Raid and Lobengula's Return to Esigodlweni

Figure 31. An Artistic Impression of Sara the Dutch Girl with Prince Lobengula Upon Spotting Potgieter's men. Courtesy of Author Lynn Bedford Hall.

Lobengula lived amongst the Mpangana Malaba people until 1847 when he was presented back to his own father Mzilikazi by Mncumbatha just before the skirmishing that occurred between Mzilikazi and Hendrik Potgieter, uNdaleka. It is cited that Mncumbatha had gone down from his Enkantolo homestead to Esigodlweni to report the local sightings of uNdaleka (Hendrik Potgieter) who had been seen hovering in between the Matopo and Figtree areas. However, legend presents a Mpangana who had always been in anticipation of Potgieter's raid on the Mangwe Pass and surrounding areas either through his supernatural prowess, through some BaKalanga travellers or some intelligence agents. At some point it appears Mpangana was spending a lot of his time upon the hills preparing the isathiyane concoction on the hills. One of the Makalanga woman was heard exclaiming,

"Have you not noticed of late how old Mpangana goes every day to the look-out on Inungu hill and keeps his eyes fixed towards the south, as if he expected some stranger to come? And where has he been all to-day and all yesterday? Perhaps he has himself sent for them to come and kill Mzilikazi, so that the Makalanga may get back their country" (Hall, 2013).

Naturally, the freedom of the kingdom of Bukalanga was certainly old Mpangana's inclination, but according to one informant, mainly because he was viewing the Malaba people's relationship with the Matabele from a physical, as opposed to a spiritual sense. The interview with the informant, interestingly highlighted that the unyielding reality was that the Matabele were not simply phantoms to just be expunged from Bukalanga. Their presence in this part of the world was that they would become an active fact of the everyday lives of the BaKalanga. Therefore, the presence of both the Malaba clan and Mzilikazi's Matabele in the kingdom of BuKalanga after showing up nearly at about the same period, was according to the informant, far more than a mere coincidence. It was to a significant degree a spiritually arrangement by Mwali than it was a mundane encounter.

In all the Malaba physical journeys in history, it is noteworthy to mention that the main determinant was the responsibility to fulfil the spiritual obligations. Therefore, for the Malaba clan, the Matopo hills felt to have answered an increasing imaginative need to be united with Mwali, the rain god. To the Malaba people, Njelele was far from a belief in heaven on earth, but of course, the shrine, regarded as a sister hill to the Biblical Mount Sinai, was a piece of heaven. It deserved not only to be revered and canonized, but to be jealously guarded and be defended, yet on the other hand the Njelele divinity was strictly against war and/or the spilling of blood. As Nyathi noted, "graves and what they represent, that is death, are the antithesis of the Njelele Shine and what it stands for, which is fertility. Fertility is about life, its extension and sustenance, whereas graves and death are the very opposite. The colour red is prohibited at Njelele and when it is raining because it symbolizes death" (Nyathi, 2019). The Njelele strict prohibition against the spilling of blood was derived from the Jewish Torah that portrayed murder as a capital crime and having a few points describing in detail the moral understanding and legal implementation of the consequences.

The Malaba clan's link to the Torah is further backed by the theory that, the Lemba tribe, who evidently were trailing the path of their relatives from up north, arrived in Southern Africa bringing with them some remnants of the Biblical Ark of the Covenant. According to Steve Vickers of the BBC, a wooden object claimed to be a replica of the Biblical Ark of the Covenant and belonging to the Lemba people of Jewish ancestry, went on display at a museum in the Zimbabwean capital city of Harare at some point (Vickers, 2010). Parfitt, a professor of Modern Jewish Studies at the University of London's prestigious School of Oriental and African Studies argued that it was indeed remnants of the Ark of the Lord. He argued that the original Ark of the Covenant may have been destroyed when the Babylonians invaded Jerusalem in 586 B.C., and that several copies likely were made and that one was taken to Ethiopia by Prince Menelik, the son of Solomon and the Queen of Sheba (M. Wood, 2010). It was how another could then have found its way to ancient Zimbabwe through the Lemba migrants (Fig. 32).

Also, according to the BBC, colonial officials had originally put the vessel on display at a museum in Bulawayo, being last photographed in 1949, but during the war of independence it was hurriedly taken to Harare with other artefacts for their protection. Its transfer was apparently forgotten about and the Lemba people thought their sacred relic had been lost (Vickers, 2010). Parfitt says that according to oral traditions, the Lemba were among peoples who left Judea in biblical times and migrated through Yemen to east Africa, Ethiopia and beyond, bringing the ark with them (Vickers, 2010). One of the 10 commandments contained in the Ark of the Lord was that "whoever sheds the blood of man, by man shall his blood be shed, for God made man in his own image". This was the basis of the belief that the Njelele shrine should never be associated with the spilling of blood. In one of his writings, Ranger argued that Mwali was, ' fifthly,' a God of peace and plenty and never, in the knowledge of the natives, he has posed as a God of war (Terence O. Ranger, 1999).

According to a culturist informant, it was therefore, out of the attempt to resolve the religious and political contradictions that Mwali brought Mzilikazi and his Matabele in the equation. Hence, for the Matabele embracing the Mwali religion on their arrival was not capitulation, neither was it for the Malaba clan's acceptance of the Matabele rule, but it was a matter of taking life on its own terms. According to the Malaba orality, Mwali had plans for the nations, plans to prosper them, and give them hope and a future.

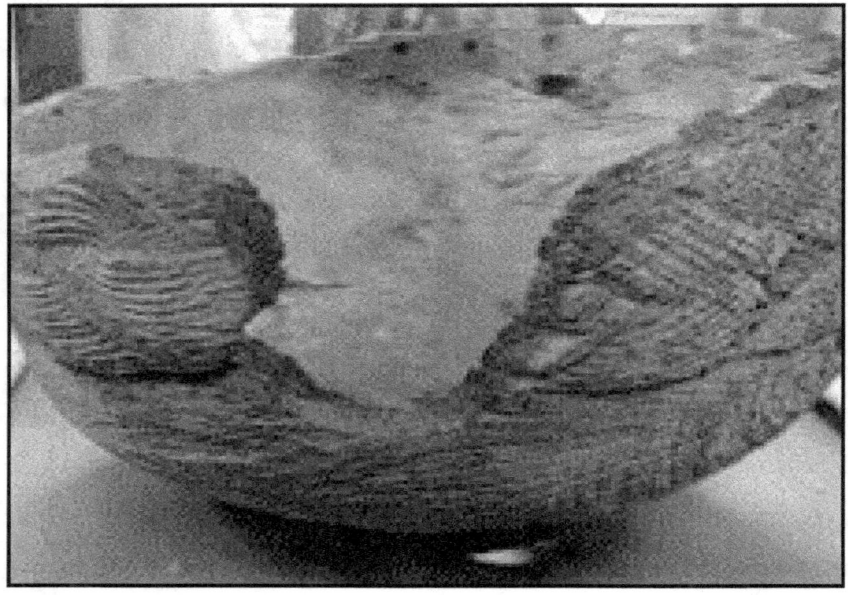

Figure 32. The wood object is thought to be oldest ever found in sub-Saharan Africa (Photo Courtesy of the BBC)

Correspondingly, Mzilikazi's establishment in the area was driven by his passionate dream to build a nation out of people of different ethnic formations, nevertheless, the Matabele, a fiercely warrior tribe, apparently had a divine role to play as Mwali's army in the safeguarding of the institution of the Mwali religion in general and the Njelele shrine (Malaba-informant, 2019). The informant argued that their theory was veritably backed by several historical events and manifestations. Before anything else, the Mwali priests and the rest of BaKalanga did not ultimately submit but acknowledged the Mzilikazi reigning over Bukalanga without further hostility. Secondly, in the face of the fact that the Mwali religion in general and the Njelele shrine conventionally detested war and the general shedding of blood, a new shrine of Dula, known as the shrine of the Red Axe or *Ilitshe lemikhonto or Ihloka elibomvu* emerged forthwith in the eastern Matopos. It was upon that materialization, that Mzilikazi appointed Mtuwane Dlodlo, one of his *abeZansi* representative to work together with some BaKalanga priests as one of the shrine guards.

The natural disagreements between the Mwali priests and Mzilikazi were in the main, hinged on Mzilikazi's spilling of blood at Ntabazinduna. Based on that fact, an agreement was permanently reached though that King Mzilikazi would, thenceforth, honour Mwali by sending black cattle to the shrine of the Red Axe annually. Although the Dula shrine site was traditionally under the custodianship of the Mufukwa family, part of the arrangement was that the powers of making war as well as of calling for peace bestowed upon a Dlodlo family. Mzilikazi's trust of the Dlodlos emanated from long back in the period when Mpangazitha Hadebe, a Dlodlo ancestor, was Mashobana's *inyanga* (traditional healer). Later, Mtuwane Dlodlo, was given the power of war as a continuation of the role of the Dlodlos in the Dula shrine and later succeeded by Queen Lozikeyi Dlodlo.

Mzilikazi's ultimate intimacy with the Mwali religion is depicted by Becker in his book*, Path of Blood* where he records that, Mzilikazi the Black Africa's Biggest

Conqueror and often equated to Napoleon, "regarded the Mwali priests with the deepest respect, and never attempting to injure them, and lavishing gifts regularly upon them" (Becker, 1966). The fact that often the Matabele heard Mwali speaking oracularly in the Matopos, was a signification that they did not only embrace the religion in their settlement there, but also became an embodiment of it, broadly not by choice. Most of the senior Matabele figures, from Mzilikazi, Lobengula, Mbiko, Dlodlo and others, became somehow part of the religious practices relating to Mwalism especially the rainmaking ceremonies. According to Bhebhe (2019), when asked whether the Nguni people who came with Mzilikazi from South Africa were ever part of the custodians of the Njelele shrine, Thenjiwe Lesabe responded, "one day the shrine said, "I want my son to come here." (Lesabe, 2019).

Then the people who were sent, the chiefs, asked "How shall we know who your son is?" He said, "Amongst the royal boys you will find one who has sores on his head." That was Hlangabese. The shrine did take some of Mzilikazi's children to its own. They became the children of the shrine like, Lobengula, Dlodlo and Hlangabese was. The mother of the late Chief Sigombe Mathema was also daughter of the shrine. These were both Khumalo boy and Khumalo girl but once possessed they became Thovhela, which is the totem of the shrine. Bhebhe, however, emphasizes that Lesabe clarified that, except for those possessed by the Njelele spirit, the AmaNdebele would naturally not get involved in the issues of custodianship. "First, it is not our culture. It's not our tradition" she said (Lesabe, 2019).

As of Mbiko kaMadlenya Masuku, Thomas writes about his 1865 encounter with him after he had been suffering from "dropsy of the abdomen for about two years" highlight the Matabele intimacy with the Mwali religion (Thomas, 1986). Thomas narrates that "when told that I could not help him, he wept pitifully, and said that 'Jolie', (meaning Mr John Moffat), had told him to seek *Jesu* (Jesus) and his guidance, and that *Jesu* had told him to go to consult the Amakalanga God (Mwali), and that the god's reply was that 'no one but Tomasi could cure him." Another unity of purpose is also practically illustrated in the fact that the Mwali priests like Lubimbi and Tshimba-Mbikwa, and traditional healers and magicians like Mpangana and his son Hhobhodo/Hhoba, enjoyed the privilege of being summoned periodically to the King's capital to give advice on important political, social, and religious matters.

....

Back to the story of Henry Potgieter uNdaleka-one bleak and glaring day in 1847, in the hills that later were known as the Malaba hills, it is assumed that Lobengula was demonstrating to Sara how to skin an animal, when suddenly, a stream of white men was spotted down below (Hall, 2013). It is told that upon seeing the Boers riding on horse backs, the Kalanga people in the area were heard exclaiming, *mmuka dzakabhabha bana!* (Animals are carrying babies on their backs)

"They are my people. The white people!" Sara exclaimed.

Legend has it that before that Sara and Lobengula had spotted old Mpangana Malaba having a chat with the Boers in the mountain. For some strange secret reason, which he would have found it hard to explain, Lobengula made no mention of Mpangana's presence in the Boer camp (Hall, 2013). It was all about trust. Trust that Mpangana's intentions were always to do the right thing and trust in Mpangana's mysterious ways of conducting business. In retrospect, also his father Mzilikazi, prevalently trusted the decisions or actions by Mpangana Malaba. Nevertheless, this was the time! Potgieter had apparently tracked Mzilikazi down and coming from the direction of the BaNgwato who he surprised and attacked.

What had ultimately enabled him to track down the Matabele was a report, brought down to Potchefstroom by Bechuana hunters, who had it from some natives, that a Dutch woman was being kept as a prisoner in the Malaba homestead and the Matabele were using her as a slave.

According to legend, at that moment Sara, the white Dutch girl, found herself stuck in an impossible long search for self-realization and identity. The presence in the Boers of Potgieter UNdaleka left her with multiple questions that jostled each other in her head, all of them seeking her attention. Did she belong to the Boers, her race? Or to Mkhaliphi Khumalo the Matabele warrior who picked her up after the battle at the foot of the Zoutpansberg mountains? Or to Nyumbakazi her Matabele caretaker mother? Or to *Ngwali* (Mpangana Malaba) the mystery man who gave her a home, refuge and took care of her and the young Lobengula? Or to prince Lobengula, her adopted son? For Sarah at that time, it was a situation in which a difficult choice had to be made.

Potgieter, uNdaleka, reached the Ndebele territory accompanied by a force of some Tswana helpers. His first tip over was on the Mncwazini Village that was situated on the upper Tshatshani river and run under Chief Mtotobi Mlilo. Here Potgieter raided herds of cattle before advancing inland towards the Sizinda villages where he also conducted an onslaught, raiding herds of cattle and thereafter heading deep towards the sunny delectable Matopo hills. When he reached the Mangwe Pass area where the Malaba people were settled and Mpangana's son Hhobhodo Malaba was newly appointed chief, it is alleged some Bakalanga women had spotted him upon the mountains, and informed Mpangana who instantly summoned prince Lobengula, briefing him before making him dash down and report Potgieter sightings at Mncumbatha's Enkantolo residence at the foot of the Matopo hills. (Fig. 33) is a picture of Hendrick Potgieter and his wife Susanna.

Figure 33. Picture of Hendrik Potgieter and his wife Susanna Maria Duvenage, courtesy of the Zousternburger

Lobengula reached Enkantolo and reported the presence of Potgieter in the vicinity to Mncumbatha as per arrangement with Mpangana Malaba.

"You have done well, Nkosana (prince)," Mncumbatha said, addressing Lobengula for the first time by a title of rank.

"Now the hour has come for you to be seen by the King, your father, who for many years has believed you to be dead. Come with me" (Hole, 1926).

When the two arrived at eSigodlweni, Marshall Hole pictures that Mncumbatha told king Mzilikazi that "because uNdaleka has now followed us here, Nkosi, and many Boers with him, this young man has seen them this very day and has run through the night to give us warning." Mzilikazi is believed to have feigned ignorance of Lobengula's existence on earth,

"And the young man, who is he?"

"Does the old bull know all the calves that he has sired? May there not be some that he has forgotten? King, it is your own son, the son of your wife Fulatha, whose father was Malindela, the Swazi chief."

The account state that Mzilikazi was visibly stunned. He muttered, looked this way and that and took several pinches of snuff before he spoke again.

"Where has he been hiding all this time?" Mzilikazi pretended.

"King, when you came back from the Great River your heart was black, and I feared you would have him killed. All these years therefore I have kept him in a secret place. But if I have done wrong kill him now, and kill me also, my father!"

It is outlined Mzilikazi then turned to Mbiko Masuku, one of the chiefs who were present and spoke.

"Mbiko, this shall be your business. Call out your impi at once. This young man shall go with you and guide you to the Boers. If he fails you will strangle him, but if he fights well and bloods his assegai, I will take him back as my son. Be off at once, for UNdaleka moves quickly, and thinks he will catch us asleep."

Apparently, the Boers of Hendrik Potgieter were certain that Mpangana would be against the Ndebeles of Mzilikazi because from their prerogative, Mpangana Malaba perceived the Matabele as occupiers of the land of Bukalanga, and old Mpangana's wish was to have both parties destroyed. Some of our Malaba informants appeared reluctant in dismissing the claim, insisting that there was no reason why Mpangana could not have used his tjathiyane/sathiyane magic to fend away the marauding Boers of Potgieter, except that he was strategically hoping that the circumstances could provide an opportunity to drive the Matabele out of the land of BuKalanaga. Based on that belief too, it is argued Potgieter uNdaleka consulted Mpangana on how to attack Mzilikazi since Mpangana had inside information. However, it was a miscalculation that would lead to the demise of Potgieter's men.

In this regard, Lobengula had been handed to Mbiko Masuku, the expectation would have been that he was going to be enrolled in the Zwangendaba regiment. The Malaba oral narrations mentions that Tshada Malaba, who earlier on had been enrolled in the Amahlokohloko regiment as a guarantee for Lobengula's safe stay in the Malaba homestead, reported to his father Mpangana about the conscription of Lobengula in the Amahlokohloko regiment geared to face uNdaleka's Boer army. Amahlokohloko regiment popularly known as Inyoniyamahlanga, (the weaver bird) was led by Mbambelele Hlabangane and stationed not far from the original kraal, below the junction of the Umguza and Khoce rivers.

Potgieter second guessed Mpangana's languish for the freedom of Bukalanga and was aiming at taking advantage of it. Nevertheless, like a foe he real was,

Mpangana was gathering strategic intelligence about Potgieter himself and passing it to the Matabele camp through the young prince Lobengula. The battle against uNdaleka was led by Mbiko kaMadlenya's Zwangendaba regiment. Mbiko is declared to have fought valiantly earning himself praises as

Umazembazemba wakithi omnyama

Owazemba ozingeni, wazemba ngomdikadika

Kwanuka umswane ka Ndaleka (The warrior who destroyed Potgieter's marauding army)

In the battle against Potgieter uNdaleka, young Lobengula fought heroically and blooded his assegai and by so doing, earning his kingship from his father Mzilikazi. After the heroics Mzilikazi consequently allowed Mbiko Masuku to marry his daughter Zinkabi. In June 1866 Mbiko Masuku is declared to have paid twelve hundred cattle to Mzilikazi and married Zinkabi, a fair and favourite daughter of the king. Potgieter's Boer army was defeated and retreated south. This consequently led to a peace treaty later signed between Potgieter and Mzilikazi on 8 January 1853. Part of the agreement was to ban the smuggling of weapons to both Matabeleland and the Transvaal.

After the encounter with his father Mzilikazi, Lobengula did not return to the Malaba homestead. Instead, he was sent to temporarily stay under Gwabalanda Mathe at KweSikhulu. Gwabalanda Mathe was under instructions to keep Lobengula preoccupied and herding cattle, which was already a task Lobengula would perform with expertise. The Malaba people referred to him as *tjiyisana tjakalisa* (a skilled herd boy). The name Tjakalisa (Tshakalisa) was later conferred to his son Sintinga. At KweSikhulu, to start with, he was first given the lighter responsibility of looking after the calves and later the bigger responsibility of herding the grown-up cattle.

Sara Liebenberg died of a snake bite in the Matopo hills and had no children when she died. As a matter of fact, through Sara, both the Ndebele nation in general and the Malaba clan became one of the pioneer authentic experiments in racial harmony in Southern Africa.

The frequently visitations to Mzilikazi's palace on healing and advisory mission, earned Mpangana a wife in return of his service. Despite that this spectacle still puzzle the Malaba oral historians for the reasons that neither the wife nor the children borne in the kraal by Mpangana were ever identified.

The narrative regarding the incident is still circulated just as an unverified account although there is a hazy belief in some circles that his children could be some section of the Jahunda people known now as the Moyo Nhliziyo whose totems that go like, *"ENcube eBalugwe Mvumi Mvumi zehore Bagudu. Bembe Bagudu baNjelele Tombo lisingapoteleki Lingapoteleka konaya mvimbi"* are closely like those of the Malaba people. An interview with some of the Moyo Nhliziyos reveal that their forefather emphasised their Ncube background. Nevertheless, the Ndebele continued to live shoulder to shoulder with the BaKalanga as illustrated by the map in figure 34.

As indicated earlier on, Mzilikazi had sought Mpangana's expertise in magical defence in case of a marauding Dingani Zulu pursuing him. Dingane son of Senzangakhona had been born in 1795 to Chief Senzangakhona. Dingane's mother Mpikase was Mlilela Ngobese's daughter and she was also the sixth wife of Senzangakhona. With the help of his half-brother Mhlangana and servant Mbopha, Dingani assassinated his brother Shaka Zulu on the 22nd of September 1828 to become king of the Zulu nation.

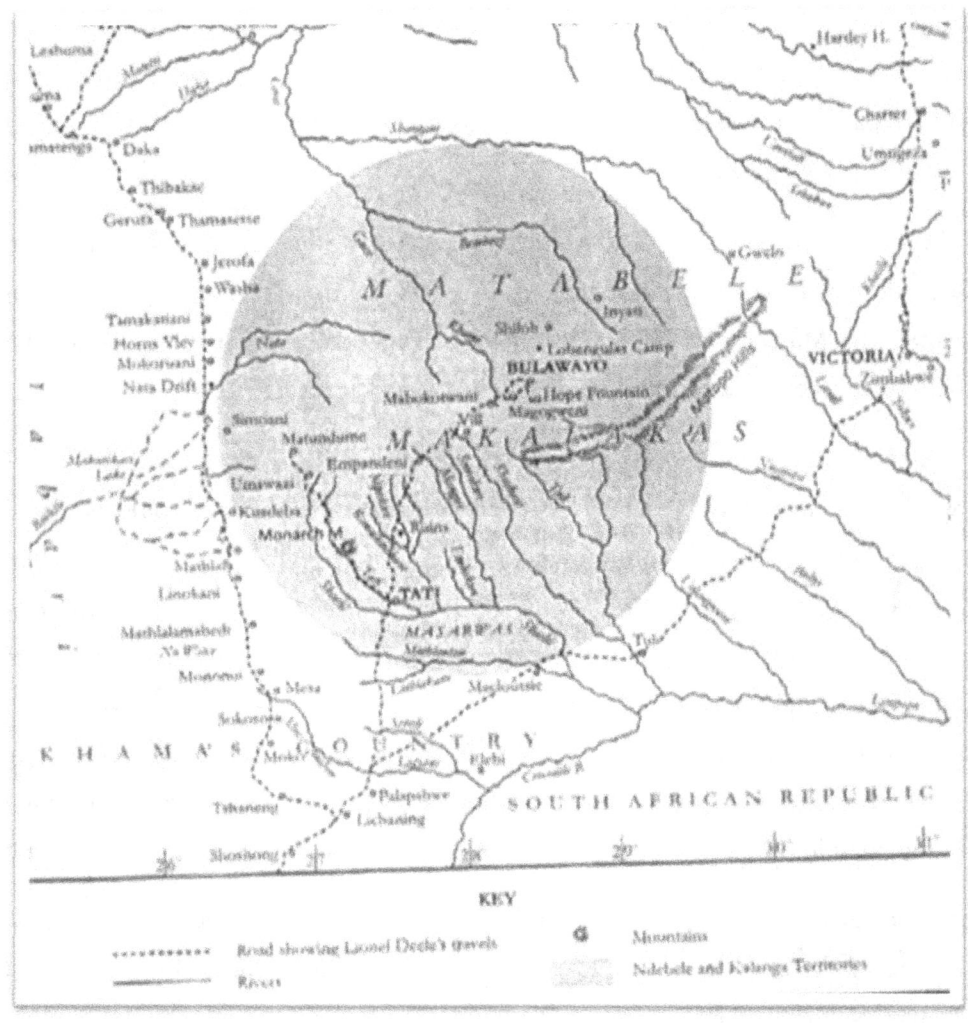

Figure 34. Pre-colonial Map showing indicating Kalanga and Ndebele areas. Source; University of Rochester Press

4,5. The Malaba Traditional Leadership

At their Bukalanga settlement, Mpangana was still in possession of both the traditional and religious responsibilities of the Malaba clan. According to legend the medicine bag, '*gobhodo lemiti*' had amongst its contents, two knobkerries (*swimbo*). The two knobkerries symbolized legitimacy of a traditional leader's authority. Only a divinely chosen Malaba traditional leader was authorized to strike the knobkerries against each other (*loba nlayo - ukutshaya umthetho*), before making a judgment that involved or would have repercussions on the clan. Incontestably, the legitimate traditional leader of the clan was Tshibi or his elder son, of which both were not available at some point in time. Therefore, despite Mpangana being a national figure and a *nkumbudzi* (advisor) to King Mzilikazi, he was more of an appointed than a divinely chosen traditional leader of the clan as per religious custom. The instructions from the Great Luvhimbi to Mpangana in the aftermaths of the Maneledzi pool contest was that Mpangana should exercise all his authority against the clan but at no time should he ritually put the two knobkerries into use *(ukutshaya umthetho/loba nlayo)*. He was to remain just as their custodian until the time when Tshibi had reached the age of maturity permissive to take over the clan leadership as per the ancient culture of the Malaba people.

Duly, determined to revive the house of Tshibi, and to follow the clan traditions, Mpangana had instructed one of his sons Hadledzi, to embark on a long journey to find a woman amongst the Phuthi people of the BaBirwa or Tswana origin. The woman may have been from amongst the Muleya Phuthis at Siyoka or just lived amongst the Babirwa people at Maribeha and at the basin of the Tshatshane river. She is said to have been a direct descendant of Khwadalala, a BaBirwa leader. Hadledzi embarked on an arduous journey and came back with a woman. There has been several arguments and counter arguments on the choice of MaPhuthi.

Some argue it was more by design than by accident. MaPhuthi may have been a descendant of the Siyokas, who in turn, were evidently descendants of Sioka of the ancient Bukusu clan. Upon the availability of MaPhuthi, it was agreed that the house of Kuyani in its capacity as the second senior house of the Malaba clan was to look after the woman MaPhuthi to enable the recreation and continuation of the Mwali-chosen house of Tshibi.

The agreement was based and or done in accordance with the Malaba traditional norms and customs and not before long, Mpangana's aspiration came to fruition. A son of Tshibi Malaba was born. Moyo (2018), in his Midlands State University research thesis entitled *A Social and Cultural History of The People Under Chief Malaba (Matobo District) 1890-1980*, makes an attempted reference to the incident (albeit with a number of mixed-up facts) as he writes, that Mpangana had seen the need to follow the traditions. He sent Hadledzi to go and look for a woman. "(Tshoko) Hadledzi brought a woman, BaPhuthi of the Tswana origin" and old Mpangana asked his son Kuyani to look after his brother's widow. As a result, it led to the birth of (Tshidada) Tshidada" (Moyo, 2018, p26). Tradition spells out that there was nothing untoward in the circumstances because widow inheritance was a custom common with the Luhyia (Bukusu) people in general and the Malaba clan. Furthermore, according to ancient Jewish law, *Halaka*, a man must marry the widow of his childless brother to maintain the brother's line. This Levirate marriage also had subtle similarities with the Malaba customs of widow inheritance.

Mpangana' occupation as a renowned traditional healer and a nkumbudzi (advisor) in the Mzilikazi's kraal highlighted him in the form of a habitual nomad because of his numerous regular mission trips. When Tshidada was born in 1845, Mpangana was elsewhere and on that account, it was chief Hhobhodo/Hhoba who made an appearance on the day. Oral traditions have it that it was in exultation that Hhobhodo/Hhoba named him Tshidada, a name expressing some exhilaration over young Tshidada's birth. As an interview with old Tshemane indicated, Hhobhodo/Hhoba was saying *"Ndodada ndengumba yomfowethu yamuka nasi"* (I am so pleased by my brother's house that have been revived). Once more, through Tshidada, the Malaba legacy was revived and once again, through a process of recreation. Yet, as per custom, a decree was issued clarifying to every member of the Malaba clan that Tshidada (Tshidada) was none other than the son of Tshibi born to serve as a continuation of the ancient *Wele* Malaba legacy.

As Mpangana was reaching advanced age, of which oral traditions adds that the old age was coupled with some sort of early dementia, circumstances called that he passed the medicine bag *"Gobhodo lemiti"* to his older son Hhobhodo/Hhoba, to lead the clan. Hhobhodo/Hhoba, although from third house, had to take over the power because as the oldest of the boys he had been Mpangana's apprentice and had learnt and inherited Mpangana' astute and shrewdness in as far as traditional medicine practices and religious custodianship was concerned. After some thorough traditional rituals, Hhobhodo/Hhoba assumed seniority of the clan. If Marshall Hole's testimony is anything to go by, old Mpangana Malaba died in 1847. According to the Malaba orality, he is buried in a the Malaba mountains cave in Gurumane Nkalange area of Marula, in the *Bulilima gwa Mengwe* (Mangwe) district. Although in his historical novel, some oral traditionalists contend that Mpangana was shot by the Boers of Hendrik Potgieter, UNdaleka, during the Mzilikazi-Boer battles, the Malaba oral traditions demonstrate that old Mpangana died of natural causes in Marula at around the age of 77 and is buried on the Malaba mountains in Gurumane.

Coupling it with the chieftaincy trust upon him by Mzilikazi, Hhobhodo/Hhoba finally takes full control of the Malaba clan, notwithstanding, with notable family disputes. Despite Hhobhodo/Hhoba being a powerful man through his appointment to the role of high chief and King Mzilikazi advisor, his assumption of the Malaba traditional leadership was just on placeholder basis. His role was equitable to just safeguarding the tradition until that time when Tshidada had reached the age of maturity fit enough to run the clan. Unlike Hhobhodo/Hhoba's chieftaincy, which was an accolade from King Mzilikazi for his and his father's brave competitiveness and unparalleled skills in traditional medicine passed to him by his father Mpangana, Tshibi's position was not hereditary but a divine appointment.

An appointment by Mwali to lead, and lead beyond the mere clan functionalities but dutifully transcending to a national and international commitment. Hhobhodo/Hhoba's reign was going to cover the whole of the Marula area and yonder to other areas in the land of BaKalanga, including the Mangwe Pass, which fundamentally made him the frontier guard or a sentinel responsible for admissions into the Ndebele kingdom for both King Mzilikazi and King Lobengula thereafter. As such, the Ndebele State was organized into regiments and villages, which were led into battle by chiefs and military commanders, therefore, with that role, chief Hhobhodo/Hhoba effectively assumed the role of military village commander. This led to villagers such as the Malaba to be known as *izihlabamkhosi* or whistle-blowers.

………………………..

On a parallel episode regarding the Bango clan, when the Matabele took over the Kingdom of Bukalanga, Mzilikazi did not forfeit Bangojena's chieftaincy in the Lupane area, however, still, Bango and his clan refused the decision of resettling them in the Lupane area. For fear of losing their chieftainship in Lupane, which was then a Ndebele dominated area they instead requested that they be accommodated among the mainly BaKalanga speakers (Dube, 2015). In the Gurumane, Nkalange Marula area, Hhobhodo/Hhoba found himself sharing the jurisdiction with the Bango Dube clan who had Nimahamingo Tshilise Dube, son of Bangojena, as chief. Before long Nimahamingo Tshilise was killed by the Swazi and wherefore succeeded as chief by Tshilale or Tshilase. At first Bango was not recognized as chief as he was outside his chieftain jurisdiction of Lupane but after he had established himself in the Marula area, Chief Hhobhodo/Hhoba Malaba and other BaKalanga chiefs later deliberated with the district commissioner to institute Tshilale Bango as chief in the neighbouring area.

As precedingly indicated, the relationship between the Bango and the Malaba was perceived to be of significance and was carefully crafted and maintained through an alliance of intermarriages. Therefore, in a move that was reminiscent of the Mpangana-Bangojena deal of the past years where Mpangana gave his daughter to Nimahamingo Tshilise Bango, Chief Hhobhodo Malaba also gave his first daughter to Tshilale Bango as wife. The culture of that alliance was maintained and sustained as Chief Ntelela Malaba also gave his daughter as wife to Jeremiah Ngugama Bango, the son of Nsimbi (Fig 35). Chief Tshilale was succeeded by Kangangwani, but when Kangangwani died, the heir, Nsimbi, was still too young to take over the role leading to Habangana becoming regent. Habangana's brother Gulumbalayi took over from him later succeeded by Tawunhla. Nsimbi Bango later took over from Tawunhla to become chief until he was succeeded in 1924, by Mbubi who acted for Ngugama, the heir.

Figure 35. Chief Ngugama Bango; photo courtesy of Werbner, 1991

4,6. The Last Days of King Mzilikazi

It was after his favourite wife Loziba died in 1861 that Mzilikazi left Inyathi, moving inland to a new great place that he called Mhlahlandlela, named after his previous stronghold. These were hard times for king Mzilikazi and his Ndebele nation as they endured a great drought and an outbreak of smallpox and measles. Lung-sickness, which the native Blacks believed was brought in by the infected cattle of missionaries and hunters, killed off the Matabele cattle. Suffice in some period, strife between contesting groups led to civil war that weakened the Ndebele Empire. Through its shrine priests like Npininga Lubimbi, Njelele was consulted by King Mzilikazi as per custom and Mwali showed mercy to His people. It is chronicled that in the rain season of 1863, prosperity returned to Matabeleland. Rains fell, harvests were plentiful, and the raiding Matabele regiments were returning with large herds of cattle.

………………………………..

It was 27 years since Mpangana Malaba had died and chief Hhobhodo/Hhoba had succeeded him thereby inheriting the holistic Malaba legacy. One strange day a messenger came from Mzilikazi to Chief Hhobhodo/Hhoba informing him that he and probably other *inyangas* (traditional healers) were being summoned at the King's kraal. Thoughts raced through Hhobhodo's mind, *'he has fallen ill yet again! Its old age.'* In truth, there was nothing untoward about chief Hhobhodo being summoned at the King's kraal. As Hole also illustrated, "Far and wide as their ravages extended there was one locality which Mzilikazi and his people treated with profound respect, and into which only those who had urgent need of super-human help were bold enough to venture. Anyone with none of the superstitions of the tough Matabele, cannot shake off a feeling of awe amid the grim solitudes of the Matopo mountains, which stretch for fifty miles from east to west like a vast jagged scar across the face of the country. This vague being had, from time immemorial, been venerated, under the name of Mwali, by the Makalanga tribes, who believed it to possess the power of causing sickness and death; of controlling the weather; of arranging the success or failure of the crops, and of bringing about victory or defeat in battle. To woo the favour of the Spirit and to consult it in domestic or national crises they had for generations made a practice of visiting the wizard's cave at Njelele in the Matopo hills.

Their profession of intermediary was a lucrative and influential one. The priests, wizards, or prophets—there is no English word which exactly fits them, but they were known to the natives as *Ziwosana*—were a close corporation of men of exceptional ability and intelligence chosen from special families, and before they were deemed competent to practice their art, they had to undergo a long course of probation and training. Generally, they were skilful ventriloquists with an intimate knowledge of medicinal herbs, poisons, and remedies, and were shrewd observers of the weather" (Hole, 1926). Therefore, together with some priests and the Matabele *izanuses* (masters of the healing profession), Mpangana Malaba was amongst those consulted on occasions including the appointment of a successor to the chieftainship (Thomas, 1986).

In his writings Thomas, also highlights that to increase his influence and the people's awe of him, Mpangana had trained Hhobhodo/Hhoba, his apprentice son, to be a successor rain doctor. In evidently referring to the 37-year-old Hhobhodo/Hhoba who had succeeded Mpangana in 1847, Thomas (1871), records that "one of these young men (Hhobhodo Malaba), covered all over with ornaments, which consist of buttons, (Mapela and Mapungubwe-type) green glass beads, bangles, shells, and various kinds of charms, entering a village or town so overawes and allures the inhabitants, that they are soon entirely in his power. That his favour may be secure, presents are heaped upon him, while in turn, finding that he has become the real lord of the place, does as he like, - commands, orders, sends, or calls whomsoever he pleases, and even eats their food without scruple. A night dance and feasting complete the entertainment and the visit" (Thomas, 1986). On the royal Malaba family, Thomas also emphasizes that if the rain doctors were of good service to Mzilikazi, they were treated like royalty.

Thereafter, Mzilikazi had a deep respect for Mwali priests, he "… never attempted to hurt them and contributed his annual offering of black cattle to Mwali, the great god, speaking oracularly in the Matopos. In fact, the *aMakalanga* magicians enjoyed the privilege of being summoned periodically to the king's palace to give advice on important religious matters" (Becker, 1966). Such was the significance of Mpangana Malaba's role in the Ndebele Kingdom and establishment.

Ensuring, Chief Hhobhodo snatched his *gobhodo lemiti* (medicine bag), promptly throwing it over his squared broad shoulders and quick as a flash, headed towards Ingama village near Bulawayo. His arrival was met with a little surprise because although Mzilikazi lay sickly in his soft hide mat, unlike on most occasions, did not seem to necessarily require Chief Hhobhodo's medicinal services. In point of fact king Mzilikazi's hopes and trust had been redirected to the white doctors, particularly the Inyathi mission party that consisted of J. S. Moffat and his wife, William Sykes, and Doctor Thomas Morgan Thomas. Although it was a rivalry that the white doctors had clearly won, in his book *Eleven Years in Central South Africa*, Thomas Morgan still expressed his utter dislike of the Malaba people whom he described as deceitful. Nevertheless, on this day Mzilikazi just sought a candid chat and chat they did.

Legend say that King Mzilikazi always acknowledged the Malaba clan for the period crown prince Lobengula lived amongst the Malaba people. Hhobhodo too had always been proud of the role he played in the welfare of young Lobengula in the period he was in the Malaba homestead. Though, king Mzilikazi's take on the whole issue was sometimes obscure and therefore, always unpredictable, it was particularly this unpredictability that made the relationship complicated. It was a complication emanating from the fact that such a relationship could easily turn out that someone is guilty of a crime, and hence, in case of a brawl, given the fundamental power Mzilikazi possessed over Hhobhodo, there was always going to be one underdog. Basically, both understood that and the distinct individual powers that they possessed in their own spaces. Their relationship, good as it appeared, was also bordering on a game of thrones and it had always been the case right from the time when old Mpangana was still alive. In essence, for many Matabele chiefs, with king Mzilikazi it was always a life of balance between trust in natural rationale and fear of a moment of madness.

Despite the uneasiness between the two figures, Mzilikazi confided in chief Hhobhodo that given his age, he was naturally preparing for a future leader. The story goes that when King Mzilikazi started acknowledging his advanced age as well as his health issues, he sincerely begun preparing for the nation's life after he was gone. By virtue of having momentarily looked after the young Lobengula, it was just proper that Mzilikazi had a word with chief Hhobhodo at personal level. The two had a candid discussion that led to Mzilikazi asking chief Hhobhodo about who was the heir-apparent in the Malaba clan leadership. When chief Hhobhodo mentioned Tshidada, it is reported Mzilikazi asked,

"Is he your first-born son"?

"Not at all", replied Chief Hhobhodo.

"Therefore, why is he inheriting the chieftaincy"? Wondered King Mzilikazi.

Chief Hhobhodo then took that opportunity to explain the Malaba chieftaincy conundrum. According to oral traditions Mzilikazi was puzzled that young Tshidada was serving in the Ndebele army at his age. Tshidada's brother

Hhabanahe had also been conscripted in the army with him so that he could keep an eye on him. Tradition has it that King Mzilikazi was stunned by the fact that the young Tshidada with such an influential traditional role coming his way, was saving in the army. He was dumbfounded by both the fact that Tshidada was too young to be conscripted in the army as well as based on being heir to the throne. The reason for that decision was later revealed. Tshidada was conscripted into the army as a way of giving him some sanctuary from a threat that was arising from amongst some of the clan members.

Vultures were hovering over the head of the young Tshidada Malaba. It could have been some power struggle from those harbouring some leadership ambitions or just pure envy of the boy who was to take over the paramount Malaba throne, with some, questioning his authenticity, a trend that happens in every society. A group of pretender hunters had earlier on made a murder attempt on the young Tshidada hence, he was sent to join the army to be away from the domestic threat. They had pretended to be going out hunting with the intention of killing the young man and falsely report him as having been a victim of a marauding lion.

The plan was subsequently foiled. It was then suggested Tshidada be conscripted in the Matabele army at an early age not only for the rationale of having him gain military discipline, but primarily for protection, before he took over the Malaba chieftaincy baton stick. King Mzilikazi's worst fears was that young Tshidada could be harmed, captured or, at worse, killed in some battles. Therefore, upon learning that Tshidada was in line to the Malaba clan throne, Mzilikazi used the powers vested in him to veto the command and rationale in keeping Tshidada in the army. Young Tshidada was ultimately relieved of his army duties and was brought home amid some delays.

4,7. Finding Tshidada Malaba

The years passed at a breath-taking pace, and a period came that the Malaba clan had to resuscitate and re-enact the house of Tshibi to its social and religious position as the senior house. Three messengers provided by king Mzilikazi were immediately dispatched in search of Tshidada the young army recruit. Legend has it that the search was arduous, stretching all the way from Marula to Manyikaland and further beyond, until word was sent that Tshidada was in the Ndebele regiment operating somewhere towards the Chilimanzi (Chirumanzu) area at that time (Fig. 48). Tshidada's Ndebele regiment was led by Mpondo one of Mzilikazi's confidantes and was stationed at Chilimanzu (Chirumanzu) for the purposes of aiding Chizema of the Chirumanzu dynasty who had an unsuccessful attempt to win a new land for himself in southern Buhera. Chizema son of Chirumanzu the Govera ruler, who earlier on had been so prominent in raids on the Ndebele, had to surrender to Mzilikazi in 1857 and from then until 1889 became a strong ally of the Ndebele (Beach, 1974).

The delegation reached the area and approached the regiment induna and informed him of the message from the king. The messengers were to find this lanky and seemingly down to earth young man and wondered why the king wanted him back so urgently. Nevertheless, tradition say that because the delegation sent was exclusively a Ndebele one who had never seen Tshidada's person before, rather at first instance said to have instead brought his brother Hhabanabe the son of Kuyani, and only for chief Hhobhodo to take it upon himself to embark on a journey to go find Tshidada.

Therefore, Tshidada was granted military leave in about 1867 and decommissioned to go attend to the clan commitments. He was leaving all in the hands of Chief Hhobhodo Malaba the then holder of the Malaba senior traditional leadership to arbitrate on the question of the pending Malaba traditional leadership. Chief Hhobhodo had thought that the time was right and deemed it fit to re-install the clan leadership to the house of Tshibi. Prior to the above events, chief Hhobhodo had arranged an extraordinary meeting with all the Malaba houses to ponder the issue of leadership and the way forward. It was during those talks that chief Hhobhodo is alleged to have informed Tshidada of his intention to hand the leadership role back to the Tshibi house, and to Tshidada himself, on account of him (Tshidada) as the legitimate heir apparent to the Malaba clan traditional and spiritual leadership. The ceremony to install Tshidada as Chief Malaba was held, and chieftaincy conferred. The ceremony of conferring Tshidada as chief involved the spreading of a softened lion skin whereby the newly installed chief was left to sit on it as he was assuming the Malaba clan traditional leadership.

Tshidada and Hhobhodo then reached at a compromise package that called attention to the fact that the new chief Tshidada considered chief Hhobhodo as his 'father' therefore proportionately he was not going to reign over the entire land and leaving Hhobhodo commanding no jurisdiction after he had led the clan with dignity for all the years gone by. It is maintained that the proposal received the blessings of king Mzilikazi too and therefore, chief Hhobhodo was afforded the remaining area of Nkalange towards Marula, Mangwe to reign over. The phenomenal situation resulted in two Malaba brothers holding two chieftaincies in two different areas. This was not a common occurrence save for the few circumstances whereby clans like those of the Ndiweni which Mzilikazi had strategically planted as chiefs in several different areas for security reasons. As opposed to popular belief in scholarly writings that Mzilikazi's mother was Nompethu KaZwide Nxumalo, Mzilikazi's mother was Cikose Ndiweni. The

Ndiweni chiefs scattered in many parts of Matabeleland now are Mzilikazi uncles originally there to safeguard the tradition and protect the king, including chief Mpini Ndiweni who was to circumstantially have the Hhobhodo Malaba's as his subject.

It was a done deal, leading to the Malaba people producing two chiefs, a phenomenon that is in existence to this day. The two Malaba chieftaincy encompassed the Hhobhodo Malaba chieftaincy situated in the Marula area of Mangwe and the Tshibi Malaba chieftaincy that existed and still exist in the vicinity of the Matobo district. The Mangwe chieftaincy had been endowed upon to Hhobhodo Malaba by king Mzilikazi as an honorarium after Hhobhodo's father, Mpangana Malaba had performed some magical dramatics before and in the process pleasing king Mzilikazi. Hhobhodo Malaba's bestowal is revered for its uniqueness as the first and only non-Nguni chief office ever appointment by King Mzilikazi at his earliest period of rule. In different circumstances, the Tshibi Malaba chieftaincy came about through a reversal of role from the stopgap house of Hhobhodo/Hhoba Malaba onto the senior and legitimate house of Tshibi Malaba.

For nearly forty-seven years, the third house of Mpangana Malaba, had the retention of the Malaba clan leadership as a place holder before Hhobhodo/Hhoba, an apprentice of Mpangana who had been accredited with, inter alia, the technical knowhow on the use of the deadly *tjathiyane/isathiyane* concoction, handed it back to the senior house of Tshibi via Tshidada. The use of *tjathiyane/isathiyane* as an instrument of both defence and attack did not end with the Mpangana era but Hhobhodo/Hhoba had perfected the art of its use. This is how it resurfaced once again later in the period when Hhobhodo/Hhoba was chief. Nyathi (2000) writes in his book, *Alvord Mabena, the Man and His Roots,* that Sicwayiza Mabhena

"Of the proud Insukamini used to talk about scald marks on his thighs. Men from his village plus some from Imbizo were sent in a raid. King Lobengula Khumalo advised them not to attack chief Malaba people who lived among the Kalanga to the south of the Ndebele state. His ancestors had come from Vendaland, across the Limpopo River. It was them who brought the Njelele shrine into Zimbabwe" (Nyathi, 2000).

Figure 72 is a sketchy art on the wall of Hhobhodo school showing chief Hhobhodo brewing tjathiyani/isathiyane. King Lobengula Khumalo's men initially obeyed the order and went to raid yonder on the baTswana. Their raid was successful, and they brought back several heads of cattle and young girls. On their way back, they made temporary shelters with the intention of milking the wet cows. Thereafter, they needed to prepare a delicious dish of *tjathiyane*/isathiyane. The dish is a mixture of boiled milk and sorghum meal. The men from Imbizo and Insukamini saw granaries in the rocks. These belonged to chief Malaba's people. Without permission, the returning *amabutho* (regiment) went to take sorghum from the granaries perched on rocks. They went ahead and prepared *tjathiyane/isathiyane*.

Hell broke loose. Suddenly, the boiling *tjathiyane/isathiyane* bizarrely ran amok against the men as it landed on their bodies and scalding them. Some sought refuge in pools of water not as soon as they would resurface, the *tjathiyane/isathiyane* landed on them in a demented situation. This is how Sicwayiza Mabhena got the scald marks that he often talked about. As a gesture to remove the spell, King Lobengula Khumalo is cited to have paid a large herd of cattle to chief Malaba. Cattle payments were common especially in relation to the members of *Umphakathi* (the King's Advisory Council).

Gatsheni, (2008) notes that the members of *umphakathi* were the richest as they were given cattle by the king to make sure they did not constitute a threat to the king. The royalty received reflected authority from the king (Gatsheni, 2008). This is the *tjathiyane/isathiyane* sika Malaba story acknowledged among the Matabele communities. Sicwayiza Mabhena used to say, when swearing, *"Ngingalumba ngani ngingeMalaba?* (What can I do since I do not possess the Malaba magic?)" He was referring to his helplessness against Chief Malaba's magical concoction of *tjathiyane/isathiyane*" (Nyathi, 2000). When it was time to take his place as a chief, Tshidada relocated from Marula to occupy his Matopo area jurisdiction. For starters he instead went to live amongst his mother's Babirwa people along the Shashane river towards the Mtshelanyemba area of Kezi.

The village was given the name Malaba indicating that he was already a chief by the time he settled there. Later a dip tank was constructed in Tshidada's former Shashane home and it's still known as *'kudibha laka Malaba'* (Malaba dip tank area) named after him. Although Tshidada was installed as chief before Lobengula was anointed king, in the 1870s, he stayed behind amongst his mother's Babirwa people until around 1899 when, in the sequel, he then had some kinfolks accredited under his arbitration and eventually relocating and hereafter establishing his new Malaba native located close to the Nyahongwe (Nyashongwe) area of Kezi on a place currently known as the Malaba ward.

Chief Tshidada Malaba's reign covered one of the largest *ntunnu/isigaba* ever to be allocated to an individual chief in the Ndebele kingdom. His jurisdiction was to stretch from the contemporary Bidi, Mayobhodo, Bango area and all the way to the Shashe river, incorporating various wards and villages amongst them, Shashane, Malundu, Beula, Seula, Tshelanyemba, Malaba, Sigangatsha, Mfila and Mazwi (Fig, 36). The Chief Bidi area was originally a Malaba jurisdiction until the 8th of February 1923 when it was divided through the *Trebhalayini* (Tribal Demarcation Line Road) to demarcate the other side to chief Bidi Ndiweni who had left the chief Mpini area to settle in the Matopo area. The Mayobhodo area was also transitionally a Tshidada Malaba jurisdiction only apportioned to Hhobhodo Malaba to enable a continuation of his Mzilikazi appointed chieftaincy.

The Bango area was designated to Nimahamingo Tshilise Dube to uphold the Bangojena chieftaincy. Including chief Tshidada and Hhobhodo Malaba, one of our informants mentioned that all together there were currently six chiefs who were descendants of Dzibagulu-levula in Zimbabwe. Most of them were found amongst the descendants of Kaluba and Nyamukoko who had migrated into the contemporary Mashonaland territories.

After the installation of Tshidada, every Malaba clan member was provided with a decree to pay reverence, appreciation, and respect to Tshidada as the rightful bona fide cultural and traditional leader of the Malaba people. This was meant for the smooth transfer of clan seniority from the Hhobhodo to the Tshibi house. To assist in achieving that, the emphasis was that every clan member was to take cognizance that Tshidada was not only the ultimate authority but also a *de facto* son of the Mwali chosen house of Tshibi Malaba.

Tshibi had been divinely chosen at Maneledzi pool incident in VhuVenda, and the installation of Tshidada was an appropriation of the ancient Malaba legacy that stretched as far back to the ancient era of *Wele* Malaba. Therefore, it was against that backdrop that an instruction was issued to the effect that the integrated Malaba houses shall thenceforth swear allegiance (*'funga'*) to the new Malaba name.

Cheekily as it sounded, it was to be, because it was after that point that every Malaba person, be it from the house of Tshibi, Kuyani, Hhobhodo/Hhoba, Hhadledzi, Tshada, Mkhubazi, Lungombe, Bhule, Manusa, Tihhani or Manyele, when trying to prove the validity of any issue or case, would swear by "*Malaba or BaMalaba tjose*". It became a norm amongst the clan. The '*BaMalaba*' appellation was not a new creation but an evolution of the primeval 'BaMalaba' label that in the prehistoric era referred to 'those of Malaba'. The 'BaMalaba' designate did not only promote unification amongst the Malaba houses but also fortified Tshidada's position as the legitimate traditional leader of the integrated Malaba houses that collectively constituted an august Royal Malaba Family.

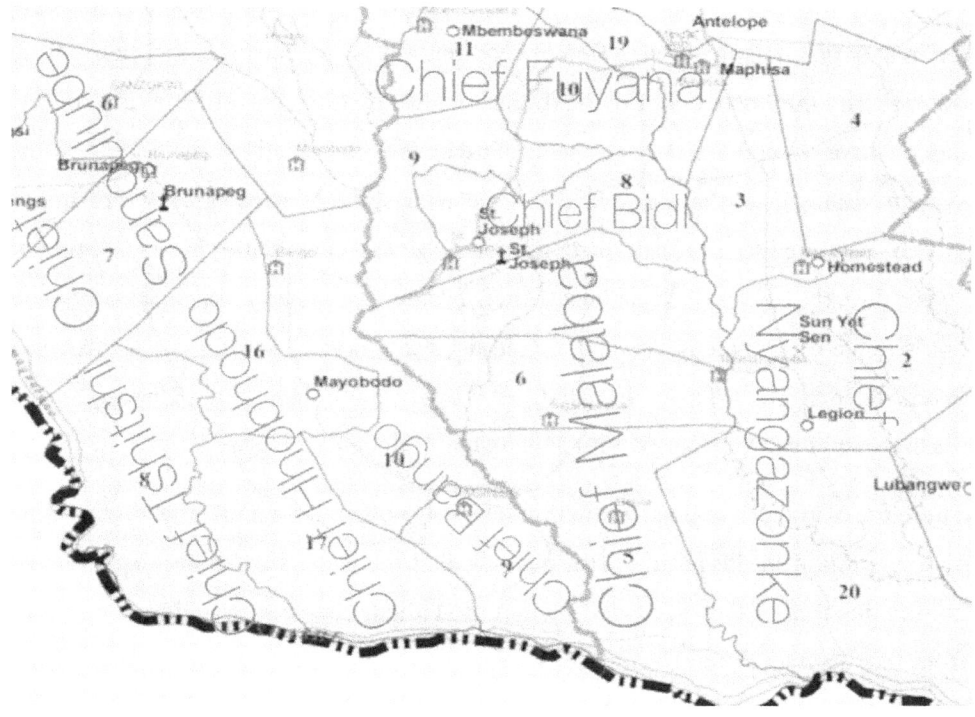

Figure 36. Map showing the jurisdiction of Chief Malaba & Chief Hhobhodo (Wards, 5, 6, 7' respectively). Adapted from Matabeleland South province https://www.humanitarianresponse.info/sites/www.humanitarianresponse.info/files/ZWE_MatSouth_Province_A0_v1.pdf

According to Tshemane narration, conventionally, in another clan setup, Kuyani, as older boy from the second house, could have been handed down the legacy from Mpangana, nonetheless, the Malaba royalty was not by its own nature capable of being inherited in conventional ways. This was on the grounds that the Tshibi Malaba house was chosen by Mwali at the Maneledzi pool contest to lead, hence by any means it was mandatory for the legacy to be persevered and continued in the manner determined by Mwali which is not outside of the Tshibi genealogy.

However, there are clear signs that the legitimacy of the Malaba traditional leadership was at some point a fiercely contentious issue, because, apparently from other family members opinion, the traditional leadership legacy had taken too long before it was handed back to the legitimate house. Family divisions got out of the system yet again at that period. This time with some Malaba houses refusing to swear allegiance to Tshidada through the *BaMalaba* designate, instead opting to swear directly by the birth names of their brothers or sisters. For reasons beyond one's range of knowledge or understanding, some houses went a step further and even disengaged their acknowledgement of chief Hhobhodo/Hhoba and/or disapproved their genealogy with Mpangana Malaba to the greatest extent.

There are also clear indications that cracks were expanding and signs disharmony also prevailing in the family. There is talk that the issue was so major that some houses like that of Kuyani, sided by that of Hadledzi began distancing themselves from the rest and, at some point, even deciding they would rather break away from the rest and retrace their steps back to the land of their forefathers in VhuVhenda. Legend has it that they were only held back by the presence of a number of heavily pregnant women in the family.

Kuyani's first son was named Mcingelwano later known as Hhabanahe, loosely translated as 'they have no legitimate leader'. It is argued that the name implied the clan was leaderless. This was most likely a dig aimed at the Malaba leadership that was then being held by chief Hhobhodo, who was from a third house of Mpangana. Yet again, Kuyani bore his second born son who was named Wubhatamakumbonholounabeni, loosely translated as 'he is just holding on to the legs because the head has its legitimate owners'. This also was interpreted as some form of a protest in reference to chief Hhobhodo Malaba leadership, presumably implying that Hhobhodo/Hhoba was dressed in borrowed robes.

It is believed the Tshedu house also decided to move away from the conflict and went to live *seli kweporo* (the other side of the railway line) somewhere far beyond to become part of the BaLilima. As mentioned in advance, the Mangwevu family from the Phando house was left behind and later trekked back to the Kezi area with the rest of the Malaba houses earning themselves the title of 'the lost house of Tshedu". However, all this, as a rule, had little importance attached to it as it merely signified some common disagreements found in any family setup.

4,8. Lobengula is King.

An interesting narrative on the death of Mzilikazi is given by Marshall Hole in his book *Lobengula* as he writes about Thomas Morgan Thomas, Mzilikazi's acquired white doctor's visit. "Morning and evening for several days the missionary came and ministered to the King, whose life was slowing ebbing. One morning he found him semi-conscious, unable to raise himself or to speak, unable to swallow the draught which Thomas held to his lips. When he left, the indunas were still sitting in the courtyard, but when he returned, just before nightfall, they were no longer there. At the sound of his horse's hoofs several women peeped timidly from neighbouring doorways and, after a hasty look, withdrew. Two of the bodyguard, in capes and head-dresses of black ostrich plumes, stood as usual, like statues of ebony, before the entrance to the royal quarters, their hands resting on their long shields. They gazed at him in silence, but their looks seemed threatening and resentful.

An air of mystery hung over the place, and, as Thomas stood hesitating, he saw a great grey owl, of the kind they call '*ingqungqulu*', rise from the thatch of the Kings hut. Slowly it circled outside the enclosure, passing so close to Thomas Morgan that he heard the soft whisper of its wings and felt a cool breath of air as it rustled by. He shivered, and, drawing his reins through his fingers, mounted his horse. He knew, without being told, that Mzilikazi had at last crossed the Great River" (Hole, 1929). All was not so well for the Matabele kingdom as in 1868, 9 September, Mzilikazi had died at Ingama, Matabeleland, near Bulawayo.

Nevertheless, after Mzilikazi's death, the succession of Lobengula was not easily accepted. In June 1870 Lobengula faced a fierce rebellion. The main internal opponents of Lobengula were the Zwangendaba, Induba and Nyamandlovu regiments, all of which lay in the northern half of the kingdom. They all were under the influence of Mbiko Masuku, son of Madlenya son of Zikode, who was the commander of Zwangendaba. Different reasons are given on Mbiko's resistance against Lobengula's ascension, some argue that Mbiko's resistance may have been because he felt excluded by the faction led by Mncumbatha and Bhudaza that represented Lobengula's claim and the selection of the successor, or it may be that there was some personal animus between Mncumbatha and Mbiko Masuku, a quarrel that could have sprung from long standing political frictions (Cobbing, 1976). Example being that, during the conflict, even when Mbiko sent two messengers to Lobengula and Mncumbatha to soliciting a peaceful settlement after sensing danger, Mncumbatha is believed to have "sent back the word to Mbiko that they would not accept surrender", and sarcastically stating that the king himself was coming to "surrender" to Mbiko himself (Campbell, 1926). Oral traditions further highlight a Mbiko who believed that Nkulumane, elder son of Mzilikazi was still alive and the search for him was not done adequately. This assertion is backed by the actions of the Zwangendaba kraal under Mbiko who "again refused to come, giving as their reasons that "there was no king, because a Nkulumane lived" (Campbell, 1926).

To top it all off, by 1872, Mangwane one of Mzilikazi's sons, backed by some of the izinduna, defied Lobengula again. Nevertheless, Mangwane's own following evaporated altogether by end of 1872 because his claim that Nkulumane was still alive was no longer holding any water. It was also gradually coming out clear that the rumour of Nkulumane existence was just a hoax perpetuated by one Theophilus Shepstone, who was popularly known as Usomtswewu, a Secretary of Native Affairs in Natal. The person being exhibited around as Nkulumane was in fact a mere pretender by the name Khanda, who was effectively an employee of Shepstone. In a letter to Thomas Morgan Thomas, the Relieving Native Commissioner and Assistant Native Commissioner of Matabeleland, dated 11 March 1872, Lobengula categorically states that "the man is not Nkulumane, but an imposter" and Mangwane "is the prime mover in the whole matter" (Thomas, 1986). Mangwane never returned to Matabeleland, thence died in the Transvaal.

Although the assault against Mbiko's Zwangendaba was mounted by regiments numbering to ten, according to the Malaba tradition, it is the eZimnyama regiment that was summoned as a vanguard for combating Mbiko Masuku's rebellious Zwangendaba regiment. Right from 1840, it had not only become a pattern that the young and able-bodied men from both the Malaba and sometimes the Bango clans would be conscripted within the eZimnyama regiment. The eZimnyama regiment being commanded by Mtsamayi Ndiweni, was initially a well-known Nguni elite regiment but by the time of Lobengula's initiation the eZimnyama regiment had virtually become a non-Nguni key force occupying an important frontier post at the Mangwe Pass, literally becoming a border patrol at the gate of the Ndebele kingdom. Lord Grey, the Administrator of Matabeleland described the Mangwe pass as "the key to the country". The eZimnyama were normally identified with their peculiar song,

"*Kulomsebenzi koMatshobana,* (.... there's work to do at Matshobane's*),*

Umsebenzi womkhonto" (...... Work for assegai...).

It is a song still popular amongst the Malaba to this day.

Mbiko kaMadlenya Masuku and his Zwangendaba Regiment had remained a powerful force against Lobengula's ascension but, both Mbiko and the Zwangendaba Regiment were indeed overwhelmed and pacified. Unfortunately, on the other hand, this civil war was taking place at the same period when the British imperial expansion was starting to threaten the very essence of the Ndebele power.

Despite born of a female helper, Fulatha Tshabalala on behalf of the Great Queen, Prince Lobengula (pictured with one of his wives in Fig 37) had been installed as king in 1870 after a brief interregnum during which the nation was governed by a council of indunas. Mncumbatha is recorded to have delivered the speech saying,

"There is the country o thy father, his cattle and his people - take them, and be careful of them; those who sin, punish; but those who obey, reward" (Thomas, 1986).

The Matabele under king Lobengula ruled from Zambezi to Limpopo and, also "between the desert of Makgadikgadi salt pans to the west and the realm of the Soshangana, the Save River, to the east" (Frame, 2018). Despite the issue of Nkulumane existence being regularly attributed to Mbiko's opposition to Lobengula's ascension, according to the Malaba narration, it was the question of Prince Lobengula growing up 'outside of the royal kraal' and therefore, missing out on how state affairs are run, that was high in the list of Mbiko's grievances. Like detailed in previous chapters, by virtue of having been temporarily residing in the Malaba homestead, Lobengula had not been brought up like other Matabele young males. Under Mzilikazi's ruling system, the youth of the nation were trained into tough battle-hardened men and by the time they reached manhood they would be fearsome warriors.

But although an Imbovane trainee, Lobengula had escaped a larger percentage of this kind of drilling. In childhood, living amongst the Malaba people who to him were not only mentors but a fountain offering to him wisdom and knowledge, "he had been forced into what was to all intents an exile from his tribe, and brought up under less violent influences, the mothering protection of the Boer girl, Sara, and the insidious tuition of the 'Malaba', who were a class by themselves, the product of many generations of inherited wisdom. His natural intelligence was above the common level, and instead of being arrested, as almost always happened with African natives before they attained manhood, it had been allowed to expand" (Hole, 1929).

Figure 37. A picture of King Lobengula and one of his wives – Courtesy of Zimbabwe Environmental Consultancy & Heritage Tours

4,9. The Malaba and the Nketha Census

Figure 38. A drawing depicting the Inauguration of King Lobengula - From a drawing by Thomas Baines.

When Lobengula got into power after Mzilikazi's death in 1868 (Fig 38), he decided it was indispensable that he conducted a population tally for the 30-year-old Ndebele nation. The objective of the census was to measure how much the nation had grown or dwindled in both population and mighty, since its establishment in 1840 under king Mzilikazi. The answerability of this official survey was invested on chief Hhobhodo Malaba's shoulders and between 1873 and 1874 Malaba coordinated a team of census collectors that went straight to work using a simple method of counting.

Literally, the identified and chosen enumeration methodology involved just the counting of huts and subsequently multiplying the statistics by three and thereby arriving at the population figures. Burdened with documenting the figures was chief Hhobhodo Malaba's consistently consistent friend by the name of Johannes Loedwickus, actually-known-as John Lee. John Lee was a Boer born in 1827 owning some of the land in the Marula area under chief Hhobhodo's jurisdiction.

John had arrived in Matabeleland from South Africa in 1858 in an elephant hunting expedition in the Shashe river area but in 1866 he ended up making his permanent camp at Mangwe where he was later joined by his wife. Unfortunately, the wife died in childbirth in 1870. Trusted by Mzilikazi, and Lobengula the same, John worked in partnership with Chief Hhobhodo Malaba and Chief Manyami, as their assistant officer, assisting with correspondence and carrying out administrative tasks at the Mangwe Pass (Figure 39) and the Tati, respectively.

Many of the travellers, hunters, and missionaries, especially the Europeans on transit would stopover with John Lee whilst waiting for permission to be "given the road", which meant being given permission to enter Matabeleland. He was a popular socialite and a well-known teller of tall tales. At some point in time as the war between the Matabele and Rhode's BSAC settlers raged on in 1893, John Lee was subpoenaed to serve under the BSA Company as a guide or interpreter. He refused to do the job, leading to his Mangwe farms, including the one under Hhobhodo's jurisdiction, being confiscated by the BSAC and offered to one, Jimmy (James) Dawson. John Lee later died in 1915.

This scene from the Rhodesian Tapestry shows Mangwe Pass Fort embroidered by the Marula Women's Institute. The border upper left has John Lee's house; centre is Mangwe Pass, right is John Lee's grave. Lower left are granite kopjes typical of the area; right is the Pioneer Memorial at Mangwe Pass. The motif is the Grey Lourie ("Go-away" bird)

Figure 39. A painting showing the Mangwe Fort/Pass, painting courtesy of Marula Women's Institute, 1923.

After the census, the feedback to King Lobengula by chief Hhobhodo Malaba and his team of census enumerators entailed that, while the general population of the nation had grown significantly since the creation of the Ndebele state, the population of the *Abezansi* and *Abenhla* groups were diminishing due to social integration and generic inclusion. Some argue that it was for those reasons that Lobengula ordered a re-stratification of the Ndebele state. The new program meant that the heterogenous Ndebele society was divided along caste lines into *Abezansi*, *Abenhla* and *abeLozwi* referring to 'those of the Rozwi empire, otherwise derogatorily called *Amahole* or *Abedlanondo*. *Abezansi* consisted of those of Nguni blood who hailed from KwaZulu, and *Abenhla* comprised those assimilated along the way while *Amahole Abedlanondo* encompassed the native inhabitants including the BaKalanga, Venda and others. "*Kwakhethwa kwehlukaniswa abetshabi* (people were separated on caste lines) and this was called *iNkethabetshabi* (tribalism) shortened to Nketha" (Damasane). In spite of that, the Nketha suburb in Bulawayo got its name after the existence of chief Malaba's official department of census and statistics at the location. In addition, men of all classes were also organized into age groups that served as fighting units.

Conspicuously, some Malaba informants argue that the Malaba people were exempted from the mandatory stratification for a number of reasons. Firstly, their recent arrival from vhuVenda was linked to neither the Matabele collective nor the native BaKalanga and Shona natives. Secondly, merely because chief Hhobhodo, like his father Mpangana, was a traditional doctor and a *nkumbudzi* (advisor) at the king's palace, and thirdly, because Hhobhodo had capacity to exempt himself and his clan after being awarded the answerability of conducting the census and subsequently implementing the stratification policy.

Although in the caste the Venda fell on the *AbeNhla* and the Kalanga on the Lozwi category, it is however no clear where the Malaba people would have spontaneously fallen under such circumstances as they were of Kalanga-Venda origin and had arrived virtually at the same time as the Matabele contingency nevertheless not as part of the Matabele movement. The determination was that they were affiliated to neither of the above castes, and as Cobbing argues, these "were terms denoting geographical origin not caste" and it was "the obsession of the British conquerors with class" that reimagined these as class divisions and indicative of nobility or the absence thereof (Cobbing, 1976). An interview with George Mkhwanazi (2020), gave a different perspective on the purpose and objectives of the stratification (Mkhwananzi, 2020).

Mkhwanazi argues that the stratification predated the reign of King Lobengula and had a positive strategic value to the preservation of the identity, culture, and language of the nation's core group. He argues that the stratification system was equivalent to the modern-day classification whereby residents are classified as temporary and permanent residents until they could be fully embraced as citizens. Amongst the Matabele, though the categorization largely stayed, accessing national privileges was not permanently forbidden. As soon as assimilation could be proved to be sufficient any member of the Ndebele Nation could be anything they aspired.

The categorizations themselves were nothing more than geographical identifications of the places where those members of the nation had joined it. Those who came from KwaZulu were not called *abeNguni* but *AbeZansi* (Southerners), which is a cardinal point on the Campus. The same applies to those who joined the nascent nation north of KwaZulu, *abeNhla* (Northerners) even though a significant number of them qualified to be called abeNguni especially the Ndebeles from kwaNdebele. *Amaholangubo* (Blanket Draggers-shortened to *Hole*) described the manner of dressing of Leopard skin by the people of Mambo whilst the country was initially referred in geographical terms as eBudlanondo (where people eat the Mopane tree caterpillars) (Mkhwananzi, 2020).

Mkhwanazi argued that the 1888 census was just a review of the national building policy which was meant to give recognition to the population expansion through the assimilation of other ethnic groups who had to be fully acknowledged as the dominant constituents of the nation, however, "whilst protecting the core values of the original group" from Zululand. Mkhwanazi also argued that the positives of the census included more non-Zansi clan members like Dakamela Myinga Ncube, Nkantiwo Sibanda, Tategulu Moyo, Huwana Ngwenya, Sihuluhulu Mabhena, Sivalo Mahlangu, Sikhombo Mguni being advanced to "senior positions in the state".

"The ban on intermarriage was, furthermore, relaxed which saw not only ordinary Matabeles marrying across the social boundaries, including King Lobengula who is rumoured to have married a MaDumane, a Kalanga woman who became his queen" (Mkhwananzi, 2020).

Although the stratification had some nation-building objectives, the social and political caste policy in the Ndebele society in principle survived the death of both Mzilikazi, Lobengula, but it disastrously led to divisions. At worse, it created a culture of bigotry and narrow-minded fanaticism in the Ndebele nation where some section of the Ndebele society considered themselves more equal than others.

The policy of stratification was ostensibly a resettlement exercise as well as national policy, nonetheless, adversely affecting the principles of respectability by insinuating that there were respectable people and not so respectable people in the nation. For instance, if a Hole murdered a Zansi, the crime would be punishable with death, while in case where a Zansi murdered a Hole, the verdict would most likely be homicide sometimes punishable with only a fine (Thomas, 1986).

The very act of naming other ethnic groups using degrading names also reflected the disunity that existed between the Matabele and the BaKalanga and other native tribes. This resulted in the use of the word AmaNdebele (Matabeleland) as a way to promote a much broader Ndebele identity than that predicated on Zulu as a prestige variety (Baldauf Jr and Kaplan). As duly, the Malaba people remained stationed in their original settlement of Nkalange in Marula until the time they were forcibly resettled by the colonial rulers in 1899, after 63 years of occupying the place.

4,10. The Death of Mbikwa Tshimba

The dramatic events of the death of Mbikwa Tshimba Thobela is orally narrated by the Tshimba orality. According to the Tshimba oral traditions, it was the year 1880 after King Lobengula's pregnant wife, Queen Xhwalile had a miscarriage. Lobengula was upset and summoned all the *Ababelethisi* (midwives) demanding to know what could have given rise to the queen's miscarriage. It was at that point that some bizarre tidings were broken to Lobengula. The Ababelethisi informed King Lobengula that the cause of the miscarriage was witchcraft.

"*Who has caused this deed?*" Lobengula demanded.

The women delivered news was shocking and unexpected!

"*Yindlovukazi, udadewenu*" (it is the she-elephant, your sister), they said.

As one would imagine, there are no befitting superlatives to describe the intensity that ensured thenceforth, nonetheless, evidently this was not going to be someone's day. The king could not believe the evidence of his ears. The news was so absurd it was unthinkable. King Lobengula immediately demanded information to indicate whether it was true that indeed it was his sister Princess Mncengence who was culpable of the child's death. For an answer to that demand, Gulukudwana Zondo, one of the witch doctors came out. Gulukudwana commanded respect amongst his peers because he previously had counselled Shaka Zulu before travelling north with Mzilikazi (Nyathi, 2010). He was holding a small oval locket (*ingqongqo/mpalela*) a cheap Brummagem thing. King Lobengula knew it well! It was one which he himself had bought from a trader and gave it to Princess Mncengence as a present some time ago.

"From the child's throat we drew forth this. And in one of Princess Mncengence's bags we also found this", adds the other *inyanga* who is assumed to have produced a dead toad, pierced with a wooden skewer. According to the Malaba orality, Mncengence quickly dashed to consult their clan elders regarding the crisis, from where she brought back a message that, not she, but Lobengula's brother had bewitched the king's wife. However, it is said that Mbikwa, son of Tshimba, had also cast the magic bones and found out that indeed Princess Mncengence was the culpable one. Legend has it that in consequence, Lobengula boiled with anger that he gave immediate orders,

Lobengula is said to have declared that he did not want Mncengence to ever look at his face again. Since witchcraft was customarily punished with death, the deed was done. It was that impasse that generated an unspeakable disharmony especially between the *inyangas, izanuse* and the *indunas*. Mbikwa Ncube son of Tshimba, son of Thobela Mbedzinkulu was one of the *inyangas* and/or, because of his descent, was probably authoritative over the traditional medicine institution. Unanticipated, the blame was laid squarely on his doorstep. Some of the indunas convinced king Lobengula that Princess Mncengence's death was because of some manipulative intentions. The Matabele section of the *inyangas* argued that this was entirely because of the other jealous *inyangas* who had constantly proven to be in competition with her for the everyday attention of the king.

It was also at this point that the events took a dramatic twist. Oral traditions have it that despite the utmost fame and influence of the Malaba people during King Mzilikazi's reign, the impact of some of Hhobhodo's representatives, especially the hosanna priests, seemed to be diminishing during Lobengula's monarchy. There were instances in which, despite their fame, were denounced and sometimes "roughly handled" especially "very soon after the inauguration" (Thomas, 1986).

According to the Tshimba orality, despite having watched over him in his youth growing up amongst the Malaba clan, without hesitation, Lobengula ordered Mbikwa's demise. However, oral tradition substantiates on the account that it has always been suspected by some uncomfortable section of other nyangas that for far too long Mbikwa had been acting as a 'secret intelligence service' for the BaKalanga Mwali priests and several Matabele chiefs were finding him periodically too inquisitive and as well as secretive for their liking. All this prompted the jealous of the other indunas leading to Mbikwa being marked out for destruction as soon as any chance could present itself. Actually, this secretive and withdrawn nature of Mbikwa was originating from his role that he had been holding since he was a young boy from Venda. In the Malaba clan he was responsible for evaluating and assessing the threats, risks, harm, vulnerabilities, and opportunities which may exist to harm the clan. Nevertheless, in that event in 1880, Mbikwa Ncube, son of Tshimba-Bhangwa, son of Thobela Mbedzinkulu, was certainly phased out on Lobengula's instructions. It was the person of Faku Ndiweni who was sent to execute Mbikwa's death.

It is told that Faku who was known to have shown a smouldering hostility towards the Mwali religion in general and its priests, saw and seized the opportunity to massacre Mbikwa's entire family and thereby banning all public performances associated with the Hosanna within the Ndebele Kingdom (Bhebe, 1979). Frank Sykes had recorded the contempt with which Faku regarded the Mwali religion and how he would speak to the likes of Mbikwa with the scorn appropriate to an oweZansi speaking to a Hole. The circumstances were however, just because of a jostle for the attention of the king between the Mwali priests and some of the Ndebele chiefs. Faku is considered to have detested the Mwali priests to a point that even when the Dula shrine declared war against the Europeans in 1896, he ostentatiously become 'loyal' to the settlers.

However, some of our informants argued that Faku's collaboration was simply because he wished to maintain an illegal inheritance of which he succeeded in 1901 as the Native Department assisted his son, Nyangazonke to become chief in the present-day ward 1, 2 and 20 of the Matobo district area.

More so, Faku managed to execute Mbikwa but not his family members. According to researcher Cobbing, Faku was a man with vaulting ambitions. When Tunzi became involved in the Mangwane-Kanda invasion of 1872, Faku is reported to have gone to inform Lobengula leading to the execution of Tunzi in 1875. Concurrently, more other Mwali priests are reported to have cheated death by running away, some fleeing as far as to Magutu's (Gutu) in that same year (Cobbing, 1976).

1880 was a year of turbulences regarding cases of witchcraft and accusations of witchcraft tendencies. Anger and acrimony became the new normal. Gatsheni (2008), notes that it had become common that "the accusation of witchcraft was used as a political weapon in moves for favours. The prominent and powerful members of the Ndebele society tended to manipulate and abuse their power and positions in the *umphakathi* and *izikhulu* to eliminate one another by accusing each other of witchcraft and plots against the king" (Gatsheni, 2008). Gampu Sithole was also exiled on a charge of seducing one of Lobengula's daughters. Lotshe Hlabangana was in 1880 charged with witchcraft but survived for a while only to be executed in September 1889 on a charge of having misleadingly commended the Rudd concession to Lobengula (Ndlovu- Gatsheni, 2008). Mhlaba Khumalo son of Mncumbatha and his brother Sidlodlo were executed in June 1892 for favouring Nkulumane in 1868-72 and for trying to overpower Lobengula's queens with the intention to rape them.

Earlier on Mpanjwana had been killed on Lobengula's orders because 'he killed people without permission' (Cobbing, 1976). Manxeba Khumalo and Mpondo who were both eliminated on charges of witchcraft yet their "real crime, however, was that they were too close to Mzilikazi to the extent that they generated jealousy from their colleagues who also wanted to be nearer to the king" (Gatsheni, 2008).

In different circumstances the death of Mbikwa who was also known as Tawulo occurred as a blessing in disguise to some of the Tshimba family in general and the Sekudza family. It triggered a memory of an unresolved case in history. The story goes that a couple of years before, when the old Tshimba died, he had left behind a young wife. Sekudza, one of Tshimba's sons, saw a potential wife in his father's young wife. The shenanigans led to the birth of a son whose name was Mzila, of whom Mzila primary school in the Sigangatsha area of Kezi is named after him. Although this was a familiar phenomenon, for some reasons Sekudza's affair with his father's young wife did not go down well with his brother Mbikwa-Tawulo.

It was as a result that Mbikwa arranged for Sekudza to be killed by accusing him of an overzealous act of witchcraft and then reporting him to the then king Mzilikazi. In fact, the report was based on trumped-up witchcraft charges including claims that in his secret closet, Sekudza kept horrible apparatus including human skulls. It is told that in one way or another, the young Mzila overheard the rumour regarding the plan to eliminate his father. He foiled it by tipping off his father. Hence, before the deed was carried out Sekudza took a flight to Botswana in some strange fashion.

One cool morning, some women from the Tshimba family were seen hovering in the bushes pretending to be performing some domestic chores. They were keeping their closeness to a large herd of cattle in the pastures close to the Mwewu river in Kezi. With the aim of confusing the enemy, they appeared to be fetching water or gathering firewood but as a matter of fact they were driving the herd of cattle out of Matabeleland into Botswana, and ultimately finding refuge in a place they called Sowa near the Dukwe area of Botswana.

Nonetheless, now, in the early 1890s, that both Mzilikazi and Sekudza's brother, Mbikwa were dead, Mzila went down to fetch back his father's people who ultimately relocated to the Simphathe area of Kezi where they are still located under chief Malaba's jurisdiction.

Nevertheless, in around 1880s, the Lobengula-Malaba relationship had manifested itself in a graceful way. Oral traditions have it that, in 1869, King Lobengula bore a second son and named him Sintingantinga senkosi. In honour of the Malaba people who he regarded as his spiritual parents, Lobengula later renamed his six-year-old son Tshakalisa (Tjakalisa) pictured in Figure 40 below. The name Tshakalisa, a Kalanga name, came from the Malaba people, as his isiNdebele name was Sintingantingasenkosi or shortly Sintinga. Sintingantingasenkosi means the King's most favourite son. As narrated by Tshemane, Lobengula went back to the Malaba people and said,

"I have been blessed with a son" and it is said that the Malaba people, filled with joy said to the king.

"You shall name him Tjakalisa", in reference to Lobengula, who as a young man used to look after both people and animals in the area. The name Tjakalisa, literally meaning 'the keeper or guardian of people' could also have referred to the role of Malaba as Lobengula's spiritual father. Tshakalisa's mother was Mbhida, the daughter of Lodada Mkhwananzi whose village was in Inqobo in the Ingwingwisi valley.

Figure 40. Prince Tshakalisa Sintinga; Photo Courtesy of R.S. Roberts

It was during this visit to the Malaba people that Lobengula took time to familiarize himself with the area covered by chief Malaba's arbitration. Over the period in question, the area which stretched from the Bidi area down to the Botswana border of the Shashi River, was under chief Tshidada Malaba's reign. Lobengula, on a horse ride, travelled south towards the Shashe river where he identified an unoccupied land. It is then that Lobengula exchanged opinions with chief Tshidada Malaba on a matter regarding his in-laws, the Mkhwananzi, who needed land in the meanwhile, occupying the uninhabited area.

The affiliation between Lobhengula and the Beula Mpande Mkhwananzi people was emanating from Lobengula's first wife Mbhida, the mother of Tshakalisa, who was from the Mkhwanazi clan. Lobengula had married Mbhida before he became King. Nevertheless, Mbhida was regarded as one of the most important and favoured wives of Lobengula coming only after Lozikeyi and Xwalile. The present occupants of the land are presently known as the Beula Mpande people. They apparently assumed the Mpande title which presumably is just an extraction from their praise name (*isitemo*) for Mkhwanazi people. '*Nkwali yenkosi, Mpande yamadoda*'. It was on the backdrop of that interrelationship that chief Malaba favoured and appointed Beula as his kraal head (*umlisa*). Beula Mpande is still one of chief Malaba's headmen today. However, some associate the Beula people with a Moyo family originating from the Matopo area. The family is declared to have gained favours from Lobengula after proving that they were high level medicine men.

CHAPTER 5

THE MALABA LEGACY AND THE TEST OF TIME & THE EFFECTS OF THE NDEBELE WARS

5,1. Cecil John Rhodes

Figure 41. Cecil John Rhodes (1853-1902) is a painting by Granger.

All things considered, since their settlement in the Kingdom of Bukalanga in 1836, despite intermittent occasions of calamities, the Malaba clan managed to live a serene life. In all fairness, right from the Mzilikazi period to Lobengula's tenure, the Khumalo-Malaba alliance was an effective one and hence, correspondingly, the Malaba people found themselves naturally constituting a section of the population that was ordinarily privileged and favoured by the Ndebele state machinery. Author (Becker, 1966) put it more distinctly as he writes that the Mwali priests who "led the tribe in the worship of Mwali, had an extraordinarily high reputation for their prowess in witchcraft and magic" and "Mzilikazi regarded the Mwali priests with the deepest respect, and never attempting to injure them, and lavishing them with gifts regularly upon them".

There is a general consensus amongst those interviewed that the Mwali priests were never compromised by the invasion of the Matabele, because their connection with Mwali was steadfast and protective of them so that while all around were demolished, they enjoyed solitude and immunity from aggression. Moreover, whenever king Lobengula felt that the Malaba people had been violated in any form or fashion, he would shell out heads of cattle as compensation for the infringement. Therefore, despite life's general peaks and valleys, the Malaba clan essentially lived in the lap of luxury. In other words, life generally went on unperturbed. Even Sicwayiza Mabhena the commander of Insukamini when swearing used to say that *"Ngingalumba ngani ngingeMalaba?"* (What can I do since I do not possess the magic of the Malaba people) (Nyathi, 2000)

Then entered Cecil John Rhodes! (Fig 41). A man whose calculated mendacity and neo-fascism was matched only by his vaulting Cape to Cairo ambition. Cecil John Rhodes was born 5 July 1853 in Bishop's Stortford, England. A mercenary by nature, Rhodes arrived in Durban, South Africa on 1 September 1870 when he was only 17 years old. In his purse he had only three thousand pounds borrowed from his aunty which he later invested it in diamond mining (Rotberg, 1998). In 1873

Rhodes was enrolled at Oxford University where the philosophy of John Ruskin is argued to have greatly influenced him and reinforcing his own attachment to the cause of British Imperialism. In 1877 Rhodes wrote in his *Cecil Rhodes "Confession of Faith"* that he was attracted to the idea of creating a 'secret society' of British men who would be able to lead the world and spread the spirit of the Englishman to all corners of the globe.

Although writers like Maylam (Maylam, 2005) argue that Rhodes was driven by only the pursuit of material gain, Harlow, and Carter, (2003) were convinced that Rhodes was more of an ultimate imperialist who believed that the Englishman was the greatest human specimen in the world whose only rule would be a benefit to all. It was Rhodes' view that the native population of Africa existed 'in a state of barbarism', and that it was the Anglo-Saxon's obligation to subjugate and govern the continent. As he put it: 'the more of the world we inhabit the better it is for humans." He further commented that "it must be brought home to them (African natives) that in future nine-tenths of them will have to spend their lives in manual labour, and the sooner that is brought home to them the better" (Harlow & Carter, 2003).

When gold was discovered in the Transvaal in the early 1880s, it sparked what was later known as the Witwatersrand Gold Rush. Rhodes is cited to have considered joining the rush to open gold mines in the region, but his lifetime friend and business partner Charles Rudd, convinced him that the Witwatersrand was merely the beginning, and that far greater gold fields lay further to the north, in Matabeleland and Mashonaland.

It is therefore that in 1888 Rhodes arrived in Matabeleland.

Matabeleland fell squarely in the territory which Rhodes hoped to conquer, from the Cape to Cairo, in the name of the British Empire (Fig. 42). It also was believed to hold vast, untapped gold fields, which Rudd believed would be of far greater value than those discovered in the Witwatersrand. Afterall, the 'Scramble for Africa' was also already well under way and Rhodes became convinced that the Germans, French, and Portuguese were going to try to take Matabeleland prompting him and his men to prepare to get Matabeleland under British control as quickly as they could.

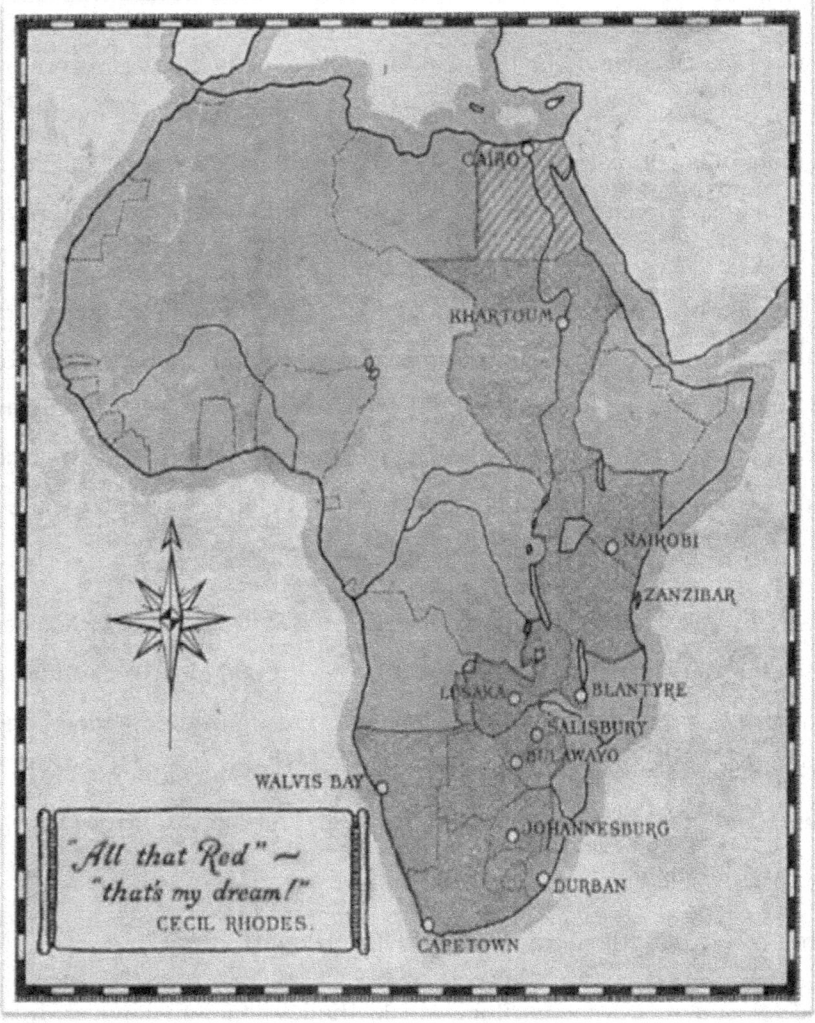

Figure 42. Rhodes' vision was British dominion "from the Cape to Cairo". Picture courtesy of the Rhodes Foundation.

5,2; The Rudd Concession

It is noteworthy to point once again that the chief Hhobhodo/Hhoba Malaba supremacy stretched from the end parts of the Matopos, right across the Marula-Figtree, and in the process encompassing the indispensable Mangwe Pass up to the border with the Bangwato. To a degree, in the second half of the century the route to the capital of the Ndebele state ran through chief Hhobhodo's jurisdiction. At Marula, which is forty-four miles from Bulawayo on the Plumtree Road, the Mangwe Pass side road led away to the south through fifteen miles of grand rock scenery, forming the southern gateway to the heart of Matabeleland. The BSAC settler travellers, hunters, traders, concession seekers and missionaries, passed by the western edges of the hills, by the way of the Mangwe Pass which was under chief Hhobhodo Malaba and the Manyami kraal under chief Manyami. Here, they would wait for the king's permission to proceed.

Since Hhobhodo's chieftaincy covered this area, he essentially became the watchman for the King. In fact, king Mzilikazi had conscripted him to that post as a position, and as indicated in Robert Moffat's writings, chief Hhobhodo was the 'permission messenger' and the gate keeper or frontier guard while chief Manyami was the register keeper from the BaNgwato side. Both were responsible for admission to the Ndebele kingdom through the wagon-road that ran between Shoshong and Bulawayo, a thoroughfare which the follow up settlers in Southern Rhodesia passed through. Manyami, known as 'the black one' was a Bangwato lechaba or soldier.

Explorer and geologist Mauch also writes that, "On the 20 September we arrived at Mosilikatsi's (Mzilikazi) last subjects at the southern guard post of his property under the command of the chief Manjami (Manyami) The passport office is here for all those arriving from the south. From here the name of each traveller as well as his purpose is reported to headquarters by runner and here too, the answer has to be awaited" (Mauch, 1871). In *The Matabele Journals of Robert Moffat 1829–1860, Vol. 1,* Moffat accounts that after having been screened at Chief Manyami village on Saturday 15th July 1854, had not proceeded more than four miles before they were requested by the chief man of a BaKalanga village to halt and 'till a messenger should come direct from headquarters.' According to Moffat, the chief resided in a village called *Malabe*, which he thought was "named after a river" (E. W. S. Wallis, 1946). On Saturday 21st October 1854, Moffat again confirms being detained at Manyami's village for two days (E. W. S. Wallis, 1946). The concessionists would normally pass through the peculiarly grand and sublime hilly country of BuKalanga and at last reaching the Matabele ground. Often, Chief Hhobhodo, as the chief of the area and a military village commander, would be the natural bearer of the message to the King.

Nonetheless, it was the calamitous situation of 1888 that the then 78-year-old chief Hhobhodo Malaba, found himself engrossed in. This is in reference to the infamous period of the Rudd Concession on 30th October 1888, when the Cecil John Rhodes team of Francis 'Matabele' Thompson (nicknamed Matabele because of his fluency in the Ndebele language) and Charles Rudd, fraudulently descended in the area with the intention to get the concession signed by king Lobengula.

It is recorded that, from left, right and centre, favour after favour was being sought by the concessionists and Lobengula was growing weary of the continuous flow of these concessionists together with the big-game hunters who were frequenting his royal kraal. Historian Rotberg records that fed up Lobengula even went to post a notice at the entry point to his territory on the Tati River, "proclaiming that his *impis*, or regiments, would stop any white man they found on the road". Not even this cautionary advice was enough to deter a team of three men, Charles Rudd, a man experienced in negotiating with Boer landowners about gold mining claims, Francis "Matabele" Thompson, a manager of black labour compounds at Rhodes' diamond operations and was fluent in Setswana and James Rochfort Maguire, a barrister by occupation who Rhodes had known at Oxford University back in England. Maguire is referred to by author Rotberg, as the "odd man out" on this expedition, conversant with legal documents but unfamiliar with discomforts of the African bush" (Rotberg, 1988).

Point is made that Rhodes was very much aware that for his quest to conquer Africa to succeed, he needed to smash the Ndebele kingdom, whom, because of their battle-hardened nature, he regarded as a stumbling block to his 'Cape to Cairo' ambitions. Rotberg, quotes Rhodes' letter to a friend which read that "someone has to get the country, and I think we should have the chance. I have always been afraid of the Matabele king. He is the only block to central Africa, as, once we have his territory, the rest is easy". Therefore, for Rhodes, a war against the Ndebele was a matter not able to be avoided when all was said and done. Apart from the letter, and £1000 in gold sovereigns, the concessionists were carrying with them the usual consignment of hard liquor as gift for King Lobengula (Rotberg, 1988).

Consequently, under the pretext that they were on to have an official business meeting with a missionary, a so-called John Smith Moffatt, the three, Rudd, Thompson, and Maguire, ostensibly made an entrance into the territory. According to the Malaba oral traditions, at that time King Lobengula, with a team of his chiefs that included, Hhobhodo/Hhoba Malaba, were preoccupied with the rainmaking ceremonies at the Njelele shrine in the Matopo Hills. The concessionists had customarily used the route that went through the Mangwe Pass and journeying over the Marula area from the direction of Bulilima towards the Royal kraal of Bulawayo. Word of these journeyers awaiting entry into the Matabele territory reached chief Hhobhodo on the morning of the 19th of September 1888 prompting chief Hhobhodo to hastily leave the Njelele shrine ceremony and en route to his Marula homestead.

As a renowned skilful medicine man, chief Hhobhodo Malaba was readying to perform his exceptional magical powers to stop the Rudd convoy from proceeding towards the king's kraal. The wizardry seemed to have responded to the affirmative, as the Rudd convoy's ox-driven carts got stuck in the Mangwe river. In reference to the incident, Baxter (2018), writes that at that point, progress was halted by an AmaNdebele border guard that informed Rudd of a royal decree forbidding any white man from proceeding into Matabeleland without the prior and express consent of the King. Rudd and his convoy tried every manoeuvre to liberate their carts from the entanglement but to no avail. For unrecognized reasons, the strong oxen just could bring out their pulling power to get the carts moving. They were stuck in a quagmire and a boggy area of the river sand that was gradually giving way underfoot.

But as Rotberg reports, nonetheless, King Lobengula was gradually getting weary of the constant nagging by the concessionists to an extent that the chances of him giving in to the demands of a meeting, were nothing but inevitable (Rotberg, 1988). Therefore, upon learning of the event in the Mangwe Pass (Fig. 44 & 45), Lobengula's command was relayed to chief Hhobhodo that he let the concessionists proceed towards his kraal. It was in due course that, chief Hhobhodo, accompanied by interpreter John Lee, approached the travellers by the river where they were stuck. As oral tradition would say, he cheekily asked them what their trouble was, of which they answered,

"We are stuck in the middle of nowhere".

"Don't you know it is disrespectful and sacrilegious to visit the royal residence without sending a forerunner as a harbinger?", chief Hhobhodo further questioned them.

"We are on way to visit our dear friend, John Smith Moffatt, the missionary", they answered.

Chief Hhobhodo found their version hard to believe however, king Lobengula had already sent a directive to accord a thoroughfare to the three men, apparently deciding he might as well receive the Rudd party as they were already in his country. Little did he know that 'the Mangwe Passage which Baxter describes as 'the scorching suicide months of October and November 1888' (Baxter, 2018) was to symbolize a passage to Lobengula's tragic downfall, together with the entire Ndebele nation.

With a directive from king Lobengula, chief Hhobhodo felt an obligation to assist the crew. He approached the men and according to the Malaba oral traditions, chief Hhobhodo ultimately got to the men, with him a bullwhip made from braided leather attached to a wooded rod known as *tjimi* and *umchilo* in the Kalanga and Ndebele languages, respectively. As confident as Hercules, chief Hhobhodo firmly held the lower end of the bullwhip rod which was balanced leaning against his broad shoulders. The wooded rod buckled from the weight of the attached long braided leather string adopting a rainbow arc shape over his raised shoulders. Without warning, he elevated the bullwhip high and swung it in several circular motions before its shape drew a trilogy, then to the left and then to the right and in the centre before letting out a cracking and deafening thunderous sound, accompanied by a pristine whistle (*nlidzo/umvokloklo*).

It is told that the oxen, upon hearing the strange noise, lifted their heads up high and were sent scampering and in the act, hauling the carts out of the quagmire. Rudd and company stood there in amazement and before they took off, they donated some carts to chief Hhobhodo and some of the carts are still there today on a hilltop previously known as the Malaba mountain, where Hhobhodo/Hhoba lived (Fig. 43).

Figure 43. A wheel from one of the concessionists carts is kept by the Malaba people as a monument in a hilltop in Marula (Photo Courtesy of R. Doko)

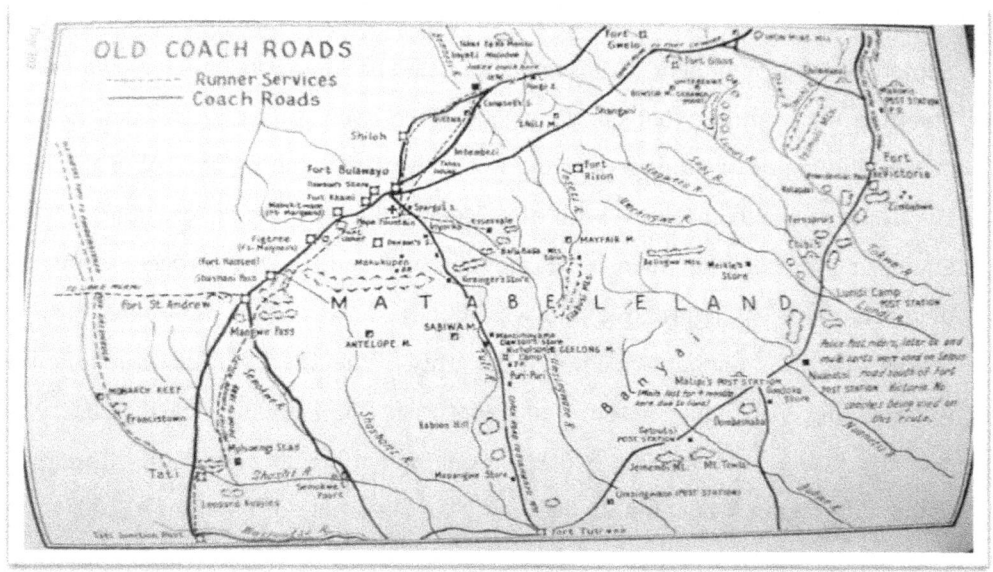

Figure 44. An Old Map of Matabeleland – source unknown

Figure 45. A picture of the Mangwe Pass – Courtesy mapio.net

At last, Thompson and friends arrived in Bulawayo close to noon on 20 of September 1888 and thereby presented their case to King Lobengula, albeit, falsely claiming that, unlike what the Transvaal Boers were doing, their backers were merely in pursuit of mining gold and not interested in taking control of the land. By contrasting themselves with the Boers, the British concessionists were attempting to deliver themselves favourably and in the process depicting themselves as less aggressive and less greedy. It was after all, ironic that Piet Joubert, the Commandant General of the army of the South African Republic had warned king Lobengula before citing that, "an Englishman once [he] has your property in his hand, then he is like a monkey that has its hands full of pumpkin seeds – if you don't beat him to death, he will never let go" (Meredith, 2007).

The suspicious Lobengula who seem to have sensed danger was initially defiant, as he had been recorded to have spoken to the Rev C.D. Helm observing that "The Boers are like the lizard, they dart about quickly, but the English proceeds more cautiously. Did you ever see a chameleon catch a fly? The chameleon gets behind the fly and remains motionless for some time, then he advances very slowly and gently, first putting forward one leg and then another. At last, when well within reach, he darts his tongue, and the fly disappears. England is the chameleon, and I am that fly" (Keppel-Jones, 1983). This led to the negotiations being prolonged until October 1888 when a key figure to the negotiations arrived. His name was Sir Sidney Shippard and was Commissioner of neighbouring Bechuanaland. Shippard, who had enthusiastically bought into Rhodes' ambitions, repeated the warnings about the Boers to king Lobengula and advanced the cause of the Rudd party.

What prompted King Lobengula to gain interest in Shippard was because Shippard, as "a representative of the Colonial Office, more importantly, provided a central link to the white Queen across the seas". From his royal position King Lobengula naturally perceived dealing directly with the British monarch as of importance as in comparison with dealing with the capitalist private businessmen. The document, which was apparently an agreement which allowed the British to prospect over all the territory under Lobengula's control in exchange of a gunboat on the Zambezi, rifles, ammunition, and a payment to Lobengula of £100 a month, was signed (Coltart, 2016). Little did Lobengula know that Shippard and his colleague, a Sir Hercules Robinson in Cape Town were also agents of Cecil Rhodes. The whole deal was all a phony ploy.

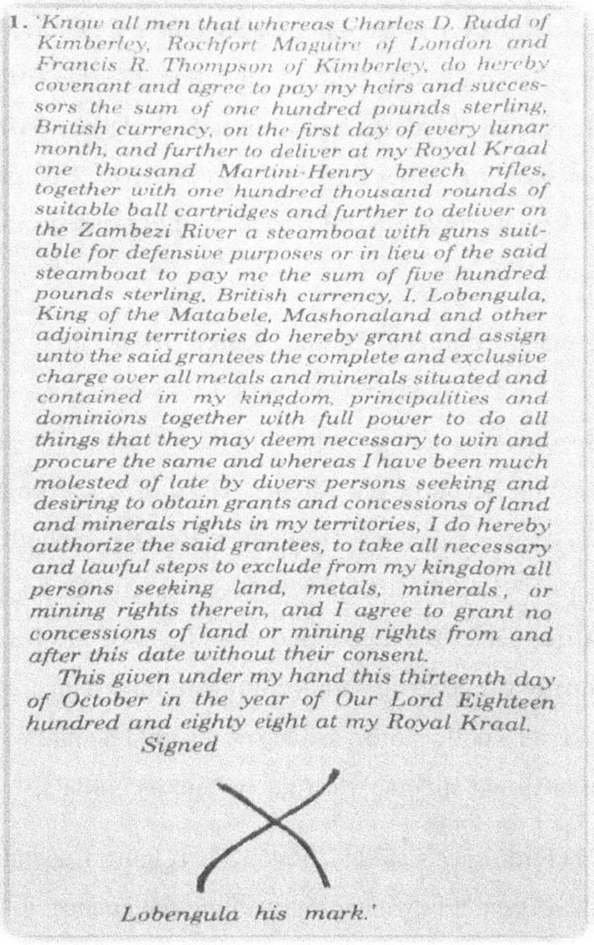

1. 'Know all men that whereas Charles D. Rudd of Kimberley, Rochfort Maguire of London and Francis R. Thompson of Kimberley, do hereby covenant and agree to pay my heirs and successors the sum of one hundred pounds sterling, British currency, on the first day of every lunar month, and further to deliver at my Royal Kraal one thousand Martini-Henry breech rifles, together with one hundred thousand rounds of suitable ball cartridges and further to deliver on the Zambezi River a steamboat with guns suitable for defensive purposes or in lieu of the said steamboat to pay me the sum of five hundred pounds sterling, British currency, I, Lobengula, King of the Matabele, Mashonaland and other adjoining territories do hereby grant and assign unto the said grantees the complete and exclusive charge over all metals and minerals situated and contained in my kingdom, principalities and dominions together with full power to do all things that they may deem necessary to win and procure the same and whereas I have been much molested of late by divers persons seeking and desiring to obtain grants and concessions of land and minerals rights in my territories, I do hereby authorize the said grantees, to take all necessary and lawful steps to exclude from my kingdom all persons seeking land, metals, minerals, or mining rights therein, and I agree to grant no concessions of land or mining rights from and after this date without their consent.

This given under my hand this thirteenth day of October in the year of Our Lord Eighteen hundred and eighty eight at my Royal Kraal.
Signed

X

Lobengula his mark.'

Figure 46. Picture of the Letter signed by King Lobengula. Courtesy of South African History online

The very historic moment when king Lobengula placed the X at the foot of the paper (Fig. 46), was not only a moment that represented some truly extraordinary times but also paralysis at the heart of Ndebele nation. Legend has it that, turning to his companion Thompson, Maguire smiled like a Cheshire cat and muttered the words, "Thompson, this is the epoch of our lives" (Keppel-Jones, 1983). In addition, other present concessionists like Helm and Dreyer were asked to add their signatures too as witnesses. At that instance, the Rudd concession had been completed, signed, and sealed. However, after King Lobengula's signature, the Rudd Concession document was, right off the bat, distorted by the British government and leading to the Ndebele kingdom being virtually declared a British protectorate and the Treaty was used to charter the British South Africa Company (BSAC). In October 1889, Queen Victoria granted Rhodes and his British South Africa Company (BSAC) a Royal Charter.

This happened after the Rhodes' company Central Search Association, was combined with the London based Exploring Company Ltd which was also capitalizing on the expected mineral wealth in parts of Mashonaland. The first directors of the BSAC included the second Cecil Rhodes, Duke of Abercorn and Albert Beit who was the South African financier. The town of Beit Bridge built by Dorman Long in 1929 to form the political border between South Africa and Zimbabwe is named after Alfred Beit. The terms and conditions of the BSAC operations were that the Company would trade with local rulers, form banks, own and manage land, and raise and run a police force, as long as it would do that while respecting traditional African laws and endorse free trade within its borders.

It was just a matter of time before reports started flowing into King Lobengula kraal informing him that he had been hoodwinked into selling the country to the Concessionists. Lobengula was so aggrieved that, instantly, he wrote a protesting letter to the Queen of England. According to Copell-Jones in the book *Rhodes and Rhodesia: The White Conquest of Zimbabwe 1884-1902*, the letter read:

"I hear it is published in all the newspapers that I have granted a Concession of the Minerals in all my country to CHARLES DUNELL RUDD, ROCHFORD MAGUIRE [sic], and FRANCIS ROBERT THOMPSON.

As there is a great misunderstanding about this, all action in respect of said Concession is hereby suspended pending an investigation to be made by me in my country".

Lobengula.

……………………………

As alluded before, from 1840, it had not only become a pattern that the young men from both the Malaba, Osabeni and sometimes Bango clans would be conscripted within the Ezimnyama, a regiment that had started as a Nguni elite regiment, but with the Malaba and Usaba clan dominance, had virtually become a non-Nguni regiment by Lobengula's time. However, when the Malaba later militarily became under chief Gampu Sithole's command, the young men from the two clans had also become indispensable to the Amagogo annex, a section of the Igabha regiment under Gampu Sithole. Gampu commanded a force of about 15000 men divide into dispersed detachments. Further down the line, for some reasons the Rudd Concession saga particularly, fractured the relationship between Gampu Sithole and chief Hhobhodo Malaba.

Legend has it that Gampu was so riled by the Rudd concession that some rumours spread amongst the white residents of a freebooter force in the South African Republic. The force allegedly committed to coming to Matabeleland to support chief Gampu Sithole in overthrowing and killing Lobengula. The concessionism problem, however, was not the main reason for the breaking down of the relationship between Lobengula and Gampu Sithole. Some scholars reveal that the friendship between Lobengula's and Gampu was broken in 1887 because of Gampu's affair with the Lobengula's daughter, Hlomela, who was being reserved to be the wife of the Gaza King, Gungunyana. After the misunderstanding, Gampu is cited to have relocated to Transvaal with the assistance of some Boers resulting in the rumours that he had gone to Transvaal to seek aid to overthrow king Lobengula (J. G. Wood, 1893).

Based on principles of loyalty, chief Malaba would naturally disagree strongly to an idea of overthrowing Lobengula. Although Hhobhodo Malaba was directly or indirectly involved in the Concession saga, his steadfast loyalty to Lobengula was not only originating from their administrative roles in the king's kraal, but from the family history. Therefore, this was always going to be some testing times of faith, allegiance, and patriotism for the Malaba clan in general and chief Hhobhodo Malaba in particular. The animosity between Gampu and Hhobhodo Malaba was exacerbated by the fact that Gampu was at the time also being supported by Mpini Ndiweni who most BaKalangas perceived to be holding strong views and a bigot.

5,3. The First Ndebele War

After the Rudd Concession deception, King Lobengula decided to act and act quickly. This much, a determination was reached that Chief Babanyane Masuku, Chief Mtshede Ndiweni, Edward Maund and linguist and interpreter Johan Colenbrander were to be sent to England instantaneously. The envoy is alleged to have left the Capital of Bulawayo for Cape Town end of the month of November 1888 and Sir Hercules Robinson who happened to have an audience with the Matabele as the embarked on the *Moor* on the 2nd of February 1889 said the gentlemen told him that their main mission was to find out for the King, whether England and the Queen existed or not. However, it is known that the king's message to be delivered to Queen Elizabeth was an unequivocal information on that the rephrasing of the Rudd Concession, thereafter, turned it into a deceptive document that represented neither the King's words nor those of Rhodes' men at the time of signing. The British Times newspaper reported the details of the journey, and *The Launceston Examiner* of 23 April 1890 also carried an article about Babanyane and Mtshede's visit to Buckingham Palace, reported by a journalist named Barry Brown.

Amid that state of bewilderment, King Lobengula took a far-reaching verdict to deny the British South African Company (BSAC) access to the areas under his control. Following the embargo in 1890 Rhodes ultimately took his men and in due time occupied the Mashonaland territory where they were met with little or no resistance. However, the settlers hunted for gold but to no avail. Coupled with Rhodes' Cape to Cairo ambition and Starr Jameson's hunger for war, by 1893, the British South African Company (BSAC) had decided it was the time to attack Matabeleland. And to a degree, in July 1893, a chance presented itself.

Legend has it that in May 1893, the people of Headman Gomala from under Bere, a MaShona chief, were found to be guilty or rather were accused by the BSAC of cutting some telegraph wires. Furthermore, there was an accusation against the people of chief Bere himself having stolen Jameson's cattle near Fort Victoria. Some oral narrations contend that the telegraph wires were, in point of fact, taken down by the people belonging to the hungry-for-war Starr Jameson, as a calculated move to brew trouble by setting both chief Bere and headman Gomala against King Lobengula.

It was thenceforth that the settlers demanded a payment for their stolen goods, and it was on that occasion that Gomala paid the ransom using King Lobengula's cattle, the cattle that were supposedly stolen from Umgulugulu Hill between June and September 1893. For King Lobengula's sphere of influence stretched as far as areas that lied as far as Mazoe and Save Rivers. Writer Campbell confirms that at that time some MaKaranga had certainly raided some Inxa cattle at the Silonda Hill, beyond the Lunde River and the spoor was traced to chief Bere's homestead (Campbell, 1926).

Traditionally, such a deed as done by Chief Bere and Gomala would, by and large, lead to a hefty fine or at worse a retaliatory raid. Wherefore, it was after the incident that on 12 June 1893, King Lobengula resolved to send a small regiment led by Chiefs Manyewu Ndiweni and Mgandane Dlodlo to Chief Bere's homestead to inquire about the incident. Without any further ado, the regiment began with a raid further east by attacking the Karanga of Zimundu, who had also been implicated in the embezzlement of the cattle. This was done before approaching the other Karanga speakers to the west and north of Victoria. When Lobengula's regiment breezed in to Chief Bere who lived only some twenty miles west of Victoria they got the ear that he had already reported to the whites that the Matabele were on way to raid his own cattle.

Much to their astonishment, on arrival, the Ndebele delegates came eyeball to eyeball with Chief Administrator, Doctor Leander Starr Jameson, who ordered an ultimatum for the Ndebele group to leave the Mashonaland Protectorate. The delay in responding to Jameson's demands proved fatal for the Ndebele convoy. As they stood transfixed there, Captain Lendy shot at and killed Chief Mgandane Dlodlo. In a state of shock and disbelief, the rest of the group promptly made a reverse journey into Matabeleland and reported what had transpired. The news was unfortunate as, according to Cobbing (1976), at that time Lobengula had no intention, at least that winter, of taking aggressive action against the white settlers (Cobbing, 1976). All the same, he at that point in time, appreciated the full nature of the emerging Whites -Shona coalition against him.

As historical novelist Hole would dramatize it, the Ndebeles felt that their pride had been largely wounded. One and all, the entire Ndebele nation felt as a man stung by a scorpion would feel, a wild burning desire to crush and kill (Hole, 1926). The work of the entire five decades was potentially in tatters. It was in those circumstances that Lobengula probably remembered the irony of 1890 when the BSAC started moving across the Limpopo, the Voice of Mwali at Njelele had told him that he was "a small man killing others" and was instructed to look at Mwali's "white sons" crossing the river.

A letter, that can be found in Shaw's 1893 Review of Reviews and World's Work, Volume 8, shows that Lobengula was left in a state of bafflement by the actions of the BSAC. It also gives a picture of how King Lobengula felt about the whole situation at that time as he wrote.

"You said before that you would not punish my Amahole, but now that I send to punish them for you for harm done to your telegraph wires you resent it" (Shaw, 1893).

Nonetheless, at this point, rumours of war were already spreading across the nation like measles in a country school. Thereupon, readying for battle, King Lobengula made a pronunciation to add Insukamini, Jingeni, Inxa and Moreni into the resident regiment of Ameva, that despite the awareness that he was facing an uphill task. As news of the impending White settler invasion of Matabeleland became even more widespread, Shona adversaries of the Ndebele from Gutu, Zimundu, Madziviri, Chirumanzu and, least surprisingly, from Chivi, came forward to offer their services and collaborated (Cobbing, 1976).

The battle lines had been drawn and the big battle was almost and certainly inevitable. Consequently, King Lobengula and the War Council concluded that the invading forces were to be attacked now they were crossing the rocky uMguza River, 'because that would be when the mobility of the laager and horses was at their lowest point' (Hensman, 2016). It was on 25 October 1893 that the clashes occurred. Figure 47 is a map of the October/November 1893 Ndebele War campaign. The Ndebele regiments fought gallantly however, they were never going to be any match against the newly acquired heavy artillery of the Martini Henry rifle and the Maxim machine gun whose extreme lethality was employed to devastating effect.

The report on the casualties normally differs from scholar to oral traditions, but presumptively, over 1,500 Ndebele fighters were killed in this battle. Records reveal that only 10 BSAC soldiers died or were wounded. Another decisive battle followed in November 1893. They were 700 BSAC soldiers fighting off some 5000 Ndebele warriors with just five Maxim guns. The battle was so fierce, that on 6th of December the King fled north and got to the Shangani River.

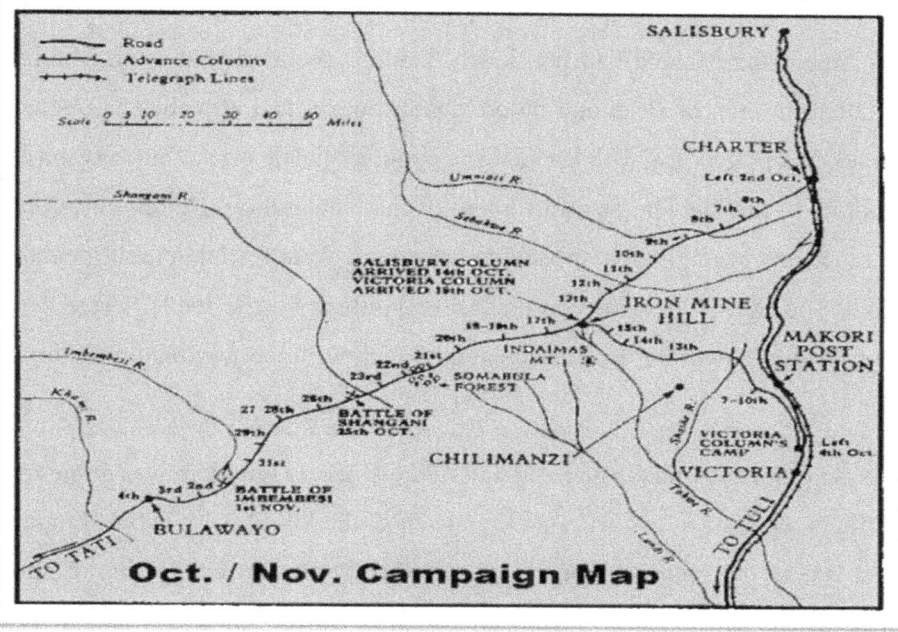

Figure 47. Map of The October/November 1893 Matabele War Campaign, Picture courtesy of Dennis Bishop

Legend has it that the custodians of Njelele gathered and performed some rituals that caused heavy rains to fall, and the Shangani River flooded overnight. Growing up in the Mwali priestly homestead, Lobengula himself had been schooled to be a rainmaker, and as king he was essentially the Great High Priest of the nation. Europeans called Lobengula 'the clerk of the weather and the Rainmaker General of the country,' for he was good at making thunderstorms, had powers to cause rain and knowledge of the moon phases (Lesabe interview in (Bhebhe, 1979). The rains caused the Shangane river to flood and making it impossible for the BSAC's Major Allan Wilson and his troops to cross in their pursuit of King Lobengula. In the jaws of defeat, Sihuluhulu Mabhena and Sivalo Mahlangu were given a signal by the king to set the Capital Bulawayo alight and king Lobengula disappeared without trace. According to the Malaba tradition, the *gobhodo lemiti* had worked its magic just as Mpangana Malaba had previously made a declaration to king Mzilikazi before, that no man of flesh and blood was to pursue and apprehend Lobengula Khumalo. In an interview with Ranger, the popular Njelele priest, Sitwanyana also corroborate to the incident as a fulfilment of that declaration. He reiterates that a reassurance had been given to the young Lobengula from the Njelele shrine that "I will hide you. I will go with you and leave you among the reeds" (Terence O. Ranger, 1999). Therefore, his disappearance without trace was testimony to that claim.

All the same, for the Malaba clan, the fall of the Ndebele kingdom was going to be a significant episode in history. In a literal sense, the fall of the Ndebele kingdom in 1893 was in the same way heralding the Malaba clan's own decline in power and influence. Their inherited legacy and ultimate power relating to the nature of Mwalism in general, and the rainmaking custodianship, was dwindling and like a shot, the intestinal fortitude of the acquired chieftain too, was sharply diminishing. As already indicated, their relationship with the Ndebele kingdom was interpreted by some culturist as based on some divine connections.

While the national spiritual lives of the nation were in the care of the Mpangana Malaba, who author, Hole (1926,) illustrate as having been the second most important person in the nation after Mzilikazi, the leadership security of that spiritual realm was under the safeguard-ship of the Matabele artillery (Hole, 1926). Therefore, prima facie the defeat of Lobengula manifested some clipped wings for the Malaba clan. The flying start of the disempowerment is captured in the verbatim accounts of W. A. Wills and L. T. Collingridge, in their work, *"The downfall of Lobengula: the cause, history, and effect of the Matabele War"*. The two diarists narrate about when the news of the defeat of the Ndebeles were broken to them for the first time. They were in their journey back from Botswana moving into Matabeleland, where, as the Matabele war was ragging on, Rhodes' man Sir

Henry Loch, had requested with success, the help of Khama's army to march against the Ndebele of Lobengula and he managed to march back into Matabeleland with 1,000 men for reinforcement.

W. A. Wills, who, as a protocol, was passing through the Malaba territory wrote that, "on 3rd November I moved on to a good site, close to Empandeni Kraal. On 5th November 1893, just as I was in spanning preparatory to moving on towards Mangwe, the Chief Khama informed me that neither he nor his people could go on any farther, that smallpox had broken out among his people, and that unless he could get back to his own country his people would be dying in the veld. Within a few hours of Khama's leaving, I received a deputation from the MaKalanga Chiefs Hhobhodo Malaba and Manyami of the BaNgwato, stating that they were reinforcing protection for their people. They also informed me that the Column from Mashonaland had a battle near Bulawayo, that the Matabele had been beaten, and that King Lobengula had fled". Wills and Collingridge also mention an incident about when the other impis, on hearing the news from Bulawayo had fled in the direction of the Gwayi River. *"On 6th November 1893 I received a message from Doctor Jameson confirming these reports...."* he wrote.

The Wills and Collingridge's communication assist in portraying the shrinking Malaba power, particularly the gatekeeping role at the Mangwe Pass, which, veritably, was still there but not there anymore as the power was being reduced significantly. After the defeat of the Ndebele, the white settlers ultimately advanced to the capital Bulawayo on 4 November 1893 where the union flag was raised. On the first of June 1894, Dr Leander Star Jameson, the Administrator for Matabeleland marked the official opening of Bulawayo as a town with the following speech:

"It is my job to declare the town open. Gentlemen I do not think we want to waste any talk on it. I make the declaration now. There is plenty of whiskey and soda inside so come in." (Nyathi, 2019).

The victorious Dr Leander Starr Jameson then raised the British South Africa flag signalling an apocalyptic death knell for the Matabele kingdom. Matabeleland, formerly BuKalanga and Mashonaland were then merged into Southern Rhodesia.

Figure 48. Haddon and Sly Limited, picture courtesy of Rhodesianstudycircle.org.uk

Unlike so many other colonies, the white settlers were hereby settling for life and therefore, investing heavily in constructing a solid infrastructure (Coltart, 2016). Within a short period of time, trade in Bulawayo was booming. Competition was at such a high level that by 1894, businesses like Haddon and Sly Limited were forced to merge their businesses to suppress competition from other entrepreneurs

(Fig. 48). The first bank in Matabeleland, The Standard Chartered bank, emerged during the period, starting off under a tent at the Bulawayo Laager, now known as the Bulawayo large City Hall. Figure 49 shows the town of Bulawayo in Rhodesia with several homes, shops, and military buildings on display.

By March 1895, barely six months after the foundation of the Rhodesian Native Department, the settlers conducted their own census that followed the one previously done under the leadership of Malaba under the instructions of king Lobengula in the Nketha base. The Rhodesian Native Commissioners used a similar method as that used by Malaba and his team of census collectors but this time around, the new team going a step further and counting the people as individuals, mainly done for the purposes of taxes.

Although the number of black natives was not absolute, Rhodesian archives show that on 1st of March 1895 the findings were that the population of Matabeleland was 126 491 people. There were 1,232 white male and 164 white female adults in Bulawayo alone. Comparatively, a follow up November 1895 Salisbury (Harare) census however revealed 507 white males and just 88 females. The population for blacks in 1900 was estimated to be at 692,000, consisting mainly of Mashona and the Ndebele. By 1911 the Rhodesian archives in the National Gallery of Zimbabwe (NGZ) showed that the native population in Southern Rhodesia had increased to numbering about 700,000.

………………………..

Most of the whites who were recruited in the BSAC army mainly from South Africa had been promised mining prospects. As their hopes of discovering gold waned, Rhodes and the BSAC began expropriating African land, labour, and cattle.

For example, settlers who had participated in the war were granted lavish farms and mineral claims, both of which soon passed to speculative syndicates. A land commission perfunctorily set aside the Shangani-Gwayi reserves for the Matabeleland people on some poor soils.

Figure 49. This photo shows the town of Bulawayo in Rhodesia with a number of homes, shops, and military buildings on display. Photo Courtesy of the Daily Mail.co.uk

The Rhodesian administration made a solemn declaration that they were not conceding to a revival of the Ndebele monarch again. Therefore, Lobengula's sons were never going to be granted an opportunity to assume the Ndebele Kingship. According to a Zambian author, after crossing the Shangani River, Lobengula marched on and finally arriving at Luangeni, Ngoniland in Zambia in 1894.

Lobengula considered Ngoniland as a safe net because, according to Gwakuba (2017), its ruler, was Lobengula's cousin Mpezeni, son of Zwangendaba. It is alleged that after Zwangendaba's death, his clan split up dividing itself under the leadership of his sons, Mpezeni, Mperembe, and Mbelwa. Mpezeni's people moved southbound and ultimately settling near the modern-day Chipata in Zambia. This is evidenced by the fact that Lobengula even gave his son, born in 1880 the name Mpezeni. Lobengula's son Mpezeni died young on 9 December 1899. According to the author, Lobengula's settlement still exist today and is called Mashanga, which is a corruption of Mahlanga. Author Gwakuba (2017) reveals that in early 1980, an elderly Ndebele man whose totem was Msimanga appeared at the PF ZAPU headquarters in Lusaka, accompanied by a boy of about eight or nine years. According to Gwakuba, the man found Andrew Mafu and another man where he said that he had been sent by the Ndebeles to inform ZAPU leader Dr Joshua Nkomo that he needed to go and see the grave of Lobengula before returning home to Zimbabwe. It is recorded that Dr Nkomo found it impossible to return to Zambia at that overly critical time as he was on a campaign mission in Zvishavane (Gwakuba- Ndlovu, 2017).

As a matter of course, the BSAC government identified and blocked Lobengula's sons Njube, Mpezeni, Nguboyenja (pictured in Figure 50) and Sidojiwe who were born when Lobengula was king, because those were eligible to claim the kingship. In 1894 the three were extracted from Rhodesia and sent to Cape Town to be 'educated' in Western culture under the care of the State, ostensibly to divert them from focusing on their own culture and the potential revival of the Ndebele kingship. Having born before Lobengula had become king, Nyamande and Sintinga, the Malaba's own God son, actually known as Tshakalisa (Tjakalisa), were not eligible to become king according to traditional customs. However, it is important to note the fact that there are arguments qualifying Nyamande as heir to the throne. Those who hold that notion argue that Nyamande was born in 1873, three years after Lobengula's coronation and that Nyamande succeeded Lobengula at some point.

A thesis by researcher Cobbing reveals Nyamande as being coronated king at Entumbane on 25 June 1896 two years after Lobengula's defeat (Cobbing, 1976).

Five-year-old Sidojiwe could not go to Cape Town because he was still too young. Later when some Ndebele elders demanded Njube, the eldest of the boys to come back home to become king, the Rhodesian government made it clear that they would not grant Njube such permission and he was not going to become the new Ndebele king. In January 1898 James Makunga also applied to the BSAC Administration on behalf of Lobengula's wives for permission to proceed to the Cape Colony and see their sons. As interpreter Makunga indicated at the time, Lobengula's wives desired to proceed to the Cape accompanied by Mtshana Khumalo, and with him, Makunga as a guide (Makambe, 1979). That request too was not successful.

Together with the likes of John Grootboom, John Makunga was one of the well-known black Rhodesian collaborators during the Ndebele uprising. According to Makambe (1979), it was interesting to note that Makunga may have been forgiven by his Ndebele kinsmen for his part in the *Umvukela wamaNdebele* uprisings, and thus continued to maintain friendly contacts with them in the post-1896 era (Makambe, 1979). Njube died in South Africa in 1920 and his young brother Nguboyenja, had been made to die a destitute earlier on in 1908 after having been Rhodesia's first qualified black lawyer but barred by the colonial regime from practicing as a lawyer. Had Nguboyenja (Fig. 49) been allowed to be a legal practitioner, he would have become the first black barrister in Southern Rhodesia fifty years before Herbert Chitepo (T. O. Ranger, 1972). As reported in the Bantu Mirror of 21st June 1944, when Nguboyenja was being buried close to his grandfather King Mzilikazi, there were rain showers and two large rainbows emerged, one over King Mzilikazi's grave and a smaller one over Nguboyenja's grave, signifying his symbolic social status (Terence O. Ranger, 1999).

Figure 50. Lobengula's sons; Prince Nguboyenja (Left), Prince Njube (Centre) and Prince Mpezeni (Right) in 1900. Picture Courtesy of R.S. Roberts

Prince Tshakalisa (Tjakalisa) later lived on the southern bank of the Shangani River in Nkayi. Having come under the influence of the London Missionary Society (LMS), Tshakalisa built a home with huts displaying Inyathi-inspired architecture. He even sent his two sons Dabulamanzi and Qedilizwe to Inyathi Mission to receive western education before the 1920s. No one knows exactly what happened to the last born, Sidojiwe who was the youngest of the four 'royal' sons of Lobengula having been born in 1888 by Ngotsha at Nsindeni. Some accounts say he was put away quietly by the Rhodesian authorities, but the Bantu Mirror reported that Sidojiwe died on 13 July 1960 and was buried at Entumbane near to Mzilikazi and Nguboyenja.

5,4. Umvukela WamaNdebele -The Ndebele Uprising

William Elliot Thomas, the Bulilima-Mangwe Native Commissioner who grew up among the Ndebele people and got to know their customs and traditions, argues that assertions that normally create an association between Mwali and the politics of violence are too simplistic. His line of reasoning is that Mwali, the god of seasons and crops, could never have been involved in the rebellion. He characterized Mwali as a god of peace and plenty and further arguing that never in the knowledge of the natives had Mwali posed as the god of war. He contends that even when Mzilikazi entered the country Mwali did not help the BaKalanga to withstand the Matabele, nor did Mwali ever pretend in any way to assist the Matabele impis which went out to war during Lobengula's time, nor did He ever assist Lobengula (or ever pretended to do so) when the whites advanced against him in 1893. Mwali blossomed forth as a god of war for the first time during the late Matabele rising in this present year, and even to this day the natives in Matabeleland say: 'who ever heard of Mwali being a God of war or armies? (Thomas, 1986).

Although a sound argument, Thomas' line of reasoning remarkably misses the point. In fact, preceding the rebellions around the turn of the century, there is overwhelming evidence that the Mwali religion had for a long time, been associated with intertribal affairs. At least, as far as the Malaba orality is concerned, Mwali has always been associated with the legitimation of political authority. Equally, Daneel, who is well known to have been fluent in the local languages, argues that the interest of the Mwali religion in ethnic group politics dates to the time when the Lozwi begun using the religion as a "centralized service" as well as a means of consolidating their own dynamic rule over the surrounding ethnic groups (Daneel, 1970). There is evidence that these political uses of the oracle continued after the arrival of early Europeans in the southwestern part of the country in the early 19th century.

Before all else, an argument about whether the Mwali religion advocated war or not, is a simplification of an otherwise complex issue. The argument itself is a fallacy of composition that commits an error by assuming that what is true of a member of a group is true for the group. Therefore, the most feasible approach to the subject matter could be to first dissect the holistic Mwali religion into separate shrine components. By all means, the shrine of Njelele was a peaceful shrine that shunned the spilling of blood since the days beyond recall. This is the reason the Dula shrine was introduced in the eastern Matopo hills in the late 19th century.

Hereafter, like the Pentagon, the Dula Shrine became the department of defence headquarters of the Mwali religion where the oracle was consulted in political and matters of national defence. This is the reason the *Umvukela wamaNdebele* rebellion was dubbed *Impi Yehloka Elibomvu* (The War of the Red Axe). Some scholars like Ranger (1999) even argue that Dula was established as late as just before the *Umvukela WamaNdebele* uprising, nonetheless, there are records of its existence prior to that as Mzilikazi was "allowed" the Red Axe shrine once he had paid a certain number of cattle (Clarke, 2010) and that was way before the uprising.

After its establishment, the Dula shrine, known as *Ilitshe lemikhonto* or *Ihloka elibomvu* was bestowed the powers of making war and making peace (Terence O. Ranger, 1999). Like it was argued in the early chapters, the coming of the Matabele nation into the Mwali epicentre of the Matopos could have been to institute this department of defence which, prior to that, was either missing or just irrelevant. In a nutshell, the Njelele and Dula point of convergence is where the BaKalanga and the Matabele nation met in terms of spiritual functionality and purpose as a nation.

In conclusion, the Mwali religion is a national symbol and a religion of everybody, whatever their tribe as the 1896-1897 rebellion show that the religion had an intertribal nature as it fulfilled the role of an intelligence service. Although the spilling of blood was a taboo in the Mwali religion, the creed certainly advocated for the legitimation of political authority and distasted the disabling conditions for an individual while favouring the fulfilment of enabling conditions for the people.

Ranger (1999), writes that when he interviewed Joshua Nkomo in July 1988, Nkomo indicated that Njelele was the only site for his great rally in February 1980. Mrs. Thenjiwe Lesabe also insists that ZIPRA was so powerful because Joshua Nkomo was getting his support for the war from the Dula shrine. In her interview with Ranger (1999), she also insists that the Voice promised invulnerability to Nkomo as it was heard saying "before you are settled, in this part of the country, there is really going to be bloodshed. But you, son of Nyongolo, great son of Maweme, you will lead this nation. When you go into the river, I will be with you. When you climb trees, I will be with you…. Whenever you are, I will be with you until this war is over. Nobody will touch your body. Let us go to the war together" (Terence O. Ranger, 1999).

……………………………

After the disappearance of king Lobengula in the 1893 war, a Land Commission was set up by the British South African Company in 1894 as it meant to find a solution to the conflicting interests between the people of Matabeleland and the European settlers. A recommendation was made to allocate two tracts of a waterless land uninhabited at the Gwayi and Shangani reserves which had had become the first native reserves under the provisions of the Matabeleland Order In-Council of July 18, 1894. The people of Matabeleland flatly refused to settle there, as Earl Grey, the then Administrator of Rhodesia, admitted in a book, stating that the Reserves were 'cemeteries and not homes.'

Then in 1895 a drought ravaged Matabeleland. A rumour that Njelele had prophesied that the 4000 white settlers were the cause of all misfortunes started circulating, and according to the white settlers themselves, being leaked through the shrine priests.

However, it is important at this point to revisit the assertion that the Mwali religion was a creed that was against the spilling of blood. Even immediately after the establishment of the Njelele rainmaking shrine, author Ranger (1999) indicates that Mpangana Malaba and Sabaswi Lubimbi sent their son Hhobhodo/Hhoba and Npininga to instruct king Mzilikazi about the expectations of the Mwali religion - which was to stay peaceful. According to culturist Cont Mhlanga, Mzilikazi was even 'castigated' by Njelele for his role in the killing of *izinduna* at Ntabazinduna (Terence O. Ranger, 1999). This is what led to King Mzilikazi ultimately agreeing to honour Mwali with annual gifts, through an offering of black cattle, and requests for rain. Mzilikazi was 'allowed' the creation of the Red Axe shrine, known as *Ilitshe lemikhonto* or *Ihloka elibomvu*, at the Dula shrine in the Matobo Hills once he had paid a certain number of cattle. According to Mhlanga (Conti Mhlanga, 2018), this occurrence was related to the spilling of blood in Ntabazinduna vis-a-vis the perception by Mwali of such an event as a taboo.

These contrasts in cultural backgrounds and customary beliefs were sometimes causing visible damaging cracks and fissures between particularly the BaKalanga and the Matabele. For instance, two years before the Ndebele uprising, in February 1894, some of the BaKalanga population never answered the call to turn out and fight the whites but remained in their fastnesses. They instead sent representatives to the whites to ask for peace. Part of the reason of the reluctancy was that the BaKalanga still perceived both the Matabele and the White settlers as enemies of the BuKalanga state. Selous writes that, for instance, Umfezela even sent his own son to the Kalanga of the Marula area, calling upon them in the name of racial solidarity to make common cause against the whites who were 'killing all the black men they can catch' (Cobbing, 1979). The Marula residents also refused to act. Nonetheless, according to the Malaba traditions, the reluctance to participate in the early stages of the war was exacerbated by the fact that the BaKalanga, particularly the Marula residents under chief Hhobhodo Malaba, were against Umfezela's ambition to become King after the disappearance of king Lobengula on 4 November 1893 rather than a refusal to fight the white settlers. The Malaba felt that Fezela Khumalo's candidature was being imposed by Mlugulu Khumalo who claimed to have been entrusted by Lobengula to be chief priest and restore the monarch, together with some older *izinduna* like Gampu Sithole. Malaba and his people of Marula instead supported Lobengula's eldest son, Nyamande the brother of Tshakalisa, because they too considered him as their spiritual son.

Therefore, when summoned to join the war preparations, the Malaba and other BaKalanga merely replied that the 'people don't wish to fight; they wish to sit still'. And sit still they did. Another reason was that the Njelele rainmaking shrine priests were of Venda origin and only recently domiciled in the Matopos. Like Ranger (1999), notes, the Venda-Kalanga priests were not therefore able to co-ordinate an uprising because as noted before, Mwali was, ' fifthly, 'a God of peace and plenty and against the spilling of blood (Terence O. Ranger, 1999). Therefore, the Malaba, Lubimbi or Tshimba priests although participated in the physical battles, however, were reluctant in leading a battle, therefore, the *Umvukela WaMaNdebele* commanders were drawn from shrines such as the shrine of Dula, as well as Manyanga, Manyangwa and other Mwali shrines and not from the Njelele shrine. Cobbing (1976) however, believed that the Njelele shrine had later re-emerged with a revolutionary role in contrast to its previous role of arts of peace. His conclusion could have been influenced by the generalization of the Njelele name in reference to all the other Mwali religious shrines including Dula the shrine largely associated with the revolutions (Cobbing, 1976). Upon realizing some signs of peace and reluctancy to fight in this part of the country, the white settlers arrived at the Mangwe area wholesomely. Firstly, they found refuge in a dilapidating Mangwe Fort (Fig 38) which had previously been constructed by Lieutenant-Colonel Goold-Adams, commander of the Bechuanaland Border Police (BBP) during the 1893 war. The Fort had been deserted after the BSAC victory of 1893 as the column ultimately moved on to the capital of Bulawayo. It was the Fort Mangwe establishment that in 1893 led to several Ndebele chiefs accusing Gampu of not taking his chance of annihilating Goold-Adam's column in the Mangwe Pass, possibly in the hope that he would be made paramount chief of the new colonial order, they claimed.

When the Ndebele rebellion broke out in 1896 (Fig 56), white families from the nearby areas cramped into the deserted Fort. According to Bishop in his work Artless Imperialism, The Conquest of Matabeleland, 1893, there were one hundred and fifty Europeans who crammed in the rat plagued Mangwe Fort for a period of three months, including forty-two children and six babies who were born during its occupation. When the Fort was not attacked during the *Umvukela wamaNdebele* rebellion, a further chain of six more Forts were constructed at intervals of about sixteen kilometres. These were Fort Luck, Fort Halstead, Fort Molyneux, Fort Marquand, Khami River Fort and Fort Dawson. The colonial settlers were erecting these forts and using them as strongholds and representatives of a show of force and colonial domination. The forts even officially fell under the safeguarding of the Protection of Natural and Historical Monuments law. As the 'disharmony' and discontent seemed to persist, the whites further tried to capitalize on it by calling for an indaba with the Kalanga chiefs, but every time they approached the area everyone would disappear into the mountains. The mistrust became more and more significant and more and more pronounced. The Rhodesian government then turned to Native Commissioners, who, once the war had broken out, had practically acted as the Rhodesian army's chief intelligence officers. A group of Native Commissioners, some of them the chief native of Matabeleland Herbert John Taylor, Johan W Colenbrander, the Native Commissioner of the Bulilima-Mangwe district William Elliot Thomas, and the Native Commissioner of Matopo district Hugh Marrison Gower Jackson, were asked to prefer a solution to the dire situation. According to the Malaba oral narratives while the general notion was that the Ndebele were being frustrated by the Marula Makalanga's lacklustre response to the call for war against the Rhodesians as petitioned from the Dula shrine, the Native Commissioners were conversely noticing a trend they deemed to be a strange one. For example, they observed a sudden unexplained surge on the Malaba men joining the Amagogo regiment.

However, more surprisingly, it is alleged that at that point the Bango young men were withdrawing from several of the Ndebele Regiments en masse citing reasons including that Kangangwani Bango's son, Habanahe, had been killed by Lobengula in 1872 for aiding the supporters of 'Nkulumane'. Believing that knowledge is power, the British South African Company (BSAC) had examined the history, culture, and customs of the black natives including the BaKalanga, the Matabele and the MaShona to an extent they would understand some cultural elements even better than black people themselves. Therefore, the Native Commissioners considered and concluded instantly that the slow response to the call to fight by the Marula residents was not actually a refusal to fight the white settlers but just a protocol for the Mwali religion that the custodians of the rainmaking shrine of Njelele should not be duty bound to lead a war. For the Njelele shrine was a shrine of peace and a shrine that was against the spilling of blood. However, as indicated before, this was rightly compensated as that defence duties were left to Dula, the Pentagon of the Mwali region. The Native Commissioners then produced a white paper on the influence of the chief priests of Mwali in the Matopos.

After an agreement that the shrine priests were chief troublemakers, the Native Commissioners and BSAC started identifying and pegging all areas they deemed to be run by potentially volatile traditional leaders. The conclusion by the Native Commissioners was that the Malaba were a big national threat and imposed a serious hazard to white rule. The map drawn of the Matabeleland identified and marked a 'Malaba mountain' (Fig. 51). This unique modus operandi by the Native Commissioners was aggravated by their unveiling of the fact that a number of young men from the Malaba and other neighbouring clans were being secretly sent to join the civil disobedience against the white settler rule. However, at this period, all the blacks had potentially become nationalists regardless. The anger against white rule was there but just being bottled up until things were desperate. Blacks could no longer tolerate the intolerable as desperate times called for desperate measures. Hence, the rebellion.

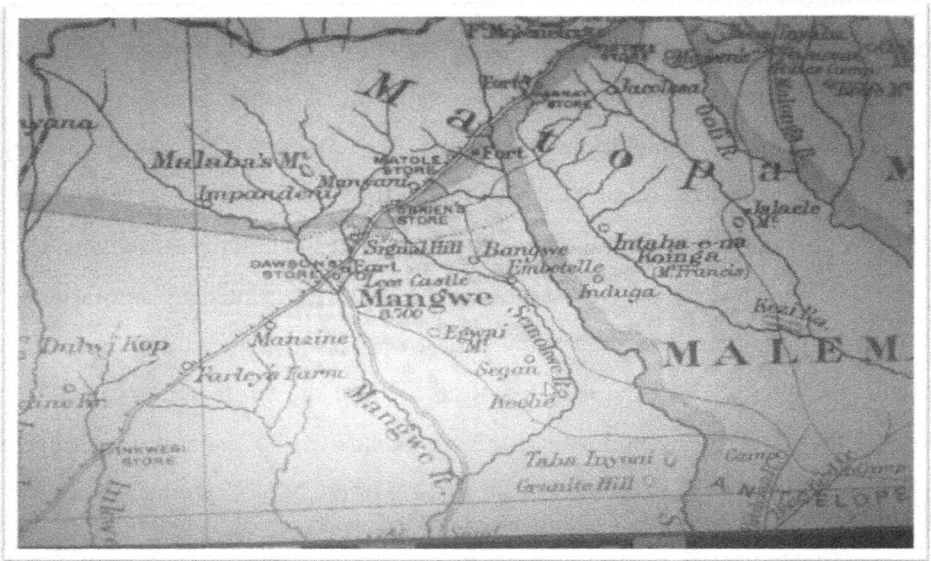

Figure 51. A map shows a place that was pegged as Malaba Mountain as a way to keep an eye on the Malaba people during Umvukela waMaNdebele. Map Courtesy of Fletcher and Espin's map of Matabeleland by Robert Alexander Fletcher

Through his role at Mangwe Pass, Chief Hhobhodo Malaba was one of the military village commanders that included, among other village commanders, Thebe, Mtshana, Ndiweni, Mphoko, Malisa, Msindazi, Mgandane, Sithole, Mafu, Fuyane, Mguni, Masunda, Mapanzure, Nhema, Fusi Khanye Mathema, Mkwananzi, Gwebu and Masuku in other areas. All these village commanders and others naturally became targets of British Pioneer Column led by Cecil John Rhodes. Chief Hhobhodo Malaba had another role, the role of being a traditional doctor and chief administrator in the King's kraal. However, in terms of military operations the Bulilima district to the south-west of Bulawayo was under chief Gampu Sithole, who was also chief of Amagogo within the Igabha regiment.

The chiefly town ruled by Gampu was Ndikimbela, in Nata Reserve, present-day Bulilima Mangwe district. His father chief Maqhekeni had been a leading chief under King Mzilikazi and was one of the chiefs that constituted *umphakathi*, the inner circle of chiefs that King Mzilikazi consulted on important issues. Based at Emagogweni, his chief village, chief Maqhekeni oversaw several newly established villages. He had become the head of Igabha when the Ndebele were still in the Limpopo Province of South Africa. Sotho incorporates were enlisted into villages that came under the authority of chief Maqhekeni. However, later in the 1896 the antagonism between the Malaba people was reaching crisis levels following instructions from Njelele to fight the whites and chief Gampu Sithole's reluctance. Therefore, militarily, chief Hhobhodo Malaba's village arbitrarily fell under the jurisdiction of chief Gampu Sithole. Besides the eZimnyama Regiment which had a number of the Malaba and Bango men and Amahlokohloko that had Tshada the brother of Hhobhodo/Hhoba in it, most Malaba men were by and by conscripted in chief Gampu Sithole's regiment although the regiment was basically known for recruiting more Kalanga man of Usaba and Lulwana clans.

This is the reason why the Christmas day battle that wiped out the Allan Wilson Patrol at Pupu had, according to the Malaba oral traditions, many the Usaba and

Lulwana clans and Malaba people who fought gallantly to fulfilling Mpangana's prophecy on Lobengula's invincibility. The battle of Pupu was led by both Mtshana Khumalo's Imbizo regiment and Gampu Sithole's Amagogo regiments from the Marula area. Many BaKalanga sons including the Malaba, Usaba and Lulwana clansmen are said to have heroically fallen in this battle. The clash is still referred to as 'the battle that was won in a war that was lost'. At this point the number of the Bango young men in the Amagogo regiment had been reduced to next to none as the then chief Hobane Bango, refused to join the Ndebele in the uprising citing his anger over Lobengula's killing of Kangangwani's son, Habanahe, who was killed for being actively involved in the hunt of Nkulumane as heir to the throne after the death of Mzilikazi. Amongst the White settlers themselves, there was a rumour that was circulating and instructing that the whites were never going to win the war if Jenje Thobela Lubimbi the Mwali High priest was alive. Hinged on this rumour, the BSAC resolved that the solution to the situation was to eliminate The High Priest Jenje Thobela. The first attempt to kill Jenje was in June 1896, after Colonel John Antony Speckley had brought some news to Major General Sir Frederick Carrington that the chief instigators of the rebellion Mkwati Leya-Ncube, the child of Mwali, and Jenje Siginyamabele Thobela, the High Priest of Mwali were stationed about one hundred and thirteen kilometres north-east of the capital Bulawayo at Ntabazikamambo or Manyanga. Lt. Col.

Herbert Plumer was dispatched to go for a blitz. Plumer, was a seconded Imperial officer who had been raising a force of Boer and British volunteers in South Africa, of which the unit also incorporated the Matabeleland Relief Force upon complete formation. His record on the incident states that at the dawn of 20 June 1896, Plumer and company stormed the Ntabazikamambo position from three different points and heavy fighting ensued leading to "recovering of cattle and grain loot which was found stored away in the recesses of the caves" (Plumer, 1897). Both Jenje and Mkwati escaped unhurt. Burnam seized the prized asset and presented it to Baden-Powell as a souvenir. Baden-Powell personalised the material and used it to display spiritual prowess, consequently keeping it until his death. It was after this foiled attempt at Jenje and Mwati's lives that a sharpshooter was hired to go and kill Jenje Thobela who they know was permanently based at the Njelele Shrine. The sharpshooter's name was Frederick Russel Burnham, an American scout and world traveling adventurer. Burnham was the influencer of Baden-Powell's popular Boy Scouts Campaign hats of the Stetson 'Boss of the Plains' type which became popular not only in Africa but in the USA and Canada. In one of his diaries, Russel narrates the entire modus operandi including the names of those who assisted him carry out the assassination.

"A young man came to me in June in 1896. He told me his name was Armstrong a Native Commissioner stationed at Mangwe. He proposed that we go together to find the cave where chief priest lived and kill him and put an end to the source of our troubles with the natives" (Baden-Powell, 1896).

Before Burnham and Armstrong went for the siege, they communicated with Matopo Native Commissioner H.M. Jackson inquiring about the name of the shrine priest of which he however, responded,

"I have been told the name of the priest at Njelele, but have forgotten it" (Cobbing, 1976).

As a result, in the still of the night, Native Commissioner Armstrong took the hired assassin Russel Burnham to within point blank range of Jenje Thobela, after which the sharpshooter shot him dead in cold blood. His verbatim transcripts and account of the killing takes up full ten-page chapter in his book. On the 23rd of June 1896, the two men had tethered their horses to a thicket before crawling cautiously by means of branches held before them and entered the Njelele cave. They surreptitiously waited until the priest entered the cave and started his rituals.

"I saw with surprise", Burnham narrated, *"that a man striding in advance of the others was not a Matabele at all, but a pure Makalanga".*

Jenje Thobela was son of Npininga son of Sabaswi Lubimbi, son of Thobela Mbedzinkulu who were of the Mbedzi Venda clan. Getting mixed up with Jenje's relation to Mpangana, researcher Cobbing recorded him as Habangana, presumably a corruption of the name Mpangana or just confusing him with another considered troublesome man, Habangana of the Bango totem. The Ndebele called Jenje Siginyamabele and was from the shrine priest clan of Ncube yaka Lubimbi section of the Mbedzi Venda group that included Mpangana Malaba, Tshimba and Tshawwila. On arrival, Burnham remembered Carrington's command, "Capture him if you can; kill him if you must". Therefore, upon reaching to the cave, Burnham took aim at Jenje and pulled the trigger shooting him just below the heart and callously killing him instantly (Fig. 52), heralded the end of the ancient Sabaswi Thobela Lubimbi family priesthood legacy at the Njelele shrine. Burnam ransacked the Njelele rainmaking shrine seizing a handful of prized assets that included a knobkerry-type walking stick. walking stick which he conferred to Baden-Powell as a souvenir. Baden-Powell personalised the stuff which he used as a symbol of spiritual prowess, keeping it till his death. In his own words, unrepentant Baden-Powell wrote, "I was sorry for him-he was a fine savage; but I signed his warrant, directing that he should be shot at sundown" (Baden-Powell, 1896).

The Lubimbi orality present a Jenje who evidently left no male successor to the throne of the Mwali priesthood. On the Bulilima-Mangwe side, another relative of the Malaba was also being a victim of the war. He went by the name of Njenjema, but his childhood name was Mbengwa Tjabulula Nleya from the Nleya clan of Nilikawu. His mother was BaSabaswi or BaLubimbi, who was a descendant of Sabaswi- Lubimbi, a brother to Mpangana Malaba. Njenjema had been named after his uncle Jenje because he was predestined to succeed him as an acclaimed Mwali priest. Nevertheless, Njenjema became a powerful hosanna in charge of a small rain shrine (daka) known as Zondani, located not far from Tokwana School in Bulilima District. Hs divine career had all begun when one day the chief of Dombodema was visiting one of the Mwali shrines and heard a voice:

"I will now visit you through Njenjema (Mothibi). You must no longer come here but go and tell Njenjema that I will come through him" (Rodewald, 2010).

This was how Njenjema assumed his religious specialist role (ntungamili) and served as guardian of Mwali's place. In 1896, during the *Umvukela WamaNdebele* war, Njenjema was killed by the white settlers. After the realization that a number of young men from both the Malaba and the other Kalanga clans were joining Chief Gampu Sithole's regiment en masse in preparation of the uprising, the white settlers struck again. Like cattle to the slaughterhouse, seven other unarmed men led by Jobani or Tjobani (Tshobani) Bango Dube were marched to the hills, shot, and killed in cold blood. Tjobani was of Bango totem and a leader of the struggle however, not a Mwali priest based at the Matopo hills shrines.

Figure 52. Depiction of Burnham and Armstrong after the assassination of Mwali high priest Jenje Lubimbi. Matabele warriors in hot pursuit, drawn by Frank Dadd. Pic, Courtesy of WikiVisually.com

Upon learning of the death of Jenje the Mwali priest, Cecil Rhodes walked unarmed into the Ndebele's stronghold and persuaded the Impi to lay down their arms. According to Ranger (1999), an indaba was arranged with the Ndebele indunas on the 21 August 1896. Rhodes came along accompanied by his two interpreters John (Jan) Grootboom and James Makunga. John Grootboom, one of the blacks who loyally fought alongside the BSAC was a Xhosa from the Cape Colony who had come up to Matabeleland either before or after 1890, but before 1893 as he fought against the Ndebeles in 1893. He had arrived and took employment as a driver to the London Missionary Society minister, the Rev. C.D. Helm. Helm was one of the Rudd Concessionists. John's original surname was likely to have been Mthimkhulu, which was translated to Grootboom, an Afrikaans equivalent (Terence O. Ranger, 1999).

At Mlugulu's in the eastern Matopos on 21 August 1896 Rhodes held his famous indaba in the hills with the Ndebele leaders that included Sikombo, Dhliso, Somabulana, Umlugulu, Nyanda, Nconcobela, Sikota, Ntweni, Nhluni, Mabesa, Nyanda, Babayane, Mtshana, Nhlukoniso Faku, Gampu and Kaal Khumalo (Fig. 53). He thereafter referred to the period as "one of those moments in life that makes it worth living" (Milner, 1953). However, the meeting failed to yield any positive results. Although the term indaba had always been a reference to an important conference held by the izinduna of the Zulu, Swati, and Xhosa peoples of South Africa, it was this event that led to the word finding its way into the Oxford dictionary (Cont Mhlanga, 2020).

The murdering of Jenje Thobela at the Njelele shrine did not only create an unattended shrine, but also a vacuum in leadership, a vacuum that was filled by an emergence of none other than Mkwati-Leya Ncube. Based in the Manyanga shrine that was in the present day Bubi district, Mkwati is argued to have originally been a member of the Toka-Leya tribe but had adopted the Ncube surname after his marriage to Tenkela Ncube who was a sister to the Manyaga priest Whunya Ncube.

According to Clark, towards the end of the seventeenth and beginning of the eighteenth centuries the Leya who are under Chief Mukuni had migrated south from their original homelands in the southern Congo Basin. They were an offshoot of the Lenje tribe. The word 'Leya' is said to mean 'to keep out of troubles' (Clark (1952).

By 1896, led by Mkwati, an all-out rebellion sanctioned by Mwali from the Dula shrine, broke out against the white settlers. It was later to be known as *Umvukela wamaNdebele* and involved all native language speakers like the Ndebele, Kalanga, Shona, Chewa, Chibarwe, Koisan, Nambya, Ndau, Shangani, Sotho, Tonga, Tswana, Venda, and Xhosa. From his Jingeni base in Bubi, Mkwati became a key figure in the *Umvukela wamaNdebele* war, being influential in encouraging people to fight against the white settlers. For the maiden attack, the Mwali voice had given a command for the planned war to wait until the night of 29 March 1896 which was the first full moon. This was the right time for surprise attack in Bulawayo which would be immediately after a ceremony called the Big Dance. However, a number of young Matabeleland men were overly anxious to go to war, and the rebellion started prematurely. On 20 March, Matabele rebels shot and stabbed a native policeman and killing several white settlers over the next few days. Mkwati was declared a *persona non grata* by a force under command of Roben Baden Powell, Mkwati was forced to flee from Matopo only to go back to his Ntabazikamambo or Manyanga base.

To intimidate and put fear into the Ndebeles, the British South Africa Company identified a tree outside the fortifications of Bulawayo where a total of nine Ndebele men were hung from the tree for rebelling against Rhodes' British South Africa Company (Fig. 53 left). The tree was later to be known as the 'Hanging Tree'. There is also documented evidence of some members of the British South Africa Company celebrating the hangings. For example, a Mr Labouchere, who was the editor of the Daily Graphic reproduced the letter in his paper as well as another in which the writer wrote of it being "quite a nice sight" to see men shot as spies, and a photo taken from these hangings were so cherished by Robert Baden-Powell that he kept it in his diary and entitled it 'The Christmas Tree'.

The Baden-Powell statue done by sculptor David Annand (Fig 53 - right) was unveiled in Poole England on 13th August 2008, at the island site of Baden-Powell's first 1907 camp which is seen as the start of the Scout and Guide movement. However, after the death of George Floyd, an African American man who was killed by the police in Minnesota's major city of Minneapolis, the statue was boarded up on 12th June 2020 to protect it from the Black Lives Matter protesters who had scheduled to remove it on the 18th of June 2020 after enlisting it as a racist symbol.

Figure 53. Fig. The execution of some Ndebele men at the 'Hanging Tree' in Bulawayo. Photo extracted from Olive Schreiner's book entitled Trooper Peter Halket of Mashonaland and below it, Statue of Robert Baden-Powell holding on to Jenje's walking stick in Poole England

Determined to fight on, Mkwati fled to chief Lomagundi in Makonde, Mashonaland where he incited the Mashona rebellion. In response, within a week, records show that 141 settlers were killed in Matabeleland, another 103 killed in Mashonaland (see Table 2). Although the Ndebeles had managed to acquire around 2000 Martini Henry rifles and large stocks of ammunition, they were naturally far less dangerous with rifles than with assegais. In addition, the Matabele still lacked the firepower, mobility, and communications that would have been needed to pacify their enemy. The *Umvukela wamaNdebele* rebellion was ultimately crushed, and in 1898 Matabeleland and Mashonaland were combined as one country leading to the birth of Southern Rhodesia, born in honour of Cecil John Rhodes. At the very least there is a conviction that local Black Natives were hit so hard it took them short of a century to attempt at standing up and fight the settlers again. After the war, the provisions of the 1894 Order-in-Council were extended to the whole territory. Native Commissioners started demarcating African areas throughout Rhodesia. For the Malaba clan, it was another decade and another new start.

Figure 54. Picture: Ndebele chiefs and representatives gather for a meeting during umvukela wamandebele. (Photos by W. Rausch; Courtesy of the Daily Mail, UK).

Figure 55. A sketch of the 1896 peace Indaba. (Sketched by Lord Robert Baden-Powell).

Rotberg, writes that after the indaba (Fig 55), Rhodes, rode unarmed again and again into the Matopos, on one occasion stumbling upon the granite dome of Malindandzimu of which he chose it for his burial. "I admire the grandeur and loneliness of the Matopos in Rhodesia, and therefore I desire to be buried in the Matopos on the hill which I used to visit and which I called the 'View of the World'" (Rotberg, 1988). Ranger argues that, due to the spiritual power of the shrine, the ambitious Rhodes soon came to think of Matopo as a place that makes it worth dying too (Ranger, 1999).

After Rhodes visited England in 1901, he was already ill and on his return to Cape Town in the early months of 1902 and he died on 16th March 1905 at his seaside cottage in Muizenberg, Cape Town. In his will he asked to be buried on the 'View of the World' hill in the Matobo district, Matabeleland. The location of Rhodes' grave (Fig 56) that is atop the Malindadzimu Shrine (resting place of spirits) but not on it.

Although Rhodes had wished to be buried in the most powerful place spiritually and the Malindadzimu Shrine was the most fitting, some informants revealed that upon coming to the hilltop, African labourers, even at threat of a gun, still defied and misdirected the funeral procession to an empty space nearby and professed it was the Malindandzimu shrine point.

The Malindandzimu cave was where "the bones" of the Mwali priests were buried and was in a "cave only a few hundred yards from the Rhodes' tomb" (Terence O. Ranger, 1999). In a square to be cut in the rock on the top of the hill, covered with a plain brass plate, were these words thereon: 'Here lie the remains of Cecil John Rhodes'. Such was the significance of Njelele seen and believed even by the missionaries as well as the white colonialists themselves who in public denounced the African cultures and customs.

Figure 56. Picture; The burial of Cecil John Rhodes. Photo Courtesy of Rhodesia.me.uk

Figure 57. Picture taken in March 1896; the Matabele revolted against the authority of the British South AfricaCompany (pictured. (Photos by W. Rausch; Courtesy of the Daily Mail, UK).

Table 2. Summary of Casualties in Matabeleland and Mashonaland 1896-1897, Data Adaptedfrom Beach, 1975

	Rhodesia incl.volunteer forces	Imperial troops	BSAC	Total
Killed in action	47	8	4	59
Died of wounds	17	3	5	25
Died of other causes	70	11	22	103
Murdered by rebels	262	1	1	264
Total Deaths	**396**	**23**	**32**	451
Wounded in action	121	29	8	158
Wounded accidentally	15	1	-	16
Wounded at commencement of uprising	14	-	-	14
Total wounded	150	30	8	188

NB: the above list refers to Europeans only.

CHAPTER 6

THE MALABA PEOPLE AND LAND DISPOSSESSIONS

6,1. The Empandeni Settlement

"Kudala kwakunganje,

umhlaba uyaphenduka,

kwakubusa uMambo loMzilikazi.

Sawela uTshangane saguqa ngamadolo,

inkos' uLobengula yasinyamalala."

Translated - (Things were not like this in the past. The world is changing. King Mzilikazi and Mambo used to be the rulers. We got to the Shangani (river) and knelt down on our knees. Then King Lobengula disappeared.)

This is generally a sad national song. For the Malaba people it is classified as a clan's sad song. In culturist Cont Mhlanga's own words, "it is a sad song because it's a depiction of when both the Ndebele and the Malaba power story ended. It is a song that relates the stories of *kudala* (once upon a time). A song that is reciting the events regarding the forces of destabilization and destruction, whilst it is also pregnant with historical information. At the time of its composition in 1896 during *umvukela wamaNdebele* (the Ndebele uprising), Lobengula's disappearance in 1893, marking the gradual crumbling of the Ndebele state, together with its traditional values, culture, and general way of life that their Kings Mzilikazi and Mambo before him, had taken so long to build," narrates Mhlanga. Some scholars argue that the song was a Nguni war cry, but the Malaba clan narrative contend that the song is neither a Nguni ethno-music nor a Ndebele war cry. Reason for this being that the song is characterized by the lack of the rhythm and speed of Nguni ethnic-music, and over and above, the absence of rhythmic elements such as *'zhiii yaa hoo'* or *'zhiya helele'* et cetera, does not by its own nature disqualifies but certainly distances the song from other typical Nguni war cries. Apart from that line of reasoning, researchers have found that those associated with both king Mzilikazi and Lobengula's esigodlweni were either not privy to the song or disassociated it from other definitive Nguni war cries. Although it is not clear who composed the song or the circumstance around its composition, the song was made popular by the post war activities. For the Malaba clan who, at the time of their arrival from Venda were not only acknowledged but also embraced and incorporated into the leadership mainstream of the Ndebele kingdom, this was a blow. A juggernaut! It was like a dark cloud emerging from the horizons of hell, infiltrating itself into a smiling sunshine spell and causing its destruction and thereby giving way to demoralization, doom, and cheerlessness.

The Malaba people always had traditionally supernatural prowess associated with both rain-making and other wonders. While the medicinal supremacy and the will power was a greatness born of them, the political ascendance was power attained from Mzilikazi's admiration of their acute skills in medicinal craft. It was a greatness thrust upon them rather than acquired. The 1893 crumbling of the Ndebele kingdom was, over and above, the crumbling of the Malaba political power and the weakening of their religious significance and influence and social status. Historically, the Malaba were a people that had before, forced to fight back against some often unsurvivable odds. They had defied and escaped the wrath of their bitter enemies before them, surviving gruelling journeys through deserts and wildernesses, all the way to achieve the greatness they now possessed in being part of the Matabele and BaKalanga's Mambo kingdoms.

One of the greatest achievements by the Malaba clan over the years was the unwavering awareness of who they were and not changing it a bit. Despite the test of time, the Malaba people never broke faith with their language and culture. They epitomised a people that understood that their language was a vessel that contained the triumphs and tribulations of their past and the ammunition of their future. To them the Kalanga language was complexly interweaved with their religion and culture, evolving together to ultimately define what it is to be a *Mbedzi, Malaba, Thobela, Kumbudzi, Batombo tjisipotelekwe tinopotelekewa kukabemibvimbi.* Though still powerful in those aspects, by 1896 the Malaba people felt they had lost a large chunk of their social honour amongst the BaKalanga community as well as the powers bestowed upon them by King Mzilikazi amongst the Ndebele nation. The powers included religious powers (as custodians of the Njelele shrine), Traditional powers (as chiefs appointed by the King) and Political powers (as BaKalanga chiefs and gate keepers at the Mangwe Pass). The Malaba people who had arrived in this land at the end of the Mambo rule, had played an integral role at the very formation of the Ndebele nation, been a fundamental part of its administration and governance, and at this moment experiencing being casualties of its nervous breakdown.

The Malaba oral traditions gives a specified account of when in the month of September 1896, instead of going to Njelele as per custom, the clan gathered at a place called Nkalange in Marula. It is narrated that they indulged and drowned themselves into song and dance, lamenting, and counting their losses. They were performing the Malaba traditional dance called *'tjangwiii'* (thin sound) whereby they play a drum by scratching it with a wooden stick to produce a sound a *ngwii* sound, hence dubbed tjangwii. According to their oral traditions, the performance was correlated to a lamentation song called *Kudada kwakungenje umhlaba uyaphenduka*, a song signifying a sad period of great loss. In chronicling their journeys, from Yemen to the Sinai, from the Sinai to the Lake Victoria Peninsulas, to Bukalanga, to VhuVenda and back to Bukalanga, the memories of their trials and triumphs were now folding, but this time inside just one bag of shambles. It was like the more the realization of the imminent fall of the nation, the louder they beat the drum.

It was not only in the community of the Malaba people where the beating of a drum was an integral part of religious observance, but in the whole sub-Saharan Africa. The African drum acted as a vehicle to transporting the participants into the spiritual world where they would be enabled to communicate with the departed spirits of their ancestors. As Oosthuizen (2016) notes, traditional African societies generally acknowledged that the drum had a spirit and character that was observable and that voices of great ancestors were hidden somewhere within the realms of possibility and could be accessed whenever the sound of a drum is heard (Oosthuizen, 2016). When Africans were sold as slaves in places like America, it is assumed that drum beating assisted them surviving the rigours of a life of hardship and toil. For example, upon realizing the significance of these drum beating occasions, slave masters outlawed drum beating in many slave communities in the United States. "When slave "masters" and overseers in the United States discovered that drums could be used as a secret means of communication, they were banned" (Toyin Falola, 2020). Such was the power of an African drum beating.

....

By end of 1899, the Madla family from the Hhobhodo/Hhoba house had instead found themselves in the Simpathe and Mambale area by interest of their herdsmanship and game hunting tendencies. A young adventurous young man by the name Nyawo, son of Hhobhodo/Hhoba, had left the Empandeni area exceedingly early in the settlement and went on to live in the now Sigangatsha area of Kezi. Young Nyawo was known for travelling long distances and love of adventure, hence the name Nyawo, a traveller. Word went back to the Mangwe area that the Sigangatsha area was a good fertile area, good for both agriculture and cattle grazing. It was when Nyawo's elder brother, Madla, heeded the word about the fertile breeding land and relocated to the Simphathe area before moving to the Sigangatsha area. But it is told that before he went, chief Hhobhodo had a message for Tshidada who was now living along the Shashane river. Likewise, chief Hhobhodo saw an opportunity to begin a gradual process of moving the Malaba people to be under Tshidada Malaba's jurisdiction. He began with those remarkably close to him because they were more likely to be more submissive to his motion. By 1900 only those biologically closest to Hhobhodo like the Mathumo, Madla and the Mangwevu had taken Hhobhodo's directive and settled under Tshidada's chiefdoms. Hhobhodo's brother Manusa also moved to settle towards the Malaba area under chief Tshidada. The other Malaba house that heeded Hhobhodo's memo were the Lungombe (Velaphi) House who settled in the Beula-Seula end towards the Shashi River. The seniority of the house of Tshibi Malaba had re-emerged, materialized, refined, and fully fledged once again. Madla who had been born in 1866 and was known as Nquge died in 1940 and is buried in the Sigangatsha area of Kezi.

....

A rural clinic which was spearheaded by a white medical doctor nicknamed BaMalaba was later established in the Mambale area in 1985. The white doctor's real name was Dr Idah, a popular expatriate Germany doctor who came to work in Brunapeg's St Anna and St Joseph's hospitals (Fig. 69) in the 1970s and 1980s, respectively. Due to her hard-working principles and professionalism, empathy and integrity as well as taking ultimate responsibility for difficult decisions in situations of clinical complexity and uncertainty, she was nicknamed BaMalaba (daughter of the Malaba people). According to Dr Idah the name BaMalaba was a way of illustrating the professional conduct which manifested itself amongst the Malaba people in general, and of which Dr Idah seemed to also manifest in her daily duties as a medical practitioner. With their divergent traditional roles, the Malabas were practitioners of tradition, religion, and politics in the Mthwakazi Kingdom. They fulfilled different social and political roles in the community, including divination, healing physical, emotional and spiritual illnesses, protecting warriors, counteracting witchcraft, and narrating the history, cosmology, and myths of the traditions of the kingdom. The Roman Catholic Church had established the Brunapeg Mission in 1954. Although of European descent, Dr Idah carried the Malaba name with pride.

There were a number of reasons on why the Malaba clan were amongst the earliest natives to be affected by the forced removals of Black Africans, ranging from the role of Njelele in the *Umvukela wamaNdebele* rebellion, the new land legislations aimed at relocating the natives, as well as the introduction of the railway line which pushed on through Mafeking, Palapye, Francistown and through the Marula settlement to the capital Bulawayo. After establishing themselves, the colonialist BSAC, led by Cecil John Rhodes had started formulating and implementing some new land legislations. Initially, most of these were just mere settlement agreements than completely developed legislations, but substantially a commission was afterward set up to divide land between the BSAC and the Ndebele. The Lippert Concession of 1889 that allowed would-be settlers to acquire fertile land rights from African lands, had been introduced before the actual occupation of Matabeleland in 1890.

The Native Reserves Order in Council was over and above passed in 1898, introducing the blacks only Native Reserves. It was at this stage that the white settlers began massive land appropriation while forcing Africans to move from their original homes. The Native Reserves became what were called communal areas, meaning places where all Africans lived together in various isolated villages, on a large scale, on extremely poor and unproductive land (Brownell, 2020). To the whites, the Native Reserves were meant to prevent the extinction of the indigenous people while at the same time guaranteeing that settlers got the lion's share of fertile land.

Through a settlement agreement that was brokered between Rhodes and some Matabele chiefs chief Faku, as well as the Native Reserves Order in Council Act of 1898 and other land legislations, the Malaba people were forcibly moved from their Marula settlement in 1899. There was also an introduction by the Estate Trustees of a concept of committing the Matabele on the Estate lands to specified labour periods in lieu of paying rent. In Clause 81 it stated that:

"The company shall ...assign to the natives inhabiting Southern Rhodesia land sufficient for their occupation, whether as tribes or portions of tribes, and suitable for their agricultural and pastoral requirements, including in all cases a fair and equitable proportion of springs and permanent water".

A formal contractual arrangement along these lines was eventually signed by several Matabele chiefs. Although the eviction clauses contained in the agreement began to be put to regular use largely around February 1908, the Malaba clan, were already had been forcibly settled in the Empandeni and near Embakwe areas.

In spite of, the Malaba people being finally evacuated from Marula by the year 1899, the push had begun earlier on. The colonial regime was determined that the original villages were never to be revived again.

As Webner interview with Tobela Bango reveals,

".... from the time when we lived in Marula, we were pushed, bit by bit. The train dropped donkeys, taken off at Marula, in April when the sorghum was (white) and ripe. The donkeys ate in the fields until they finished the grain"

People went to tell Thomas who was the Native Commissioner at the time.

Thomas replied, *"Remove from the way of the train. Go far off. Do not live near the train"* (Werbner, 1991).

Creating difficult circumstances from which there was little escape because of mutually conflicting conditions, was a prevalent BSAC strategy applied against the natives.

Likewise, guided by vicious calculations, the BASC regime of Cecil Rhodes had detected that there was a strong spiritual and physical link between the Matabele resistance and the Mwali religion. Therefore, to achieve good results, it was logical that the two foundations be sabotaged simultaneously. Gathering evidenced from the 1896 uprisings, the Rhodesians had learnt that annihilating the Matabele royal house alone while sidestepping other relevant institutions like the Mwali religion and its priests was synonymous to leaving their mission unaccomplished. For as historian Marshall Hole expresses, by 1847 "next to Mzilikazi himself, Mpangana Malaba was the second most powerful individual in the whole of Matabeleland". Therefore, the Malaba people's forced resettlement to Empandeni was not only an issue of land expropriation and dispossession, but a calculated move to suppress elements of resistance to white rule by dislocating the influential natives.

The choice of Empandeni as resettlement point for the Malaba clan was two-fold. Besides being a barren land with a toxic, infertile soil and nothing to offer agriculturally, it being a Catholic station was also a convenient and fertile environment for religious indoctrination and forced divergence from Mwalism.

According to the Administrator of Rhodesia Earl Grey, there were two principal causes of *Umvukela wamaNdebele*. Firstly, it was the incompleteness of the Matabele Nation in 1893 which left elements like the Mwali priesthood still in operation. Secondly, it was the warlike and aristocratic race who had no intention to give up on their old habits and all their confidence was based on the extraordinary influence of the Mlimo and the physical plagues which He all attributed to the continued presence of the white men in the land. The Roman Catholic Church was one of the first churches to penetrate the Zimbabwean plateau towards the end of the 19th century although Catholicism had first come to Zimbabwe in the fifteenth century with a Portuguese priest, Father Gonzalo da Silveira, though for a long time this church remained in the Mashonaland region. The first Catholic priest to arrive in Matabeleland and Bulilima-Mangwe was Father Prestage in 1884. He was directed to Sindisa Mpofu's Empandeni area by Lobengula whose aim was to try to prevent him from influencing the Ndebele in Bulawayo with his faith and practice of the Roman Catholic Church.

From the point of view of the Rhodesians, like the Ndebele kingdom of Mzilikazi and Lobengula, the elements of Mwalism deserved to be obliterated. Therefore, a forced enrolment into the Empandeni Catholic station was to get the Malaba clan trained out of their traditional beliefs and be converted into Catholicism. The approach was a determination to carry out David Livingstone's idea that 'civilization and Christianity should go together.' With its principle of Pax Romana, Catholicism was like Mwalism in its all-embracing nature and tolerance to a wide variety of cultures, customs, and values. As a matter of fact, the word Catholic means to be diverse or to be all-embracing. Like the Catholic Church with its strict hierarchy, or ranking according to authority, from parish priests to bishops and archbishops to the Pope himself, Mwalism hierarchy ranged from messengers, Hosannas, shrine priests to custodians and to Mwali God the Almighty. The Rhodesians were, however, much aware that there would be a catch.

Catholicism was veritably a foreign religion which emphasized on white civilization and with a shared white perception that African spirituality was dark and primitive. They even brought new religious concepts like Satan which was normally an absent twist in the Mwali religion which emphasized much on evil spirits than Satan the prince of evil abstraction. The reference to *uSatane weRoma* (the Roman Devil) became a popular cliché and a proverb. Therefore, in this case Catholicism was being used as an opium to the Malaba as a people and as a clan. Besides being taught what they did not need, they would be trained to forget what it was they already knew. They were to be taught the importance of faith, to follow the scriptures to the letter, but in the process losing their essential spiritualism and the historical essence and being, and morally becoming a colonial invention. Conversion into Catholicism was to be some kind of faithfulness aimed at creating parochialism and narrow mindedness. They were to be pushed through faith until they reached a spiritual dead end or reach a calculated point that would have them cut off from their being or selfhood. The ultimate aims and objectives of that calculated system was social control actively implemented by the colonial Native Commissioners, who at that time were planted all over the districts.

The formulated land legislations were not fundamentally implemented immediately after the conquest because initially the BSAC focus was mainly on mineral exploitation than agricultural development. Therefore, beside the land appropriation, the main reason for the disintegration of the Malaba homestead in Marula was because of their participation and active role in the *Umvukela wamaNdebele* revolt in 1896 and the Matabele war of 1893. It was a common occurrence as historian Nyathi also observes that those who were perceived to have played major roles in the war were immediately targeted.

Nyathi (2016), accounts about Chief Manondwane Tshabalala of Insukamini who "crest and bruised, continued living in the Gwelo (now Gweru) area. The Native Commissioner, knowing the role that Insukamini and its leaders had played in resisting colonization, poisoned Chief Manondwane Tshabalala who however, managed to get to his home to tell the sad story to his wives. He died and was gone with the memory of iNsukamini Regiment of the *isathiyane sakoMalaba* fame, that epitome of gallant resistance against colonialism" (Nyathi, 2016). The mention of isathiyane by Nyathi also highlight another significance aspect of Mpangana Malaba's *isathiyane* concoction as a formular of war during the times.

The native eviction exercises were normally characterized by forms of brutality. The people were not allowed time to gather their belongings, and as they left, the settlers even looted not only their land but their homes too. Some people died of cold, hunger, and disease on their way to the new settlements. The Malaba clan was finally resettled at Empandeni where Mhlotshana Primary School is currently located. The area was under a chief Tshitshi. Chief Tshitshi had succeeded Sindisa Mpofu in 1890. Sindisa who was a Shava/Mhofu hailing from Seke, was a Nyai who had impressed Lobengula with his prowess in battle. But according to oral traditions amongst the old Kalanga communities Sindisa was appointed chief of Empandeni after he had poisoned and killed Khanda, the infamous Nkulumane's impersonator.

Few years after the Empandeni settlement many of Mpangana's older sons from his different houses including Chief Hhobhodo, died in the Empandeni area and was buried next to his father Mpangana in the Mangwe area in a cave on the Malaba Mountains. According to the royal Malaba tradition clan heads were buried in caves because the soil must never touch their remains. There are some of the Malaba forefathers that include Mpangana, Hhobhodo/Hhoba, Hadledzi and others that are buried in the Malaba mountains in Mangwe. Bangojena of the Bango Dube clan is also buried in the Malaba mountains, presently known as the Hhobhodo hills in Nkalange. At the Empandeni area, Hhobhodo's son Mahango (Hhoba II) born around the 1840s, became the clan leader and 'chief', albeit for a noticeably short period of time.

Life at this part of the world was not easy for the Malaba clan. The Marula area where they were forcibly moved from, was an area that had fertile soil with sufficient ability to sustain crop yields. The clan had enjoyed sustained and consistent yields of high quality in original Marula homestead. On the contrary, the Empandeni land was barren landscape, dry and bare and consisting of soil that was so poor that farming activities were almost a futile exercise. But astonishingly, in the area, there were bushes of thriving Mopane trees extensively covering the area. However, a Mopane, a type of tree in the legume family (Fabaceae), grows in hot, dry, low- lying areas and does not grow well outside hot, frost-free areas with summer rainfall, growing preferably on fine-grained sand and within arid zones. The newly settled people found the contrasting performance between the blooming Mopane trees and the failing agricultural output hard to explain. The outcome of it were the composition of a song that they would sing and dance during the distressing times.

The song contained lyrics that went-

'Aye aye bhani lakaloyewa'

uboyekela ukusebenzela abanye

bhani lakaloyewa"

(Hey! Hey, you bewitched Mopane tree.

We should liberate ourselves from colonial slavery bewitched Mopane tree).

The song *bhani lakaloyewa* attempted to express the confound bewilderment at their new but distressing life.

The Malaba people's stay at Empandeni was cut short. It did not take long after their arrival in the area that the Catholics started an attempt to instil into the clan some Catholic ideologies. The ultimate objective by the Catholics at the time was to coerce the whole clan to finally act and think based on the Catholic Christian ideas. These attempts were met with some resistance from the Malaba clan among other Kalanga clans, however, with unpleasant consequences. The objection to comply becoming straight in the catechism led to the Malaba people being accused of drunkenness and polygamy and were labelled obnoxious natives before expelled from (Empandeni) mission stations.

In the wake of the Empandeni expulsion, most of the Malaba people found themselves in the wilderness, neglected and abandoned. Desperate for land, Mahango Malaba and his people, as well as other BaKalanga agreed to the land offer under chief Mpini, son of Mpukane Ndiweni, in the Thegwani area. Mahango Malaba all the same continued recognizing himself as chief despite arbitrarily falling under chief Mpini Ndiweni's jurisdiction. He later died in the early 1950s leaving behind two sons, Matsambani and Thela. Matsambani was the older son and Thela the younger son. Matsambani, who was supposed to succeed Mahango died while his father Mahango was still alive and a chief, meaning that after the death of Mahango, Thela, the surviving son, succeeded him as chief. However, chief Thela Mahango, together with other Mangwe chiefs were again demoted from chieftaincy by the whites in 1951 for resisting and defying the colonial government and were made mere headman administratively under chief Tshitshi.

According to the Zimbabwe Local Government documents, the district of Mangwe was as a result restricted to three chiefs instead of five which made the duties of the remaining chiefs difficult until Simon, son of Thela Hhobhodo Ncube, was officially reinstated on the 23rd of July 2007 at the age of 74. The year 2007 saw the restoration of other BaKalanga chiefs as Madhlambudzi, Kandana, Masendu, and Tjankuluba (Sangulube) being installed as well. Simon Thela died in December 2013 and was succeeded by his son Adolph Ncube who was installed as chief in 2014 at the age of 54 after a public wrangle between the Matsambani and Thela families over who should take over. The Matsambani descendants believed that the chieftaincy was their birth right and according to them, were eager to correct what had gone wrong in the 1950s before and after the death of Matsambani.

....

An interview with Fredrick Nhlanhla Ndiweni, reveals that Bidi Ndiweni arrived in the Malaba area of Kezi on the 8th January 1923, apparently fleeing the Chief Mpini area. Bidi arrived with his Osabeni clan that comprised the Madlila Namate, the Vakas, the Mlevus, the Sigabades and some Ngwenyas who ultimately settled where the Bidi family cemetery is now located in the Gubungano area of the Malaba territory. This was at around the same time the Hadledzi and the Kuyanis also resettled in the area after their relocation from Empandeni. While the other Malaba families were condemned by the Catholics to live under Chief Mpini Ndiweni as personae non gratae without their own land, the Kuyanis together with the Hhadledzis had remained put at Empandeni, despite the harsh environment, managing to live in the so-called Catholic station.

The Kuyanis had managed to strike a rapport with the Catholics ultimately holding important roles such as Roman Catholic religious positions in the Catholic church. One of the Catholic stations was later established at St Joseph's in the Kezi area and another at St Sebastian in the Sigangatsha area of Kezi. The Kuyani and the Dihwe house of Hadledzi had arrived immediately after the Osabeni clan in 1924 when the new St Joseph's Catholic station was established in the south of the Matopos. The Kuyanis commanded both the St Josephs and the St Sebastian Catholic stations through one Kuyani Catholic official at the St. Josephs station and Kubani Kuyani Malaba at the St. Sebastian station. Owing to the time of their arrival, the Dihwe and the Kuyani arbitrarily found themselves classed under Bidi's jurisdiction where the land was available for them upon arrival. Nevertheless, some like the Msitheli Kuyani family subsequently moved across and settled on the Chief Malaba jurisdiction. Before that, the Kuyanis had temporary settlements in places like Botela and Matopos where Kuyani died and is buried in the Tshapu area of Matopo. The Dihwe family settled adjacent to the Montgomery Farm in the area.

The Hadledzi tell stories of incidents that they witnessed on arrival to the area, especially the story of the white farm owner, Montgomery, who died after being devoured alive by a marauding lion in his farm in the year 1924.

It is worth mentioning that several scholars and oral narrations observe that at some point, there was an agreement between Chief Mpukane Ndiweni of Osabeni and the Southern Rhodesia Native Affairs Department, that if the chief was able to fulfil the requested assignment of recruiting military personnel for the Rhodesian Army which was fighting on the British side against the Germans in the then German West Africa, now known as Namibia, and that if the British won the war, Chief Ndiweni was to be rewarded by having two of his sons appointed as chiefs in the areas which were headed by some Kalanga chiefs. The directive in the case of Bidi's installation in the Malaba area was coming from the then Plumtree Native Commissioner's Office, however, a referral was later made to the Native Commissioner based in Kezi who later became the case worker. Bidi's jurisdiction is bounded by Shashane River in the east and Semukwe River in the West. It stretches from Marinoha Hills in the north, where it shares a boundary with Chief Fuyana and ends in the south at Tribal Demarcation Line Road (Tribal line, corrupted to Threbhalayini), where Chief Malaba's area starts. In all fairness, unlike the sour relationship encountered between the Mpini Ndiweni and the Malaba people in Mangwe, Bidi Ndiweni's relationship with the Malaba in the Kezi area was amicable and steadfast, as it may be, because Bidi was a Malaba relative from the maternal side.

When the Malaba people were evicted from The Empandeni Catholic station and settled under chief Mpini Ndiweni, life was never a bed of roses. Although the clan had endured the test of time and continued migrating and settling as a folk since the departure from Venda and several stop over settlements that included Malungudzi (Beitbridge), Tjizeze/Chizeze (Zezane), Kumbudzi Nhawebezi (Mtshabezi), Makwe, Marula and Empandeni, it was the settlement under Chief Mpini that was the main source of the ultimate disintegration of the Malaba clan, with several clan members separated ending up scattered in various locations of both South and North of Matabeleland.

Some members of the Hhobhodo house remained put under Chief Mpini Ndiweni while others like Tshada and Mkhubazi, ending up being forcibly settled under chief Sangulube in the present Sanzukwi area in the Mangwe. Before that, together with the Bango people, the Malaba had trekked back to the land of their forefathers near the Marula area, finally settling on the Taylor's Block and Roy along the Marula Kezi road, respectively. However, in the 1934 the Plumtree Native Commissioner triggered a lot of migration from farms that were privately owned by the whites into the Native Reserves. The Hhobhodo and Bango people comprised some of the huge groups of people forcibly moved to different locations when these private owned farms began to change hands, albeit a predicament in settling them. The period is reflected in Webner's interview with Tobela Bango where Bango explained that a white farmer, Kesbaum Teit, just came and informed the people that he had bought the land "from the place at Bango up to Malaba there at Mbakwe near Empandeni" (Webner, 1991). Regardless, Teit did not evacuate the people instead making them pay tax to him in return to being allowed to stay in the land. However, before they knew it, the land had exchanged hands again as an Afrikaner bought the land from Teit, consequently pushing the Natives out to live on the other side of Ndadza (Webner, 1991). In less than no time they were forced out yet again from Ndadza by Kala, another European who had also acquired the land. At one-point John William Posselt, the Acting Magistrate and Native Commissioner Charter, wrote, in reference to the Hhobhodo and the Bango people:

"I have received a letter from Mrs Rose Taylor requesting me to give Immediate notice to Natives on Taylor's Block and Roy to remove (the Hhobhodo people). A number of male Natives affected is 88 on Taylor's Block and 18 on Roy. These people are part of the following of Chief Bango who lives on the adjoining property known as Smith's: Block, now in the Market. It is conceivable that Chief Bango and his following may soon be similarly served with notices to quit in the near future. I am at a loss to know where these Natives will be settled."

By 1939, Posselt, the Native Commissioner, is recorded to have made a real push for the Bango and the Malaba people to be evacuated. A determination was made that the Bango people, were to be relocated back to the Lupane area where they had originally come from. "Chuchu, majaha…now this country is for farms. The government has given you lands on the other side of the farms at Lupane", Posselt told the Bango people who are said to have been thoroughly aggrieved by the decision.

"What wrong have we done? We have no fault, no court case. We did not bring ourselves here, Nkosi. We came by your word." (Webner, 1991).

The exhausting negotiations then began and went on until a compromise was finally reached with a deal that involved an establishment of a new Special Native Area. Thus, chief Bango were resettled in the 46000 hectares Sanzukwi Special Native Area where Bango continued to be a chief over his people, nevertheless, after splitting into two groups. In 1938 the other Bango group led by Headman Mgulatshani son of Sikafu later went to resettle in what is now the Semukwe Communal Lands in the Matobo District (Werbner, 1991). Mgulatshani, officially remained a Headman under chief Ngugama Bango all the same, an arrangement that still stand to this day.

By 1947 the two chiefdoms of Bango and Hhobhodo Malaba were compressed together on the Crown Land between the Semukwe, Shashi and Ramaquabane Rivers, in the process resulting in their political power being adversely compromised. In consequence, the area between Chief Tshidada Malaba and Chief Hhobhodo Malaba was created as chief Bango Dube territory and was to be known as the Sanzukwe Special Native Area. Thus, chief Bango and his people migrated down to the Matopo area, then Marula area before they were resettled in the 46000 hectares Sanzukwi Special Native Area where Bango continued to be a chief over his people, nevertheless, after splitting into two groups. In 1938 the other Bango group led by Headman Mgulatshani son of Sikafu later went to resettle in what is now the Semukwe Communal Lands in the Matobo District (Werbner, 1991). Mgulatshani, officially remained a Headman under chief Ngugama Bango all the same, an arrangement that still stand to this day.

Chief Bango Dube finally reigned over the area, a tract of land that currently sweep like a snake along the Semukwe river from Tjebakadzi, Kheme, past number 3, Cross-roads to Khalanyoni, via Emkhonyeni, and incorporating Nsuthu store and Kepu hills up to Tshatshi river otherwise known as Ward 10 in Mangwe District. As the elders would normally say, "the Malaba names are talking names", John Posselt was known as Mafohlela (the invader) for constantly dispossessing the natives of their land. The name Mafohlela became popular amongst the Malaba people as Tshemane, one of Hhobhodo's grandsons, gave the name to one of his sons, the current Malaba headman, Herman Mafohlela Tshemane. Equivalently, Mafohlela's father Tshemane's original name was Njini (Engine) because he was born in 1896 during when the railway line for the Bechuanaland Railway Company reached Bulawayo and heralding the beginning of forced removals of African people from their land. Amongst the clan, names were another way of documenting history. Probably in relation to his birth circumstances, Tshemane seemed to have developed some inert interest for engines as he later on, through some friends, initiated and facilitated the instalment of a dip tank and a generator run water pump which was later to be known as the Sigangatsha dip tank facility.

In reference to the evictions, Ruwitah, (1988), also noted the adverse impact of these forced migrations as he wrote that, "It is interesting to see how the mere appropriation of land from the Africans had led to the near disintegration of the once compact chiefdoms even before the modern involuntary and related population movements under examination. Further disintegration was to occur in the areas of resettlement due to the fusion of the various ethnic groups from different parts of Matabeleland as these were compressed together owing to the shortage of land" (Ruwitah, 1988).

The chief in question at that time was Thela Hhobhodo Malaba who at this point had been demoted to the headman role and was now arbitrarily under chief Tshitshi. By 2020 a large population of the chief Hhobhodo people had their identification documents still registered under chief Tshitshi's chiefdom. The chief Hhobhodo area in the new Mayobhodo area currently cover kraals such as Dayintambo, Mswiliswili, Lumahwe, Roscommon, Thegwane and Gurumane. Although the Malaba and Bango people were forcibly moved from the Nkalange area giving way to the white settlers' farms, the farm owners without question respected the cultural value of the space. A larger part of the Nkalange-Gurumane area is still a wilderness. Furthermore, visiting the place today is still a daunting task because the area is uninhabited and infested with dangerous reptiles like poisonous types of snakes. Most of the elders consulted on the subject attributed the untapped nature of the area to the aboriginal Malaba spirituality and divinity.

Nonetheless, the effects of the Native Reserves Order in Council (1898) were significantly evident. By the 1914 period, the whites who constituted 3% of the population controlled 75% of the economically productive land while the Blacks who constituted 97% of the population were forcefully confined to 23% of the land scattered into several reserves (Njaya, 2010). Although the country's population consisted of 836 000 African natives and 28 000 Whites, by the eve of World War One in 1914, the apportionment of land was as follows:

Africans owned 24 000 000 acres.

The BSAC owned 48 000 000 acres.

Individual white settlers owned 13 000 000 acres.

Other Private Companies owned 9 000 000 acres

……………………………………

In the Bulilima-Mangwe area, as matter of fact, most of the Kalanga speakers generally began to go against Chief Mpini's chieftaincy as they viewed him as a Nguni chief imposed over a predominantly Kalanga area. Some documents during this period reveal one Kalanga Chief, Madlambudzi, challenging the powers of Chief Mpini. Consequentially Madlambudzi was demoted from his chieftaincy, an occurrence that increased his resolve as he refused to attend Chief Mpini's courts and in the process influencing his kraal heads to boycott Mpini's meetings too. The 1965 Delineation Report also highlights the support by most BaKalanga, including the Malaba people, toward the defence of Madlambuzi's chieftaincy which they viewed as representing the Kalanga identity. The primary source of the disharmony was the arrangement to replace Madzete Madlambudzi Ncube with Mpini, an incident that proved to be disagreeable with the expectations of the Kalanga people and tribal custom. The BaKalanga people were said to be unable to perceive how the Government could completely abolish the chieftainship and impose a 'foreign chief' rather than install Madzete who was the heir apparent to the Madlambudzi chieftaincy.

After being relegated to the headman's position, Madlambudzi was not paid for his role. The whole exercise was further made worse by some political disharmonies of the times. As Landman recorded, traditional authorities also found themselves in a difficult position because of the liberation struggle. On one hand, they were compelled to support the Rhodesian Front as they were agents of the government while on the other hand, they faced accusations by the guerrillas of supporting the suppressive rule of the colonial regime. Their position was further made worse by the deliberate attempt of the colonial regime to empower them as tribal authorities during the period of Community Development. During this period, traditional authorities had their judiciary authority over land restored and this was followed by an increase of allowances to the chiefs. For example, the African Affairs Act of 1966 gave chiefs new punitive powers, including powers to arrest, as government paid messengers. With all these provisions, chiefs were left with no choice but to dance to the tune of the colonialists. But as the waves of nationalism spread throughout the country and the war intensified, most traditional authorities had to shift their loyalty to the guerrillas.

The guerrillas generally assumed that some of the chiefs were working hand in hand with the "oppressors". For example, Headman Mrapelo Masendu Dube was killed in 1975 after the guerrillas accused him of being a sell-out (Masendu-Dube, 2012). Chief Gambu Sithole was also killed by the guerrillas for collaborating with the white government. However, some chiefs such as Madlambudzi Ncube and Hhobhodo Malaba, whose chieftainships had been abolished by the colonial regime, gained favours from the guerrillas as they strongly supported the guerrillas too in a reciprocal way. The guerrillas were usually accommodated at both Chief Hhobhodo and Madlambuzi's households and had made their homesteads political bases where villagers received political orientation by the guerrillas. It was because of his support of the guerrillas that the Rhodesian Forces sought to kill Madlambudzi, forcing him to consequently flee and seeking refuge in Botswana.

Later, in the early 1950s, Chief Bidi's brother, Ndabakayena, was literally taken from the Osabeni area and installed in the Nata Reserve following the demotion of a number of Kalanga chiefs such as Madlambudzi Ncube, Masendu, Hhobhodo Malaba, Sangulube Moyo and Hikwa Nleya. Those on Mpini's side argued that it was the deposed chiefs who sought to consolidate Kalanga ethnic identity by undermining Chief Mpini, a Nguni chief who they thought was imposed by the colonial regime in areas which were traditionally Kalanga areas. More so, there is evidence of a continued clash between Chief Mpini Ndiweni and the Kalanga speakers. For instance, in 1945, members of a Khumalo clan organization called the Matabele Home Society (MHS) wrote letters requesting a separate burial ground for the Ndebele of King Lobengula's decent and other distinguished African natives. The letter was sent to various parts of the country that had Nguni chieftainships. Mpini Ndiweni came out as a staunch supporter of the idea which was considered as literally an insult to the BaKalanga in general.

In a letter to the provincial Native Commissioner, Mpini is cited to have written that "one does not bury a dog near his fathers' grave" (Dube, 2015). By a 'dog', Mpini was referring to the non-Nguni people who had been assimilated and incorporated into the Ndebele identity. These utterances were justifiably perceived as vitriolic and utterly disrespectful, consequently prompting a desire by non-Nguni people to separate and form their own ethnic associations. Matabele Home Society was a movement created to succeed the formation of Nyamande Khumalo's National Home Movement which was mainly a voice fighting for a separate Ndebele homeland.

6,2. Chief Ntelela Malaba

While the struggle between the missionaries and the traditional Malaba people in the Empandeni and Thekwane areas continued unabated, a similar struggle was also taking place in the Matobo area where the Tshidada chieftaincy covered. According to the 1948 Native Affairs Department Annual journal, this Nyashongwe section of the Semokwe Reserve and Mambale Area was a 180,000-acre land with a population of 4,250 people being headed by chief Ntelela Malaba (NADA, 1948). It is recorded that in the 1940s the missionaries had strengthened their efforts of undermining Njelele and other Mwali shrines. The missionaries would occasionally send the black Christian converts into the Njelele shrine to destroy the shrine contents in the dead of the night as a way of sabotaging the Mwali religion in the region and thereby allowing Christian ideologies to swiftly overtake it. there are also some indications that the whole exercise was just a sinister strategy by the colonialists to demolish and politically pacify the African natives by diverting their attention away from politics. This exercise caused despair amongst the traditional priests as many of them began losing faith in the power of Mwali to rid the country of the BSAC. Nevertheless, the Mwali religion made some further gains in political influence in correspondence with the rise of nationalism in the 1950's.

There was a problem though as the religion also suffered competition from Zionist church leaders. Daneel (1970), refers to an individual called Joel who was a Zionist, and whose derogation of Mwalism as wizardry and witchcraft and his denunciation of ancestor honouring reflected the radical attitude of most Zionist groups (Daneel, 1970). Their constant attack on traditional forms of worship often culminated in the identification of Mwali of the Matopos with Satan himself. However, Ranger (1999) records that the circumstance became more significant during Ntelela Malaba's chieftaincy. A prominent Zionist church leader, through the adaptation of his church practices and liturgical patterns, scored some considerable success in supplanting the three main functions of the shrine, namely promoting crop fertility, healing, and the great influence on tribal and national politics (Terence O. Ranger, 1999). Actually, in 1948 the Matobo District Commissioner, Noel Robertson, celebratorily documented that 'Zionist prophets had been attracting many converts in Matobo' and the 'Native Department was pleased to note tension between the sect and Ndebele chiefs.' This however, led to bloody clashes between the Zionists and the Chief Ntelela Malaba people. Feeling that the core principles of the Mwali religion was being overshadowed by these Zionists, one day, Chief Ntelela (pictured in Figure 58) decided to fight back.

He one day ordered a raid on the Zionist sect regularly stationed on the Hhowuyawa hill where the Zionists usually conducted their ceremonies of umlindelo. Hhowuyawa is a hill located on the Kezi side of the Semukwe River adjacent the Semukwe bridge. As Ranger (1999), records in his book *Voices from the Rocks; Nature, Culture & History in the Matopos Hills of Zimbabwe*, the Ntelela people surrounded the hill but in order to not frighten the children and cause a stampede, waited until dawn, and when they had the praise and worship singing and shouting, they pounced and arrested the Zionist preacher. Legend has it that the preacher was tortured, and his traditional Zionist long beard was set alight with fire. Ironically, later in his life, Ntelela became a member of the Zionist church himself, a membership he held until his death.

Some informants attested that chief Ntelela's activism was not particularly directed against the mushrooming churches per se, but rather he viewed their association with western culture as aiding some colonial policies. For example, chief Ntelela is said to also have had unending skirmishes with Noel Robertson, the Matobo District Native Commissioner who was known amongst the locals as Nkomiyahlaba. Although Robertson Nkomiyahlaba and chief Ntelela Malaba naturally belonged to different political ideologies, theirs was mainly a war of ideas, ideals, ideologies, and lifestyle concepts.

Nkomiyahlaba had been transferred from Gwanda District due to his unscrupulous business, social and political dealings. He is said to have been running a secret parallel government enforcing the people to pay taxes directly to himself and his businesses. In the midst of his transfer to Matobo, Nkomiyahlaba is said to have reduced his offices to ashes in an attempt to distract an audit on his financial dealings. However, as the newly appointed Native Commission of Matobo District, Nkomiyahlaba was still the same old neo-fascist. It is said that when he arrived in Kezi/Matobo district he introduced several policies including the Rural Councils, the anti-erosion farming, and the training as well as the supply of *omlimisi* (agricultural extension officers).

Most crucial of his ambitious policies was the anti-erosion farming and the training and supply of agricultural extension officers, and it was those particular policies that got him in loggerheads with chief Ntelela Malaba. Chief Ntelela Malaba is said to have been an advocate of agricultural methods that were culturally different from those of Noel Nkomiyahlaba Robertson. Therefore, as a tactic to frustrate his methods, Ntelela banned his local men from attending regular meetings normally arranged by Nkomiyahlaba. There is a recorded incident about when, attending his fifth Shashane Board agriculture meeting held in March of 1934, to his utter shock, Nkomiyahlaba had arrived at the meeting only to find exclusively women in attendance.

The meeting had been arranged to instruct the local people to desist from using the land 'in a wasteful manner' and 'are reluctant to accept advice on overstocking,' and it was 'better that it be divided into small farms for sale to those Natives who wish to live there.' The locals were also instructed to follow the example set out by their

Mashonaland counterparts and make use of the so-called Native Purchase land before they could be considered for any further communal land.

Through his all-female meeting attendees, chief Ntelela turned down the Native Commissioner's proposal arguing that the Native Purchase land policy was not relevant to the problems of the local people. Despite all the altercations, it was chief Ntelela Malaba's sustainable agriculture methods and farming practices that won the day as in 1947 chief Ntelela Malaba was awarded the Bledisloe Medal for being a 'very progressive and influential chief' as well as for being a 'Master Farmer'. The medal was presented to chief Ntelela by His Majesty the King George VI on his visit to Rhodesia on the 14th of April 1947 (NADA, 1948).

Figure 58 shows a portrait of chief Ntelela Malaba, with his personal signature, done by D.J. Avery in 1947. The Bledisloe was a Medal originated in 1930 by the Viscount Bledisloe, former Governor-General of New Zealand. It aimed at awarding individuals who had made an outstanding contribution to his or her chosen field of expertise. The medal presented to chief Ntelela is said to bear on its obverse the figure of a native Afrikander bull with the inscription "Southern Rhodesia *Mutungamiri/Umtungameli*", meaning leader or guide. The reverse bore an ear of maize and the inscription "The Bledisloe Medal for the Advancement of Native Husbandry".

Chief Ntelela Malaba was born in 1878. In 1968, when he was approximately 90 years of age, in reference to the trio of Mpangana Malaba, Tshimba-Bhangwa and Sabhaswi-Lubimbi, he was quoted by Cockcroft (1972), confirming that his forefathers had come into present day Bukalanga as youth, and confirming that the establishment of Mwalism as a religion had taken place long before their arrival from BuVenda (Cockcroft, 1972).

This confirms the Mwali religion being in existence and operational in Bukalanga even before the Malaba clan came with the rainmaking shrine of Njelele in 1836. As historian Ralushai argues, in ancient times, whenever the Luvhimbi failed to cause rain to fall from their southern base, they would send their messengers to Malungudzi (Beitbridge), where the Malungudzi Mbedzi would contact Mwali (Great God) (Matopo) on behalf of the South African vhaMbedzi (Luvhimbi), implying, as stated above, that although the Malaba people brought the rainmaking Njelele shrine in particular, the worship of Mwali at the Matopos in general was an old practice.

Joshua Nkomo in his book, *The Story of My Life*, writes that Ntelela Malaba was an especially important man peculiarly on Wednesdays the day of his weekly courts. Wednesday was *tjisi* (Holly Day) day and anyone who did ploughing or any other field work on Wednesday was brought before the chief and fined, ''perhaps having their ox span and plough confiscated for a month'' (Terence O. Ranger, 1999). Men and women would come to his *nnanga/enkundleni* (court) and Nyongolo's role and those of other men would be to act as assistants. As mentioned before, Tshidada had Beula Mpande as his headman on a mutual arrangement agreed upon with King Lobengula. Figure 59. Reflects the traditional Zimbabwean system of governance. Over and above Tshidada's appointment of Beula Mpande, during his tenure as chief, Ntelela also appointed Mdumuli Makawule (otherwise known as Mpamadzi) to be *uMlisa* (headman).

However, at some point in time the unfortunate incident that involved three Makawule headmen dying in succession led to the herdsman-ship being transferred to the Sigangatsha Ndlovu family, who, like Makawule, was also a nephew (*abazukukulu/bazekulu*) of the Malaba. The Sigangatsha Ndlovu family still holds the *umlisa* (herdsman) position till today.

Figure 58. Picture - Chief Ntelela Malaba Portrait by D.J. Avery. Photo Courtesy of the Tshidada Family.

> **Constitutional Court** (Inkantolo yoMthetho-Sisekelo/Khutha yenlayo nkulu)
>
> **Supreme Court** (Inkantolo Enkulu/Khutha wulu)
>
> **High Court** (Inkantolo kaMehluleli/Khutha ipehhugwi)
>
> **Magistrate Courts** (Inkantolo kaMantshi/Khutha dzemitinnu)
>
> **Chief** (induna/He)
>
> **Herdman** (Mlisa/N/A)
>
> **Kraa**l (Sobhuku/ N/A)

Figure 59. The traditional Zimbabwean system of governance

....

Besides the showdown with the Zionists, there was another contentious issue, the concept of observing Wednesday as the day of rest alongside the Sunday. This was a belief in line with Mwalism as well as the ancient Malaba Divine Trinity and it was brought into the land of BuKalanga from Venda by the Malaba clan. The problematic part of it was that it was a foreign custom being introduced amongst the majority by the few, and in an entirely new world.

Another issue was that of rural nationalism that was spreading beyond its original founders to the peasant farmer masses. This gave weight to the ideology of Njelele which became a tool used to rebuke and repress the acquisitive aspirations of the contemporary Christian entrepreneurs. This expressed itself through a campaign to enforce the Njelele rest day of Wednesday but to achieve that was a real struggle. Despite it had several Jewish worship elements, characteristics and behavioural traits, the monotheist belief in Mwali was a new and foreign religion in this part of the world.

Le Roux, records that in 1867, German missionaries Merensky and Wangemann were astonished to find the Malaba clan reciting the creation and flood narratives and professing the existence of the Jewish God the missionaries recorded as Mwali. Also, elsewhere, the journals of an early missionary Knight-Bruce (1888-1892), record surprises as well as his own view of what constitutes religion, on finding no one working in the fields on Wednesday, which was called Mwali's day. It is also recorded that on this day chief Ntelela Malaba and other chiefs would send a man up a hill to shout that, *"It is Mwali's day, God's Day, and no one works"* (Le Roux, 1997, 1999), and surely no one would go to work on Wednesday.

The belief that Wednesday was a holy day spread and grew for years as Ranger (1999), records that on 10th January 1959 this provoked both clarification and indignation from the church evangelist RM Mhlanga, based at Vizhe School. He expressed his greatest horror of his life about the issue of Wednesday treated as a day for rest. Mhlanga went on and blamed the people of Insiza for observing Wednesday as holy while working on Sundays. He lamented that, worst still, the chiefs had made it a rule (Terence O. Ranger, 1999).

"Uneducated chiefs are a danger to the African community because they do not know how to read the Bible" Mhlanga declared.

However, Mhlanga was fighting a losing battle. Before he knew it, on 17th of January 1959, the Bantu Mirror revealed that the observation of Wednesday had significantly grew wider and had spread further into the Semukwe Reserve in the Matopo. Chief Ntinima the son of Bidi, son of Mganyulwa, son of Mpukane had told a gathering that he was one of the people who used to plough on Wednesdays until a delegation went to Njelele to ask for rain. Mwali is believed to have told the rain seekers that their chief (Bidi) cultivated his land on a Wednesday, and therefore, they should go to him and ask him to supply them with rain. Chief Bidi went on to tell the gathering that he had experienced great phenomena which proved to him that he was doing wrong by not observing Wednesday as a resting day. He ordered those cultivating on Wednesdays to stop henceforth and observe the day as holy (Terence O. Ranger, 1999). Ntinima Bidi Ndiweni whose chieftaincy coronation was in 1929, was later assassinated in January 1978.

A prosperous trader in the area, JM Dube summoned a counter meeting and denounced chief Bidi's order. With the help of the missionary evangelists, JM Dube even went on and performed a taboo by invading the Njelele shrine at some point. In an August 1990 interview conducted with Ranger (1999), Dube confirms the incident and further highlights that he was not impressed by what he encountered in the inside of the Njelele shrine. However, he admitted that his unorthodoxy actions made him an enemy of the locals, and during the liberation struggle, neighbours denounced him to every Zipra guerrilla group. As Ranger (1999), noted, despite all that, the Njelele shrine continued being central to nationalism and increased as opposition to the white regime, increasingly taking the form of the first sabotage and then armed violence (Terence O. Ranger, 1999).

....

Ntelela's first son was Joseph born in 1911. Joseph served as a BSA Police for ten years. He also was a holder of Master Farmer Certificate. He acted as a chief during his father reign from 1960 to 1971 and finally became official as chief after his father died in 1969. Unlike his father Ntelela who was hot tempered, Joseph is said to have been soft spoken.

Figure 60. Picture - Chief Joseph Malaba. Photo Courtesy of the Tshidada Family

When chief Joseph (pictured in Figure 60) died on 20 February 1986 at the age of 75, his son, David Christopher, born 02 February 1938, was installed on the 13th of August 1988 in a ceremony officiated by Joshua Mqabuko Nkomo (Fig 61). Besides being related, Joshua' father, Thomas Nyongolo Letshwantso Nkomo, had become close friends with Ntelela Malaba during their school days at Tiger Kloof Educational Institute, a school near Vryburg in South Africa. The mother of Thomas Nyongolo was a BaMalaba from the house of Tshedu. In his book, The Story of My Life Nkomo writes that his family moved and settled into the Malaba area of Kezi by way of chief Ntelela's invitation (Nkomo, 1984). At some point Joshua Nkomo went to live in the Malaba homestead where he spent most of the time as a herd boy under the tutelage of Chief Ntelela Malaba. Maheleni Malaba (Maheleni, 2015), confirms that chief Ntelela used to tell a story about an incident involving Joshua Nkomo that stunned both the Malaba and the Nyongolo communities.

As herd boys, Joshua and other boys set off to herd Ntelela's cattle at the Shashi River pastures, towards the present-day Zimbabwean border with Botswana, riding on donkey backs. As the boys were wandering around and stumbled almost blindly through the deep, black forest of the Shashe river area in search of the cattle, they realized that one of them was missing. It was young Joshua. Panicking, they called his name as loud as they could but the only response, they could get was the echoes of their voices. Having given up, they headed home to report Joshua to the elders as a missing person.

Since the area was a wilderness infested with all sorts of dangerous animals, they believed that it was most certain that the young Joshua had become meat to the pride of marauding lions operating the area. What stunned the elders was when reporting the incident to Joshua's parents Thomas Nyongolo and Mlingo Hadebe, their reaction to the incident was unexpectedly relaxed. His father's words were just that, the boy was always mysterious and there was nothing they could do about it at that particular point.

They were very much appreciative that, much the same as with Lobengula Khumalo in the preceding years, it was just another training day for the young

Joshua. Nonetheless, feeling guilty, men from the Malaba village organized themselves and embarked on a thorough search of the area. They pushed their bodies through the dense forest and due to the thickness of the bush, they could only see faint glows through the dense and gloomy leaves scattered on the ground. They treaded lightly on them, cautiously and afraid of the many spooky and mysterious noises that come from all directions, surrounding them in curiosity.

Until suddenly, a silhouette, big and dark appears from across their path, startling them into shock and almost fear. It was the young boy, Joshua Nkomo seated on a low branch, eating some wild berries as if his life depended on them. Just yonder to him were the two donkeys which appeared to be relaxed. Joshua was taken back home and to his parents. This is one of the many mysterious stories attributed to the larger-than-life figure of Joshua Mqabuko Nyongolo Nkomo, who later became a Zimbabwean revolutionary who led the Zimbabwe African People's Union from 1961 until the 1987 Unity Accord with Robert Mugabe's Zimbabwe African National Union to form ZANU–PF. Nkomo also served as Vice-President of Zimbabwe from 1990 until his death in 1999.

On 19 May 2004 Chief David Malaba was elected deputy president of the Council of Chiefs, a position that effectively made him a Member of Parliament representing the interests of all chiefs. He was still chief at the time of writing. His mother was Veronica Ndlovu. The heir-apparent to the Malaba chieftaincy is his son Henry Thobela Malaba who was born on the 13th of September 1978 and attended Embakwe secondary school.

Figure 61. Picture: Joshua Mqabuko Nyongolo Nkomo Statue on Main Street Bulawayo renamed to Joshua Mqabuko Nkomo Street. Courtesy of RMF

CHAPTER 7

THE NJELELE AND THE MALABA PEOPLE

7,1. Mwalism

The Njelele rainmaking shrine, a component of the Mwali religion, was established upon the arrival of the Malaba clan in the Matopo hills area in 1836. In spite of that, the site known as Mabweadziba had existed for many centuries. On balance, Mwalism is a religion based on the concept and worship of Mwali, who is the God Almighty, who is a high God with a spiritual presence. Although Mwali, God, Allah, Yahweh are the names of the same being, the superlatives and attributes associated with Mwali praises are those of an imminent and transcendent being, ever present in his own creation. Mwali is involved and concerned about the activities and social welfare of his people on earth and in heaven. There is never any distance or gulf between him and his creation, and as Daneel adds, "Mwali has not totally lost sight." Mwali never stays away from his people, he provides for their social needs. He was, and remains, the one God available for consultation and prayer (Baxter, 2018). and the monotheistic concept of Mwalism was never at any time associated with idolism. Baxter notes that even in the recent times, when being sworn in at a court of law, blacks always swore to Mwali as the deity, although their hand would rest on a Bible and the Christian god was naturally implied (Baxter, 2018).

In Venda culture Mwali was sometimes referred to as Raluvhimba a name that emphasizes a monotheistic deity. The Venda and BaKalanga people believed that Mwali/Raluvhimba was a universal God and that he was the only creator of mankind on earth. In the Venda language they, therefore, referred to Him as

Mutumbuka Vhathu (creator of mankind). Mwali was also the protector and defender of the people, he is however, from the BaKalanga people's perspective, being more predominant as the provider of rain which people depended on for their survival.

The vhaVhenda believed that Mwali used to visit his people and that his arrival was preceded by the sudden cracking of thunder up to the sky. The people would look up in the sky, ululating and dancing while welcoming the arrival of Mwali. The Luonde website mentions that for example in 1917, a meteor which bust during daytime made a thunderous noise along the Soutpansberg mountain range leading to people believing that Mwali was visiting Vendaland. This highlighted the extent of their belief in Mwali, a deity who art in the heavens and his Mosaic elements of being associated with the mountains or high places which according to Moyo is a feature of the God of the Bible and of the Semites (Moyo, 2012). Mwali is thus, Yahweh, the universal God who brings into existence whatever exists. Like Yahwehism, Mwalism nevertheless gave acknowledgement to the existence, though not necessarily the worship, of other customs like traditional healing by worshippers but as long as it is done outside the devotional services of Mwali.

Writer Baxter also acknowledges that the general view of what Mwali represent is not that dissimilar to Yahweh or Jehovah (Baxter, 2018). Therefore, the standard definition of Mwalism as a cult by some foreign writers is as invalid and faulty reasoning as it is deceptive. Though early European missionaries rejected the worship of Mwali as superstition (Bhebhe 1979), according to Rodewald (2010), even a casual biblical scholar cannot help but notice a relationship between people and deity reminiscent of the Israelites and Yahweh as found in the Old Testament. Such as, the Mwali religion's belief in God the Almighty possess a number of elements similar to those of the Jewish religion. Common to the Semitic world was the concept of God – *Il, El, Ilu, or Allah*, (Moyo, 2012) which God had varying degrees of monotheism associated with Him. Such monotheistic characteristics found in Mwalism was not generally shared by the Bantu everywhere in Africa and did not at all exist in Southern Africa in particular.

In reference to the newly arrived Malaba clan, in his *The Matabele Journals of Robert Moffat 1829-1860* book, Moffat, notes that 'some of their' customs were peculiar and not like "any tribe of which I have knowledge" (E. W. S. Wallis, 1946). Similarly, in his book, *The Rebirth of Bukalanga: A Manifesto for the Liberation of a Great People with a Proud History,* researcher Moyo (2012), also notes that this very monotheistic concept was foreign to the Bantu, so was that of the name of God as Mwali, Muari, or Muali, which is presumed a corrupt form of Il, El, Ilu or Allah, the God of the Semitic peoples (Moyo, 2012). Muali is associated with wind and high places which is a feature of the God of the Bible and of the Semites.

The derivation of the name Mwali could, as according to van Ordt, been derived from the Arabic *'Allah'* as a result of Islamic cultural influence during the migration from north to the south, or as Moyo notes, the term came from *Muali –* in Kalanga *Mu-ali-iye* (He who is) as in Exodus 3;14 when God declared, (Yahweh) "I am who I am" (Moyo, 2012). By way of explanation, the names Yahweh and Mwalie possess the same meaning except that Yahweh (I am who I am), is a first-person narration while Mwalie (He who is), is in third person point of view. In his writing, Moyo further notices that Njelele is associated with strict observance of the seventh day, and there was no cosmic basis for such an observance except this concept emanates from within Judaism where there is the observance of the first and seventh days in the lunar month (Moyo, 2012).

Moreover, the Malaba people had Wednesday as another holy day certainly introduced as part of the trilogy phenomenon. As noted by Mothibi, contrary to supplication of Mwali through ancestral gods, the Malaba oral traditions stress that those who threw bones and divine (through the ancestors) were prohibited in the proximity of the Njelele shrine (Rodewald, 2010). These included traditional healers, diviners and/or herbalists, although they sometimes were considered to exist amongst a definitive list of Mwali given attributes. The above-mentioned actuality is highlighted, for example, during the Njelele factional fights of 1992 which involved the locals, chiefs, politicians Herbert Ushewokunze and Dr Joshua Nkomo. Ranger documents that the villagers who were against Sitwanyana Tshimba Ncube's candidacy argued that "Njelele is not a *n'anga* (traditional healers) thing and never has been. It is purely a rain shrine…" (Terence O. Ranger, 1999). The only initiation allowed at Njelele was the Hosanna initiation only and no visit from *'abantu bamadlozi'* (spirit mediums) was allowed (Nthoi, 1995). In effect, before the arrival of the Malaba clan in 1836, even the initiation of hosanna was not carried out within the practice of the Mwali religion.

Ancestors were not used as intermediaries in the worship of Mwali. This does not mean that ancestors were not included in the traditional cosmos of the Mwali religion, rather they were not allowed in the proximity or worship of Mwali. The Malaba people, through their ancestors like Mpangana, Hhobhodo, Mruthe Bhule and others, were themselves renowned traditional healers but never at any point would they create an attachment between the activities in Njelele and their traditional healing practices. They by all means accredited their traditional healing prowess to Mwali but would not for instance apply that traditional healing aptitude in the general and particular worship of Mwali. Among the Bakalanga people, there is still a distinction between the worship of Mwali and the appeasement of the ancestral spirits. Therefore, the Venda-Kalanga shrine custodians did not furthermore visit any shrine in order to have communion with their ancestral spirits but to worship, pray or give thanks to Mwali God the Almighty (Nthoi, 2006). The Malaba people for example considered and taught about the shrine of Mwali as a sacred place where the living come to the presence of the High God.

Under the custodianship of the Malaba clan, the pilgrim, being led by the Tshimba-Bhangwa hosanna priests, would approach the Lubimbi-priesthood monitored Njelele shrine in order to have a dialogue with the Voice of God and not with or through the ancestral spirits. An interview with renowned culturist and film writer Continue Loving Mhlanga, also notes and emphasizes on the fact that the history of the Malaba clan evidently goes beyond Mapungubwe and vhuVenda in general. "It is a historic phenomenon that needs tracing as far back as Mount Sinai in Egypt and yonder (Conti Mhlanga, 2018). As argued before hand, the name Mwali or Muali, so goes the claim, is argued to be derived from a pre-Christian and pre-Islam name for the idea of a High God in the Middle East. According to Mhlanga, there is also evidence that this goes back beyond Mapungubwe where trade was associated with the Arabs while the religion was associated with the Jews. These assertions assist in reconstructing and confirming the route of the Dzibagulu clan to as far back as Yemen and parts of the Ancient Near East.

Another Malaba Semitic link could be derived from the Lemba tribe who possess behavioural, religious, and cultural traits similar to those of the Malaba clan, leading to a high possibility that the two groups migrated from the same geographical and cultural location. The Lemba, a Bantu- speaking people of southern Africa, have a tradition that they were led out of Yemen by a man named *Buba*. One of their practices was the practice of circumcision and keeping one day a week holy. A team of geneticists has found that many Lemba men carry in their male chromosome a set of deoxyribonucleic acid (DNA) sequences that is distinctive of the *cohanim*, the Jewish priests believed to be the descendants of Aaron (Wade, 1999).

In an interview with the author, another informant argued that the Malaba praise name has *Thobela*, which is a Lemba (Semitic) name. He cites Robert Moffatt who stated that "some of their customs were peculiar and "not like any tribe of which I have knowledge".

Moffat gives an example of the doctor who refused eating Matabele's meat, because it was not slaughtered by their own hands. According to Moffat, this is nothing more than a Lemba (Semitic) ritual killing (informant, 2018).

The informant also believed that the Mwali religion is a Lemba religion based around a corrupted Old Testament Jewish view of God, so a mix of Old Testament stuff and a powerful rain God, arguing that even some of the names of the associated spirits have names like '*Hosanna*' '*Mwali*' (Yahweh), *dimoni* (demon; daemon) that are either Jewish, Greek, or medieval Latin. According to the informant, comparatively, the normal Shona were different as they had ancestor spirits and powerful spirit mediums. That is why the Mwali religion does not extend to northern Mashonaland by tradition and is only found in areas where the Semitic BaKalanaga have had some stronger influence (informant, 2018).

7,2. The Malaba Clan and the Njelele Rainmaking Shrine

The Mwali shrine of Njelele is located on a hill known by its Kalanga name Njelele. The name comes from an ancient migratory *'njelele'* bird, a bateleur eagle which is a bird that signalled the coming of wet season. In Kalanga, Njelele is a type of hawk which were (are) believed to, if they are in a group and fly in "continuously" (*mayile*) circular manner, symbolize imminent rain.

In order to absolutely understand the essentiality of the Mwali shrine of Njelele, the backdrop of the Malaba people need to be fully comprehended because the Njelele shrine and the history of the Malaba clan are reconcilable. Needless to say, historical evidence shows that long before the Malaba clan arrived from VhuVhenda, the Mwali religion was actively practiced by many people in Bukalanga and beyond. Indeed, the Mabweadziba place of worship had been established in the Matopo hills earlier on by Dzibalevula the Malaba clan ancestor who called himself the son of Mwali. Then, a lot has been written about the Mwali religion, as having been the unifying factor during the Tjangamire (Changamire) Dombo State, giving the Mambos, who were also appointed with divine sanction, powerful control over their subjects, and in addition the priests or mediums of Mwali served to check on the power of the Mambo people. More so, records show the ancient Gutu-Rufura and the Marumbi Karivara people annually sending messengers all the way to the Matopo hills to consult the oracular voice of Mwali as early as the 1700. They did so mainly on matters pertaining to succession and to seek spiritual guidance on issues of national importance, including praying for rain of course.

There is also a possibility of rainmaking ceremonies taking place even prior to the arrival of Dzibagulu levula implying that rainmaking rituals were not necessarily and uniquely a Mwali religious phenomenon. Historians like Ranger (1999) note that many of the earlier Khoisan cave paintings in the Matopo hills were somewhat depicting some rainmaking ceremony activities taking place even long before the establishment of Mwalism in the area. Nevertheless, Campbell concludes that although the religion may be traced back prior to the Mambo dynasty, the priest of later times was of Venda origins (Campbell, 1926), backing the information that Npininga of the Sabaswi-Lubimbi Thobela totem was the first priest at Njelele.

Although the Matopo hills existed long before as the epicentre of the Mwali religion, with related shrines such as Manyanga Wililani, Manyangwa, Zhilo, Neyile, Ntogwa and others, fact is, there is no evidence of the existence of a rainmaking shrine named Njelele before 1836, either in documentation or through any trusted word of mouth. Hence, a clear indication that the Malaba clan brought in and established the rainmaking shrine of Njelele in the Matopo hills at the time of their arrival from VhuVhenda. This is despite that, upon their arrival, the Mabweadziba place still stood where it was before as a holy place of Mwali since the times of Dzibagulu levula in the 1250ADs. In his thesis, Bhebhe, refers to an oral history interview with Thenjiwe Lesabe who argued that "to be possessed by a Njelele spirit you do not need to have been born in that family [of Njelele custodians]. The people that were known normally to possess those powers are Venda people. The rainmakers are believed to be Vendas because that is where Njelele came from. It came from Venda" (Bhebhe, 2019).

Cobbing is one of the most extensive researchers on the Mwali religion and his findings also put the lid on that the Mwali rainmaking shrine only came into the Matopos from VhuVenda. He further reveals that "no genealogical study of the priestly family from Njelele has yet revealed a firm date for the founding of the shrine, but it seems to have been between about 1830 and 1850 during the Venda upheavals of that period which sent many Venda groups north into what is now Southern Matabeleland" (Cobbing, 1976). His dates of between 1830-1850s reciprocate with the definitive 1836 date of the Malaba clan arrival in BuKalanga.

In one of his essays, he also continues with the same view as he asserts that, "virtually all my recent informants confirmed the original connection between the *cult* and the Venda (for example the Mwali-caused thunderstorms are termed *izulu le Venda* (rain from Venda), as well as stressing its fundamental alienation from the Ndebele proper" and other indigenous BaKalanga (Cobbing, 1976).

Ranger, another broad researcher on the Njelele shrine, also argue that in fact Zimbabwe was until the later nineteenth century just outside the area covered by the rainmaking religion (Ranger, 1999). Beach and Huffman have also recently argued that there is no evidence of a Mwali rainmaking shrine presence in Zimbabwe until the early nineteen century which heralded the arrival of the Thobela Mbedzi clan from VhuVenda (Beach and Huffman, 1980). Baines, for example, also discovered in the late 1860s that: 'the God in Matabeleland is the son of the one on the Limpopo'. In a way that further backs the Malaba tradition, there is a tradition obtained by AIM Ncube that because of frictions between the people of the Zoutpansberg and the Mwali priest, 'Mwali ceased to appear in Venda country so that his worshippers had to come 'to the Matopos to find him" (Cobbing, 1976).

The Njelele shrine was used for rain making ceremonies while other small shrines like, *amadaka, koMavumbuka Ncube, Kumbudzi, koDabha Ncube* or *Magubu and Dondoriya* were also intense on rain making ceremonies. Daneel, also notes that, with most of the Matopo shrines having become inactive, Njelele has emerged in the last four decades as the principal Mwali shrine. This could be because in contrast of all the other shrines in the Matopo hills, Njelele is a rainmaking shrine while others are for other religious purposes. The second reason could be that agriculture as the main source of livelihood over the decades and coupled with the arrival of the Malaba people, Njelele shrine became more significant than others. This led to the aggregate of the Mwali religious shrines to generally be tagged the Njelele title.

An interview with some informants from Mianzwi in Venda also reveals some consistence on the account that three men, Mpangana, Sabaswi and Tshimba, together with their one-breast sister Tshawwila, left VhuVenda in a hurry in the 19th century. The accounts differ only on the reason for the departure, with some believing that in truth the Malaba contingent left VhuVhenda through a calling to transfer and re-establish the rainmaking shrine from VhuVhenda to the Matopo Hills rather than because of family squabbles. However, deductible, whenever a clan member was banished from VhuVenda for any reason, the explanation given were usually that the individual had gone back home to vhuKalanga. There are several such myths, with one popular one as the Singo tradition that King Thohoyandou's disappearance without a trace in 1770 meant that he had gone to Bukalanga, the land of his forefathers.

Despite the fact of the sanctity and privacy in the Mwali religion, evidence show that, upon arrival in Bukalanga in general and Matopo hills in particular, the Malaba people were immediately embraced, assimilated, and blended back into the original religious arrangement created by their ancient forefathers. This reveals not only their historical and spiritual linkage to the shrine, but also the existing knowledge locally, of their role and responsibilities as superintendents of the rainmaking shrine. Therefore, it is logical to put across the fact that the Malaba people did not only join the custodianship of the Mwali shrines in the Matopo hills, but they also established the Njelele rainmaking shrine in the site of Mabweadziba. The BaKalanga who were already entrenched in the area, considered the Venda their "sister's children" (Werbner, 1991), hence the easy assimilation of the Malaba clan back into the Mwali religious system of the Matopos.

Albeit some few mix ups, a number of historians are in consensus that the people of Dzibagulu- levula are among those who came from the north into the land of BuKalanga with the Mwali religion. Nthoi (2006), uses the name Lubimbi and writes that this was a clan from among the Venda who, according to Ralushai, was from a ruler named Luvhimbi (Nthoi, 2006). In his work entitled *The Ikalanga Monarchy (Party 10) – The Fall),* Ramsey adds that, "Ikalanga traditions of Mwali being brought from Venda are, however, consistent with the genealogies of the Lubimbi priests of the principal Mwali shrine at Njelele in the Matopos" (Ramsay, 2016). He also mentions that the Hhonyedzapasi people were the ones who came with Mwali into the BaKalanga country. Hhonyedzapasi is an orally verifiable name that was used in reference to Mpangana Malaba. Ramsey further emphasizes that these people were of the great Mwali, and they were Venda, and they arrived in this country and found that King Nichasike ruled over the BaKalanga country, and he further identifies Sabaswi-Lubimbi as their chief priest. His argument points to the Malaba people as the clan that compatible with the Njelele rainmaking shrine.

Despite all the evidence to the contrary, nevertheless, Daneel argues that it was the Mbire Shoko ethnic group who arrived in the Matopo hills in the 14th century, having migrated from around Lake Tanganyika, and eventually, establishing the Mwali shrine at Matopo hills (Daneel, 1970. However, if as Daneel, puts it that the Mbire occupied Matopos in the 14th century, then that means their arrival was way after 1250AD when Dzibagulu and his people arrived in the area. Archaeological evidence further shows the BaKalanga already settled in the present-day Zimbabwe at about the year 900 AD. The Dzibagulu are amongst the people who constituted the first BaKalanga settlers in the present-day Zimbabwe. There is evidence that their offshoot people lived in the Zambezi Valley (Dande) as part of the Jewish Middle Eastern group associated with rainmaking way before Daneel's referred time of the Mbire arrival. Historian Chigwedere even locates the Mbire arrival half a millennium later. He then distinguishes the Bantu from the earlier non-Khoisan and non-Bantu people calling them 'Negroes', meaning dark skinned, rather than Bantu. He argues that the Dziba-Hungwe group was the first Bantu group to occupy modern Zimbabwe sometime between 700 and 800 AD, identifying themselves with water and aquatic animals and plants and so chose totems related to water creatures, such as *hove* (fish), *ngwenya* (crocodile) and *dziba* or *siziba* (pool) (Chigwedere, 1980). The Dziba-Hungwe union constitutes the original BaKalanga groupings.

The Dzibagulu levula (sometimes referred to as Dzivaguru) are the oldest groupings associated with the Mwali religion and Mwali's popular praise name is *dzibagulu* the great pool. For example, the main Mwali religion in Venda was centred at Makonde, and was established by the Dziba and Mbedzi clans, whose alliance brought with them expertise on priesthood and of serving Mwali, when they migrated from Matopo in Zimbabwe. This has also been confirmed by other scholars like Rennie and Gray, who stated that, "the first migrants from the Northern area into Vendaland were people of the Dziba (Dziba) totem" which veritably refer to the great Lubimbi migration. Therefore, Ranger's argument that the religion is assumed to have been acquainted with migrants from Venda land of the Dziba totem and was later advanced by the people of the Mbire Shoko totem, is validated. If the above reasoning is anything to go by what has been referred to as the Mbire grouping should be none other than the late arriving cousins of the Dzibagulu levula clan who came from Great Zimbabwe during the Togwa state. The Mbire Shoko evidently arrived at the Matopos from Great Zimbabwe together during the Togwa migration before manning the Wililani shrine as the first ever Mwali priests at the Matopos.

Indeed, in addition, there are visible and striking similarities between the praises of the Njelele shrine and the Malaba totem. God is addressed by His praise-names: Dziba! Mbedzi! Mwali was praised with names of honour such as Thovhele-Thobela (most highly respected one), Mbedzi (lord), and Dzibalevula (pool of water) among others (Daneel, 1970), the whole trend absolutely borrowing from the Malaba praise totems and thereby confirming the Njelele rainmaking shrine and the Malaba clan as spiritually inseparable. These clear and striking similarity between the praise totems of the Malaba with those of the Njelele shrine, also indicates that the Malaba are the clan that brought the Njelele shrine in particular to the Matopo hills. Ranger further reveals that before the arrival of the Malaba clan in 1836, Mabweadziba actually had different praise names from that of the Malaba clan. A Mwali praise poem found in 1835 hails the shrine as 'the stone from which the rain comes from…the great pool from which mist rises when one stirs the water'. Part of the Malaba praise totem that goes *"Bagudu BaNjelele; Batombo Tshisipotelekwe"*, literally mean 'the Malaba clan of Njelele, the holy hilly'. It is important to note that the shrine praises are only applicable to particularly the Njelele shrine and not to the other group of shrines like Manyanga Wililani, Manyangwa, Zhilo, Neyile, Ntogwa and others. Therefore, hinged on the above premises and many others, it is indisputable that the relationship between the Njelele rainmaking shrine and the Malaba clan is based on a special spiritual tie-up, making the two entities substantially inseparable.

As both Nyathi and Chigwedere write, today as one approaches the hill a sign that reads "*KoThobela*" is visible. The locals will also refer to the place as "*Kokhulu*". This is a reference to the grandfather's place, specifically Npininga Lubimbi who was the first Njelele priest. The Kalanga, Ndebele and Shona continued to worship Mwali at Ntogwa and Manyangwa shrines. Kalanga oral traditions indicates that, the oracle of Mwali came from Lutombo Lutema to Bambadzi, Zhomba, Chizeze, Mavula MaTshena, Njelele, Manyangwa, Njenjema and then to Ntogwa.

Apart from the Njelele shrine, the other Mwali shrines had priests, priestesses, and custodians from various clans. When king Mzilikazi was annually sending cattle to the newly established Dula after the Ntabazinduna incident, the shrine of the Red Axe, Muntuwani Dlodlo was appointed keeper of the shrine. Dula is known as the war shrine (*Ilitshe lemikhonto or ihloka elibomvu*). A Venda called Mafukwa had crossed over from the Transvaal into the modern Gwanda area during the 1840s and established the shrine at Gwenungwe, before moving further north to

Dula. According to Cobbing, Mufukwa was succeeded by his son, Maswabe in the later nineteenth century. Maswabe was born near Pietersburg in the Transvaal, and it was he who really established the Dula Shrine, where he was joined by his family (Cobbing, 1976). Like the Malaba who decided to adopt the Ncube/Wudo surname, Mufukwa family surname was also changed to Ncube. Religiously, it was of great importance to adopt the Gudo/Ncube/Wudo surname in order to easily settle as a custodian of a shrine in Matopo. The Mbire Shoko had arrived in Bukalanga in the company of Tjibundule as part of the Togwa/Tolwa state to become one of the earliest Mwali priests at the Matopos, assuming the custodianship of the Wililani shrine for centuries.

During the uprising of 1896, Naswabe fled back to the Transvaal because his shrine was in the centre of the fighting. Mabwani temporarily took over, but Neswabe returned soon afterwards and established a temporary shrine at Nambeni. After his death he was succeeded by his son, Lufu. It appears the Dlodlo influence on the Dula shrine had rescinded post 1893. The Manyangwa shrine was under the custodianship of the Mabwani Dube clan, while the Ntunjambili shrine was under that of Daba Ncube. When Daba died Mmeke is said to have taken over the Ntunjambila shrine. By 1961, the Zhilo shrine was under the custodianship of priestess Minye Ncube. The Wililani shrine had forever been under the custodianship of the Shoko/Soko clan who had arrived with Tjibundule during the establishment of the Togwa state. Tandauze who was once the custodian, like Dzibagulu-levula and the Malaba/Lubimbi before him, is described as a 'son' of Mwali and it is reported that the oracular voice in the 1960s was a Kalanga/Lozwi. He used the Ncube surname, and his father was from the Gwanda region and later became an assistant at Njelele.

In 1896 the priest at the Wililani shrine was Nkosanzana Shoko, a rain-bringer of the Mlimo *cult* (*uMtaka Mlimu*), who had lived in Nyamande's village. She later became a slave woman to Sikombo Mguni Chief of Intemba. Later, the Wililani shrine was taken over by Mbabani Nkala during the first few years of the twentieth century. Although Njelele was not the only shrine at the Matopos, it was unique and distinguishable from other shrines because it was a rainmaking shrine capable of sustaining people by bringing rain as well as the mouthpiece of Mwali. The shrine became so popular in its significance the whole Mwali religion became known by the Njelele name.

The Njelele custodianship continued under the Sabaswi Lubimbi, from Npininga to Jenje Kole Tshevula Lubimbi until Jenje was shot by the white settlers. He supposedly had no heir apparent to succeed him. Mbikwa took over the custodianship of Njelele amid on temporary basis until his death in the 1880s. Mbikwa's son, Shula Timila, succeeded him and ran the shrine until the late 1940s. It is not clear who took over from the 1940s to 1960, but there is an emergence of the Mayezane Ncube clan who consequently took over the custodianship of the Njelele rainmaking shrine in the 1960s through Gogo Ngcathu. Gogo Ngcathu Mayezane Ncube became the priestess and custodian of the shrine until she was disposed by her husband Sitwanyana Tshimba Ncube.

Sitwanyana was not a legitimate priest of the Njelele shrine as he, like Mbikwa and Shula Timile, was from the Tshimba clan whose ancient traditional roles and responsibilities pertained only to the operations of the Hosanna ceremonies. Sitwanyana was son of Matshokodo, son of Tshobuta, son of Tengani, son of Mbikwa the elder son of Tshimba of the Thobela Mbedzinkulu origin. Tshimba was the brother of Mpangana Malaba, Sabaswi and Tshawwila. The Mayezane were said to be the rightful custodians of the Njelele shrine. However, their Sabaswi Lubimbi Kole Tshevula descent which would customarily grant them the right to the Njelele priesthood, is unclear, although the name Mayezane (small clouds) and KoleTshevula (small clouds) are synonymic.

Interestingly too, the Mayezane clan claims an ancestor called Tshobuta (Tjobuta) who is also appearing in the Tshimba-Bhangwa clan lineage, leading to wild speculations that upon the tragic murder of Jenje by Burnham in 1896, there could have been an attempt to recreate the house of Lubimbi through the person of Tshobuta. However, there are no decisive confirmation to that effect as some of the Mayezane descendants claim a Zulu while some claim a Kalanga lineage. Nevertheless, there is tangible evidence that Sitwanyana was only enticed into becoming in charge of Njelele by Nationalist leaders Joshua Nkomo and Grey Bango during the Zimbabwean armed struggle for liberation.

The two nationalists assumed that, as male, Sitwanyana Tshimba Ncube, would be useful to ZAPUs struggle for liberation than the legitimate Gogo Ngcathu Mayezane. As the war was believed to being led from Njelele, particularly Dula, the patriarchal nationalist movement needed a male figure to take charge. It should be pointed out that the general competition for shrine priesthood was fierce in this period. One politician, Herbert Ushewokunze favoured a Shona speaking and ZANU PF leaning candidate known as Sipoyana. Sipoyana had been presented from Harare to the Matopos professing to be possessed by the spirit of Mbuya Nehanda. The turmoil went on unabated and again, in 1977, a committee led by chief Garret Nzuza Masuku removed Sitwanyana Tshmba from office and appointed Sili Ndlovu as the caretaker priest.

By 1995 Ngcathu Mayezane Ncube was recommended by local elders and was brought back to the shrine by chiefs as the rightful person to be the priestess and custodian of the Njelele shrine. Unfortunately, in 1999 she however, fled the Njelele shrine when her hut was struck by lightning in mysterious circumstances. One of the Malaba informants reveals that all these theatrics were performed outside of their prerogative as the custodians of the Njelele rainmaking shrine.

7,2. The Njelele Real Experiences

In his book *The Story of My Life*, Nkomo (1984) wrote that as the spirit of Zimbabwean nationalism came to the fore again in the early 1950s, he visited the Dula shrine in the Matopos Hills accompanied by William Sivako and Grey Mabhalani Bango at 3am in the morning. Nkomo claims he heard a voice from the shrine addressing him and his guides by name and asking them what they wanted.

"You son of Nyongolo and you son of Sivako and you son of Luposwa Bango, what do you want me to do for you?"

Nkomo then replied that he had come "*to ask you to give this land back to your children, the people of the land.*"

The voice replied: "*Yes, my children. I will give you back your land. It will be after thirty years, and it will be after a big war in which many will die... But you, son of Nyongolo, great son of Maweme, you will lead this nation.*"... (Nkomo, 1984)

Narratives of Nkomo's visit to Dula, which came to be widely distributed in Matabeleland, bestowed a sacred legitimacy on his leadership. In an interview conducted by Ranger with the Rev. Kenneth Nkomo of the Faith Apostle Church of Zion, Nkomo claimed *"to have visited the shrine with his son in law at the beginning of the 1993 rain reason and had heard the voice speak from the 'rock'"* (Ranger, 1999).

According to Rev. Nkomo's account the voice had been there before anyone else was. It further claimed to be the creator, to own the Bible and to have written and given the Ten Commandments to Moses on Mount Sinai. Rev Nkomo argued that God who spoke to the ancestors during the Biblical times on hills, mountains, and rocks, was the same God who still used these objects at the Njelele shrine (Fig. 62).

God spoke to Abraham on one of the mountains in the land of Moriah in Genesis 22. God spoke to Moses on Mt Sinai in Exodus 20 and spoke to Elijah in the cleft of Mount Horeb in 1 Kings 19:8-9. Moyo in his work, The rebirth of Bukalanga: a manifesto for the liberation of a great people with a proud history, notes,

".... from the ritual to the political function, the religion is integrally involved the same way we find the Yahweh of the Hebrews involved in their national life. Mwali speaks from the mountain caves where he cannot be seen; is sacrificed to in a manner much similar to that of the Hebrew God; he has priests from one tribe ministering to him; and the offerings to him are of animals without blemish, underlining some link with Yahwehism, the religion of the Hebrews, from the ancient and remote past" (Moyo, 2012).

7,3. The Hosanna Real Experiences

Figure 62. Njelele Shrine; Image Courtesy of www.chronicle.co.zw

Figure 63. Suspected Mount Sinai picture courtesy of Google images

Continue Loving Mhlanga's 2017 interview with the author reveals that it is recorded in the Mhlanga "'izitemo' (totems) that "singabako lembu elimnyama elokuceca abakoSitengwane" (we are of the red cloth the smart ones of Sitengwane). According to Mhlanga, the trade of black cloth for the Hosanna which is important in the rain dance religion is where the Mhlanga ancestry connects with the Malaba clan.

"How do we end up with a traditional dance of black cloth with the middle east name of hosanna? This brings us to the Sinai link" argues Mhlanga.

"The Mwali African religion has its last temple as Njelele and it is similar to that of the Old Testament, while the fashion is that of Arabs and Asian, especially the plastic beads." Mhlanga attested.

The Mhlanga clan was amongst the first ever Hosannas, a role that was under the leadership of Malaba's brother, Tshimba-Bhangwa. Perceiving the link between the two peoples, it is hard to dispute Mhlanga's assertion, an assertion that is also supported in the book, The Zimbabwe African People's Union, 1961-87: A Political History of Insurgency in Southern Rhodesia, in which Sibanda, notes that *"the ilitshe (stone) was what Mt. Sinai* (Fig. 63) *was to the Israelites"*.

The Black people in Zimbabwe believed there were specifically designated mountains where God could be worshipped, and those mountains were known as Amatshe, (stones) in the singular, Ilitshe" (stone). Ranger's interview with Thenjiwe Lesabe also reveal that particular association as she highlighted that nationalist Dr Nkomo was drawing on his memories of Westminster Abbey and his *"impressions and experiences of Jerusalem and Mount Sinai"* (Terence O. Ranger, 1999).

Both the Tshimba and Lubimbi people are still found and living amongst the Malaba people in various places but predominantly in the Kezi area. Their cultural traits exhibited signs of a cross breed between the Luvhimbi and the Mbedzi clans. For example, they have a rite regarding three stones representing the father, grandfather, and great grandfather further strengthening their valuing of the number three as representing the completeness and wholeness of being. According to Stayt (1968), this was exclusively a Luvhimbi rite while the Mbedzi sib used sacred cattle to connect to their ancestors.

Research findings of this book show that in order to be the Njelele rainmaking shrine custodian, to assume priesthood of the shrine or to take responsibility of the Hosanna affairs, one must have had a genetic linkage with both the great Luvhimbi and the Thobela Mbedzinkulu. The visible descendants from both families are daughters Mufanadzo and Tshawwila, and sons Mpangana Malaba, Tshimba-Bhangwa and Sabaswi KoleTshevula. Despite existing narratives that there were other characters in existence in that family, no other figure is traceable or visible in either form, space, or time to justify the perspective. Some informants attested that some of the Tshimba house broke out after bitter family squabbles. It is that section that subsequently settled at the foot of the Tshibale mountain in the Matopos and calling themselves 'Tshibale' after adopting the name of the mountain.

The Tshibale section continued with the totem '*dombo lisingapotelekwe linopotelekwa ikabe mivimbi yoga*', at the same time adopting '*banongula nenkanka/omageza ngochago* (those who bath with milk). The later totem line is said to have emanated from their downstream maternal biological association with the Mnkandla clan. The Tshibale section further reversed the artificial 'ukuqquma ubuhlobo' (marrying within the family custom) and maintained that the Malaba and the Lubimbi people are their biological kith and kin.

7,4. Does the Njelele Shrine Hold the Future Key?

Figure 64. The Njelele Shrine located at the Matopo Hills.

In an interview with researcher Ranger, one priest was uncompromising on that "no one can rule this country (Zimbabwe) unless he comes to the rock" (Ranger, 1999). The priest also believed that after a period of withdrawal and punishment, Mwali will return, take pity on creation then the sky will become pregnant by the clouds and Mwali's voice will come like a needle that will sew the earth and the stone will begin to speak again.

This book has revealed that although Njelele (Fig. 64) is known mainly as a rain-making shrine, over the course of time, centuries rather, the people, mainly of Southern Africa, has regarded the shrine with utmost respect and have used the shrine many times to ask for spiritual guidance. There is also evidence that the Mwali religion, had for a long time, preceding the rebellions around the turn of the century, and has been associated with intertribal affairs and in addition, it always had been associated with the legitimation of political authority dating back to the time when the Lozwi begun to use the religion as an "intelligence service" and as a means of consolidating their own rule over other ethnic groups. These political uses of the oracle continued in the early 19th century after the arrival of early Europeans in the southwestern part of the country.

During the Zimbabwean liberation struggle, the shrine played a significant role in helping the leaders wage the war against colonial rule. At that time, the Njelele shrine assumed higher values as when prominent leaders and liberation war soldiers consulted the oracle for guidance and security. If over such a long course of history the shrine was regarded with such esteemed authority, it is difficult to comprehend how the shrine has, in modern times, been assigned such an inferior rank or position to an extent that it has been desecrated through physical and spiritual vandalism of unprecedented proportions.

Most of the readers may not believe that the region's problems could be stemming from the mystical domains relating to Mwalism as most have been exposed to the notion that, because it is associated with African spiritualism, Mwalism is therefore a cult. However, the question remains: Does the sacred shrine of Njelele, through its Malaba clan custodians and their Lubimbi clan priests hold mysteries of how Southern African countries, particularly, Zimbabwe's welfare and prosperity could be restored?

Appendix A

The Malaba people now

Genealogy and Malaba Prominent Individuals

Accordingly, the ad hoc Malaba clan is entirely made up of the eight houses including their siblings. The Tshibi family is the first and legitimate family for the Malaba traditional leadership not only on the basis of being the first house but because Tshibi was chosen as a leader by Mwali at the Maneledzi pool contest. His sons are listed below together with those of the other 7 houses.

1,1. Genealogy

Eight Houses of Mpangana

TJIBI SONS

TJIDADA

BHUZWANI

KUYANE *SONS*

HABANAHE

HUBHATA MAKUMBO NHOLO UNABENI

HOBHODO *SONS*

MAHANGO TSHALOBA

MATHUMO

MADLA NQUGE

NYAWO

MADLANGOMBE

MAGOMBI

LUSIBA

NJELELE

JITA KWIYE

BHADU

GUMU

MANKUNI

MBENDA

HADLEDZI SONS

TJOKO

MADZIPA

TABA

NTAMBU

TJEDU SONS

MFUNDA

MAHABA

NKUWELEGWA MTSHEDE

PHANDO

***BHULE* SONS**

KERETSIYANA

MAPUNDU

GALE

THUMISANI

MURUTHE

CHINA

MDABULI

***TSHADA* SONS**

MAZWIGWA

TABOKA

***LUNGOMBE (N'ombe Phondo)* SONS**

VELAPHI

SGULA

NDONDAYI

MABANDLA

SAMBA

TONO SHONGWENI

1,2 The Malaba Prominent Figures

As was revealed earlier on in the book, the Tshibi family is the legitimate family for the Malaba traditional leadership not only on the basis of being the first house but because Tshibi was chosen as a leader by Mwali at the Maneledzi pool contest. The most notable individual from the Tshibi house is Chief David Christopher Malaba (Figure 65), who in 2004, became a Member of Parliament representing the interests of chiefs.

Figure 65. Chief David Christopher Malaba at his birthday celebration. Picture courtesy of RMF

Another notable individual from the house of Tshibi is Luke Malaba (figure 66), born 1951, and is a judge, who at the time of publishing, was serving as the Chief Justice of Zimbabwe. He was appointed Chief Justice by then-President Robert Mugabe on 27 March 2017. However, he had already been serving as acting Chief Justice since 1 March 2017, following Justice Godfrey Chidyausiku 's retirement. Previously, he had served as Deputy Chief Justice. Chief Justice Malaba, in a unanimous supreme court decision in August 2018, concurred with the other eight justices of the court, in a ruling that Zimbabwe's July 2018 elections were lawfully conducted, and had "complied with prescribed procedures". It was a judgement that dismissed the political opposition's claims to the contrary.

Figure 66. Chief Justice Luke Doko Malaba, Courtesy of www.zimbabwesituation,com

Kuyani was from the second house after the Tshibi house. His sons were Hhabanahe and Wubhata. Kuyani had a brother called Tihani who died at an early age. The third house was that of Hhobhodo/Hhoba. It is professed that Hhobhodo/Hhoba was born during the disputes regarding the Luvhimbi/Malaba leadership legacy, hence his name 'Hhoba' which implies feuds or disputes. Figure 67 shows Hobodo Primary school named after chief Hhobhodo. The sons of Hhobhodo/Hhoba were Mahango, Magombi, Bhadu, Mathumo (from the Madla house), Njelele and Jita (Kwiye). Jita was born when Hhobhodo/Hhoba was at a very advanced age. Mahango has a brother called Madlangombe, born of the same mother. Hhobhodo/Hhoba's brother, Mkhubazi had four houses made up of Tshaduma, Ndadzila, Matobo and Tshula. Tshada, was another brother to Hhobhodo/Hhoba, however, Tshada's mother was young sister to Hhobhodo/Hhoba's mother. Tshada had two sons consisting of Mazwigwa and Taboka. Tshada's brother, Manusa had sons that included Mdenge, Mabedza, Zwiphoso, Mpulo and Mpikiwa. From the Bhadu house came Abedu, Mbayiwa, Manyele and such houses as that of Gebhe which further brought forth the shrouded house of Tabengwa.

Figure 67. Hobodo Primary school named after chief Hhobhodo.

Figure 68. A sketchy art on the wall of Hhobhodo school showing chief Hhobhodo brewing tjathiyani/isathiyane.

Nsala Mili Malaba former chairman of Kalanga Cultural Promotion Society (KCPS) is one of the prominent Hhobhodo/Hhoba descendants. Nsala was born at Mhlotshana in the vicinity of Empandeni Mission in the 1930s, being the last-born son. His name Nsala means the last born. Nsala Malaba spent the 1970s working tirelessly to promote and grow the Kalanga language and culture. In 1983 he founded Mpangana Malaba Musical Choir which composed a number of Kalanga songs including translating the national anthem to Kalanga. The name of the choir was derived from the name of his ancestor Mpangana. The songs that were adopted and adapted by the choir included the traditional song BuKalanga ndiko ludzi gwedu, (Kalanga is our identity), Takabva kule nehango yedu, (we came from afar with our nation).

It was through Nsala's efforts that Kalanga musicians such as Solomon (Moyo) Skhuza were inspired to compose their own Kalanga songs. Solomon Skhuza's album Banolila, (they are crying) which was released in 1982, was therefore a continuation of Nsala's promotion of the recognition of the Kalanga people in independent Zimbabwe. Kalanga musicians such as Ndux (Nduna) Malaba and later on the Ndolwane Super Sounds were inspired by the efforts of the KCPS and also came to support the idea of the recognition of Kalanga language and culture. Nsala is known for his inspiration to some young Malaba clan members like Tshidzanani Malaba. Tshidzanani is a co-founder of the Kalanga Language and Cultural Development Association (KLCDA).

Hadledzi had four sons, Tshoko, Ntambu, Madzipa and Taba. Although Tshoko is the oldest of the sons, the traditional headship of the House seems to fall under the house of Ntambu. This is because Tshoko was born out of wedlock. Like in the case of Hhobhodo/Hhoba and Tshada's mothers, Hadledzi is believed to have gotten Tshoko through an elder sister to his wife. The name 'Tshokomudenje' (hidden behind some bushes) came because he was hidden away from the public after his birth. Legend has it that Tshoko grew up at his mother's homestead where he also had a son Tahangana. Tahangana was later taken back into the Malaba kraal where he went in to live with the Tshidada family. He died and is buried by the Malaba shopping centre next to Ntelela and Nyongolo Nkomo burial family burial shrine. The most notable individual from this house was the tshibilika musician Ndux Malax (Nduna Malaba) whose popular song entitled 'Unity' celebrated the Unity Accord. The Unity Accord was an agreement between Zimbabwe's two major political parties PF ZAPU which was being led by Joshua Nkomo and ZANU led by Robert Mugabe. The agreement was signed on the 22nd of December 1987 to form a united nationalist political party aimed at ending ethnic purging which had marred the country between 1983 and 1987.

Other figures of prominence were Jelimane and his son Hongololo who made the traditional song Jelimane a popular hit as far as Botswana where the song became an anthem in traditional functions. Tshinga Dube (2019), former Minister of Welfare Services for War Veterans, War Collaborators and Former Political Detainees records in a biography Quiet Flows the Zambezi, that the first phases in ZIPRA's military campaigned included the ill-planned attack on Zidube Ranch near Mambale, south of Maphisa. The attack was led by Moffat Hadebe, alongside others that involved Rhodes Malaba son of Mgqibelo of Ntambu from the Hadledzi house. Amongst them was also Roger Mashimini Ncube a descendant of Tshimba.

Another of Mpangana Malaba's sons, was Lungombe (N'ombe/Phondo). He had a brother called Bhunu. Lungombe had six sons, Velaphi, Sigula, Ndondayi, Mabandla, Samba, and Tono Shongweni. A prominent figure from the Lungombe family is Misheck Ntundu Velaphi Ncube whose original name was Misheck Ntunduzakovelaphi Velaphi Ncube. He was born on 25 July 1937 in Matobo District of Matabeleland South to Mfihlo, son of Velaphi. Misheck Ntundu Velaphi Ncube (Figure 69) is one of the pioneers of Zimbabwe's armed liberation struggle from its very inception. He was among the first Zimbabwe African People's Union (ZAPU) to undergo military training in Egypt in 1962.

His group took part in clandestine military operations in Zimbabwe. Their brief was to lay the groundwork for military operations, including shipment of weapons for the military wing of Zimbabwe African People's Union that is Zimbabwe People's Revolutionary Army (ZIPRA). His mission led to the first smuggling of weapons into Southern Rhodesia. One time when Misheck Ntundu Velaphi brought in the next batch of weapons in the company of Amon Ndukwana Ncube and were intercepted by the Criminal Investigation Department (CID) operatives just beyond Hwange.

Figure 69. The Chronicle cutting 5 May 2019, on the declaration of Misheck Ntundu Velaphi Ncube, as Zimbabwe's National Hero. He was the son of Mfihlo, grandson of Velaphi, great, grandson of Lungombe and great, great, great grandson of Mpangana Malaba.

Misheck Ntundu Velaphi became one of the ZIPRA cadres who fought the fiercest battles in the 1960s at Hangwe. This led to his arrest by the colonial regime. He was arraigned before the courts, convicted, and imprisoned at Grey Prison, now known as Bulawayo Prison. Considered the most dangerous man by the Rhodesian colonial regime, he was kept under close surveillance in a number of prisons. One such prison is Khami Prison, where he met President E.D. Mnangagwa.

On the 3 July 1979 during the run up to Lancaster House talks which paved Zimbabwe's 1980 elections, Misheck, Ntundu Velaphi Ncube tested what can best be described as "freedom of a lifetime" though short lived. After Zimbabwe's independence, he became the Administrator of ZIPRA's owned company Nitram Investment Holdings. During his lifetime he also occupied several positions which includes the following: Chairman of District Coordinator Committee for Area 2, Chairman for Transport and Welfare for Bulawayo Province, Chairman of Tendele Charity Trust, Acting Chairman of Welfare Society of Bulawayo, and Zimbabwe ZANU –PF Central Committee Member. At the time of his death, he was a member of the National Consultative Assembly for Bulawayo Province. He died on the 29th of April 2019, aged 82 and was declared a National Hero, (see fig. 69). He was laid to rest on May 9, 2019, at the National Heroes Acre in Harare, Zimbabwe). From Lungombe's brother Bhunu came the house of Mehlwenkomo.

The Tshedu house comprised sons, Mfunda, Mahaba, Mtshede/Mkuwelegwa, and Phando. The Tshedu house was the first of the Mpangana family to leave the Thegwane area. However, the Phando house was left behind and later trekked back to the Kezi area with the rest of the houses. One Tshedu elder once said "we have always considered the Phando/Mangwevu house to be the lost house of Tshedu" because of the separation.

The House of Bhule comprised Keretsiyane, Mapundu, Gale, Thumisani, Muruthe, China and Mdabuli. Manyele is brother to Bhule, and his sons were Lukuta, Gwamulumba, Fulukani, Makhasi and Dema. Bhule's name is presumed to have been an appeal for peace in the Malaba leadership disputes (mutiBhule mumoto, - rescue us from the fire).

Figure 70. Picture; St Joseph's Mission in Kezi; Picture. Courtesy of RMF

Later on, nearly all the Malaba houses ended up living under Chief Malaba in the Kezi area. Family cohesion is further reflected in the way the Malaba people and their relatives live and relate. In areas like the Sigangatsha area of Kezi, approximately the whole clan is living in one place as neighbouring families. Towards the southern end of the Tshemane Hhobhodo village there is a Mangwevu family hailing from the house of Phando son of Tshedu.

Then to the northeast the Jinde Mackray family hailing from the Hadledzi house are settled as neighbours. Further south is a cluster of the Tshimba clan headed by headman Maribula. The Mzila Salvation Army Primary school is named after Mzila Tshimba Ncube. In the eastern side of the Sigangatsha primary school (St Sebastian), exists the people of the Lubimbi origin, the likes of Jim KoleTshevula. Few miles away there are homesteads belonging to the Mapundu and the Mbuya from the house of Bhule. Eight kilometres from the area, the Tshibi house is found located in the Nyahongwe area, but with the particular people dotted right from the Wonyana in the Jabhi area, up to the other side of the Malaba ward. Towards the south the Lungombe (N'ombe/Phondo)) -Velaphi people are settled at the Beula-Seula areas.

These people have boundaries divided by rivers, streams, and streamlets. However, it is not by coincidence that these people come to live in one place. It is because of the awareness of their umbilical connections. Nonetheless, the disharmony that occurred under Chief Mpini sent most of the Malaba families scattering all over the region. The Lungombe family went to settle as far as places like Lupane, Pupu and Gomoza areas. Some are found in places like Zamanyoni and Beula-Seula. Lungombe is said to be buried at the Donkwe-Donkwe area of Kezi.

The Tshedu house was the first to leave the Empandeni-Thegwane settlement after, it is narrated that, they got fed up with the constant inhouse grumblings about the delay in passing the clan traditional leadership to the Tshibi house. They settled in Bulilima area and are currently settled in Madlambudzi. Therefore, currently, all the eight houses of Malaba are proportionately represented under chief David Malaba's chieftaincy through the agency of Tshibi, Kuyane (Msitheli), Hhobhodo (Madla-Tshemane), Hadledzi, Lungombe (Velaphi), Tshedu (Mangwevu), Tshada and Bhule (Mapundu and Mbuya).

REFERENCES

Abraham, D. P. (1959). The Monomotapa Dynasty. NADA, 36, 59-84.

Alpers, E. A. (1970). Dynasties of the Mutapa-Rozwi complex. The Journal of African History, 11(2), 203-220. Retrieved from https://www.jstor.org/stable/180317

Anthropology-UK. (2020). SPECIAL MILAYO OF THE RAIN-MAKING CLAN. Retrieved from http://era.anthropology.ac.uk/Era_Resources/Era/VendaGirls/Milayo/M_Rain.html

Associated-Press. (2015, 14 October 2015). Migration in reverse: Eurasian farmers migrated to Africa 3,000 years ago. The independent, Malta. Retrieved from https://www.independent.com.mt/articles/2015-10-14/world-news/Migration-in-reverse- Eurasian-farmers-migrated-to-Africa-3-000-years-ago-6736143579

Baden-Powell, B. R. S. S. (1896). The Matabele Campaign / Being a Narrative of the Campaign in Suppressing the Native Rising in Matabeleland and Mashonaland, 1896: Good Press.

Baxter, P. (2018). Rhodesia: A Complete History 1890-1980 Independently Published. Beach, D., N. (1980). The Shona: Gweru: Mambo Press.

Beach, D. N. (1974). Ndebele raiders and Shona power. The Journal of African History, 15(4), 633-651. doi:10.1017/S0021853700013918

Beach, D. N. (1980). The Shona and Zimbabwe: 900-1850: An Outline of Shona History: Heinemann.

Becker, P. (1966). Path of Blood: The Rise and Conquests of Mzilikazi, Founder of the Matabele Tribe of Southern Africa (PRE-ISBN edition ed.): Panther books Ltd.

Bentley, J. (1996). Shapes of World History in Twentieth-century Scholarship: American Historical Association.

Bhebe, N. (1979). Christianity and traditional religion in western Zimbabwe, 1859-1923. London: Longman.

Bhebhe, S. (2019). Understanding the Traditional and Contemporary Purpose of the Njelele Rainmaking Shrine through the Oral Testimonies of Local People in Matobo. doi:10.25159/2663-6670/4015

Bourdillion, M. F. C. (1972). The Manipulation of Myth in a Tavara Chiefdom. Africa: Journal of the International African Institute, 42(2), 112-121.

Brownell, J. (2020). The Collapse of Rhodesia: Population Demographics and the Politics of Race: Bloomsbury.

Bulimo, S. A. (2013). Luyia Nation: Origins, Clans and Taboos (1st ed.): Trafford Publishing.

Caiado, A. (1898). Letter that Antonio Caiado wrote from Manamotapa to another friend of his who was in another place in the same land-1561. Theal, II, 99-107.

Callaway, E. (2016, 26 January 2016). Error Found in Study of First Ancient African Genome. Scientific American. Retrieved from https://www.scientificamerican.com/article/error- found-in-study-of-first-ancient-african-genome/

Campbell, A. A. (1926). MLIMO: The Rise and Fall of The Matabele (1st ed.). Bulawayo: Books of Rhodesia.

Carmichael, D. L., Hubert J., Reeves, B., Schanche, A. (1994). Sacred Sites, Sacred Places (J.

H. David L. Carmichael, Brian Reeves, Audhild Schanche Ed. 1st ed.). London: Routledge.

Carotenuto, F., Tsikaridze, N., Rook, L., Lordkipanidze, D., Longo, L., Condemi, S., & Raia,P. (2016). Venturing out safely: The biogeography of Homo erectus dispersal out of Africa. (1095-8606 (Electronic)).

Chigwedere, A. S. (1980). From Mutapa to Rhodes: 1000 to 1890 A.D. London: Macmillan.

Christiane Harzig, Dirk Hoerder, & Donna R. Gabaccia. (2009). What Is migration history? / Christiane Harzig and Dirk Hoerder with Donna Gabaccia. Cambridge, UK: Polity Press.

Clarke, M. N., P. (2010). Lozikeyi Dlodlo: Queen of the Ndebele: a very dangerous and intriguing woman (6th ed.). Luveve Bulawayo: Amagugu Publishers.

Cobbing, J. R. D. (1976). The Ndebele under the Khumalos, 1820-1896. [publisher not identified], Lancaster. Available from http://worldcat.org /zwcorg/ database.

Cockcroft, I. G. (1972). The Mlimo (Mwari) cult. NADA., 10, 83-92.

Coltart D. (2016). The Struggle Continues: 50 Years of Tyranny in Zimbabwe. Jacana Media (Pty) Ltd. Sunnyside.

Daneel, M. L. (1970). The God of the Matopo Hills: An Essay on the Mwari Cult in Rhodesia. Retrieved from https://hdl.handle.net/2144/8949

Dube, T. (2015). Shifting identities and the transformation of the Kalanga, people of Bulilimamangwe District, Matebeleland South, Zimbabwe C. 1946-2005. (Doctor of Philosophy in History). University of the Witwatersrand, South Africa.

Frame, J. (2018). The Rhodesian Civil War (1966-1979): New Generation Publishing. Garlake, P. S. (1978). Pastoralism and Zimbabwe. Journal of African History, 19, 479-493.

Gray, R. (2015, June 5th, 2015). The Egyptian in all of us: First modern humans spread out of Africa into Europe and Asia from the Sinai Peninsula. Daily Mail UK. Retrieved from https://www.dailymail.co.uk/sciencetech/article-3101197/The-Egyptian-modern- humans-spread-Africa-Europe-Asia-Sinai-peninsula.html

Gwakuba-Ndlovu, S. (2012, 22 October 2012). The Rebirth of Bukalanga an intellectually refreshing bombshell. Chronicle. Retrieved from https://www.chronicle.co.zw/the- rebirth-of-bukalanga-an-intellectually-refreshing-bombshell/

Gwakuba-Ndlovu, S. (2017, 20 April 2017). Tjilisamhulu's fall after ridiculing Mwali. The Patriot. Retrieved from https://www.thepatriot.co.zw/old_posts/tjilisamhulus-fall-after- ridiculing-mwali/

Hall, B. L. (2013). Return to Corriebush: Random House Struik.

Harlow, B., & Carter, M. (2003). The Scramble for Africa. Retrieved from https://doi.org/10.1215/9780822385035

Hexham, I. (1981). Lord of the Sky-King of the Earth: Zulu traditional religion and belief in the sky god. Studies in Religion/Sciences Religieuses, 10(3), 273-285. doi:10.1177/000842988101000302

Hole, H. M. (1926). The Making of Rhodesia (1st ed.): Macmillan and Co., Limited, London. Hole, H. M. (1929). Lobengula. London: Philip Allan.

Hole, H. M. (1968). The Making of Rhodesia (1st ed.). London: Routledge.

Howell, M. C. (2001). From reliable sources: an introduction to historical methods. In W. Prevenier (Ed.). Ithaca, N.Y.: Cornell University Press.

Huffman, T. N. (2005). Mapungubwe Ancient African Civilisation on the Limpopo: Wits University Press.

Kakai, P. (2016). History of Inter-Ethnic Relations in Bungorna, Mt. Elgon and Trans Nzoia Districts, 1875-1997. (PhD). Kenyatta University, Kenya.

Keppel-Jones, A. (1983). Rhodes and Rhodesia

The White Conquest of Zimbabwe 1884-1902: McGill-Queen's University Press. Khumalo, P. Z. (2020, January 2020) The NDebele Kingdom/Interviewer: E. T. Sibanda. King, M. L. (1963). Strength to love. New York: Harper & Row.

Langlois, C.-V., & Seignobos, C. (1898). Introduction to the Study of History: Paris: Librairie Hachette.

Le-Roux, I. (1996). Only the words remained: A religious scientific interpretation of Venda Folk stories (Ngano). (Doctor of Philosophy). University of South Africa, South Africa.

Le Roux, M. (1997). AFRICAN" JEWS" FOR JESUS A preliminary investigation into the Semitic origins and missionary initiatives of some Lemba communities in southern Africa. Missionalia, 25, 493-510.

Le Roux, M. (1999). 'Lost Tribes1 of Israel' in Africa? Some Observations on Judaising Movements in Africa, With Specific Reference to the Lemba in Southern Africa2.

Religion and Theology, 6, 111-139. doi:10.1163/157430199X00100 Lesabe, T. (2019)/Interviewer: S. Bhebhe.

Llorente, G. M., Jones, E. R., Eriksson, A., Siska, V., Arthur, K. W., Arthur, J. W., . . . Manica,

(2015). Ancient Ethiopian genome reveals extensive Eurasian admixture throughout the African continent. (1095-9203 (Electronic)).

Luonde. (2021). VhaVenda History

Mabogo, D. (2012). The ethnobotany of the Vhavenda.

Mabuse, A. A. (2012, 28 September 2013). The significance of Domboshaba ruins to Bakalanga pre-history. Mmengi. Retrieved from https://www.mmegi.bw/index.php?sid=7&aid=14&dir=2012/September/Friday28

Magris, C. (1999). Danube: A Sentimental Journey from the Source to the Black Sea Harvill Press.

Maheleni, V. (2015, 27 February 2015) Mpangana & Malaba/Interviewer: M. Ncube. Malaba Legacy.

Makambe, E. P. (1979). The African immigrant factor in Southern Rhodesia, 1890-1930: The origin and influence of external elements in a colonial setting. (PhD). University of York, Makila, F. E. (1978). An Outline History of Babukusu of Western Kenya: Kenya Literature Bureau.

Makondo, L. (2009). An investigation in anthroponyms of the Shona society. (D. Litt. et Phil. (African Languages)). University of South Africa,

Malaba-informant. (2019, 06 August 2019) The Malaba people/Interviewer: T. Ncube. Malabalegacy.

Malikongwa, D. M. F., C. C. (1979). The history of the BaKhurutshe (the Phofu group) and the BaKalanga of Botswana. Gaborone.

Masendu-Dube, C. S. (2012)/Interviewer: Tumelo.

Mauch, K. (1871). Some Karanga Chiefs Around Great Zimbabwe 1871–1872.

Maylam, P. (2005). The Cult of Rhodes: Remembering an Imperialist in Africa: New Africa Books.

McClellan, J. E., & Dorn, H. (2006). Science and technology in world history: an introduction Science and technology in world history an introduction (2nd ed. ed.). Baltimore: Johns Hopkins University Press.

Mellet, P.T, (2018), The Peopling of South Africa, retrieved from https://camissapeople.wordpress.com/2018/12/10/the-peopling-of-south-africa/

Meredith, M. (2007). Diamonds, Gold, and War: The British, the Boers, and the Making of South Africa: Public Affairs.

Mhlanga, C. (2017, 20 October) Umthwakazi: Honouring the San (Abathwa) who tamed the land/Interviewer: P. Nyathi. Sunday News Zimbabwe.

Mhlanga, C. (2018, 25 January 2018) The Malaba people and the Ndebele kingdom/Interviewer: T. Ncube. Malabalegacy.

Mhlanga, C. (2020). Mthwakazi Wars - Izimpi ZikaMthwakazi 1890 - 1983. Bulawayo: Amagugu Publishers.

Mkhwananzi, G. M. (2020, 21 November 2020) The Ndebele State/Interviewer: T. Ncube. Malaba Legacy.

Moyo, E. N. (2012). The Rebirth of the Bakalanga: A Manifesto for the Liberation of a Great People with a Proud History (1st ed.): Maphungubgwe News Corporation.

Moyo, T. (2018). A Social and Cultural History of the People Under Chief Malaba (Matobo District) 1890-1980

Mudenge, S. I. G. (1988). A Political History of Munhumutapa: c. 1400-1902. Harare: Zimbabwe Publishing House.

Mulaudzi, F. (2015). Perceptions of the Vhavenda Regarding the Significance of IKS Rituals and Customs in Women's Health: "The Other Side of The Coin". Asian Journal of Social Science, 44, 21-27.

Muleya, S. (2018, 15 November 2018) The Sioga people of Beitbridge/Interviewer: T. Ncube. Malabalegacy.

Mwakikagile, G. (2007). Kenya: Identity of a Nation (1st ed.): New Africa Press. NADA, 1948.

National-Geographic. (2020). Africa: Human Geography.

Natural History Museum (2021), Accessed at https://www.nhm.ac.uk/discover/homo-erectus-our-ancient-ancestor.html

Ndeda, M. (2019). Population movement, settlement and the construction of society to the east of Lake Victoria in precolonial times: the western Kenyan case.

Ndlovu-Gatsheni, S. J. (2008). Who ruled by the spear? Rethinking the form of governance in the Ndebele state. African Studies Quarterly, 10(2-3), 71-94. Retrieved from http://asq.africa.ufl.edu/files/Ndlovu-Gatsheni-Vol10Issue23.pdf

Nhlapho-Commission. (2010). Traditional Leadership Disputes and Claims. Nhlapho Commission

Nickel, G. D. (2015). Dom Gonçalo da Silveira (d.1561): Christian-Muslim Relations. A Bibliographical History (Vol. 7): Drill.

Njaya, T. M., N. (2010). Land Reform Process and Property Rights in Zimbabwe: Constraints and Future Prospects (1980-2002). Journal of Sustainable Development in Africa, 12(4).

Nkala, M. (2018) The death of Prince Buhlelo/Interviewer: T. Ncube. RMF.

Nkala, S. (2017, November 11, 2019). Ndebele kingship circus in new twist. Newsday. Retrieved from. https://www.newsday.co.zw/2017/11/ndebele-kingship-circus-new-twist/

Nkomo, J. (1984). Nkomo, the story of my life. London: Methuen.

Noyes, P. (2019, 13 March 2019). What Is the Meaning of Hosanna in the Bible?

Ntelela, C. (1976) The Malaba people and their origins/Interviewer: A. Cockcroft. Malabalegacy.

Nthoi, L. S. (1995). Social Perspective of Religion: A study of the Mwali Cult of Religion: A study of the Mwali Cult of Southern Africa. (PhD). University of Manchester, Manchester.

Nthoi, L. S. (2006). Contesting Sacred Space: A Pilgrimage Study of the Mwali Cult of Southern Africa. Trenton, New Jersey: Africa world Press.

Tshemane-Madla, N. (1970) Mpangana Malaba/Interviewer: V. M. Ncube.

Nyathi, P. (2000). Alvord Mabena: The Man and His Roots: Priority Projects Publishing.

Nyathi, P. (2014). Rain dance symbolism associated with Njelele Shrine. Retrieved from https://www.sundaynews.co.zw/rain-dance-symbolism-associated-with-njelele-shrine/

Nyathi, P. (2016). Chiefs as defenders of the state: Resulting demise of same after conquest. Sunday News. Retrieved from https://www.sundaynews.co.zw/chiefs-as-defenders-of-the- state-resulting-demise-of-same-after-conquest/

Nyathi, P. (2017). At the traditional court of King Mzilikazi Khumalo: Expressions of gender, patriarchy and seniority. Sunday News. Retrieved from https://www.sundaynews.co.zw/at- the-traditional-court-of-king-mzilikazi-khumalo-expressions-of-gender-patriarchy-and- seniority/

Nyathi, P. (2019). Re-imagine Bulawayo. City turns 125 years. Sunday News. Retrieved from https://www.sundaynews.co.zw/re-imagine-bulawayo-city-turns-125-years/

Oosthuizen, R. (2016). The drum and its significance for the interpretation of the Old Testament from an African perspective: Part one. Verbum et Ecclesia, 37. doi:10.4102/ve.v37i1.1395

Parker, C. H. (2010). Global Interactions in the Early Modern Age, 1400–1800. Cambridge: Cambridge University Press.

Penrose, H. (1960). The Power of History Making Retrieved from https://www.educateplus.edu.au/2020/11/the-power-of-history-making/

Pfebe, E. (2015). Zimbabwe: who were the first settlers. Retrieved from http://pfebve.blogspot.com/2015/08/zimbabwe-who-were-first-settlers.html

Plumer, H. C. O. (1897). An irregular Corps in Matabeleland: Kegan Paul, Trench, Trübner & Co. Ltd.

Raftopoulos, B., & Mlambo, A. S. (2009). Becoming Zimbabwe. A History from the Pre-colonial Period to 2008

A History from the Pre-colonial Period to 2008: Weaver Press.

Ralushai, N. M. N. (1978). Further traditions concerning Luvhimbi and the Mbedzi. Rhodesian History, 9, 1-12.

Ralushai, N. M. N. (2003). Additional information on the oral history of Mapungubwe. Dept. of environmental affairs. Dept. Of environmental affairs.

Ralushai, N. M. N. V. (1977). Conflicting Accounts of Venda History with Particular Reference to the Role of Mutupo in Social Organisation. Belfast: Queen's University of Belfast.

Ramsay, J. (2016, 23 May 2016). THE IKALANGA MONARCHY (PART 10) – THE FALL. Weekend Post.

Retrieved from http://www.weekendpost.co.bw/25373/columns/the- ikalanga-monarchy-part-10-ae-the-fallae%C2%A8ae%C2%A8/

Randles, W. G. L. (1975). L'empire du Monomotapa du XVe au XIXe siècle: Moulton. Ranger, T. O. (1972). The African Voice in Southern Rhodesia, 1898-1930 (1st ed.): Northwestern University Press.

Ranger, T. O. (1999). Voices from the Rocks: Nature, Culture, and History in the Matopos Hills of Zimbabwe (1 ed.). Indiana: Indiana University Press.

Rasmussen, R. K. (1976). Mzilikazi's Migrations South of the Limpopo, c. 1821-1827: A Reassessment. Transafrican Journal of History, 5(1), 52-74. Retrieved from https://www.jstor.org/stable/24520287

Roberts, R. S., & Warhurst, P. R. (1975). Rhodesian History. The Journal of the Central Africa Historical Association, 6-7.

Rodewald, M. K. (2010). Understanding "Mwali" as Traditional Supreme Deity of the Bakalanga of Botswana and Western Zimbabwe: Part One. Botswana Notes and Records, 42, 11- 21. Retrieved from http://www.jstor.org/stable/23237967

Ross, E. G. (2002). The Age of Iron in West Africa. Retrieved from https://www.metmuseum.org/toah/hd/iron/hd_iron.htm

Rotberg, R. I. (1988). The Founder: Cecil Rhodes and the Pursuit of Power: Oxford University Press Inc

Roufe, G. (2015). The Reasons for a Murder: Local Cultural Conceptualizations of the Martyrdom of Gonçalo da Silveira in 1561. Cahiers d'Études Africaines, 55(219), 467-

487. Retrieved from http://www.jstor.org/stable/24476685

Ruwitah, A. R. (1988). Matabeleland After the Dispersion: A Study in Involuntary Population Movcements, Their Economic & Political Impact in the Era of Colonialism, 1893 - 1960. Paper presented at the Handerson seminar.

Santayana, G., & Gouinlock, J. (2011). The Life of Reason or The Phases of Human Progress

Introduction and Reason in Common Sense, Volume VII, Book One: The MIT Press. Schlebusch, C. M., Malmström, H., Günther, T., Sjödin, P., Coutinho, A., Edlund, H., . . .

Jakobsson, M. (2017). Southern African ancient genomes estimate modern human divergence to 350,000 to 260,000 years ago. Science, eaao6266. doi:10.1126/science. aao6266

Shaw, A. (1893). Review of Reviews and World's Work: An International Magazine, Volume 8: Review of Reviews Corporation.

Simiyu, V., Kireti, V., & Atinga, J. (1991). The Emergency of a sub-Nation. A History of Babukusu in the TransAfrican. Journal of History, 1.

Simiyu, V. G. (1991). The Emergence of a Sub-Nation: A History of Babukusu to 1990. Transafrican Journal of History, 20, 125-144. Retrieved from https://www.jstor.org/stable/24520306

Stayt, H. A. (1968). The Bavenda. London: F. Cass. Submission of the VaNgona nation to the South Africa parliament, South African Parliament, (2018).

Thomas, T. M. (1986). Eleven Years in Central South Africa (1st ed.): Routledge.

Toyin Falola, R. C. N. (2020). United States and Africa Relations, 1400s to the Present: Yale University Press.

Van Waarden, C. (1988). The oral history of the Bakalanga of Botswana. Gaborone: Botswana Society.

Vickers, S. (2010, 8 March 2010). Lost Jewish tribe 'found in Zimbabwe'. BBC Magazine. Retrieved from http://news.bbc.co.uk/2/hi/8550614.stm

Von-Sicard, H. (1946). The Tree Cult in the Zimbabwe Culture. African Studies, 5(4), 257-267. Wade, N. (1999, 9 May 1999). DNA Backs a Tribe's Tradition of Early Descent from the Jews. New York Times. Retrieved from https://www.nytimes.com/1999/05/09/us/dna-backs-a-tribe-s-tradition-of-early-descent-from-the-jews.html

Wallis, E. W. S. (1946). The Matabele Journals of Robert Moffat 1829–1860. African Affairs, 45(180), 157-158. doi: 10.1093/oxfordjournals.afraf.a093511

Wallis, J. P. R. (1946). The Matabele Journals of Robert Moffat (two volumes) (The Presentation Edition ed.): Chatto & Windus, London.

Walter, L. (2017, 24 August 2017). Re: Lewis Walter - The First White Women in Rhodesia Wentzel, P. J., & Kumile, M. (1983). Nau dzabaKalanga = A History of the Kalanga. Pretoria: University of South Africa.

Werbner, R. (1991). Tears of the Dead

The Social Biography of an African Family: Edinburgh University Press.

Wood, J. G. (1893). Through Matabeleland: The Record of a Ten Months' Trip in an Ox-wagon Through Mashonaland and Matabeleland: J.C. Juta & Company.

Wood, M. (2010). Queen of Sheba. BBC. Retrieved from http://news.bbc.c uk/2/hi/8550614.stm Young, R. (2015). Taller Than Trees: Authorhouse.

Written by:

Titshabona Malaba Ncube *(BA General (UZ. Zim)): BA. Hon. Town Planning (Newcastle University. UK): Post Grad. Dip. Town Planning (Newcastle University. UK): MSc. (Environmental Management. Derby University. UK))* is currently involved in a number of projects that includes literature writing, music and film production, journalism, and student mentoring. The novel Igazi Labafo, which was made into film, is the most notable literary work by Mr Ncube. Mr Ncube is a Town Planner and a qualified environmental management specialist based in Newcastle upon Tyne in the United Kingdom.

Dr. Matiwaza Malaba Ncube, *(PhD (University of Nottingham), MSc.Ortho (Warwick England), Bachelors & Grad Dip Dental Surgery (Australia)* – Registered Private Healthcare Practitioner/Dental Surgeon, expertise in Oral Surgery, Orthodontics, Implant Surgery & practices at own private clinic in Brisbane, Australia. Also lectures at Charles Sturt University, Australia.

John Malaba Ncube *(BA Early Childhood Education Degree, (UCLan, UK)*. Former teacher in the Lupane area of Matabeleland North, Zimbabwe between 1986 and 1987 before being commissioned to the then Union of Soviet Socialist Republics (USSR) to train as a Military Aviation Engineer (Communications Systems) from 1987 to 1992. Worked for the Zimbabwe Air Force (AFZ) Gweru-Thornhill Air Bases thereafter, before migrating to South Africa and then to the UK. Currently based in the United Kingdom.

Admire Malaba Ncube *(LLB (Hons) Law: University of Huddersfield, Post-grad Sports Law and Practice: De-Montfort University, Post Grad Legal Practice: BPP Law School Manchester.* Practicing Lawyer in England and Wales. Practice areas are Criminal law and Sports Law. A Registered (Football Agent) Intermediary with the English Football Association. Membership - The Society of Black Lawyers (SBL), Human rights Lawyers Association (HRLA) and the British Association for Sport and Law (BASL), which regularly discusses pressing sports law-related matters around the world

www.ingramcontent.com/pod-product-compliance
Lightning Source LLC
Chambersburg PA
CBHW081400080526
44588CB00016B/2565